ANCIENT PERSIAN

When ancient Persian conquerors created a vast empire from the Mediterranean to the Indus, encompassing many peoples speaking many different languages, they triggered demographic changes that caused their own language to be transformed. Persian grammar has ever since borne testimony to the social history of the ancient Persian Empire. This study of the early evolution of the Persian language bridges ancient history and new linguistics. Written for historians, philologists, linguists, and classical scholars, as well as those interested specifically in Persian and Iranian studies, it explains the correlation between the character of a language's grammar and the history of its speakers. It paves the way for new investigations into linguistic history, a field complementary with, but distinct from, historical linguistics. This title is also available as Open Access on Cambridge Core.

KEVIN T. VAN BLADEL is Professor of Near Eastern Languages & Civilizations at Yale University. He is also author of *The Arabic Hermes* (2009), *From Sasanian Mandaeans to Sabians of the Marshes* (2017), *Written Middle Persian Literature under the Sasanids* (2024), and numerous articles on Arabic, Greek, Iranic, Sanskrit, and Syriac textual traditions.

ANCIENT PERSIAN

A Linguistic History

KEVIN T. VAN BLADEL
Yale University

Shaftesbury Road, Cambridge CB2 8EA, United Kingdom

One Liberty Plaza, 20th Floor, New York, NY 10006, USA

477 Williamstown Road, Port Melbourne, VIC 3207, Australia

314–321, 3rd Floor, Plot 3, Splendor Forum, Jasola District Centre,
New Delhi – 110025, India

Cambridge University Press is part of Cambridge University Press & Assessment,
a department of the University of Cambridge.

We share the University's mission to contribute to society through the pursuit of
education, learning and research at the highest international levels of excellence.

www.cambridge.org
Information on this title: www.cambridge.org/9781009727723
DOI: 10.1017/9781009727709

© Kevin T. van Bladel 2026

This publication is in copyright. Subject to statutory exception and to the provisions
of relevant collective licensing agreements, with the exception of the Creative Commons version
the link for which is provided below, no reproduction of any part may take place without the
written permission of Cambridge University Press & Assessment.

An online version of this work is published at doi.org/10.1017/9781009727709 under a Creative
Commons Open Access license CC-BY-NC-ND 4.0 which permits re-use, distribution and
reproduction in any medium for non-commercial purposes providing appropriate credit to the
original work is given. You may not distribute derivative works without permission. To view
a copy of this license, visit https://creativecommons.org/licenses/by-nc-nd/4.0

When citing this work, please include a reference to the DOI 10.1017/9781009727709

First published 2026

Cover image: Achaemenid relief depicting tribute-bearers on the Tripylon at Persepolis.
Photo by DeAgostini/Getty Images.

A catalogue record for this publication is available from the British Library

Library of Congress Cataloging-in-Publication Data
NAMES: Van Bladel, Kevin Thomas author
TITLE: Ancient Persian : a linguistic history / Kevin T. van Bladel, Yale University, Connecticut.
DESCRIPTION: Cambridge ; New York, NY : Cambridge University Press, 2026. |
Includes bibliographical references and index.
IDENTIFIERS: LCCN 2026001863 | ISBN 9781009727723 hardback | ISBN 9781009727679 paperback |
ISBN 9781009727709 ebook
SUBJECTS: LCSH: Old Persian language – Grammar, Historical | Old Persian language – Social aspects
CLASSIFICATION: LCC PK6123 .V36 2026
LC record available at https://lccn.loc.gov/2026001863

ISBN 978-1-009-72772-3 Hardback
ISBN 978-1-009-72767-9 Paperback

Cambridge University Press & Assessment has no responsibility for the persistence
or accuracy of URLs for external or third-party internet websites referred to in this
publication and does not guarantee that any content on such websites is, or will remain,
accurate or appropriate.

For EU product safety concerns, contact us at Calle de José Abascal, 56, 1°, 28003 Madrid, Spain,
or email eugpsr@cambridge.org

*To the memory of my sister Erin (1980–2022),
dear from our meeting on the day of her birth to our farewell
on her last.*

Devenir impériale est pour une langue la plus grave des crises.
(To become imperial is, for a language, the most serious of crises.)
—Antoine Meillet, "Les nouvelles langues indo-européens trouvées en Asie Centrale"

Contents

List of Maps	*page* ix
List of Tables	xii
Acknowledgments	xiii

	Introduction	1
	Old Persian, Middle Persian, New Persian	2
	Hypotheses about the "Simple" Persian Language	3
	Linguistic History and Historical Linguistics	7
	More about Linguistic History	9
	Terminology	14
	Plan of the Book	17
1	The Transformation of Old Persian	19
	The Character of Old Persian Grammar	23
	Earlier Scholarly Explanations	32
	From Old Persian to Middle Persian	34
	The Symptoms of Middle Persian in Late Achaemenian Royal Inscriptions	40
	A Simpler Form of Persian	46
2	A Linguistic-Historical Model: Social Factors in Grammatical Reduction, Imposition, and Adoption	51
	Grammatical Reduction: Social Factors in the Loss of Inflection	53
	Three Intergenerational Patterns of Language Acquisition	61
	"Contact Languages" as Comparanda	69
	Varieties of Contact Languages	73
	State and Process in Contact Linguistics and Linguistic History	97
	Reduction and the Transfer of Features as Concomitant Factors	99
	Human Agency in the Transfer of Features and Grammatical Reduction: Three Syndromes	102
	Decreolization	108
	The Pace of Language Change and "Modern" Ancient Languages: A Note for Historical Linguistics	109
	Exoterogeny and Esoterogeny	112
	Ramifications	114

Contents

3 Middle Persian as a Byproduct of the Social Conditions
   of the Achaemenian Empire ... 116
   A Nation Morally Corrupted? ... 117
   What Happened to Old Persian? The Linguistic-Historical Model Alone ... 120
   Purely Structural Linguistic Alternatives? ... 125
   Imperial Persian, Heterogeneous Persians ... 137
   Fighters and Laborers for the Persians ... 144
   Domestic Personnel of the Persians ... 149
   The Testimony of Material Culture ... 158
   The Testimony of the Language of the Late Achaemenian Inscriptions ... 160
   Dominant Ethno-Class or Domestic Melting Pot? ... 162
   Modern Terms for Imperial Population Mixture ... 166

4 Common and Remote Varieties of Iranic-Language Speech ... 171
   Parthian and Bactrian ... 173
   Systemic Similarities between Middle Persian, Parthian, and Bactrian ... 177
   Comparisons with Languages from the Outer Achaemenian Domain
      and Beyond ... 184
   The Hypothesis of Central Iranic and Areal Features ... 187
   An Achaemenian Common Tongue? ... 192
   The Putative Role of Aramaic as an Achaemenian Lingua Franca ... 195
   Socially Remote and Socially Common Iranic Languages ... 197

Conclusion ... 199

References ... 205
Index ... 235

Maps

1.1 Achaemenid Persian Empire, with major routes. After *page* x
    Boardman (1988, map 1).

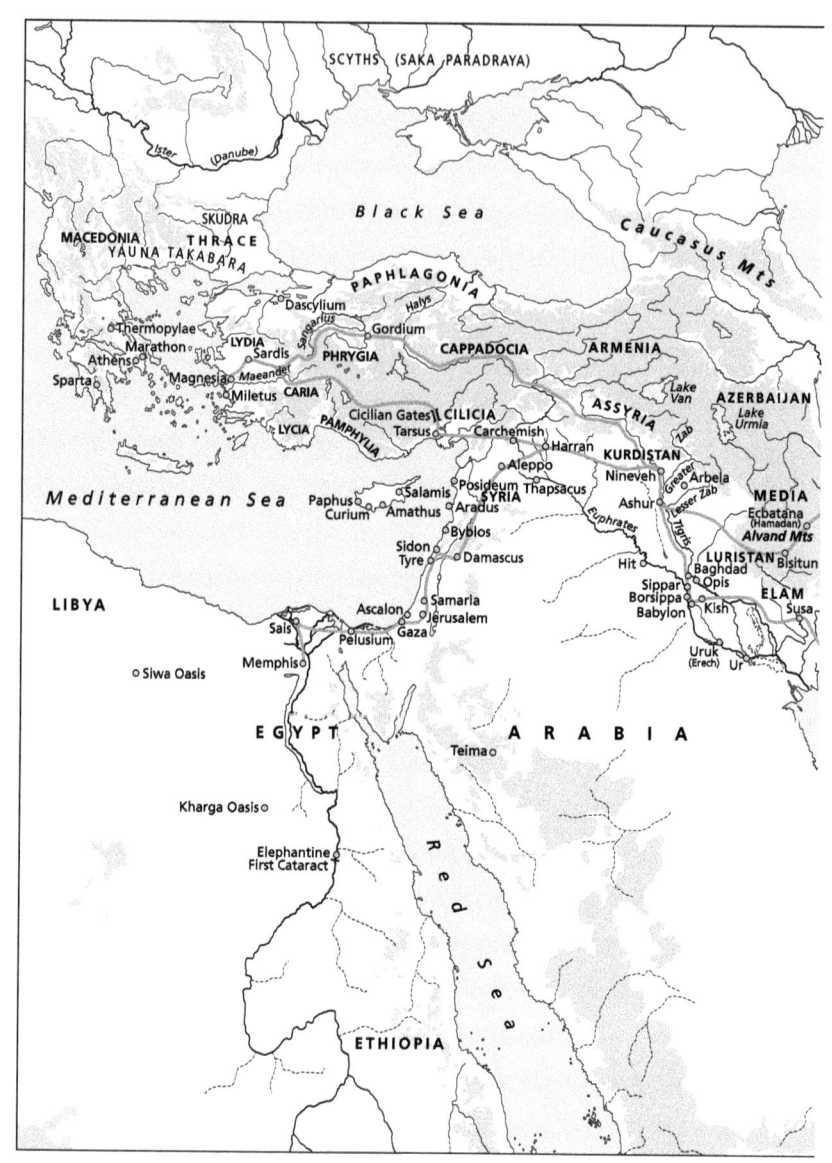

Map 1.1 Achaemenid Persian Empire, with major routes. After Boardman (1988, map 1).

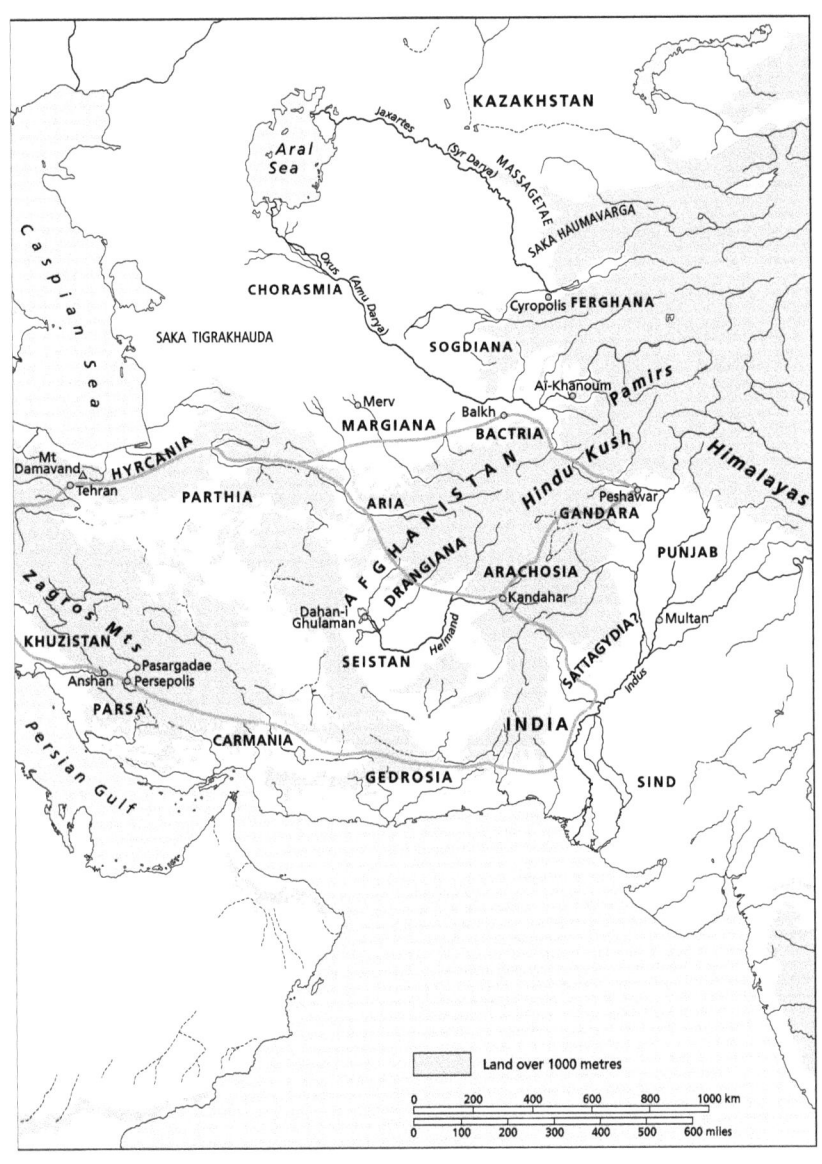

Map 1.1 (cont.)

Tables

1.1a	Old Persian noun case endings by etymological type (Singular)	*page* 24
1.1b	Old Persian noun case endings by etymological type (Dual)	24
1.1c	Old Persian noun case endings by etymological type (Plural)	24
1.2a	Old Persian noun inflection	37
1.2b	Middle Persian noun inflection	38
1.3	The Middle Persian preterit (from the ancient perfective participle)	39
2.1	"Estimated proportion of whites in various societies in the late eighteenth century" (from Holm 2004)	94
2.2	McWhorter's grid of nine types, with some of his examples	100
3.1	Reflexes of Proto-Iranic *ź in ancient Iranic languages	124
3.2	Imperfect and perfective forms in Persian and Yaghnobi, greatly simplified from Jügel (2015: 163)	127

Acknowledgments

My first debts in this work are to teachers of mine in the 1990s. It was my good fortune that Hans Henrich Hock introduced me to historical linguistics when I was a first-year college student and to Sanskrit when I studied for my master's degree in classical philology. Ladislav Zgusta (1924–2007) showed me the way into Indo-European linguistics when I never imagined that I might one day teach courses on that subject. Stanley Insler (1937–2019) introduced me to Old Persian, Middle Persian, and Parthian in the Indo-European framework. Without those teachers I would never have written this. There were others, too. Beatrice Gruendler showed me different approaches to historical linguistics in the context of Semitic and Arabic. Dimitri Gutas above all taught me the value of precision in textual scholarship and for historical research. Nicholas Sims-Williams, who encouraged me many years ago to go deeper into Iranic languages – "Why not?" was very persuasive! – has more recently earned my renewed thanks as an enthusiastic guide in Bactrian. Adam Benkato has helped me with Sogdian and provided detailed and beneficial comments on an early draft of this book. John McWhorter read an early draft of Chapter 2, which owes much to his publications, and gave encouraging feedback. The many students in my courses in Old Persian, Avestan, Middle Persian, Parthian, and Early New Persian over the years, at the University of Southern California, The Ohio State University, and Yale University, and in my iterations of the seminar "Historical Sociolinguistics of the Ancient World" at Yale, helped me to refine the argument and presentation. I offer my profound thanks to the three anonymous readers, who gave useful pointers, suggestions, challenges, and corrections, as well as encouragement. Countless others – teachers, students, friends, colleagues – helped me in too many ways to enumerate, and I ask for their grace for my not listing all of them.

I am grateful to Yale University for supporting the publication of this book in Open Access form.

Special thanks go to Michael Sharp of Cambridge University Press for his efficient facilitation of the publication of this book and to Pam Scholefield for preparing the index.

Introduction

More than two thousand years ago, the complex grammar of the ancient Persian language was drastically simplified within five generations, coinciding precisely with the period when the kings of the Persian people ruled the Achaemenian Empire – the largest empire ever created until that time, reaching from southern Egypt to Central Asia, from the shores of southeastern Europe to the Indus.[1] This book explains that correlation: how Persian imperialism two and a half thousand years ago, unprecedented in scale, triggered sudden grammatical effects that are still evident in the modern Persian language today. The Persian language was morphologically reduced and restructured as a regular and even predictable result of the

---

[1] It is often remarked that the Achaemenian Persian Empire was imperial on a scale far greater than that of any prior empire. "World empire," a nonanalytical category, has often been invoked to convey the idea that the Persian dominion was unprecedented in scale. The concept of world empire derives from the exegesis of the second, Aramaic, chapter of the Book of Daniel and ancient Christian chronography. The term entered secular historiography by the nineteenth century. The Achaemenian state was characterized as a *Weltreich* already by the geographer Carl Zimmermann (1842: 1, "Das Persische, das erste sogenannte Weltreich") and was described likewise by two of the first European specialists in Iranian studies, Friedrich von Spiegel (1871–1878: 1.1) and Ferdinand Justi (1879: 1). It was adopted in the early twentieth century in Iran: e.g., in 1933, Ḥasan Pīrniyā, a former prime minister of the Qajars, calls it *nuxustīn dawlat-i jahānī*, "the first world empire," which he glosses in French as "empire mondiale," indicating the expression's novelty and foreign origin with the need for explanation in Persian at the time (Pīrniyā 1933: 1.2). More recent examples will show that versions of this expression continue unabated: Schmitt 1983: "a multinational empire without precedent – a first world-empire of historical importance, since it embraced all previous civilized states of the ancient Near East." Dandamaev 1989: xi: "It was the first world power in history." Briant 2005: 12: "the first ancient world empire." Brosius 2006: 1: "The Persians were the first monarchy to create a *world empire* which included most territories of the known ancient world." Kuhrt 2007: 1: "The Achaemenid empire is the earliest and largest of the known 'world empires.'" Daryaee 2008: 1: "Achaemenid Persians ... created the first true world empire." Wiesehöfer 2009: 66: "the largest of all ancient Near Eastern 'world empires.'" Shahbazi 2011: 120: "the Persian state was the first 'world empire.'" Others paraphrase, avoiding the problematic expression: Llewellyn-Jones 2013: 75: "the biggest Empire the ancient world had seen." Waters 2014: xix: "the empire they forged represented something new in its scope and in its durative power," (2014: 1) "unprecedented in world history." Khatchadourian 2016: xxxi: "the largest polity the world had ever known." Llewellyn-Jones 2022: 5: "history's first great superpower."

demographic upheaval created by the Persian Empire itself. This insight prompts, in turn, meaningful revisions to the currently dominant historical narrative about ancient Persian imperial society and the ruling class of this paradigmatic empire of antiquity. The new patterns of relationships instigated by the mighty empire fostered an unplanned domestic imperial melting pot hitherto scarcely detected and understood by modern historians.

Old Persian, Middle Persian, New Persian

Specifically, this book investigates the first of the two transitions in the history of Persian, from the oldest attested stage of Persian, called Old Persian, to the subsequent stage, called Middle Persian. A word about these designations is in order. Scholars have a convention for designating stages of evolution in the history of a language by the terms Old, Middle, and New. We have, for example, the Old English of *Beowulf*, the Middle English of Chaucer's *Canterbury Tales*, and the New English still used today. The separate stages are, to a degree, artificial categories in that each stage is changing and dynamic in itself. There is dialectal, chronological, and regional variation within each stage. Shakespeare's New English is not the same as my own New English, nor is my American New English quite the same as that of my colleagues from London. Within London itself one can hear different varieties of English. Although these chronological distinctions are therefore conventional and admit much variation, linguists have sound criteria, based primarily on the grammar of English, for the division of such broad historical phases of the language. The grammar of the language in each of these three different stages is distinctly different enough from that of the others that they each can be described by separate synchronic grammars.[2]

The same convention – Old, Middle, New – is used for the historical stages of the Persian language, a usage nearly two hundred years old.[3] Old Persian is attested in the royal inscriptions of the Achaemenid Persian dynasty, which ruled their extensive empire from the sixth to the fourth centuries BCE. It was written in a simple cuneiform script specially designed

---

[2] On the appropriateness and simultaneous fuzziness of the tripartite chronological classification of English, see Lass 2000.
[3] This classification of Iranic languages into Old, Middle, and New stages began with the coining of the term Iranic (or "Iranian") languages itself (Lassen 1836: 181–185). See further van Bladel 2024: 3–4. On the continuing suitability of these three chronological designations for the Iranic languages, see Korn 2017: 609 §1.1.

to express it. Middle Persian, attested in inscriptions from the first century BCE onward, was used by the Persian kings of the Sasanid dynasty from the third to the seventh centuries CE and, until today, as a literary language of the Zoroastrian religion.[4] It was written in a much-adapted variety of the Aramaic script. The third stage, New Persian, first appears in records of the ninth and tenth centuries in Central Asia after the Muslim colonization of that region. It was written predominantly, though not exclusively, in a variety of the Arabic script, as it still is today, and it is spoken today in mutually intelligible varieties in the Islamic Republic of Iran, the Islamic Emirate of Afghanistan, and the Republic of Tajikistan (where it is written in the Cyrillic script). As with the conventional terms for the stages of English, each designated historical stage of Persian is artificial to the extent that it exhibits dialectal, chronological, and regional variations, but there are clear criteria for dividing each stage from the others. Middle Persian is different from Old Persian in specific, essential features of its grammar, and so is New Persian from Middle Persian. It has long been evident to scholars that Old Persian became Middle Persian or something close to it – using these terms in the general, imperfectly analytical ways just explained – already by the time Alexander of Macedon launched his invasion of the Persian Empire in 334 BCE. This book explains why the Persian language changed so rapidly and permanently by that time.

Hypotheses about the "Simple" Persian Language

The Persian language today is renowned as having a "simple" grammar. That is, when compared to other formerly or currently widespread languages, such as Arabic or Russian or ancient Greek, it has a simple morphology. This means it is minimally inflected: there are few changeable forms of words to express grammatical relations between words to make cogent sentences. This makes it easier for adults to learn.[5] In respect to its inflectional simplicity, Persian today is like English, a comparison often casually drawn over recent centuries. For example, the British orientalist William Jones (1746–1794) wrote in his widely read grammar of Persian for English-speakers, "The reader will soon perceive with pleasure a great resemblance between the Persian and English languages, in the facility

---

[4] Middle Persian is often known popularly as Pahlavi. This designation rests on an old error: Pahlavi meant Parthian not Persian.
[5] This point is elaborated in Chapter 2.

and simplicity of their form and construction."[6] The Swiss philologist Franz Misteli (1841–1903) compared English and Persian grammar closely in his volume of 1893 on linguistic typology.[7] He held that "historical development" of a nation changes its language, and the more removed a people is from engaging in "history," the more its language remains the same. He posited that Persian and English both similarly lost the ancient inflection of their common ancestor due to parallel circumstances (which he did not specify further).[8] Edwin Lee Johnson (1874–1947), author of an Old Persian grammar, wrote that "The relation of the New to the Ancient Persian presents something of a parallel to the relation of Modern English to Anglo-Saxon, in that an analytical language has been developed from one highly inflectional."[9] Even without a comparison to modern English, the relative simplicity of New Persian grammar was noticed by many others, too. Meerza Mohammad Ibraheem (*circa* 1800–1857), Professor of Arabic and Persian Languages at the East India College near London, wrote in 1841 that Persian grammar was "easy and simple."[10] Three hundred years earlier, the blind Egyptian Arab physician Dāwūd of Antioch (d. 1599) wanted, as a young man, to learn Persian; his foreign teacher told him that Persian "is easy for anybody, my son," and he offered to teach him rare knowledge of ancient Greek, which hardly anybody there knew, instead.[11] The Prussian philosopher Friedrich Engels (1820–1895), an educated non-specialist, wrote to Karl Marx that the acquisition of Persian grammar was "child's play" compared to the grammar of Arabic.[12]

---

[6] Jones 1809: 17.
[7] Misteli 1893: 597–608. Misteli published the comparison of the two languages earlier (1891), without drawing inferences about the reasons for their similarity.
[8] Misteli 1893: 488–489. His example of a relatively unchanged Indo-European language is Lithuanian, the implication being that Lithuanians did not undergo "historical development" so that their language remained closer to the Indo-European ancestor. The real effective factors behind Misteli's observation about Lithuanian will become evident in this book.
[9] Johnson 1917: 44.
[10] Anonymous 1857: 69. Ibraheem (spelled elsewhere as Ibrahím) was for fifteen years a Persian language instructor for lads destined to serve in the East India Company. He returned to Persia in 1844 and lived there until his death in 1857 after having served as a tutor to the future Qajar shah Nāṣir al-Dīn (Fisher 2001).
[11] Identical passages preserved by al-Muḥibbī (1966: 2.141.16–19); al-Ṭāluwī (1983: 2.36.10–13). *fa-lammā akmaltu* (*scil.* logic, mathematics, and natural science) *šra'abbat nafsī li-ta'alllumi l-luġati l-Fārsiyati fa-qāla yā bunayya innahā sahlatun li-kulli aḥadin lākinnī ufīduka l-luġata l-yūnānīyata fa-innī lā a'lamu l-āna 'alā waǧhi l-arḍi man ya'rifuhā ġayrī fa-aḥadtuhā 'anhu wa-anā bi-ḥamdi llāhi l-āna fīhā huwa id ḏāka*. The teacher was evidently quite unfamiliar with European scholarship on Greek in his time. Thanks to Ghayde Ghraowi for indicating the passage.
[12] In Marx and Engels 1983: 341 (letter dated June 6, 1853): "I am put off by Arabic, partly by my inborn hatred of Semitic languages, partly by the impossibility of getting anywhere, without considerable time, in so extensive a language … By comparison, Persian is absolute child's play."

Hypotheses about the "Simple" Persian Language

What is not widely known today is that Persian acquired most of its relative simplicity of inflection more than two thousand years ago, already at the stage of Middle Persian. As Walter Henning (1908–1967), a preeminent specialist in Iranic languages, noted in 1958, "With respect to morphology, 'Proto-Iranic' was comparable to Sanskrit or Greek, whereas Western Middle Iranic [including Middle Persian] is on a par with English."[13] But when the Persian language was first written in ancient inscriptions of the late sixth century BCE, its morphology was still quite complex. The Old Persian of that early time still had a highly inflected grammar with very many unpredictable word forms that learners needed to use to express themselves competently with native speakers. While not quite as ornately inflected as Old Avestan – an archaic Iranic cousin preserved only in a small, fixed corpus of ancient liturgical texts, maintained over centuries by daily priestly recitation – Old Persian was indeed more like ancient Greek or Sanskrit in its morphology. Middle Persian, by contrast, while not as simple in its inflections as New Persian, was already nearly so, as has been observed by Persian specialists.[14]

It may seem bold to claim that the creation of a vast empire triggered the restructuring of the very grammar of the language of its ruling elite. In fact, the claim, which this book verifies, was first articulated with respect to Persian by others as hints or suggestions, but it has never been systematically explained and defended, nor have the extraordinary implications of the claim been drawn out. Persian and Iranic language specialists such as Meillet (1866–1936),[15] Szemerényi (1913–1996),[16] and Utas[17] have intuited a connection between population contact and the reduction of Persian morphology, but they neither had the linguistic models available now nor did they provide sufficient evidence to support their tentative suggestions. The tendency in Persian studies generally, moreover, has been to focus on morphological simplicity in the evolution of New Persian, not Old or Middle Persian. The one concerted case to explain the reduction of

---

[13] Henning 1958: 89: "dem Formenschatze nach war das 'Uriranische' dem Sanskrit oder dem Griechischen vergleichbar, während das Mittelwestiranische etwa auf einer Stufe mit dem Englischen steht."
[14] Johnson 1917: 44: "In its grammatical forms and its phonology, Pahlavī [Middle Persian] is much nearer to the Modern Persian than to the Ancient Persian." Lazard 1975: 596: "Phonetically and grammatically, the degree of evolution from Old Persian to Middle Persian is considerable, the differences being comparable with the differences between Latin and French, for example. On the other hand New Persian remains in many respects quite close to Middle Persian." Utas 2013: 251: "At first glance, the differences between Middle and New Persian may appear considerable, but a closer look reveals that they are surprisingly few." Fattori 2022a: 35: "Middle Persian and New Persian are almost identical from the morpho-phonological point of view (loss of ancient inflectional endings, no distinction of case and gender etc.)."
[15] Meillet 1912: 150–151.   [16] Szemerényi 1980.   [17] Utas 2006.

Persian inflectional morphology in antiquity was made by a nonspecialist in Persian. Linguist John McWhorter's book *Language Interrupted* (2007), on grammatical reduction through mass nonnative acquisition, has a chapter on Persian, along with other chapters diagnosing the problem for other languages that have undergone similar grammatical restructuring, including English, Mandarin, and Malay.[18] That book is the most important antecedent of the present one. Although I differ with his linguistic theory in some important details, I argue in what follows that McWhorter's insight about the history of Persian is basically correct. Nevertheless, his chapter on Persian does not provide convincing historical contextualization for his arguments using primary sources, a minimum requirement for its use by historians. He likewise does not isolate the transitions from Old to Middle to New Persian clearly enough. To be fair, he addresses his fellow linguists who have largely synchronic concerns, not ancient historians or philologists, and his argument aims at general linguistic phenomena applicable to modern languages, for which Persian, like English, is merely one important example. McWhorter's tentative historical-contextual explanations about Persian are speculative, based partly on outdated surveys of Achaemenian history rather than primary sources, and are in some respects clearly mistaken. Yet McWhorter made a breakthrough, neglected by both linguists and historians, which deserves recognition and further development.[19]

What is required to explain this formative period in the linguistic history of Persian for historians and philologists is not just to explain the linguistic-historical model of analysis employed here, but also to combine relevant primary sources with that model, to demonstrate the relationship of the requisite social conditions with the grammatical change connected with the linguistic model. It is not so simple as saying that the Persian language "became imperial," as Meillet intuited. The cause and the explanation are both much more complicated than that. The outcome here is that the application of new linguistic research demonstrates social facts about the ruling class of one of the most important ancient empires. This book bridges ancient history and linguistics in a new way beneficial to both areas of research.

---

[18] McWhorter 2007: 138–164.
[19] As far as I have seen, only Nicholas Ostler's book about the future of English as a lingua franca has followed McWhorter's case about Persian (2010: 65–92), but there it is digested for a popular audience interested in the future status of English and the phenomenon of the lingua franca, rather than advancing the case about Persian per se.

Linguistic History and Historical Linguistics

Since its nineteenth-century inception, it is the field of historical linguistics that has largely controlled discussions of language change over long periods. Historical linguistic research is built on the extraordinary discovery that when languages change, they change according to regular patterns that can be expressed as systematic rules, sometimes even construed as laws of a language's development. These are especially discernible in phonology, the system of a language's sounds.[20] This discovery enabled scholars to establish the relationships of languages to one another through clinching demonstration, to elucidate the histories of words systematically, to infer prehistoric cultural facts with high confidence, and to describe scientifically change in languages over time.[21] It prepared the way for the modern understanding of the nature of language itself and for the scholarly trend of structuralism and its aftermath, effects far beyond linguistics.[22] The valid and time-tested methods of historical linguistics have offered and continue to offer sensational discoveries. But historical linguistics is founded on description, not explanation with respect to human context. At its core, historical linguistics entails describing two historical stages of a language; the systematic changes required for the prior stage to reach the latter stage are discerned and defined through the accumulation of examples and counterexamples; then these changes are named and described with special terminology as regular processes. The results can be tested and refined. The comparative method of historical linguistics, as successful as it is, does not tell us much, however, about *why* languages change as they do and when they do or *how* individuals and groups of speakers came to speak differently. It does not address the diffusion of sound changes through a population of speakers of a language who adopt those changes. It cannot address the social context of language change, just as it cannot easily address the physiology of voice production. Other methods are required for such questions. Despite some exceptions, conventional historical linguistics, by its methods, must largely treat languages as objects apart from society.[23] It is historians who are best able to narrate that social context. That said, the comparative method of historical linguistics does what it is supposed to do very well.

---

[20] Ringe and Eska 2013: 78–151; Hock 2021: 38–59. On the history of this development, see Morpurgo Davies 1998: 171–174, 226–278.
[21] Ringe and Eska 2013: 228–280; Hock 2021: 763–904. [22] Benes 2008.
[23] Ringe and Eska (2013) are notable for their effort to integrate variationist linguistics and language contact into the field of historical linguistics.

Although it is informed by historical linguistics from beginning to end, this book is not a work of historical linguistics in the sense just described. "We have to forget what it means to be historical linguists and become instead linguistic historians,"[24] as Terry Crowley (1953–2005) remarked in his careful history of the genesis of Bislama, a modern creole derived from English that became the national language of the Pacific Island nation of Vanuatu. The present book represents a project somewhat more like that one. Without forgetting historical linguistics, it comprises linguistic history. In no way is this intended as a corrective to the fundamentally sound methods of comparative historical linguistics, which I wholeheartedly endorse and continue to teach to my own students. Rather, it is complementary with those methods. It also participates in fields of linguistics concerned with language as a social medium in that it is premised on the "conviction" articulated by Thomason and Kaufman "that the history of a language is a function of the history of its speakers, and not an independent phenomenon that can be thoroughly studied without reference to the social context in which it is embedded."[25] As Croft puts it, "Languages don't change; people change language through their actions."[26] Although historical linguistic research provides necessary components of the present argument, it is already well established – many obscure details notwithstanding – that Old Persian and Middle Persian are different, how they are different, and which sounds and grammatical systems changed to which in the transition. I am therefore not outlining yet again how Old Persian and Middle Persian are formally different in a comprehensive way, nor do I seek to provide detailed grammatical descriptions of those differences. Such works, including grammars of the ancient stages of Persian, already exist in abundance and are mentioned throughout the notes and bibliography.[27] I have chosen not to include extensive comprehensive charts to illustrate Persian morphology at different stages of the language's history for this reason. I do not offer an explanation here in terms of language structure, such as we have already. My goal here is rather to explain *why* ancient Persian became so strikingly different from its immediate Old Persian antecedent and from its contemporary Indo-European relatives. The answer I propose

---

[24] Crowley 1990: 33. [25] Thomason and Kaufman 1988: 4. [26] Croft 2000: 4.
[27] Maggi and Orsatti (2018) provide a useful concise overview of the entire history of the grammar of Persian.

is functional, meaning that it examines language change from the point of view of people's efforts at communication. It has more to do with demography and social contact between groups speaking different languages than anything else. This necessitates not a comprehensive outline of ancient Persian phonology and morphology, but rather employing tested models correlating language change with patterns of population contact. The latter is primarily a historical, not a linguistic, topic.

The metaphor of a novel may work here. One can analyze the structure and contents of a novel and their variations over different editions without knowing much about the author's life or the readers of the novel. Such an analysis is valid within those constraints. That said, understanding the life and experiences of the author, and the historical context of a novel's authorship and readership and dissemination and reception will augment one's understanding of the novel in other ways that do not necessarily invalidate a structural analysis. If the ancient Persian language were a novel, this book analyses aspects of the lives of its authors that helped determine the novel's form.

More about Linguistic History

"Linguistic history" is not a rare expression in scholarship, but only limited attempts have been made to carve out a distinct domain for it as contrasted with historical linguistics, the latter of which is defined by its own rigorous methods.[28] A survey of books with "linguistic history" in their titles shows that they do quite different things. Although some studies and books already bear the designation of linguistic history, the term has seldom been clarified. I venture here to define linguistic history in a way that may be useful to others who undertake similar projects. I also wish to distinguish it from different but closely related kinds of investigation. Readers who want to get to the matter of this book without lingering on fine methodological distinctions may skip ahead.

---

[28] See, e.g., Malkiel 1953; De Mauro 1970. Burke (2004: 2–3) writes of a "social history of language," with goals similar to but distinct from those pursued here, focusing instead on "the place of language in expressing or constructing a variety of relationships" of social order, relative status, and the like. Linguistic history and the social history of language are both varieties of history that concern languages together with an account of the people who use them; in that respect they resemble each other closely.

One might think linguistic history could simply be the history of a language – but that is quite insufficient. Languages exist solely as learned systems of communication between people: adults and children, individuals and groups. Language is not an abstract entity possessing disembodied independence. Unlike speakers, languages are objects of history without agency, not subjects. Therefore, *linguistic history* must be the history of languages told through the history of their speakers as far as their languages are concerned. It cannot treat languages effectively apart from speakers, nor can it ignore the grammatical and lexical facts of their languages. Just as cultural history is impossible without the history of people interacting with the world around them, linguistic history is impossible without the history of speakers and writers.

This has consequences. For example, it is not valid, from the strictest point of view of linguistic history, to speak of the "spread" of a language, as historians and others often do casually. Rather than "spread," what occurs is the adoption of a language by new speakers, children or adults, and sometimes the shift of a population from one language to another via a stage of bilingualism. Likewise, it is not languages that move into new countries. A language's speakers are the ones who move. Persian did not "spread," but ancient Persians conquered others who had to interact with them, so some of them then learned Persian. This distinction may not matter in casual narration, but it matters greatly in linguistic-historical analysis. Furthermore, languages do not interact with each other and come into contact as autonomous entities; rather, people may use more than one language in the same life, or in the same situation, often leading to circumstances in which features are transferred from one language to another by bilingual individuals. In linguistic history people do things; languages do not. This must be a fundamental criterion of linguistic history, and its observance will help to avoid serious mistakes.

The foregoing, along with the rest of this book, may be enough to convey my intention with the expression linguistic history, but there are useful specific distinctions to be made with necessarily related fields. Linguistic history, because it concerns languages, must be informed by linguistics whenever that is relevant and possible. Linguistic history is especially closely connected with three kinds of linguistics, as the subfields are now divided: historical linguistics, sociolinguistics, and contact linguistics. It deals with some of the same problems as each of these three fields, but it is also distinct from them in its means and aims.

As already discussed, historical linguistics accounts for regular patterns of language change, mostly descriptively, and its primary tool has been the comparative method. For this reason, it has also been called comparative linguistics. Historical linguistics is diachronic by definition, producing an outline narrative of changes in the constitution and features of individual languages and reconstructed protolanguages. Because its explanations are structural, historical linguistics does not inherently need an account of the history of the speakers of a language. Normally, historical linguistics takes the grammars and lexica of languages and their components, and not their speakers, as its objects. Remarkably, the methods of historical linguistics work very well that way for its own purposes, but the relationship between social change and grammatical change – one of the subjects of this book – is thereby neglected.

Sociolinguistics, a newer field, attends to human relationships and society and their consequences for language.[29] It arose partly in reaction to the explanatory limitations of historical linguistics just described. In practice, sociolinguistics is more typically concerned with behaviors of speech, and directly observable social linguistic behaviors especially. For example, it studies language variation conditioned by social factors such as class, gender, age, place of residence, attitudes toward specific languages, or the linguistic expression of solidarity with reference groups through pronunciation and usage. Such phenomena can be studied live, in process, documented in recordings and discovered through interviews. To focus on the study of social variation and social cues and signification in living speech is to emphasize current phenomena in a relatively short scale of time, ignoring bygone societies. The methodological emphasis on directly observable social linguistic behavior explains why sociolinguistics tends not to be extensively diachronic, although any study of change is inherently historical at least on a short time scale. There is, however, a younger and lively subfield of historical sociolinguistics, also called sociohistorical linguistics. It is essentially the attempt to conduct the same kinds of sociolinguistic analysis used for present societies on linguistic usage of bygone societies. It therefore relies on written records. It continually confronts the problem that written texts do not offer the same possibilities for investigation of social factors in language use as living observable communities do, a problem philologists deal with constantly and effectively.[30]

---

[29] Coupland and Jaworski 2009.
[30] See generally the useful volume of Hernández-Campoy and Conde-Silvestre (2012), who make it clear in their introduction that the goal there is a more diachronic sociolinguistics and only incidentally history. In the same volume, Nevalainen and Raumolin-Brunberg (2012) usefully outline the history of historical sociolinguistics and try to relate it to other subfields of inquiry. As

Contact linguistics, another young subfield, is concerned with what happens to languages when they are used in the same place at the same time. Contact linguistics is therefore also concerned with human relationships in a secondary way, but the primary goal of this research is to understand linguistic effects between languages simultaneously in use in the same situation, not human relationships or societies themselves. It is, in effect, an approach to language change between languages not accounted for by the methods of comparative historical linguistics. That said, the designation "contact linguistics," referring to "language contact," is technically sloppy, for a reason already mentioned: languages mostly "contact" each other in the brains and behaviors of multilingual individuals.[31] Research in this area continues to yield important new results, mostly focused on recent times, although a growing number of philologists have been taking the findings of contact linguistics into consideration in their accounts of ancient languages.

These three fruitful kinds of linguistics are primarily concerned not with history at large but with specific aspects of language and the nature of language itself. That is because they are parts of linguistics. They stand somewhat autonomously as subfields because of their respective successes. Although linguistic history is related to all these important concerns, its goal is history, relating the history of people with that of their particular languages and vice versa, not with language as a general phenomenon. Linguistic history does have the potential to inform the study of language as such, and it will do so with well-documented instances and examples. Likewise, it will benefit from the models and methods of general

---

they write (2012: 32), "[the l]ack of linguistic materials from the more distant past and the mode of preservation of extant sources severely limit the historical sociolinguist's research agenda: the spoken language and para- and nonverbal information central to much of interactional and ethnographic research is simply not available." A conspicuous number of the major works of historical sociolinguistics concern the diachronic dialectology of English over the last several centuries, for which records are relatively abundant. The early landmark of sociohistorical linguistics, with its heavily articulated theoretical struggles, is Romaine's book of 1982, a work on Middle Scots Anglic. She argues (1982: 13) rightly that "synchronic sociolinguistic findings" are "relevant to diachronic problems."

[31] Matras 2009: 3: "'Contact' is, of course, a metaphor: language 'systems' do not genuinely touch or even influence each other. The relevant locus of contact is the language processing apparatus of the individual multilingual speaker and the employment of this apparatus in communicative interaction. It is therefore the multilingual speaker's interaction and the factors and motivations that shape it that deserve our attention in the study of language contact." Hock 2021: 631: "while it is convenient to speak of 'language contact,' actual contact does not take place between languages, but between their speakers."

linguistics.³² Linguistic history is like historical linguistics in its extensive diachrony, but unlike it in that it is rooted in the history of the speakers of a language, without which a language cannot exist or undergo change. In its focus on speakers and their relationships, linguistic history resembles sociolinguistics, but it is far more extensive in its diachrony. It necessitates the study of language contact, but its primary goal is not to discover universals of linguistic phenomena.

To summarize, linguistic history calls for explanatory pluralism but it stands on its own. It is like historical linguistics in studying language change over time, although it is different from it in addressing social change and the history of speakers simultaneously and inseparably from language change. It is also like sociolinguistics in that it attends to human relationships and society and their consequences for languages, but it is unlike sociolinguistics in using eclectic methods to access the speech and language use of speakers long gone and in its extensive diachrony. It participates in contact linguistics in studying bilingual and multilingual individuals and societies, as well as the linguistic effects due to such situations, but it is concerned with all aspects of linguistic diachrony, not with contact alone. Like all but the most recent history, linguistic history largely depends on written records of languages of the past before audio recordings of speech existed, commonly available only for about a century now. Therefore, philology in every sense of the term must be the primary methodological basis of linguistic history. This kind of linguistic history may even be considered a new branch of philology. Philology itself is not unitary; it is an umbrella term. Sometimes the name refers to textual criticism and the preparation of texts for publication and study, without which sound records for the study of language over long periods are unavailable. Sometimes it refers to comparative-historical linguistics itself, which is necessary to understand change in languages. Most broadly, it refers to the historical-contextual study of written texts, refusing to treat texts as abstracted objects lacking a contextual world that produced and preserved them. Linguistic history needs all other kinds of philology because these methods give the best access to premodern languages and speech before audio recordings. In this it is the same as historical linguistics. As Labov quipped, historical linguistics "can be thought of as the art of making the best use of bad data," bad in the sense that these data are obtained not from living subjects whose living behavior is directly

---

³² See Haspelmath 2021 on the distinction between general linguistics and the study of particular languages, and the cooperation necessary between these two related endeavors.

observable and through scientific methods of sampling, but through the vagaries of the preservation of the media of writing across the vicissitudes of time.[33] Linguistic history is in the same situation. The combination of philological methods makes the best use of such data. The power of linguistic history is due to reliably tested correspondences, one of the bases of all science: it can diagnose social history through historical linguistic data while it can also diagnose linguistic change through historical social data. (This will be explained in Chapter 2.) It does so with the models of various subfields of linguistics, at least a dose of sociology, and the methods of history and philology.

Because it necessitates explanatory pluralism, it is not always necessary to demarcate linguistic history very sharply from these other kinds of linguistic research. It participates in them, and those kinds of linguistic research do sometimes contribute directly to history. The goal of linguistic history is to produce specific histories of languages in terms of the histories of their speakers, not to address universals and general tendencies – although it should contribute to the latter and it can benefit from them, too. The linguistic history offered here, as the reader will see, is of a specific kind. While enjoying the valuable proceeds of various kinds of linguistics, this book adds new methods and models for understanding language change in history as a function of changes in human society affecting their linguistic relationships. It relates language change over a long period to social, political, and economic change, and vice versa.

Last, linguistic history should avoid propagating myths about particular languages and about language in general. Linguistic history must historicize. Because language ideologies rely on tendentious historicization, linguistic historians must be conscious of these pitfalls and try to avoid them.[34] Linguistic history should contribute rather to the demythologization of languages and the critical analysis of the stories told about languages invented by the people who speak them for their own ends.

Terminology

This project uses distinct terms deliberately in specific ways. The Persian language is one of a subgroup within the Indo-European language family commonly called Iranian in English. I refer to these languages rather by the term *Iranic* to distinguish the languages, spoken over millennia in many

---

[33] Labov 1994–2010: 1.11. [34] Milroy 2002; Watts 2011.

countries and regions, from the modern nation of Iran, its Iranian people, and Iranian culture. The term Iranic is not new and offers clear advantages for discussions of the languages involved.[35] It aligns with the English terms used in adjacent fields: English is a Germanic language, not a German language; Uzbek is a Turkic language, not a Turkish language; Sinhala is an Indic language, not an Indian language. The different English adjectives help to keep the different kinds of phenomena clearly distinct, and they contribute to holding some ideological tendencies at bay.

When Christian Lassen, followed by other nineteenth-century linguists, identified the Iranic languages as a group with common features and designated them as such (*iranisch* in German), he was drawing on the ancient endonym of the speakers of the Iranic languages, *Arya* (Old Persian *ariya*), the keyword in the etymology of the name Iran.[36] Lassen rightly distinguished the Iranic languages as a group specifically distinct from their cousin Indic languages of India, the speakers of which were also known as Arya. He called the Iranic languages *iranisch* without concern about confusion with the name of a modern state, because what we call Iran today was generally known as Persia in nineteenth-century Europe. Linguists of that time, however, assumed that the history of a language and its speakers was also a racial or national history. A language corresponded with a nation, one to one, it was assumed, and the speakers of a group of related languages constituted one race. In this connection, the idea of a distinct "Iranian people" who constituted or were a part of an "Aryan race" developed.[37]

Only in 1934–1935 did the government of King Reza Pahlavi request that foreign states refer to his country as Iran rather than Persia, a controversial decision at the time.[38] The tendency thereafter was to connect the modern nation of Iran to a whole family of languages and to call all their ancient speakers "ancient Iranians" regardless of the land in which they lived, the specific language they spoke, or their different cultures. The "Iranian" languages were then more easily appropriated as an entire group for the nonlinguistic purposes of Iranian nationalism and for the modern idea of a distinct Iranian race of the Aryan "whites" of Asia. These conceptions left an imprint within Iranian studies still noticeable today, seldom addressed

---

[35] Iranic was used, e.g., by Windfuhr (1979) and Perry (1998: 517). See further van Bladel 2024: 3–6.
[36] Lassen 1836: 105.
[37] Already Lassen (1836: 183) refers to "the national development of the Iranian peoples" ("die nationale Entwickelung der Iranischen Völker").
[38] Yarshater 1989.

directly.[39] As is well known, the term Aryan was furthermore appropriated for other political purposes and given almost irrevocable new moral connotations by the National Socialists of Germany and their Third Reich, as well as by some Iranian nationalists.[40] Suffice it to say that the term "Aryan" now bears such inappropriate signification for the study of the ancient Persian Empire and other Persian-led polities of the past that its use should be discontinued for this purpose. When there is so much ideological baggage relevant to modern history but not to ancient history, it is necessary to parse the terms carefully. Ancient Persians like King Darius I called themselves *Arya* in their own language in a context having little to do with the modern term Aryan as it is used in English. By deliberately reverting to the ancient adjective *Arya* (without the English suffix -n), I employ the term with its ancient use. Therefore, I write occasionally about Arya languages and Arya people, which is, in effect, a shorthand way to say Iranic-language-speaking peoples – without referring to "Aryans" racialized in modern ways. In this context, it should be clear that I am not referring to the speakers of Indic languages who designated themselves Arya, either. The term Arya has the further small advantage of avoiding confusion with the Christian "Arian heresy" of the bishop Arius (d. 336), another homophone apt to trip up the unwary. Those more accustomed to discussing "ancient Iranians" and "Aryans" will easily understand my purposefully modified usage of terms.

The Old and Middle Iranic languages, all of which are first attested before the advent of Islam, are conventionally regarded as belonging to "ancient Iran." The title of this book uses that convention to describe Old and Middle Persian together as Ancient Persian.

I use the words Achaemenids and Sasanids to refer to the members of their respective dynasties, the kings themselves and their descendants, treating the word ending -id as referring to the descendants of an individual. I use the words Achaemenian and Sasanian, with the more general adjectival suffix, to refer to things pertaining to their states, the people they ruled, and their cultures. For example, Xerxes was an Achaemenid, his empire Achaemenian.

I refer to this work as linguistic history. The adjective from that is *linguistic-historical.*

---

[39] See Zia-Ebrahimi 2016 for aspects of this that are relevant here. Maghbouleh (2017) provides lively examples of recent complications in the lives of Iranian Americans owing to the myth of the Aryan race.
[40] On modern Iranian nationalism in this area of historiography, see further Zia-Ebrahimi 2011 and Motadel 2013.

Plan of the Book

Chapter 1 introduces the linguistic phenomena exhibited by the Old Persian corpus of texts. It presents and summarizes what is well known to specialists but not widely known to ancient historians generally, and it introduces the major standing problem to be investigated here: how the ancient Persian language was drastically restructured within several generations. Chapter 2 lays out the linguistic-historical model that can explain the phenomena in a new way. In this long chapter I have synthesized that model, and the theory it represents, from various subfields of linguistics. The most important contributing subfield is contact linguistics, the branch of linguistics that addresses how the languages that people speak change when people acquire new languages under different circumstances and when they use more than one language in the same place. Modern cases of language restructuring are introduced to illustrate potential comparanda with Persian and for the use of other linguistic historians. Chapter 3 applies the linguistic model of Chapter 2 to the problem introduced in Chapter 1. It provides necessary historical contextualization to make sense of the data. This chapter takes a new look at long-known sources in Greek, Old Persian, Elamite, and other languages, and to a very limited extent also material culture preserved through archaeological research, to explain the linguistic history of Persian in this ancient period. It makes clear how the linguistic model presented in Chapter 2 applies to the Persian language in the time of the Achaemenian Empire and it addresses counterarguments. Chapter 4, the last, expands that application to other Iranic languages and to the historical context on a larger scale. It buttresses the findings of Chapter 3 by broadening the scope of the investigation, showing that Persian was not the only Iranic language affected by the social changes induced by the empire of the Achaemenid kings. The Conclusion summarizes the findings of this research and considers its ramifications.

The original plan of this book included a second, larger part concerning the genesis of New Persian and its evolution from Middle Persian. The social factors that conditioned the genesis of New Persian from Middle Persian are similar in some ways, but different in other, critical ways, to the factors that created Middle Persian from Old Persian. The origins of New Persian are also much better documented than those of Middle Persian, but the social history discernible from richer sources is correspondingly more complicated to analyze and to discuss. Together, the two parts of the original project grew too large to be accommodated in a single volume for today's readers and the preferences of today's presses. Although they both deal with the linguistic history of Persian using the same methods, they also deal with events separated by many centuries. They rely on different corpora of sources, written in different languages. For these reasons, and with the advice of various publishers who considered the project at its largest, I decided to separate them into two books. The second book, analyzing the evolution of New Persian, will appear in due course.

CHAPTER I

The Transformation of Old Persian

Old Persian first appeared in writing two and a half millennia ago, in the aftermath of conquest. Our story begins with the conqueror Cyrus of Anshan and the usurper Darius the Persian.

Cyrus was the royal heir of a little kingdom called Anshan, located in a large, relatively sheltered endorheic mountain basin of interconnected valleys in what is today southwestern Iran. This region is the one most properly called Persia, which ancient Greek geographers later called "Basin Persia."[1] Cyrus of Anshan created a coalition of warriors – among whom speakers of Iranic languages were prominent – and overthrew his master, the king of the Medes, an Arya people to the north. Taking control of Median treasure and resources, he conquered many other kingdoms in a series of successful and far-reaching military campaigns. Cyrus' armies marched into Anatolia and Babylonia, to the Mediterranean coast, and as far east as the steppes of Central Asia. By military force he and his son Cambyses, who subsequently added the bounteous river valley of Egypt to the conquered territories, created the largest empire ever seen by that time and adopted the ancient Assyrian and Babylonian title "king of kings." In political conditions marked by conspiracy over the dynastic succession to Cambyses, Darius, son of Hystaspes, became the Persian king of kings, ruler over lands of many peoples, as he himself declared, through a coup d'état carried out in 522 BCE. To legitimize his seizure of power, he married into the family of his predecessors, Cyrus and Cambyses, making those previous kings his in-laws, and he furthermore insisted on his sharing a patrilineal family relationship to them through his great-great-great-grandfather. The common ancestor he claimed for both families was a putative Achaemenes (Old Persian *Haxāmaniša*). We still call the dynasty of Cyrus and Darius "the Achaemenids," even though it is impossible to verify that Cyrus and Darius really did share the same distant patrilineage.

---

[1] Strabo 15.3.6: ἡ κοίλη Περσίς.

Darius immediately faced several attempts by local leaders to reassert their regions' independence in the wake of his coup. Some of them claimed to represent the local monarchies recently overthrown by Cyrus. Darius' violent and successful suppression of these many efforts to reassert independence is commemorated and justified as the defeat of imposters and military victory against rebels in a gigantic trilingual royal inscription. This appears together with his victory monument, a sculptural relief carved high on the conspicuous face of a mountain called Bisitun (or Behistun), situated along a major route through the Zagros range linking the Tigris region with the Iranian plateau, near modern Kermanshah. The relief depicts Darius victorious before captive "rebel" leaders while Ahuramazdā, the god to whom he gives credit for his success, hovers overhead. At first, only the two major written languages of the region, initially Elamite and then Babylonian, were used to write Darius' first-person account of his triumph over all his opponents and his legitimacy ordained by Ahuramazdā. Both Elamite and Babylonian had their own ancient literary traditions and had long been used for public inscriptions and records. Elamite was the language written in the kingdom of Anshan, from which Cyrus had emerged, and in the region of Elam, roughly modern Khuzistan in the southwestern part of Iran. Babylonian was the major literary dialect of Akkadian, a Semitic language prevalent in ancient Mesopotamia. It was the medium for literary traditions in the wealthy, internationally prestigious neighboring kingdom of Babylon, now a subject domain.[2] These two languages were therefore the obvious choices for a monumental commemorative inscription of a ruler from a region that used Elamite in writing after the conquest of Babylon. About a year later, however, Darius had his account etched beneath the rock relief of Bisitun in a new register, this time in his own Persian language, with some additional, supplementary information at the end of the text.[3] Most scholars agree that the simple cuneiform script used for Old Persian was an invention devised for this occasion, with thirty-six signs for sounds and several additional special characters.[4] The Old Persian cuneiform functioned rather like the simple Aramaic script and is much easier to learn than the hundreds of cuneiform signs used for Babylonian, or the 113 signs then used for Elamite.

---

[2] Tavernier 2017: 338–340.
[3] Wiesehöfer (1996: 13–21) nicely describes the stages of the development of the Bisitun monument.
[4] Fattori (2022b: 16–20) argues convincingly that the first to design and use the Old Persian cuneiform script were scribes trained in the writing of Elamite.

1 The Transformation of Old Persian

The Persian inscription of the Bisitun monument, created and augmented with addenda from about 520 to 518 BCE, is the oldest physically surviving document written entirely in an Iranic language. Because it was the language of a self-designated Persian king and his successors, who came from the southwestern part of Iran called Persia, we call that language today Old Persian, though they called it simply "Arya" (Old Persian *ariyā*), the language of the Aryas, an ethnic designation that is the etymological ancestor to the term "Iranian."[5] The Persians were one subgroup of the Aryas, like the Medes whose reign Cyrus usurped. Each Arya subgroup evidently had its own dialect of the same ancient linguistic stock. Linguists today call all the languages derived from that prehistoric ancestor language the Iranic family of languages, in turn a branch of the Indo-European language family. Because of the success of ancient Persian dynasties among Iranic-language-speaking peoples, the term Persian has often been generalized, imprecisely, for all speakers of Iranic languages and their subjects, in antiquity as often also today.

For 200 years after the Bisitun inscription, Darius' royal descendants and successors continued to employ the Old Persian cuneiform script for inscriptions in their Old Persian language that echoed Darius' words and those of his son and immediate successor, Xerxes (regn. 486–465). The Old Persian (OP) royal inscriptions after Xerxes are mostly formulaic statements emphasizing the continuity of the Achaemenid family's powerful monarchy and their devotion to the creator god Ahuramazdā, whom Darius and his descendants credited with bringing them to power. Here is an example of one of the formulae from the inscriptions.[6]

Darius I inscription DSf, lines 1–5, at Susa, Iraq, in OP, Elamite, and Akkadian	Xerxes I inscription XEa, entire, at Alvand, Iran, in OP, Elamite, and Akkadian	Artaxerxes III (regn. 358–338), inscription A³Pa, lines 1–8, at Persepolis, Iran, in OP only
The great god is Ahuramazdā who created this earth who created that sky who created man	The great god is Ahuramazdā who created this earth who created that sky who created man	The great god is Ahuramazdā who created this earth who created that sky who created man

---

[5] On the inflected form of the word used to designate the language, see Schmitt 2014: 136–137.
[6] Schmitt 2009: 123, 151, 195–196. The English translations from Old Persian are all mine unless noted.

who created happiness for man	who created happiness for man	who created happiness for man
who made Darius king	who made Xerxes king	who made Artaxerxes king
one king of many	one king of many	one king of many
one commander of many.	one commander of many.	one commander of many.

Here is an example of another, much shorter, prayer formula, expanded slightly with the passage of time to name other gods of the ancient Persians.

Darius I inscription DNa, lines 51–53, at Naqš-i Rustam, Iran, in OP, Elamite, and Akkadian	Xerxes I inscription XPh, lines 57–59, at Persepolis, Iran, in OP, Elamite, and Akkadian	Artaxerxes II (regn. 404–358) inscription A²Ha, lines 6–7, at Hamadan, Iran, and A²Sd, lines 3–4, at Susa, Iraq in OP, Elamite, and Akkadian
May Ahuramazdā protect me from what is foul and (may he also protect) my house and my country.	May Ahuramazdā protect me from what is foul and (may he also protect) my house and my country.	May Ahuramazdā, Anahita, and Mitra[7] protect me from what is foul and (may they also protect) what I have done.

The extant inscriptions are most plentiful for the early kings Darius I and Xerxes. Smaller numbers of generally shorter inscriptions survive for the later Achaemenid kings. The latest extant inscriptions are from the reign of Artaxerxes III (regn. 358–338). When the military conquest of Alexander of Macedon destroyed the dynasty two centuries after Darius I, in the 330s BCE, the Old Persian cuneiform script may have already been going entirely out of use but, whatever the real cause of its demise, it soon definitely became obsolete. The knowledge necessary to read the script was forgotten. The meaning of some of the inscriptions was summarized to a few Greek observers in that time – proving that the inscriptions were not merely symbolic, as a few scholars have supposed – but soon nobody could read the Old Persian inscriptions again until its nineteenth-century decipherment by European scholars.[8]

---

[7] I am inclined to accept the argument of Gershevitch (1964: 33–34) and Fattori (2022b: 4–5) that the unexpected <t> rather than <θ> (or even <h>) in the name of Miθra is due to a draft of the text in the Aramaic script, which does not distinguish the two dental sounds.

[8] On decipherment, see Weissbach 1895–1904: 2.64–72, Finkel 2005, and Tavernier 2013: 640–644.

The Character of Old Persian Grammar

The problem addressed in this study is that the grammar of the Persian language changed drastically in the Achaemenian period. To understand this, it is not necessary to learn to read Old Persian, but a sketch of the systems of its grammar is necessary. The Old Persian language of the early inscriptions of Darius I and his son Xerxes was characterized by a complicated system of word inflections. It was similar to its contemporary, distant cousins in the Indo-European language family, such as Latin, Greek, and Sanskrit, and very close to the ancient Iranic language of the Zoroastrian corpus of liturgy and hymns, the Avesta, particularly in its later linguistic stratum, called today Young Avestan.[9] Compared to its probably older close cousins Old Avestan and Vedic Sanskrit, Old Persian was slightly reduced in morphological complexity. For example, in Old Persian the ancient dative case was lost, and its function was taken over by the inherited genitive case. Nevertheless, Old Persian remained quite complex in the same ways as its contemporary relatives. In the earliest Old Persian inscriptions, the role of nouns in the sentence was expressed by inflections according to as many as six different case endings that varied in three grammatical genders between several different classes of nouns. Each noun belonged to one of these classes and each class had its own slightly different pattern of inflectional endings. Verbs were inflected from often unpredictable (i.e., irregular) verb-stems for different tenses and temporal aspects and with a range of special suffixes expressing person, number, mood, and diathesis. Some classes of verbs exhibited regular variation in the verb stem between the singular active and the rest of the forms. Though few in their attested instances, the ancient aorist and perfect verb systems, accounting for two of the three major ancient Indo-European verb stem types, are still somewhat in evidence – the perfect verb stem only once in the Bisitun inscription.[10] Nouns and verbs had not only singular and plural forms, but also dual forms when referring to pairs of individuals. Many different prefixes to verbs (preverbs), related to the prepositions, connoted various directions of activity or nuances of meaning special to each verb stem.

The following table of noun endings is suggestive of this complexity, but does not come close to doing justice to the intricacy of the noun inflection in this system. The biggest problem for this table is that no noun or noun class is found in all its possible forms in the limited Old Persian

---

[9] Cf. the similar comparative estimation of McWhorter (2007: 148). [10] Brust 2018: 77–78.

inscriptional corpus. Not one declension is completely known. I am sure that specialists may quibble with the way I have presented it, and they would be right to do so. That said, none of them have attempted to compile a single table to account for all the noun endings – for the good reasons I am about to explain – and it is only to demonstrate visually the complexity of Old Persian nominal inflection that I provide it in Tables 1.1a, b, and c.

Table 1.1a *Old Persian noun case endings by etymological type (Singular)*

Singular	Thematic nouns	ā-stem nouns	Athematic nouns (many subtypes)
vocative	-Ø	-ā	-Ø
nominative	-s/-Ø, *neuter* -am	-ā	-h/-s/-š/-Ø
accusative	-am	-ām	-(a)m
genitive-dative	-ahyā	-āyā	-as, -h/-š
instrumental-ablative	-ā	-āyā	-iyā/-auš/-āuš/-ā
locative	-ai/-ayā	-āyā	-i

Table 1.1b *Old Persian noun case endings by etymological type (Dual)*

Dual	Thematic nouns	ā-stem nouns	Athematic nouns (many subtypes)
voc./nom./acc.	-ā	*-ay	*-ā
dat./instr./loc.	-aibiyā	-āyā	*-biyā

Table 1.1c *Old Persian noun case endings by etymological type (Plural)*

Plural	Thematic nouns	ā-stem nouns	Athematic nouns (many subtypes)
voc./nominative	-ā/-āha	-ā	-ā
accusative	-ā	-ā	-ā
genitive-dative	-ānām	-ānām	-nām
instrumental-ablative	-aibiš	*-ābiš	-biš
locative	-aišuwā	-āuwā	-hu/-su/-šu

The asterisks refer to unattested forms. We can assume that actual forms corresponded to each of these cells in the time of Darius I. The major way in which this table simplifies the reality is that the third column of the nouns, called athematic (a technical term in Indo-European linguistics), includes several distinct types that vary according to specific rules of sound combination between the final consonant or vowel of the noun stem and the endings added to those stems. Moreover, some athematic nouns exhibit variations by case and number not just in the inflectional endings, but also in the changeable stems to which inflectional endings are added in different cases and numbers. Table 1.1 therefore does not display the real variety of several such noun class subtypes under the athematic category. Despite my somewhat reckless shortcuts in presenting it, it does give a sense of the complexity of Old Persian noun morphology through the number of cells available for noun forms. Old Persian nominal morphology formed a heterogeneous system. Even within that complex system, some attested words seem to have exceptional inflections. In addition to the streamlined pattern of noun endings presented here, pronouns had somewhat different endings in some cases, too. Personal pronouns for first and second person followed their own patterns. Third-person pronouns had pronominal endings often different from those of nouns, varying by the three grammatical genders, not to mention their application on near- and far-deictic demonstrative pronouns that had stems varying by case. The reader who wants to take in all the endings and attested forms should consult a reference work.[11]

The complexity of languages like these makes them a challenge for those who study them. That is, we adult learners experience the complexity in Old Persian morphology as a relative difficulty in learning them. These many inflectional endings must correspond grammatically to other words likewise with corresponding forms in different parts of a sentence: verbs and subjects agree in person and number, objects and indirect objects are marked to show their function in the sentence, adverbial usages are inflected in different ways, and so on. Some of these forms are not predictable by the normal patterns, being irregular. Learners of Old Persian must memorize many inflectional paradigms and irregular forms. Students today, of course, have no access to native

---

[11] Kent 1950; Schmitt 2014; Brust 2018: 47–70. Skjærvø (2009a: 72–86) presents these in partially tabular form for both Avestan and Old Persian combined, showing the range of unattested but probably real possibilities of the early Achaemenian period.

speakers of these dead languages and learn them as adults from books only or from teachers, most of whom learned them from books. Two factors make learning Old Persian in a short period feasible today. First is the relatively small size of the extant corpus of inscriptions. Only a narrow range of the grammatical possibilities of the language actually occurs in these limited texts, almost the whole corpus of which easily fits, together with a translation into a modern language, into a single volume of 200 pages.[12] Second, most students today who undertake to learn Old Persian, as I have seen, already have expertise in related fields. Usually, they have already studied closely related languages, such as ancient Greek or Sanskrit, or are Assyriologists already quite familiar with inscriptions of this type. Teaching Old Persian to students without such background – another experience I have enjoyed – shows that comprehending the grammar of Old Persian, even in its limited corpus, is far from intuitive and is indeed quite difficult.

The Old Persian royal inscriptions were displayed as symbols of Persian power and the legitimacy of the Achaemenid dynasty and commemorations for the future. Their contents were considered important, enough to be deliberately disseminated in different media. Not only were they carved in plain sight on many walls and column bases of Persian palaces at Persepolis and Susa; we know also that they circulated at least sometimes in translation. For example, a fragmentary Aramaic translation of two of Darius' inscriptions was discovered at Elephantine in southern Egypt, written on papyrus and preserved by the dry Egyptian climate, at the site of a remote garrison serving the Persian government.[13] More famously, Herodotus, in the late fifth century BCE, in the third scroll of his Greek *Histories*, a work mainly about the fraught relations of the Persian kings with the polities of Greeks, relates a version of the contents of Darius' first inscription as he knew its story and chose to retell it with other information added.

As just shown, descendants of Darius and Xerxes used and reused the same formulae and turns of phrase in their own inscriptions, with a few variations and new statements interspersed among them. Skilled masons and scribes carved Old Persian royal statements and tags elegantly into the walls and column bases of palaces, on commemorative plaques buried in foundations, and on rock faces in private parks of the kings. Such inscriptions demonstrated royal continuity. An inscription was put up in the name of Darius' predecessor, Cyrus, to buttress the idea of an

---

[12] Schmitt 2009, with German translation.
[13] Sims-Williams 1981b; Greenfield and Porten 1982.

Achaemenid dynasty that started with the famous conquerors whose kingdom Darius had usurped. Old Persian inscriptions in the name of antecedents of Darius I were made after the Bisitun inscription, and in a few instances, as it turns out, are modern forgeries.[14]

Only 100 years after Darius, however, the Persian language of the inscriptions had changed. Already by the 420s BCE, just one century after the first Old Persian inscription at Bisitun, the inscriptions seem to be getting the grammar wrong by the standard of the language expressed by Darius and Xerxes. This has long been noted. E. H. Sturtevant (1875–1952) wrote that ancient "highly inflected languages are remarkably free from gross errors in the use of case forms … in all save one: … The single Indo-European language which appears to form an exception is Old Persian."[15] Historical linguist E. A. Hahn (1893–1967) likewise noticed this, singling out the later Old Persian inscriptions. She wrote that "by the time of the three kings named Artaxerxes, especially the last one, something peculiar has happened to the language, or at least to those users of it, whether the kings in question or their ghost-writers, who composed the inscriptions purporting to come from these monarchs."[16] First, the range of nominal inflection in use conspicuously diminished. As noted by Cantera, from the reign of Artaxerxes I (regn. 465–424) onward, the range of noun cases used in the inscriptions diminished almost entirely to three (nominative, genitive-dative, accusative). The exceptions are very few: there is one locative-case noun that appears lexicalized (fixed as *wiθiyā*, "in the house"), from the reign of Artaxerxes I, and one ablative-case ending in a formulaic prayer, following a preposition that already determined the meaning (*hacā wispā gastā*, "from all that is foul"), occurring three times in the reign of Artaxerxes II (regn. 404–358 BCE).[17] Second, and at least as important as the reduction in the range of inflection, the texts begin to exhibit what have appeared to many modern scholars to be mistaken forms, with respect to phonology, syntax, and morphology, especially in the morphology of inflectional noun and verb endings. These occur even in formulaic

---

[14] Fattori (2022a) has convincingly demonstrated that several of the inscriptions alleged to have been discovered at Hamadan, including inscriptions attributed to the reigns of Artaxerxes I, Darius II, and Artaxerxes II, and long used by specialists, are frauds produced in the period approximately from the 1930s and 1950s. Until now, scholars have relied upon them for an account of later Achaemenian Persian inscriptions. In fact, the inauthentic ones copied "mistakes" of genuine late Achaemenian Persian inscriptions. I have excluded consideration of these newly unauthenticated inscriptions from this study.

[15] Sturtevant 1928: 66.   [16] Hahn 1965: 48–49.   [17] Cantera 2009: 26–28.

28   1 The Transformation of Old Persian

expressions that could easily have been copied verbatim from known earlier versions less than a century old and on display at the same royal sites.[18] For example, by the time of Artaxerxes II and thereafter, the nominative and accusative cases seem not to be clearly distinguished, and the final syllables *-ā, -aiy, -am*, and *-ām*, word endings hitherto serving as distinct grammatical markers for different specific purposes, were sometimes omitted in various nouns, pronouns, and verbs. In some instances, the inscriptions exhibit the wrong word-endings (non-etymological endings). Grammatical gender in nouns and relative pronouns seems confused. The scribes, or the authors who composed the inscriptions, were evidently aware that there should have been a specific correct ending because at times they employed hypercorrections, aiming at a perceived correct form. For example, the ending *-ām*, which was formerly the accusative singular ending of the *ā*-stem nouns, came to be used on some nouns and pronouns that would not have taken such an ending before, regardless of the older inflection or the grammatical role of the nouns and pronouns in question. Artaxerxes III (regn. 358–338) sponsored the creation of four different beautifully and conspicuously displayed copies of an inscription at the palace complex of Persepolis, A³Pa.[19] In the formula beginning with "The great god is Ahuramazdā," we find non-etymological endings on the nouns for "earth," "sky," "happiness," and "for man." The ancient accusative ending on the noun "kings" is missing in one instance, but not the other, and the word for "commander" is spelled with a different vowel quantity word-internally. One quarter of the words taking nominal and pronominal endings exhibit different kinds of grammatical problems, and they do so in all four copies of this inscription, where legible, showing that they were based on a common master-copy exhibiting these grammatical features. Scholars represent the Old Persian words of this formula in Roman letters as follows.[20] I have boldfaced the apparent oddities in the inscription of Artaxerxes III.

---

[18] Fattori (2022b: 20–21) notes that the Elamite versions in some late Achaemenian inscriptions seem not to correspond always to the accompanying Persian and were probably copied from older Achaemenian Elamite inscriptions to which they do correspond. He suggests that Elamite had probably gone out of administrative use in the late Achaemenian period, when administrative Elamite tablets are no longer attested.

[19] Schmitt 1999: 91–104; Schmitt 2009: 27, 195–197.

[20] Schmitt 2009: 123, 151, 195–196. Note that I follow the conventions of Old Persian transcription almost the same as adopted by Korn (2021: 3n6), slightly modified. Fattori (2022a) has shown that the example of this formula attributed to the reign of Artaxerxes II (regn. 404–358) inscription A²Hc (lines 1–7, at Hamadan, Iran, in Old Persian) is probably a forgery.

The Character of Old Persian Grammar

Early inscriptions		A very late inscription	
Darius I inscription DSf, lines 1–5, and Xerxes I inscription XEa	Modern scholars' rendering of the words in Roman script	Artaxerxes III (regn. 359–338), inscription A³Pa[a, c, d], lines 1–8	Modern scholars' rendering in Roman script
The great god is Ahuramazdā	baga wazərka dʰuramazdā	The great god is Ahuramazdā	baga wazərka dʰuramazdā
who created this earth	haya imām būmim adā	who created this earth	haya imām būm**ām** adā
who created that sky	haya awam asmānam adā	who created that sky	haya awam asmān**ām** adā
who created man	haya martiyam adā	who created man	haya martiyam adā
who created happiness for man	haya šiyātim adā martiyahyā	who created happiness for man	haya š**āyatām** adā martiyahyā
who made Darius/Xerxes king	haya [dārayawaʰum / xšayāršām] xšāyaθiyam akunauš	who made me, Artaxerxes, king	haya mām ərtaxšaça xšāyaθiya akunauš
one king of many	aiwam parūnām xšāyaθiyam	one king of many	aiwam parūnām xšāyaθiyam
one commander of many.	aiwam parūnām framātāram	one commander of many.	aiwam parūnām framatāram

This is just one striking example out of the whole extent of the grammatical variations of the late Old Persian inscriptions. In some late inscriptions, case endings are abstracted and superadded agglutinatively on the nominative form, as far as the spelling is concerned, creating thereby apparently unetymological word forms that had never existed before.[21] For example, in the early Old Persian inscriptions of Darius I and Xerxes I, the name of the king Darius is *dārayawaʰuš* in the nominative case, *dārayawahauš* in the genitive-dative. This proper name belongs to the ancient Indo-European athematic noun class called *u*-stems and these inflections were formed regularly according to consistent inherited ancient grammatical patterns. In the time of Artaxerxes II, the early fourth century

---

[21] On this "agglutinierende Bildung," see Schmitt 1999: 65 and 116; somewhat differently Mancini 2019. Kent (1950: 24 §57) suggested both "neologism" and "error" as reasons for such "new formations," but these are descriptions, typical of historical grammar, not explanations.

BCE, however, the genitive-dative form occurs as *dārayawaʰuš-ahyā*, a form derived by adding *-ahyā*, the genitive-dative ending of the most widespread noun class, *a*-stems, the ancient Indo-European thematic class of nouns, over the nominative ending of the *u*-stem proper name.[22] The same occurs with Artaxerxes' name already in the time of Darius II (regn. 423–405): the old nominative form was *ərtaxšaçā*, the old genitive-dative form *ərtaxšaçahyā*; but a new, etymologically irregular form *ərtaxšaçā-hyā* appears in later inscriptions.[23] In such forms as these, the most frequently occurring genitive-dative ending in the language (-[*a*]*hyā*), from the *a*-stem nouns, has been abstracted and reanalyzed as an independent suffix added to the nominative. The English equivalent would be something like writing "she's" instead of English "her" or "he's" for "his"; in both of these mistaken forms, the English genitive marker, -'s, would be added to the subject pronoun, rather than using the genitive *her*, *his*. Not only noun endings, but verb endings and syntax were affected. In different fragments of copies of a column-base inscription of Artaxerxes II at Susa (A²Sd), the ancient form of the imperfect verb *akunawam*, "I made," shows up with unetymological variants *akunawām* and *akuwnašāš* (?).[24] This inscription was available for copying from formulae in publicly visible inscriptions, but the endings are not correct by the older standard.[25]

The later the inscription, the more such inconsistencies in grammatical inflections one finds. The late inscriptions show that the authors of these texts had an idea that some word ending should be there, but they did not know which ending to apply, or at least which signs to write, in different grammatical contexts. Finally, an author of one of the latest of the extant Old Persian inscriptions, writing in the 350s BCE, partly gave up on attempting the inflectional word endings used in the inscriptions of Darius I. In one portion of the inscription on behalf of Artaxerxes III

---

[22] A²Ha (Schmitt 2009: 25, 186–188). Other examples of this are found in D²Ha (which would have been an earlier attestation of this form) and A²Hc, but Fattori (2022a) has demonstrated with overwhelming likelihood that these are modern fakes modeled on known texts.

[23] Schmitt 2009: D²Sb 2, A²Sa 2. This form occurs also in the modern fakes impugned by Fattori (2022a), omitted from consideration here for that reason. The forgers learned ancient grammatical solecisms from modern publications and used them in their forgeries, creating "inauthentic mistakes."

[24] Schmitt 2009: 26, 195. The imperfect verb in the Old Persian of Darius was used for ordinary past narrative.

[25] Mancini's different interpretation (2019: 552) will be discussed further. Fattori (2022b) makes the case that some of these unexpected Persian inscriptional spellings are due to their having been transliterated from a prototype in the Aramaic script, which was then misinterpreted on transliteration into Old Persian cuneiform. While this may have happened in some instances, not all the cases he proposes are convincing, and the theory does not account for all the irregularities that I am discussing.

(A³Pa §2), from which the comparative sample just given is drawn, proper names in the dynastic genealogy are strung together with no inflection, written entirely in the old forms of the nominative case, except for an unexpected appearance of the genitive case, intelligible to us mainly because of the text's simplicity and because we know from the ancient recurrent formulae what the later texts are supposed to say. Compare these fluently inflected genealogies from the early kings Darius I and Xerxes with the late inscription of Artaxerxes III. Words in parentheses in the English translation represent words required in English but not in the Old Persian. Note also that the Roman and Greek letters used to illustrate Persian sounds create a scholarly ideal, based on the reconstructions of ancestral Iranic word forms, and do not adequately represent the changing pronunciation of the Persian words. The later inscriptions were not pronounced as shown here; the point here is to show the change in inflectional morphology.[26]

Darius I, Bisitun (DB §2 1.3–7)[27]
θātiy dārayawaʰuš xšāyaθiya
manā pitā wištāspa
wištāspahyā pitā əršāma
əršāmahyā pitā ariyāramna
ariyāramnahyā pitā čišpiš
čišpaiš pitā haxāmaniš

King Darius declares:
My father (is) Hystaspes.
Hystaspes' father (is) Arsames.
Arsames' father (is) Ariaramnes.
Ariaramnes' father (is) Teispes.
Teispes' father (is) Achaemenes.

Xerxes, Persepolis (XPf §3)[28]
θātiy xšayaršā xšāyaθiya
manā pitā dārayawaʰuš
dārayawahauš pitā wištāspa nāma āha
wištāspahyā pitā əršāma nāma āha

King Xerxes declares:
My father (is) Darius.
Darius' father was Hystaspes by name.
Hystaspes' father was Arsames by name.

Artaxerxes III, Persepolis (A³Pa §2)[29]
adam ərtaxšaçā xšāyaθiya puça
ərtaxšaçā dārayawaʰuš xšāyaθiya puça
dārayawaʰuš ərtaxšaçā xšāyaθiya puça
ərtaxšaçā xšayāršā xšāyaθiya puça
xšayāršā dārayawaʰuš xšāyaθiya puça
dārayawaʰuš wištāspahyā nāma puça
wištāspahyā əršāma nāma puça
haxāmanišiya

"I (am) King Artaxerxes, son
  Artaxerxes, King Darius son.
Darius (is) King Artaxerxes son.
Artaxerxes (is) King Xerxes son.
Xerxes (is) King Darius son.
Darius (is) Hystaspes' by name son.
Hystaspes' (is) Arsames by name son,
  (an) Achaemenid."

---

[26] Cf. Mancini 2019: 531–532.   [27] Schmitt 2009: 37.   [28] Schmitt 2009: 161.
[29] Schmitt 2009: 196–197. See Mancini's interpretation (2019: 547–550).

The literal English translation of the last of these does not capture fully the effects of the uninflected words and missing syllables in the last Old Persian inscription, because all that is missing in the English, a much less inflected language, is the apostrophes used to indicate the genitive case in writing. There is also the use of the genitive *Hystaspes'* where the nominative is apparently wanted. Nevertheless, the reader of the English translation will sense the uninflected and incorrect English that a direct translation of each word produces.

Earlier Scholarly Explanations

The change in the language of the inscriptions has long been noted and studied. It calls for an explanation, and different explanations have been offered. A typical response of scholars of the past has been simply to describe the Old Persian of the late inscriptions as "corrupt" and "erroneous," signs of a language "in decline."[30] They were said to be merely bad compositions, or it was a language itself gone wrong. This is evidently not quite an explanation, but rather a value judgment, cohering with the once-widespread idea of historians that the state of the Achaemenids had gradually become morally decadent. Linguistic "corruption" could be related implicitly to social corruption. A few influential ancient Greek sources, which were for generations the basis of European scholars' knowledge of ancient Persian history, and which will enter discussion in Chapter 3, attributed moral corruption to the later Achaemenian Persians and their kings, perhaps predisposing modern historians to evaluate linguistic changes in this context in a similar way. The linguist Antoine Meillet, followed by several others, offered a more practical explanation. He regarded the Old Persian of the late Achaemenian inscriptions merely as the results of barbarous and partly failed attempts at Old Persian, in which the language is composed by nonnative speakers, foreigners who did

---

[30] Such assessments began almost immediately upon the decipherment of Old Persian. Oppert (1852: 205–206) regarded the late language as due to the "crass ignorance of the people" who used "barbarisms" that were the sign of a "dying language." Müller (1877: 228) saw "der Verfall der Sprache" (the decline of the language) in the late Old Persian inscriptions. Von Spiegel (1881: 126) characterized the inscription of Artaxerxes III as having "Fehler" (errors) and exhibiting "Sprachverschlechterung" (language decay). Darmesteter (1883: 1.4) described the language of the late Old Persian inscriptions as "corrumpue" and as evidence of "décomposition" in the language, exhibiting "barbarismes" and (1883: 1.117) characterized the tendencies of the language as having "ruiné l'édifice des forms anciennes." Kent (1950: 23–24 §§56–57) treats most of the changes in the late inscriptions as morphological and syntactic "errors." Citing Kent, Guha (2024: 446) recently calls the language of the late Achaemenian inscriptions "a corrupted form of the language."

not know the language well. He therefore even excluded the late inscriptions from his grammar of the language, refusing to treat them as a meaningful part of the corpus for the purposes of historical linguistics.[31] In effect, this is to explain the linguistic differences of the late Old Persian inscriptions as merely profuse mistakes with respect to a correct language that had otherwise ceased to be documented. The late Achaemenian Persian inscriptions would thus not actually represent the authentic language of real Persians, but foreigners attempting and failing to write in Persian. This explanation cannot be wholly accepted, either. It is highly unlikely that the composition of a formal royal inscription conspicuously presented at a major palatial site or garden park of the kings would be assigned to somebody who did not really know the language of the king in which it was to be written. For example, inscription A³Pa of Artaxerxes III, as mentioned, existed in at least four copies on walls at Persepolis (the others being A³Pb, c, and d). The contents of these copies are identical although b has different line divisions. Therefore, the variations in the grammar were not due to sloppiness by the masons or momentary errors by a careless person. They were a part of the composition in Persian of the final draft of the master-copy, a text with which somebody took special care. The author could copy older inscriptions and get quite a few of the ancient forms right by the older standard but did not control the inflectional morphology of that earlier form of Persian enough to write even a simple new composition with the same grammar.

Some scholars have assumed that these large, beautiful inscriptions were only for showy decoration, and that nobody could really read them, anyway.[32] Perhaps then such grammatical variation or misspellings would simply not matter. Yet this is an odd assumption. Nobody would assume that Greek or Latin inscriptions, even fancy ones, were only for show and not intended also as actual declarations and memorials. Our unfamiliarity with the language does not mean it was obscure for those who

---

[31] Meillet 1915: 20–21 §46, endorsed by Huart (1927: 102). Meillet would not use data from the inscription of Artaxerxes III for his grammar, because he deemed it too incorrect to be relevant to Old Persian grammar (1915: 22 §47). The first principle of his grammar (1915: 1 §1) is that only the inscriptions of Darius I and Xerxes can inform us about Old Persian; these alone were "correct." Similarly, Brandenstein and Mayrhofer (1964: 89) characterize the late Old Persian inscriptions as "erroneous, no longer controlled Old Persian" ("Beispiel des fehlerhaften, nicht mehr beherrschten Altpersisch"). Ghirshman (1954: 163) regards them as "bad errors, illustrating the lack of skill among the scribes." Sturtevant (1928) comes to the same conclusion as Meillet, whose view he acknowledges, but he assigns blame to Babylonian scribes specifically, apparently on the grounds that Babylonians no longer knew about case endings in their own language in the first millennium BCE and so were unable to learn case endings in Persian.

[32] Tavernier (2013: 650–652) discusses this view, with references to earlier scholarship.

encountered it. My modern students of Old Persian read its simple cuneiform letter-signs easily within a week of practice before they know even the basics of the grammar. Surely native speakers of Old Persian could learn to read these signs with equal ease, if they had a little time and the interest to know what they said, especially when the signs ostentatiously ornamented the palatial walls and columns right in front of them or even the objects in their hands: fine drinking bowls, standard weights used in scales, or glass post-sockets, to mention only inscribed portable objects that we know about because the durability of their material preserved them. We can only guess how much Old Persian writing has been lost, written on less durable objects that have not survived the centuries, but it is clear that Old Persian writing was not limited to buried foundation tablets or inaccessible mountainsides. It was visible wherever the very many followers of the kings might be.[33]

From Old Persian to Middle Persian

There is a more effective explanation of the grammatical variation just described: what changed was the living language itself, as spoken by the generality of speakers, and not merely the competence of the scribes as the language in which they were supposed to be literate. Several leading scholars have already convincingly explained the changes in the Old Persian in this way. Already in 1877, Friedrich Müller suggested that the spoken vernacular Persian no longer matched the "learned" language of the inscriptions,[34] and in 1878 Friedrich von Spiegel concluded that the late Old Persian inscriptions represented "actual degeneration in the language, not mere errors," meaning that the inflectional endings were lost in actual speech. Although von Spiegel used value-laded terms like "degeneration" (as mentioned), he considered the language itself to have changed: "Apparently Old Persian did not long survive the Achaemenid dynasty."[35] In short, native speakers of Persian in the fourth century BCE did not speak the highly inflected Persian of Darius I in the late sixth century BCE. As Schmitt put it much later, "spoken Persian had evolved into a somewhat different form, so discrepancies between everyday speech and

---

[33] Van Bladel (2024) discusses literacy in Middle Persian and how the loss of physical copies of texts may contribute to an impression of nearly complete illiteracy by ancient Persians.
[34] Müller 1877: 228, "gesprochene Volkssprache," "gelehrte Schriftsprache."
[35] Von Spiegel 1871–1878: 3.738–739: "eine wirkliche Entartung der Sprache, nicht blosse Fehler;" "Wahrscheinlich hat das Altpersische die Achämenidendynastie nicht lange überlebt . . . " Similarly, Black 2008: 64: "Competence in Old Persian seems to have collapsed – possibly because the spoken language had changed too much."

the traditional language of the inscriptions had arisen."³⁶ Marco Mancini's perspicacious article of 2019 goes furthest in convincing us that the late Achaemenian inscriptions really represent a subsequent phase of the Persian language "masked" by archaic and conventional spellings.³⁷

What was really happening to Old Persian becomes evident when we consider that Middle Persian, the next attested stage of Persian, exhibits most of the same features already appearing as "errors" in late Old Persian inscriptions, particularly the loss of most of the inflectional endings on nouns. This has been obvious to some specialists in ancient forms of Persian for some time. They have not hesitated to describe Middle Persian grammar as *reduced* and *simplified*. Such terms appear controversial to linguists, and this will be important in the next chapter, so I present here several statements by specialists in Iranic languages in anticipation of that discussion. Karl Geldner (1852–1929) wrote of Middle Persian that "The abundant grammatical forms of the ancient language are most reduced in number."³⁸ Oswald Szemerényi regarded the nominal and verbal systems of Middle Persian as "severely simplified."³⁹ Rüdiger Schmitt wrote of Western Middle Iranic (including Middle Persian) that "The grammatical system of these dialects appears to have been transformed from the ground up, since the entire inflection of nouns, pronouns, and verbs has been considerably simplified and reduced and very few of the inherited forms have survived as such."⁴⁰ Judith Josephson remarked that "Middle Persian is a language with an extremely reduced morphology."⁴¹ Nicholas Sims-Williams put it in relative terms: "As compared with the complex morphology of Old Iranian, or even of Eastern Middle Iranian languages . . ., the morphological system of Middle Persian has undergone drastic simplification. Nominal morphology was particularly severely affected."⁴² Ludwig Paul observed that "Middle Persian . . . had already lost almost all morphological distinctions of case and gender that had characterized Old Persian as an ancient Indo-European language."⁴³ These specialists have stated as a matter of plain fact that Middle Persian is quite distinctly a grammatically *simplified* and *reduced* descendant of Old Persian.⁴⁴ It has not been controversial, but rather a consensus to use such neutral descriptors.

---

[36] Schmitt 2000: 718.   [37] Mancini 2019.   [38] Geldner 1885: 655a.   [39] Szemerényi 1980: 210.
[40] Schmitt 1989b: 98. "Das grammatische System dieser Dialekte erscheint von Grund auf verändert, da die gesamte Flexion von Nomen, Pronomen und Verbum wesentlich vereinfacht und reduziert worden ist und nur wenige der ererbten Formen als solche übriggeblieben sind."
[41] Josephson 2011: 24.   [42] Sims-Williams 1981a: 165.   [43] Paul 2019: 571.
[44] Already F. Schlegel noted in his influential *Über die Sprache und Weisheit der Indier* of 1808, the work which coined the term "comparative grammar" ("die vergleichende Grammatik," 1808: 28), that Persian words were "very severely abbreviated" ("am stärksten abgekurtzt," 1808: 13). He based this

Sketching the general pattern of this simplification is necessary for the nonspecialist; specialists may wish to skip ahead. As mentioned, each Old Persian noun belonged to one of three grammatical genders in one of several distinct declensions, and each declension possessed as many as six or seven distinct nominal cases in singular, plural, and less common dual forms. The evolution of Middle Persian, however, entailed the loss of all final syllables in a pattern evidently conditioned by a strong penultimate or antepenultimate stress accent (among other phonetic changes).[45] This, in turn, facilitated the eradication of distinctions of grammatical gender and of declensional noun classes, which had been most often distinguished formally in the lost final syllables. It was not just the less common inflectional forms that disappeared, such as inflections for the dual number, which was alive with its own productive noun and verb forms still in the time of Xerxes I.[46] Nouns in Middle Persian have two grammatical cases instead of the six of Darius' Old Persian, and they nearly all belong to one simple pattern of inflection, or declension. Evidence from the orthography of Middle Persian suggests that an oblique singular inflectional ending occurred, at least on some words, as -ē (derived from the old genitive-dative singular), at the time in which the orthography of Middle Persian was established, but this was gone in pronunciation by the third century CE, leaving only a fixed, nongrammatical orthographic trace in the traditional spellings.[47] The eventual loss of the singular oblique ending resulted in a situation in which grammatical case is distinguished in nouns in the plural only, in all but a very small class of nouns mostly pertaining to family relationship. That nonnominative plural is formed almost entirely regularly, with one ending for all nouns, -ān (remaining from the ancient genitive plural), a few rare exceptions aside.[48]

The example of this one word is striking but it does not adequately illustrate the collapse of inflectional complexity from Old to Middle Persian, because it represents only one of several noun classes and it does not illustrate the loss of grammatical gender. All the many ancient noun

---

on the comparison of New Persian words with their Sanskrit cognates, believing that Sanskrit was the ancestor of Persian and European languages.

[45] Salemann 1895–1904: 275; Meillet 1900; Gauthiot 1916–1918; Back 1978: 30–32; Sundermann 1989: 108; Huyse 2003. I discuss the causes of the loss of final syllables in Chapter 3.

[46] Kent 1950: 65 §189, 76 §229.

[47] Huyse 2003; Cantera 2009. I agree with Mancini (2019: 544–545) that the genitive singular ending -ē is likely masked, in effect, by the genitive singular endings in the late Achaemenian Persian inscriptions. See also Fattori (2023a) on the possibility that the oblique singular -ē survived until the first century BCE.

[48] Sundermann 1989: 154–156; Durkin-Meisterernst 2014: 199–201 §422.

Table 1.2a *Old Persian noun inflection*

"man"[49]	Nominative	Genitive-dative	Accusative	Instrumental-ablative	Locative	Vocative
Singular	martiya	martiya**hy**ā	martiyam	martiyā	martiyai	martiya
Dual	martiyā					
Plural	martiyā	martiy**ān**ām	martiyā	martiyaibiyā martiyaibiš	martiyaišu	martiyā

[49] All the inflectional endings in Table 1.2a and b are attested with different Old Persian nouns, but not for the specific noun *martiya*-. Dual forms of this noun paradigm are attested in Old Persian only for natural pairs like hands and feet. Forms here are given only as an illustration of the range of possible case forms in nouns of this class. The form ancestral to the Middle Persian would be **martya*-, without the epenthetic vowel found in the dialect of the inscriptions giving *martiya* (Kent 1950: 14 §25, 203; Brust 2018: 283–284). See the subsequent discussion of the outcome of **xšāyaθya*.

Table 1.2b *Middle Persian noun inflection*

"man"	nominative	oblique
Singular	*mard*	*mard(ē)*
Plural	*mard*	*mard**ān***

systems of Old Persian – not just *a*-stems but *ā*-stems, *i-/ai*-stems, *u-/au*-stems, the rarer *ī*-stems, *r*-stems, and different kinds of athematic consonant stems, each of these with its own partially attested paradigms in the extant inscriptions – were reduced to this simple, single Middle Persian paradigm alone, with only a few slightly exceptional nouns, none of which are inflected for more than these two cases and two numbers.

It is not normally mentioned in studies of the historical phonology of Persian that the omission of final syllables does not account for all the losses of grammatical inflection in the development of Middle Persian. Nominal case endings like *-aibiš* (instrumental plural *a*-stem) should have given the form *-aib* if the loss of syllables was the only factor. Expressions like *hadā kamnaibiš asabāraibiš*, "together with a few horsemen,"[50] occurring in the Bisitun inscription, should have resulted eventually in *had kamnaib asabāraib*, other regular sound changes pending – but such forms never occur. Clearly there was more at work in the formation of Middle Persian morphology than the loss of final syllables. Rather, it is evident that the entire system of forms was reduced not merely by the loss of final syllables, a phonological change, but also by the disappearance of whole grammatical possibilities ("paradigm cells" in the jargon of morphological theory).[51] These are two distinct kinds of loss in change.[52] As mentioned, cases apart from the nominative, accusative, and genitive disappeared from productive use from the time of Artaxerxes I onward – except a few other noun cases in fixed expressions after prepositions.[53] Then there was also the systematic loss of final syllables.

The morphology of the Old Persian verb likewise became radically simplified. The aorist verbal system, which was represented infrequently

---

[50] DB §20, lines 201–202 (Schmitt 2009: 50).
[51] The ablative-instrumental plural still has its reflexes in some modern Iranic languages of Afghanistan spoken by remote populations: from *-aibiš* there is Munji -*af*, Wakhi -*әv*, Pashto -*o* (Geiger 1895–1905: 315; Morgenstierne 1938: 2.123; Kreidl 2024: 225). Therefore, it was not as if this form was predestined to disappear in Iranic languages.
[52] H. Sims-Williams and Baerman 2021.   [53] Cantera 2009: 26–28.

From Old Persian to Middle Persian 39

in early Old Persian, is not found after Xerxes (apart from the aorist verb *adā*, "he created," occurring in the common inscriptional formula introduced previously until the end of the Achaemenian Persian record), but the ancient imperfect verb, the normal form used in Old Persian for ordinary past narration, disappeared in Middle Persian with very few exceptions: an originally imperfect form of "to be" and the survival of a few examples of imperfect verbs, some disputed, in two third-century-CE Middle Persian inscriptions.[54] Besides these rare late survivals of the imperfect, possibly reflecting a more insular dialect, Middle Persian verbs have two stems each, one for present (imperfect aspect) and modal verbs, one for preterit verbs based on the ancient verbal adjective (perfective participle of the patient) formed from the ancient suffix *-ta-*. In place of many different ancient Iranic verb classes with different patterns of endings, thematic and athematic, only one of several ancient Persian classes of verb endings, with the suffix *-áya-*, has been generalized in Middle Persian to nearly all indicative present verb stems, regardless of their etymological verb class.[55] The preterit (past-tense) verb itself is completely uninflected for all persons and numbers, as shown in Table 1.3. Nothing else is required if the patient of the verb is third-person singular or inanimate plural; otherwise, the auxiliary verb "to be" is needed to agree with the patient of the verb to indicate the patient of the action, and even this verb "to be" bears forms created by analogy to make it accord regularly with other verb forms regardless of their etymological class.

Table 1.3 *The Middle Persian preterit (from the ancient perfective participle)*

šud, "went"	Singular		Plural	
1st person	*šud ham*	I went	*šud hēm*	we went
2nd person	*šud hēh*	you went	*šud hēd*	you (pl.) went
3rd person	*šud*	he, she, it went	*šud hēnd*	they went

---

[54] Henning 1958: 101–102; Skjærvø 1989: 347–353; Skjærvø 1997b. Besides the form "was," these examples of the imperfect verb likely represent a conservative, regional, or local dialect of Persian – or, much less likely, "a literary tense" and "an archaizing device," as Skjærvø interprets it (1989: 353) – as they are not found in the royal inscriptions or Manichaean Middle Persian texts of the third century. Such variation is addressed in Chapter 4.

[55] Skjærvø (2009a: 87–88) and Brust (2018: 71–72) list these stems neatly. On their reduction to one type in Middle Persian, see Meillet 1900: 266–267; Tedesco 1923: 302; Durkin-Meisterernst 2014: 243 §489. The explanation for these endings was partly discerned already by Müller (1877: 225). For exceptions in the third-person singular present, see Gershevitch 1970.

The verb "to stand" can be used for a copula instead to give the preterit perfective sense.[56] It is the simple copula, however, and not the main verb, that is inflected. Furthermore, the Old Persian derivational affixes such as preverbs have become fused with their stems in Middle Persian through various regular sound changes, losing their status as independent morphemes and greatly reducing the derivational flexibility of Persian. Indeed, Middle Persian productive derivational morphology, unlike that of Old Persian, is exclusively a matter of transparent noun compounds and a very few verb suffixes added agglutinatively (i.e., without change to the basic word stem within one of the two tenses).[57]

In short, Middle Persian, compared with Old Persian, was paradigmatically quite transparent.[58] It had one completely regular verb conjugation,[59] one class of nouns exhibiting two nominal cases, no distinctions of grammatical gender, and nouns showing only two case distinctions, without case distinction in the singular noun by the third century CE.[60] One general suffix marked oblique nouns in the plural: -ān.[61] The inflections of Middle Persian are, as the many scholars just cited already have attested, extremely simple as compared with the Old Persian of Darius I.

The Symptoms of Middle Persian in Late Achaemenian Royal Inscriptions

The changes in usage and spelling, and especially the hypercorrections, in the late Achaemenian Persian inscriptions demonstrate in two ways that, with respect to its grammar, Old Persian was well on its way to becoming Middle Persian already during the Achaemenid period. This is also the consensus of current scholarship. The language of the late Achaemenian Persian inscriptions is correctly understood as Proto-Middle Persian,

---

[56] See Skjærvø 2009b: 218–221 for a concise summary.   [57] Weber 2007.
[58] The expression is from Finkel and Stump 2009.
[59] The third-person singular of "to be," *ast*, is the sole exception, and that is normally a predicator of existence, not a copula.
[60] A few exceptional Middle Persian nouns, mostly referring to family relations such as father, mother, daughter, brother, sister, exhibited a distinct ending for the oblique singular and nominative plural. E.g., "father," sing. nom. *pid*, obl. *pidar*/pl. nom. *pidar*, obl. *pidarān*. See Durkin-Meisterernst 2014: 199 §421, 202 §423).
[61] Rare traces of ancient inflectional types (-*i* and -*u* stems) survived in early examples of Middle Persian in the oblique noun endings -*īn* and -*ūn* (Durkin-Meisterernst 2014: 199–201 §422). Sometimes these were added to nouns or pronouns where those endings do not reflect the etymology. Fattori (2023b: 114–116) counts just fifteen occurrences of such words in Middle Persian, twenty-three in Middle Persian and Parthian together.

a term already employed by several scholars for this stage of the language.⁶² First, the choices of scribes writing Old Persian show that the living Old Persian language had indeed lost its final syllables by the time of Artaxerxes III. This is the simplest and strongest explanation for the irregular omission of final syllables together with the application of various and irregular nonetymological final-syllable inflectional endings as well as the simple omission of such endings. Second, the irregularity of the grammatical word endings applied in late Old Persian inscriptions demonstrates that their scribes really were trying to achieve an older epigraphic form of language in writing by copying some formulae and spellings of words from older inscriptions. That they did so incorrectly so often, by the pattern of the more ancient grammar, shows that they did not know those word forms intuitively or fluently. It is equally important, however, though less often remarked, that they often did use them correctly, from the point of view of the older texts. This means that the late Old Persian inscriptions were to an extent based on a perceived orthographic standard, and that when the scribes achieved that standard, they have hidden from us other changes affecting the language at their time. That is, their inconsistency indicates that the late inscriptions do not adequately and transparently represent the regular changes that had occurred in the living language. For it is a principle of historical linguistics that the sounds of a language change regularly and not haphazardly within a language, bearing ordered ramifications for the whole language according to specific conditions.⁶³ It is certain, therefore, that the living state of Persian in the time of Artaxerxes III had changed even more considerably than is evident from the inconsistently archaizing representation of the words in the late Old Persian cuneiform signs.⁶⁴ The morphology of Persian was more radically simplified by then than the writing shows. Mancini argues that the cuneiform spellings of the late Achaemenian Persian inscriptions are regular "masks" for a Proto-Middle Persian word-forms, in effect historical spellings of individual morphemes. Thus, unexpected written forms that modern scholars have read as, such as *dārayawaʰuš-ahyā*, "of Darius," represented by the letters <d-a-r-y-w-u-š-h-y-a>, would represent, in Mancini's

---

[62] Schmitt 1980: 75; Lazard 1983: 52; Huyse 2003: 27; Skjærvø 2009a: 47; Mancini 2019; Korn 2021: 2; Fattori 2023a. Cf. Skjærvø 1999a: 159.
[63] This was demonstrated in the nineteenth century and remains valid. See Ringe and Eska 2013: 78–83 and Hock 2021: 38–59.
[64] Mancini 2019. Cantera (2009) and Korn (2013: 85) both try to establish a chronological order of stages in the reduction of inflectional endings. Cantera hypothesizes a gradual collapse of the case-system and Korn proposes ordered sound rules for the gradual reduction of endings.

interpretation, a Proto-Middle Persian from "/dāraywē/" or the like. The nominative spelling stands for the Proto-Middle Persian direct-case form, putatively "Dārayw," with the letters in the word-ending <-h-y-a> representing the Proto-Middle Persian singular oblique case -ē shown in Table 1.2.[65] This is certainly possible. It would mean that the scribes of the late Achaemenian Persian inscriptions were not so much making mistakes as they were consciously employing a conventional and somewhat conservative orthography for their present language. The evaluations of late Achaemenian Persian inscriptions as "corrupt" or "barbaric" would thus be doubly wrong.

Some of the expected evolutionary changes show through against the scribes' general successes. Middle Persian entailed simplifications of Old Persian not just with respect to morphology, but also changes in phonology, which provides a few examples. Take the word for "king," Old Persian *xšāyaθiya*, or rather the more conservative, trisyllabic form not attested directly in the Old Persian inscriptions, **xšāyaθya*.[66] In Middle Persian this became *šāh* (the form retained in modern Persian to this day) through a combination of three regular sound changes. The regularity of sound changes means that they affect all Persian words with the same features. (1) The initial consonant cluster *xš-* was simplified to *š-*.[67] (2) The sequence *-āya-* regularly contracted to *-ā-*.[68] (3) The consonant θ regularly became *h*.[69] As mentioned, another change affecting not just this word, but the entire language, was the loss of all final syllables. In this word, the ending *-(i)ya-* was furthermore lost without a trace.[70] Thus, a word of three syllables beginning with a peculiar consonant cluster became one syllable with no consonant cluster. Simplification is a suitable word for the sum of such changes. Complex features were lost, and syllables were reduced, although the loss of inflectional endings is the most crucial change of all.

The relative chronology of these changes remains a problem, but there is strong evidence that many of them had taken place before the end of the Achaemenid dynasty.[71] For example, even as the scribes of the late

---

[65] Mancini 2019, esp. 552.   [66] Korn 2021: 17–20.
[67] Darmesteter 1883: 1.85; Hübschmann 1895: 232–233 §125a; Back 1978: 99 §33.4.
[68] Hübschmann 1895: 167–168 §58; Back 1978: 74 §22.1.3.   [69] Hübschmann 1895: 203–204 §95.
[70] The *-i-* here is an epenthetic vowel particular to the Old Persian phonology of the royal inscriptions, in which proto-Iranic *CyV* regularly became, or was represented as, *CiyV* (Kent 1950: 14 §25; Brust 2018: 169). It did not have phonemic status, at least in the dialect of Old Persian antecedent to Middle Persian (Klingenschmitt 2000: 203–204; Korn 2021). The antecedent form of *šāh* is trisyllabic **xšāyaθya*.
[71] Korn (2021) had produced the most detailed analysis of the order of these changes.

Achaemenian inscriptions sought to write something like the standard that they could see in earlier inscriptions, the second of the three regular phonological changes just mentioned was clearly underway by the time of Artaxerxes III. For in one of his inscriptions, one word clearly shows that *-āya-* was already being reduced to *-ā-*. The "misspelling" of the word for "happiness" in an inscription of Artaxerxes III was already mentioned. In the accusative singular, the old form was *šiyātim* (or rather *šyātim*) but here it is spelled as *šāyat-ām* (the letters *š-a-y-t-a-m*). The generalization of the ending *-ām* is one of the symptoms of the loss of final syllables, and consequent hypercorrections, already discussed, but the anomalous noun form *šāyat-* calls for further remark. The noun *š(i)yāti-* actually evolved to *šāt-*, written in the conventional historical spelling of Middle Persian of the first century BCE, *š't-* (as the first component of a noun compound);[72] the pronunciation by the third century CE was *šād*, as represented clearly in the Manichaean script of that time; the word still survives as *šād* in New Persian;[73] Armenian and Greek borrowings of Persian words likewise exhibit the earlier stage with the voiceless dental consonant *t* in *šat-*, σατ-, also with one syllable.[74] Schmitt rightly infers that this late Old Persian spelling *šāyat* was a scribal back-formation in which *-āya-* represents *-ā-*.[75] That is, the scribe has interfered with the spelling in an attempt to represent the actual word-internal sound *-ā-* with a pseudohistorical spelling. This is a kind of hypercorrection, too. The only reason that *-āya-* would have been used to represent *-ā-* is that the Old Persian standards of spelling in the inscriptions already entailed writing the sound *-ā-* word-internally by the signs for *-āya-* in other words. *Xšāyaθiya* is a conspicuous word of this kind, but the evolution of Middle Persian demonstrates that the change *-āya-* to *-ā-* was a regular rule. The Persian language in the time of Artaxerxes III must therefore already have undergone that change, otherwise no scribe would have written unetymological and otherwise inexplicable *-āya-* to represent *-ā-*. Now, if the word ending had been lost, as well, as the evidence already discussed makes practically certain, and the initial *xš* was pronounced as plain *š*, and *θ* was pronounced *h*, then the

---

[72] This word, spelled simply *š't* in Aramaic letters, is attested already as a morpheme in a word apparently meaning "drinking-bowl" in the oldest known Middle Persian inscriptions, dated to the first century BCE (Skjærvø 1997a: 93; Sims-Williams 2021: 3–5), but it is also known from Elamite, Akkadian, and Greek renderings of Persian names in which *šat-* was a component (Tavernier 2007: 317–319).
[73] This point was carefully explained before by Schmitt (1999: 114).
[74] Hübschmann 1895–1897: 1.211–212; Benveniste 1966: 119–121; Schmitt 2011: 320–323; Korn 2021: 20.
[75] Schmitt 1999: 96–97, 114; 2004: 718. The counterarguments of Fattori (2022b), although persuasive for some words, have not convinced me that Schmitt is mistaken about this word.

word for "king" had already become *šāh* by the time of Alexander's invasion beginning in 334 BCE.[76] The late Achaemenian Persian form would therefore be, in effect, almost the same as if not identical to the Middle Persian form and, in this case, even the modern Persian form. Nevertheless, an attempt to establish the chronology of the sounds changes from Old to Middle Persian raises thorny questions. They deserve further detailed investigation, but they are not the object of the present study, so I set them aside here.[77]

The point with this difficult but decisive technical example is that the apparent misspellings in late Old Persian inscriptions sometimes allow us to infer that specific phonological changes characteristic of Middle Persian, and not merely an abbreviation of the word-final inflectional morphology, had already occurred in the language before the end of the Achaemenid dynasty. We can be certain, therefore, with the benefit of hindsight, from the point of view of Middle Persian, that the changes that show through the late Old Persian inscriptions represent the direction in which the Old Persian language was evolving as used by native Persian-speakers themselves, not only incompetent foreigners, under Achaemenid rule.[78] The late

---

[76] Thus also Mancini (2019: 548).
[77] Korn (2021) applies a similar analysis to the spelling of **paraded-*, "private park, paradise," with the signs <p-r-d-y-d-a-m>, where the -y- indicates a monophthong rather than a VCV sequence (2021: 24–25). See differently Fattori 2022b, who connects the spelling of that word to the transliteration of a possible original in Aramaic letters.
[78] Fattori (2022b; cf. Mancini 2019: 529) convinces me of the possibility that the late Achaemenian Persian inscriptions were first written in Aramaic letters before they were transcribed into Persian cuneiform, but I am skeptical of specifics of his proposed Aramaic reconstructions. While his theory – elaborating proposals by Herzfeld – would account for some of the oddities in the late Achaemenian Persian cuneiform, not all proposals he offers are persuasive. To give one example, he notes (2022b: 31) that *apadāna* "palace" or *apaniyāka* "great-grandfather" occur in late Achaemenian Persian cuneiform with unexpected initial *upa-* <u-p-> (Schmitt 2014: 264–265). These late Achaemenian Persian forms are normally regarded as errors because they are not etymological (cf. Schmitt 2014: 264–265). The question then is what kind of errors these were. Fattori argues that these can be most plausibly explained as mistranscriptions from a prototype in Aramaic letters, which would be written with the initial letters <ʾp> (and Schmitt regards this as possible, too). Two readings of those Aramaic signs were conceivable, *upa-* and *apa-*, so the mistakes would be due to ambiguous writing. While I agree that this is possible, there is another viable explanation from the phonological history of Persian. Old Persian initial *u-* became become *a-* in Middle Persian, at least before labials: e.g., Old Persian **upa-ay-* "to approach" became Middle Persian *abāy-* "to be necessary" (Cheung 2007: 155) and Old Persian *upari* "over" became Middle Persian *abar* "over." Cf. Hübschmann 1895: 125 and Henning 1933: 223–224. This sound change could readily prompt a hypercorrection in late Achaemenian Persian of initial *a-* to *u-*, if the initial *u-* was already losing its rounded character and becoming *a-*. This is particularly so if the sound change was in progress at the time of writing. That is, the confusion of the initial vowel may reflect a sound change in the fourth century BCE tending toward the later attested Middle Persian forms. Fattori's solution would seem to require that the scribes did not quite know the Persian word; the phonological solution may be superior in conceding to the scribes some knowledge of the language they wrote. It is also possible that both sorts of ambiguity – graphic and phonetic – were factors simultaneously. In any case,

Old Persian inscriptions therefore do not present just a case of scribes becoming sloppy or misunderstanding grammatical rules of composition, or of "barbarians" producing "improper" Old Persian. This was, rather, Persian well on its way in evolving into what we know as Middle Persian as spoken by all Persians. Other scholars have made similar remarks since the nineteenth century.[79] Schmitt, who has devoted more effort to the analysis of such features in the late inscriptions than any other, put it just so: "By [the late Achaemenian period], spoken Persian had evolved a somewhat different form, so discrepancies between everyday speech and the traditional language of inscriptions had arisen."[80] What the changes in the grammar of the Old Persian inscriptions show is that the living Persian language really changed, and changed drastically, in just over one century of Achaemenid rule.

All this is well established by the few specialists in this area of research. The remarkable fact here – and, in a sense, the main problem addressed in what follows – is not that the Persian language had changed. All languages are changing all the time. Rather, it is that this drastic transformation, entailing the loss of most inflectional endings and the consequent restructuring of the syntax, the birth of an entirely new form of Persian language, apparently occurred in no more than four generations after Darius I (d. 486 BCE), glaringly evident in inscriptions from the reigns of Artaxerxes II (regn. 405–358) and Artaxerxes III (regn. 358–338), with the onset of such changes showing through not much more than a half century after the first Old Persian inscription. The scribes of the later inscriptions or those who dictated to them simply no longer spoke the same Persian language as

---

Fattori (2022b: 31n62) agrees with the majority that "Il fatto che il persiano stesse muovendo verso una semplificazione morfologica è certo."

[79] Already Hübschmann (1875: 329) assumed, after considering the late Old Persian inscriptions, that Persian had lost all case endings by the time of Alexander's invasion, and that it had basically arrived at the state of inflection in Middle and New Persian. Willy Foy explicitly recognized the late Old Persian inscriptions as a symptom of the evolution of Persian (1898: 57–58): "Was wir zuletzt behandelt haben, ist das früheste kapitel der zwischen der altpersischen und mittelpersischen periode wirkenden auslautsgesetze, durch die allmählich alle endsilben des Altpersischen verloren gingen, und somit sind uns in den Inschriften der beiden könige Artaxerxes II. und III. noch nicht zur genüge gewürdigte denkmäler der persischen sprachentwicklung erhalten." Herzfeld (1937: 49), too, held a similar view about Old Persian, stating that already between Artaxerxes I and Artaxerxes II (thus the period 465–359), that "die sprache ist tot, sie 'wird' nicht mehr, sie 'war.'" He added, "But the true Middle Persian forms are discernible" ("Aber die echt mittelpersischen formen sind erkennbar."). Herzfeld's further view that the Old Persian texts already from the time of Darius represented an archaic literary language no longer spoken must be rejected (cf. Henning's review, 1940: 504). Brandenstein and Mayrhofer (1964: 14) and Kent (1950: 99 §313.II), like Foy, rightly saw the first steps toward the evolution of Middle Persian already in sound incipient changes evident in inscriptions of Xerxes I, son of Darius I.

[80] Schmitt 2004: 718.

Darius I and his son Xerxes. The complexity of the inflectional endings of Old Persian was lost, for the most part, dropped from ordinary usage, so that young users could no longer produce the old forms or understand them as they had been just a few generations before.[81] The language had rapidly undergone extensive morphological reduction. In this sense, the later scribes were not getting the language wrong, strictly speaking. The scribes were using a form of Persian as they knew it, but they could not create inscriptions with the same inflectional endings and forms that had been used when Old Persian was first written, older inscriptions still easily available to them.[82] Again, the texts make it clear that they were, however, sometimes making genuine mistakes, in the form of hypercorrections, when they attempted to use the old-fashioned language as it was in the time of Darius I, and superadded inflectional oblique endings wrongly to nominative endings, or generalizing the accusative singular ending -*ām* from certain specific nouns for all nouns. This is because they did not know the archaic form of language fluently any longer, as their forefather Darius I had used it.

A Simpler Form of Persian

The low level of inflectional complexity in Middle Persian, as compared with the language of Darius I, is evident from how one studies ancient languages today for the purposes of research. I can give personal examples. To learn Greek and Latin, for example, I needed, for each, one year of university instruction, exercises, and drilling in forms of grammatical inflection before I could begin to read real, original, extensive texts slowly with the aid of a dictionary. There were hundreds of inflected word forms to learn, and they required constant review. By contrast, when I first studied Middle Persian under the instruction of Stanley Insler, he gave the students a one-page handout presenting the few inflections in the language, concisely explained the major elements of the historical phonology within an Indo-European and Indo-Iranic framework, and we

---

[81] Cf. Korn 2013: 84, "the data seem to imply that word-final vowels and diphthongs were lost by this [late Old Persian] stage."

[82] Skjærvø (1999a: 159) makes the point that we are not "entitled to judge diverging spellings as errors" (2009: 47). This is generally true, but not in the case of hypercorrections. One part of my argument here in line with his: the language had changed, so that nobody spoke "the King's Old Persian," as he puts it, if by the king we mean Darius I. (Schmitt [1989a: 60] similarly refers to the older stage, as seen by the later kings, as the "Sprache der Väter.") Nevertheless, the late Achaemenian inscriptions show evidence of failed attempts to reach the standard of Darius' language as it was known at least from his inscriptions.

started reading original texts in the same session. I had to learn the rules of Middle Persian syntax. Beyond that, it was a matter of looking up and memorizing the minimally inflected words, trying to discern the conventions and idioms of the language, and understanding passages that were preserved in a fragmentary state or were ambiguous because they were without known parallels. The main hindrance was not the language itself, but the small size of the surviving corpus of texts and the innumerable questions about particulars left unanswered because only a small number of scholars had studied it before, not to mention the relative inaccessibility of much of the research on ancient Iranic languages, especially before the availability of texts in electronic format.[83] There was no comprehensive dictionary and there was no adequate reference grammar at the time. The script, too, is notoriously difficult because of its ambiguity and the use of Aramaic words as allographs, virtually as logograms. The inflectional morphology of Greek and Latin slows the acquisition of those languages, solely for the purposes of reading, by months, but for Middle Persian inflectional morphology was scarcely a consideration by comparison.

The study of the evolution of Old Persian into Middle Persian is hindered by the long gap of time in documentation. After the Achaemenids, the earliest extant clearly Persian texts are two short Middle Persian inscriptions made in *pointillé* on silver bowls in a style archaic by comparison with the later corpus of Middle Persian. These have been dated to the first century BCE. Sims-Williams has dubbed the inscriptions Persis 1, which labels its ownership by Persian princes,[84] and Persis 2, which commemorates its bestowal as a gift by the holders of some Persian office.[85] Both exhibit archaic Middle Persian orthography in Aramaic letters. In the period of these two early inscriptions, after Alexander, new dynasties of local kings ruled the different formerly

---

[83] Scholars from other fields interested in engaging with ancient Iranic philology should know that much research in this field is published by private presses in expensive, limited-edition volumes of collected miscellaneous articles often bearing vague or misleading titles like "Nugae antico-persianae" and "The Survival of an Ancient Term." These articles are often organized and written with the author's, not the reader's, convenience in mind, based on papers delivered at occasional international conferences to a close circle of established colleagues and their students, and in *Festschriften* and memorial volumes (occasionally more than one for an individual) dedicated to each other. The volume editors are often the authors of one or more of the articles they themselves are selecting for publication and editing. Such patterns of publication make it a field difficult to navigate. These are symptoms of a field with a small number of specialists who constitute nearly the entirety of their own audience, which in turn fosters a master–disciple guild structure. It is a field in need of resources and personnel.
[84] Ed. Skjærvø 1997a; differently Sims-Williams 2021: 6–8.
[85] Ed. Sims-Williams 2021. See also Fattori 2023a.

Achaemenian territories. Pārs, in the southwest of Iran – roughly the modern province of Fārs – where Darius had originated, had its own local dynasty that had to contend with the overlordship of Macedonian Seleucid and Parthian Arsacid kings. We know little about these local Persian rulers, one line of which were called by the title *frataraka*.[86] Their independently minted coins are almost the only historical source about their reigns. Although the two bowl-inscriptions are short and difficult to read, and hint at features of the language that would go extinct in later Middle Persian, they are nevertheless distinctly Middle Persian texts, characteristically lacking complex ancient word-inflections such as those used by Darius I in his Old Persian. It is not until the early third century CE, however, that we begin to find more extensive Middle Persian texts, when a new Persian dynasty, the Sasanids, usurped overlordship from the Parthian Arsacids. When they achieved Persian hegemony over a vast territory, then they began to create new royal inscriptions of their own.

The discontinuity of the textual record of Persian between the Achaemenids and the *frataraka*s of Persis is one reason that the rapidity of the change in Old Persian itself has not been immediately obvious. The later Achaemenian inscriptions are few, and they are shorter than the early ones of Darius I and Xerxes. Their formulaic character allowed their scribes to copy older models and thereby often to get it right, so to speak, by an older grammatical standard obsolete in ordinary Persian speech in their own time. In those specific formulae, it is rare to find endings that are "wrong" by the standard of the old inscriptions. By the time of the inscribed silver bowls just mentioned, however, it is clear that Middle Persian was practically as different from the Old Persian of Darius I as early modern English was from the Old English of Beowulf. Leading Iranologists have made similar comparisons several times, but no convincing explanation for this special situation has been offered.[87] As already mentioned, the Middle Persian language by this time had become

---

[86] Cf. Old Persian *fratara-*, *fraθara-* (Schmitt 2014: 177–178), Greek πρότερος. Wiesehöfer 1994; Skjærvø 1997a; Wiesehöfer 2000; Callieri and Askari Chaverdi 2013: 698–709; Wiesehöfer 2013. The term should mean something like "first man, superior, *princeps*."

[87] Darmesteter (1883: 1.117) explicitly compared the simplicity of later stages of Persian with its early complexity, in these terms. Meillet (1912: 150) considered Iranic languages of the first century CE as farther from the Indo-European prototype than modern Romance or Germanic. Gauthiot (1916–1918: 61) regarded the "structural" difference between Avestan (similar to Old Persian) and New Persian to be greater than that between Latin and French. As mentioned in the Introduction, Henning (1958: 89), compared "Proto-Iranic" with Sanskrit and Greek, holding that the ancient Middle Persian language, by contrast, "is on a par with English."

grammatically among the simplest known of the ancient Indo-European languages. It is far simpler in its inflection than ancient Greek or Latin or even than standard modern varieties of Spanish, German, French, Dutch, and Italian.

All languages change over time, but what makes the problem here especially striking is the *rapidity* of the *drastic* change within Persian. One might have guessed that the five centuries in which Persian was not well documented, between the end of the Achaemenid dynasty and the beginning of the Sasanid dynasty with its royal inscriptions, was the period in which the language underwent such radical simplification. One might imagine that a half millennium should be ample time for these changes to accrue gradually as a matter of random drift toward simplicity. One might suppose that even the three centuries between Alexander and the two Middle Persian silver bowl-inscriptions just mentioned could be enough time for incremental changes to accumulate that would turn Old Persian into Middle Persian. As just explained, however, the consensus is that the Old Persian inscriptions themselves show that changes leading to Middle Persian were advanced by the end of Achaemenid rule. The radical trimming of noun and verb endings was probably substantially complete, entailing the restructuring of Persian syntax. By the time of Alexander's invasion in the 330s, Persian-speakers were evidently already speaking an early stage of Middle Persian, a form of the language shorn of most of the grammatical inflection that had characterized the language about 520 BCE, in the time of Darius I.[88] Whether we use Schmitt's term "late Old Persian" (*Spätaltpersisch*) to designate the later Achaemenian inscriptions as on the verge of transition,[89] Skjærvø's "Pre-Middle Persian," emphasizing that the language of the later Achaemenian inscriptions "is neither Old nor Middle Persian,"[90] or the "Proto-Middle Persian" of others on analogy with the naming of earliest attested samples of other corpus languages,[91] the meaning is the same. I would rather avoid imposing on ourselves the need to designate specific grammatical differences by which we classify categories that are, in the first place, primarily descriptive and conventional. My purpose is not to classify in grammatical terms but to explain grammatical change. Therefore, I propose the designation *late Achaemenian Persian*, which I have been using already. Terminology aside, it is generally agreed that language of the latest Achaemenian inscriptions was near to the

---

[88] Skjærvø 1999a: 159.   [89] Schmitt 1999: 111–118. The term was also used by Back (1978: 4).
[90] Skjærvø 2007: 853. The term is also used by Korn (2021: 38) for a stage in the history of Persian phonology.
[91] Mancini 2019, esp. 524–525n3; Fattori 2023a.

Middle Persian known from later centuries, a highly simplified species of ancient Iranic language.

How did this drastic simplification happen to the Persian language in a period less than two centuries, while the Persians were at their most powerful, controlling a vast empire? The answer to this question is accessible with answers and insights from linguistics developed in recent decades, long after the genesis of historical linguistics. As I will show in Chapter 3, applying these gains in linguistic science does more than explain the grammatical changes to Persian. It illuminates an aspect of the history of the Persian Empire otherwise overlooked.

CHAPTER 2

A Linguistic-Historical Model
Social Factors in Grammatical Reduction, Imposition, and Adoption

When analyzed with a new approach, the Old Persian inscriptions tell us something important about changes to the constitution of the Persian *people* as a group and their culture during the reign of the Achaemenids. The radical trimming of the inflectional complexity of the Persian language in about one and a half centuries – from the complex inflections of the language of the Bisitun inscription of Darius I in 521 BCE to the much-reduced inflections that peek through the inscriptions of Artaxerxes II (405–358) and Artaxerxes III (r. 358–338) at Susa – points to a *demographic* transformation. This chapter explains how we can determine this through a composite model synthesized for the use of historians from several related subfields of linguistics: historical linguistics, contact linguistics, creole studies, language acquisition research, and studies of bilingualism and grammaticalization. The model, which is based on the combination of observed patterns of language change in population contact and in second-language acquisition, is the main factor that distinguishes the present attempt to account for the evolution of Persian from other attempts, giving new results.[1] As I will show in the subsequent chapter, this model will help us to understand the history of the Persians and their first empire. The same linguistic-historical model will apply, necessarily with a different application and a different outcome, to my account of the origins of New Persian, which is the subject of another book to appear after this one.

This linguistic-historical model is not a tentative hypothesis. Rather, the linguistic phenomena on which it is built have been documented in numerous places and times. The model offers robust inferential explanations and reliable predictions on a par with the predictions offered by

---

[1] Gerlee and Lundh (2016) provide a clear introduction to the concept of a scientific model and different methods that fall under that category.

comparative historical linguistics.[2] I claim that it describes universal tendencies in specific socially conditioned varieties of language change.[3] It derives from the distillation of hundreds of articles and books, of which the bibliography here is merely representative, written by researchers whose main interest is not in Persian or other specific languages to the exclusion of others, but in these kinds of general linguistic phenomena. Its bases are recent in scholarship but not new. Those who wish to probe the foundations of the model synthesized here will need to pursue the works listed in the notes, but I hope to have simplified the task of reapplying the synthetic model presented here to other linguistic histories. The study of second-language acquisition, bilingualism, language contact, creoles, and historical linguistics all concern related phenomena, but these subfields of linguistics seem to interact minimally, so they have sometimes generated idiosyncratic jargon differing from linguistic subfield to subfield.[4] Such differences made synthesizing their respective findings a more challenging task, but the good news is that they often independently corroborate each other's findings, too, in a way that can be overlooked when subfields develop separately. The result will probably not satisfy any linguist, as it participates wholly in no subfield of linguistics, being intended to serve linguistic history. For the sake of nonspecialists, I have eschewed some of the jargon entailed in different subfields of linguistics except where I deem technical neologisms useful, in which case I explain the terms.

There are two main parts of this linguistic model, but the two interact enough in their application to linguistic history that I conceive of them as one complex whole that tells us more when they are combined than we can see when they are kept separate. The first part is the most immediately relevant to the problem of the evolution of Old Persian described in the previous chapter. It concerns the social factors triggering grammatical reduction in a language, particularly the loss of inflectional morphology. The second part deals with social factors in linguistic mixture – more precisely the transfer into one language of features from one or more other languages, not always

---

[2] See Muysken 2017 for a discussion of the use of established sociolinguistic scenarios to illustrate historical linguistic patterns and vice versa.
[3] I use the term universal tendency as Haspelmath proposes (2019: 5), because, while I do not know of any exceptions to the processes posited here, I do not claim that there are no exceptions. This makes the history of Persian studied in this book quite relevant for comparative linguistic purposes. If no exceptions exist, as we may suspect, then this model describes a universal characteristic of human language change under the specified conditions. In that case, the history of Persian studied in this book would be a good example for general linguistics.
[4] E.g., Muysken (2013: 193) observes that, "what is needed is a book in which findings from bilingual processing studies are fully integrated with those from language contact studies."

a reciprocal process. As concerns the evolution of Old Persian, this second part of the model turns out to be less decisive, but it guides us away from errors in analysis and substantially refines our understanding of the social circumstances that transformed Old Persian. Both parts comprise contributions of innumerable other scholars, but I have not seen them combined and applied to linguistic history as follows in this book.

The composite model employed here is incomplete as it cannot explain or predict all linguistic history, nor is it intended to do so. I do not offer a master theory of all social factors in language change. The model can and should be refined and expanded in the future, integrating new findings and new components. Nevertheless, I believe that the analysis of the history of ancient Persian here, using these tools, resolves an old problem in linguistic history productively. In this chapter, however, I will seldom refer to Persian, the subject of this book. Partly this is deliberately to separate the presentation of the model and its application. Partly it is in the hope that this chapter will be useful by itself as a synthesis of research findings for other linguistic historians interested in correlations between language change and social change but who are not concerned specifically with Persian. Strictly speaking, one does not need to know about ancient Persian to understand this chapter.

Grammatical Reduction: Social Factors in the Loss of Inflection

How does a language lose its inflectional morphology?[5] The findings of various branches of linguistics most relevant to this problem can be approached through five steps, to be explained in order, with basic bibliography at each heading.[6] After explaining these five steps and then illustrating their outcomes with examples from modern circumstances, I will discuss a few more critical factors in the topic of socially induced language change.

(1) Languages vary in their relative grammatical complexity. Some have more complex grammars than others, specifically in inflectional morphology. This is a realization that has faced ideological barriers on two sides.[7]

---

[5] Sims-Williams and Baerman (2021) offer a subtle typology of grammatical loss in change.
[6] Winford (2003) provides a careful general introduction to the field of contact linguistics.
[7] Kusters 2003; Winford 2003: 52, 217–219; Dahl 2004; DeKeyser 2005; McWhorter 2005: 43–48; Shosted 2006; McWhorter 2007: 21–58; Wray and Grace 2007; Miestamo, Sinnemäki, and Karlsson 2008; Siegel 2008: 18–25; Sampson, Gil, and Trudgill 2009; Trudgill 2010b; McWhorter 2011a: Trudgill 2011; 64–102; Szmrecsanyi and Kortmann 2012; Trudgill 2012; McWhorter 2013b: 415–417; Fenk-Oczlon and Fenk 2014; Baerman, Brown, and Corbett 2015; Dixon 2016: 125–146; McWhorter 2018: 90–109.

Those who learn or teach many languages already know this from direct experience, not as mere intuition. Complexity has many senses, but what I mean by complexity here is straightforward, practical, and descriptive: here, higher complexity in a language means that it is more difficult for adults to learn and to use actively and communicatively.[8] Such complexity can reside in morphology and syntax, lexicon, and other subsystems of a language. Complexity includes grammatical overspecification, structural elaboration, and irregularity.[9] Simplification in a language is an increase of regularity.[10] Inflectional morphological complexity is only one kind of linguistic complexity, but it is by far the most relevant here. It is perhaps the easiest to quantify meaningfully and it is the factor in language complexity that matters more than the rest for adult learners. Complex inflectional morphology burdens the learner with many semantic distinctions to be correlated formally on the spot while using a language in live communication. It is difficult for a new adult speaker of a language to conceive and produce several correctly inflected word forms that correspond with other words' disparate and grammatically heterogeneous forms beyond their phrasal constituents in a sentence, and to pronounce them correctly, spontaneously within a few seconds to keep the listener's attention, and in a way that conveys the intended meaning.[11]

To illustrate such a discrepancy in inflectional complexity between languages using descriptive grammatical terms, compare the ancient Greek verb of Plato's Athens with the verb in ancient Aramaic of Achaemenian Mesopotamia at the same time. Ancient Greek verbs were very complex. Each Greek verb was inflected, potentially, for many hundreds of forms, considering three persons, three numbers (singular, plural, and the rarer dual), seven tenses (present, imperfect, future, aorist, perfect, pluperfect, and future perfect), three voices (denoting verb diathesis, such

---

[8] Cf. Kusters 2003: 6–9; Trudgill 2009 and 2010b: 311. The nature of difficulty itself is debated in the study of second-language acquisition; see DeKeyser (2005) for clear answers.
[9] These three are emphasized by McWhorter (2011a: 1–2; 2018: 93–99). All of these are hindrances to adult learners. The factors accord inversely with Trudgill's (2010a: 4–5; 2010b: 307–308) characterization of simplification: "the regularization of irregularities," "increase in lexical and morphological transparency," and "the loss of redundancy."
[10] Romaine 1988: 32.
[11] Through various avenues of research into second-language acquisition, Slabakova (2008; 2016: 389–415) proposes that it is precisely inflectional morphology that forms the "bottleneck," or most severe difficulty, for adult learners of a language to traverse. Finkel and Stump (2009: 139–140), seeking a definition of inflectional complexity, posit that "the complexity of an inflectional system is the extent to which it inhibits motivated inferences about the word forms realizing a paradigm's cells." In other words, it is the factor that prevents people who do not know a language well from being able to deduce or guess the right form of a word by analogy or other deductions.

as transitivity and intransitivity, or a relationship of propriety between the subject and object), and four moods (indicative, optative, subjunctive, imperative). The ancient Greek verb was relatively paradigmatically opaque, with six and sometimes as many as eight frequently unpredictable (irregular) verbal stems to be learned individually for each verb, known as the "principal parts," conveying three different temporal aspects among them.[12] In addition, there is a smaller group of frequently used verbs, called athematic, that require a quite different set of inflectional endings, to be learned and applied only to that class of verbs, with accompanying inflection of the verb stem itself. Moreover – still part of verbal morphology – there are adverbial prefixes or *preverbs* that diversify a verb stem's meanings in often unpredictable ways. This furthers opaque lexicalization, as the meaning of the English word *understand* cannot be deduced from the components *under* and *stand*. Then there are participles formed from every verbal stem, each for a different verbal aspect and diathesis, not to mention other sorts of inflection omitted here.

By contrast, ancient Aramaic had verbs with two verb stems each (one perfective or punctual, one imperfect or potential), many of which have regularly formed factitive and causative variations as well as a regular mediopassive variation. There are also two participles (verbal adjectives, active and mediopassive) that do much verbal work. Almost all verbal roots follow one type (three root consonants), and verb stems are largely predictable from their roots. Aramaic verbs are inflected to agree with subjects according to three persons and, in the second and third persons, two genders. When one of the three radical consonants in a verbal root is a semivowel or another of a few evanescent consonants, some further contractions of syllables occur that are almost entirely regular. The Aramaic verb is not sheer simplicity, but by the measure of verbal morphology alone – to say nothing of the complex noun inflection of Greek and the extremely minimal noun inflection of Aramaic, with two genders and no nominal cases – the grammar of the verb used by a Greek Athenian in the fourth century BCE is exceedingly more complex than that used by their neighbors in contemporary Assyria, then under Persian rule. This is self-evident from the discrepancy in the time it takes to teach the grammar of these two different languages to post-adolescent learners today, as I have done for both in university settings. Why should one natural human language be so much more complex in its morphology than another?

---

[12] For the concept of paradigmatic transparency, see Finkel and Stump 2009.

That is a question addressed in recent scholarship, and some of the available answers are summarized and applied here.

Despite the obvious disparity in the inflectional complexity of the grammars of languages, it was for much of the twentieth century, and still is for many today, a widespread assumption that all languages are, rather, equally complex. This has been dubbed the "equal complexity hypothesis."[13] Some linguists and nonspecialists have assumed that morphological simplicity is made up for by higher complexity in another area, such as syntax or phonology. All languages are assumed to be equally complex in an unidentified fixed sum of unmeasured factors between the subsystems of a language.[14] For example, a language with simple verbal morphology should be more complex in its syntax or in some other system of language, to compensate somehow for the unadorned morphology. It is hard to understand why linguists would have assumed this without an attempt at measuring these factors, especially when it is contrary to common experience.[15] Perhaps it arises from a reaction against antiquated moralizing and implicitly racial teleological evolutionary views of linguistic philosophy at the dawn of linguistics. Wilhelm von Humboldt (1767–1835), for example, a leading contributor to the formation of linguistics, held that languages evolved from a primitive isolating type to a more advanced agglutinative type and finally a developed, higher, synthetic inflectional type possible only in a nation of greater "mental power," leading to inspired literature.[16] Perhaps it is due to the more recent tendency of major branches of linguistics to focus on the search for universal grammar and the cognitive underpinnings of all language, worthy objects of attention that happen to distract linguists from what makes languages different in their quest to find what is common to all of them.[17] One can only assume that those who hold a priori that languages are all equally

---

[13] Szmrecsanyi and Kortmann 2012: 6–7; Oczlon-Fenk and Fenk 2014. See also Trudgill 2012, who calls it the "equicomplexity hypothesis."
[14] References in McWhorter 2001: 127. For a notion of linguists' sensitivity to the issue, see the 221 pages of response by a dozen other linguists, mostly objecting to the argument summarized in McWhorter's title ("The World's Simplest Grammars are Creole Grammars"), in issue 5.2–3 of *Linguistic Typology* (2001) that, in the words of its editor, Frans Plank, "got out of hand."
[15] This has changed in recent years. The more recent debates are about what kinds of phenomena should be measured as complexity in morphology, how they should be measured, how complexity is "stored" mentally, and still other issues. See especially Baerman, Brown, and Corbett 2015, out of the references to step (1).
[16] See Morpurgo Davies 1998: 111–114. The point is explicitly clear in Humboldt's posthumous publication of 1836 (see Humboldt 1999: 88–89).
[17] Kusters 2003: 3–4.

complex have not pursued working proficiency in or taught different languages of different kinds as adults or studied current research on second-language acquisition, focusing instead on the application of general theories of linguistics to illustrative examples in the quest for universals.[18] By contrast, recent efforts in the linguistic typology have directed renewed attention toward differences among languages. Many studies have definitively demonstrated what adult learners of multiple languages have always known: that some languages really are more complex than others, and they are so according to different criteria of complexity. Complexity is not a given quantity, allocated as a fixed sum to each language, distributed to its different systems in shares having somehow the same total in every language. Some languages have far more grammatical forms to learn and to apply than others, and measurable compensation for simplicity in one area is not necessarily found with complexity in others.[19] Most importantly here, it has been amply demonstrated through studies of second-language acquisition that complexity in some modules or features of a language is more difficult for learners than others. The single biggest challenge for learners is contextual inflectional morphology: the inflection determined by syntactic relations. Purely morphological or inherent inflection, such as the use of different noun classes or declensions to which nouns are assigned without playing a role in syntax or semantics, is also difficult.[20]

---

[18] Trudgill (2011: 16) even writes, I think half-jokingly, about the doctrine of equicomplexity of languages that, "obviously this was a propaganda ploy that was vital for combating the 'some languages/dialects are primitive/inadequate' view that has been widespread in our society." This would suggest that some linguists knew that the idea was false but adopted it publicly to avoid providing inadvertent support to the notion that some people were inferior by virtue of the minimal inflectional morphology of their language.

[19] Kusters 2003: 9–12; Shosted 2006.

[20] DeKeyser 2005: 5–6: "Difficulty of language form is largely an issue of complexity. ... [The] problem of L2 users' failing to use morphology, even in comprehension, is so fundamental that it has by itself spawned entire bodies of literature." On the concept of contextual inflection, see Booij 1993 and 1996 and Marzi, Blevins, Booij, and Pirelli 2020: 229–230. Compare Myers-Scotton's "outsider system morphemes" (2006: 269–270), essentially the same concept with different jargon. To explain why these are resistant to transfer from one language to another, she writes (2008: 38), "these morphemes are seen as making the primary arguments in any clause transparent. This insight about their importance in the structuring of clauses helps explain why morphemes of this type are unlikely to be open to transfer or copying in contact situations. They are tied into an agreement system that structures the clause such that undoing the knot is difficult at best." Notably, Myers-Scotton, coming from the subfield of bilingualism studies, with a focus on defining constraints in code-switching, arrived at these results using her own names for the phenomena, and she did so without any reference to the terms "contextual inflection" or the publications of Van Coetsem on language contact, although these other lines of research describe the very same phenomena.

I have learned in talking with others about this research that it is necessary to address this further, to dispel some common misconceptions. The existence of variation in languages' complexity comes as an unwanted surprise to some because of the long-lived, well-meaning effort to dispel the intuitive, popular, but erroneous connection people draw between complexity of linguistic forms with sophistication of thought. Saying one group speaks a language less complex than another's is sometimes assumed to imply that they are also less complex in their minds or, in a word, stupider. This other, more repugnant, mistake has indeed been used at times to buttress racism and bigotry or beliefs in national linguistic superiority, promoting the false notion that speakers of morphologically simpler languages are simpleminded or unsophisticated, or even that they deserve to be ruled by sophisticated colonizing nations whose languages are complex in a way corresponding to their manner of dominating the world. It is not hard to find examples, particularly from generations long gone by, such as this one from a French military officer's essay on Guinea-Bissau Creole Portuguese, published in 1849: "It is clear that people used to expressing themselves with a rather simple language cannot easily elevate their intelligence to the genius of a European language."[21] Or take the example of William Churchill in 1911, who supposed quite mistakenly of certain South Pacific peoples that "the islanders do not know how to think comparatively" because, in their secondary pidgin English language, comparative forms of adjectives did not exist.[22] It is in the face of these bold errors, rarely if ever offered by serious scholars in the last few generations, that some sensitive observers sidestep the issue by assuming that all languages are not just evaluatively equal as natural phenomena, but *equally complex* – just as the generality of people share the same mental capacities in potential. This is, however, arguing against a repugnant fallacy with a more appealing fallacy. The correct counterargument to such bigotry is that an individual's intelligence (whatever that should mean) has no correlation with the inflectional complexity of that individual's language or languages. As William Greenfield, not a soldier but an aspiring linguist, noted already in 1830 about another creole language, "The human mind is

---

[21] Bertrand-Bocandé 1849: 73: "On conçoit que des hommes accoutumés à se servir, pour manifester leur pensée, d'un idiome aussi simple, ne purent facilement élever leur intelligence au genie d'une langue européenne." Translation from Holm 2000a: 23. Hock (2021: 728) easily rebuts such views.
[22] Churchill 1911: 27.

the same in every clime; and, accordingly, we find nearly the same process adopted in the formation of language in every country."[23]

The proposition that all languages are, one way or another, equally complex has, in any case, failed against empirical fact, as some of the studies cited in note 7 in this chapter demonstrate, and as experience in learning and teaching different languages proves. To make this less distasteful, it is useful to recall that intelligence and the complexity of the language one uses are not in fact correlated. Despite the classical scholars who have been heard to boast of the sophisticated complexity of ancient Greek, stating that its complex morphology made it more suitable for philosophy and high civilization, languages with simple inflectional morphology are not more "primitive" and their speakers are not more stupid and less intellectually gifted.[24] Russian inflectional morphology, for example, is clearly more complex than that of Mandarin Chinese or American English or modern Persian, but that does not make it better or worse, or more or less sophisticated, than the others, nor does it make Russians more intelligent and discerning than Chinese Mandarin-speakers or Anglophone Americans or Iranian Persian-speakers.

In one respect, the argument of this book does not require accepting that some languages are simpler than others, even though many Iranic language specialists, cited in the previous chapter, in describing Middle Persian morphology as greatly "reduced" or "simplified," are simply stating the obvious. Perhaps someone will insist, instead, that Middle Persian is just as complex grammatically as Old Persian in some invisible, unmeasurable, counterintuitive way, despite all the estimations of the specialists cited in the previous chapter who did not think twice about asserting that Middle Persian was an exceedingly simple language in its morphology, especially as compared with Old Persian. Such a person will still accept that the two earlier recognized stages of Persian, Old and Middle, are fundamentally

---

[23] Greenfield 1830: 51; Holm 2000a: 22.
[24] Trudgill puts it well (2011: xvi): "However, after many decades of academic linguists agreeing, and asserting, that there is very definitely no such thing anywhere as a primitive language, it now seems safe to consider this issue in print without having this suspicion arising." Ringe and Eska (2013: 55) make a similar point, that "nineteenth-century notions of linguistic 'superiority' have proved to be based on nothing more than Eurocentric bigotry, and observation readily shows that there is no correlation between the structure or typology of a language and the political fortunes or material or mental culture of its speakers." (I would qualify the latter, for indeed the political and material fortunes of the speakers of a language may create circumstances of rapid linguistic change, as I shall explain in the case of Persian.) McWhorter (2013a: 177) reverses the issue, calling into question the positive evaluation of linguistic complexity: "Opaque derivation ... is cherished by no one as a measure of expressiveness or nuance, and thus a claim of its absence in a language cannot be interpreted as implying its inferiority." Cf. McWhorter 2007: 272–274.

different, and that Old Persian changed radically before the end of the Achaemenian period, and that inflectional variety was greatly reduced. That striking difference, noted by all specialists, lacks an explanation. Nevertheless, complexity of inflection does matter. This kind of complexity is the critical issue and ought to be recognized because degrees of such complexity can tell us about the history of these languages and the histories of their speakers. It is a feature of diachronic language variation that can be used to identify historical demographic changes, as I will explain now.

(2) Children and adults learn new languages differently. Children naturally learn the grammars of languages to which they are regularly and continually exposed as they receive them, in all their complexity. Adults, by contrast, generally lose their capacity to learn new languages well (in all their inflectional complexity, without an accent, fluently). That is, adult learners of a new language cannot be native speakers. Instead, they usually acquire new languages imperfectly, from the point of view of native speakers, often introducing features from their first language (imposition) and regularizing unpredictable variation in the newly acquired language. They tend to simplify the grammar of the new languages they learn to speak, especially by reducing inflectional morphology.[25]

(3) Mass adult language acquisition produces a grammatically simplified common vernacular. When large enough proportions of a population speaking a language are nonnative adult learners, such as large groups of immigrants or colonists, then the language they have just learned will be restructured because the simplification that they give to it, in whatever degree, becomes normal and regular to the extent that their restructured variety of speech becomes pervasive. Thus, a new variety of an old language, or even an entirely new language, emerges rapidly.[26]

---

[25] Klein and Perdue 1997; Winford 2003: 222–223; Dahl 2004: 293–295; Birdsong 2006; Myers-Scotton 2006: 323–368; Labov 2007: 349; Slabakova 2008; Matras 2009: 68–86; Trudgill 2010a: 184–192; Trudgill 2010b: 310–313; Trudgill 2011: 33–40; Adone 2012; Ringe and Eska 2013: 32–35; Morgan 2014; Hartshorne, Tenenbaum, and Pinker 2018. The mechanisms of grammatical reduction are addressed later in this chapter. The difference in outcome between first-language acquisition by children and nonnative acquisition by adults is acknowledged generally, but scholarly debate about the phenomenon typically focuses on the search for the reasons behind it and the variation in effects of age on the learning of different modules of language. Those factors are not the object of this study.

[26] Milroy and Milroy 1985; Field 2004; Holm 2004; Wray and Grace 2007; Lupyan and Dale 2010; Trudgill 2011; Bentz and Winter 2013; Ringe and Eska 2013: 45–58.

(4) Children acquire newly simplified common vernaculars as native languages. When a recently simplified form of language is pervasive in the environment of children, those children will acquire the restructured, inflectionally simplified form of the language natively, and the changes introduced by a previous generation of nonnative speakers then become normal and native. The subsequent generation will learn a restructured, simpler, pervasive variety of speech in the same way as their native, normal language.

These three steps should be explained together even as they are recognized as separate components. The first (2) is a biological factor in language change; the second (3) is social and demographic; the third (4) describes a result of their combination. They constitute an area of widespread new agreement among linguists who study languages affected by population contact. Taken together in this way, they comprise the most important contribution of the field of contact linguistics to the discipline of history. The fifth step will be explained in the next section.

Three Intergenerational Patterns of Language Acquisition

Steps (2), (3), and (4) are most easily understood when we consider patterns of language acquisition between generations. Linguists with these concerns have shown that changes in language structure and complexity correlate with patterns of language acquisition and social relationships.[27] This realization, still relatively new, will have major ramifications for historical linguistics and philology as well as social history.[28] It is not that "language structure mirrors social structure," as some twentieth-century structuralists maintained. That vague and ill-defined attempt at a correlation was mostly abandoned long ago.[29] The relevant pattern is specifically based in patterns of language acquisition over more than one generation. For the sake of

---

[27] Thurston 1987; Trudgill 2009. Dahl 2004: 296: "this evolution [...] is by and large independent of the processes that are usually meant when speaking of 'cultural evolution,' and may even be negatively correlated with the rise of large-scale societies with highly mobile populations. Thus, there is evolution in language, but not in the way that 19th century scholars thought."

[28] Cf. Yakubovich 2008: 210–211: "The study of language contact represents a vigorous branch of modern linguistics, which has received an enormous boost in the last fifty years. The scholars of ancient societies wishing to decode their ethnic history must avail themselves of the achievements in this field." Ringe and Eska (2013) put nonnative acquisition and multilingualism at the fore of their recent introduction to historical linguistics.

[29] For example, Benveniste rightly pointed out that the Russian revolution transformed Russian society, but the Russian language remained largely the same grammatically. It was the lexicon that changed to respond to new needs and politics. See Laplantine 2023, studying and translating a presentation of Benveniste to this effect from 1970. When Lupyan and Dale (2010), however,

discussion, we can simplify these patterns into three broad types, necessarily ideal types found nowhere purely and exactly as described.

A typical pattern in language acquisition belongs to a mostly monolingual community. I propose to call this *intergenerationally stable* transmission. The morphology of a language in such a community remains mostly stable and changes relatively little when learned normally only by children of native speakers within a closed community. By closed, I mean that they accept few outsiders into their midst for any reason. It could be physical isolation of the linguistic community or the deliberate social exclusion of others. It could be that outsiders have little interest or incentive to join their linguistic community. In any case, children do introduce new, little changes into languages as they learn them, even as native speakers, but they are seldom drastic systemic changes. Older speakers correct children's mistakes. Children become fluent, native speakers of the language before attaining adulthood and most grammatical quirks of early childhood usage, such as leveling of grammatical irregularities, are eliminated as they interact with older users of the language. Unless their language acquisition is interrupted, their first-language acquisition never requires the leveling of complex inherited paradigms. Rather, the children in such a community learn the language of those who care for them, often their parents, and, typically in history, especially their mothers, with a high degree of exact replication, including any degree of linguistic complexity to which they are regularly exposed. The grammars, lexica, and other major features of such languages, used by closed communities, therefore change little over time. When they do change, intergenerationally stable languages normally retain complex features and even grow in complexity slowly over many generations.[30] This sort of language best characterizes populations that have been joined by very few new outsiders over time, populations that are insular, isolated socially or geographically.[31] This pattern seems to be the one historians often assume casually about their historical subjects: language and community are enduringly linked across generations; distinct communities defined by their distinct languages persist without a change in that link for centuries, so one can talk about "Arabs" or "Hungarians" in

---

declare in an important article that "language structure is partly determined by social structure," they do not define "social structure," nor do they address the long history of discussion of the topic of "social structure." That said, their clear finding that large-scale adult learning of a language correlates with reduced morphological complexity is valid and contributes strongly to the model presented here.

[30] Some communities may deliberately differentiate their languages from those around them to exclude outsiders. See Thurston 1987 and Good 2023.

[31] Milroy and Milroy 1985; Trudgill 2011; Milroy and Llamas 2013.

the fourteenth century and in the twentieth century as if these communities were intrinsically or essentially the same over seven hundred years; a language correlates with and defines its people; intergenerational changes affecting such peoples are primarily in their external circumstances, not internal and constitutional.

A different situation with a similar outcome sometimes obtains when a population includes many speakers of more than one language over many generations, possibly an entirely bilingual or multilingual community. In this second, *intergenerationally multilingual* transmission pattern, in the long term, the multilingual members of the community will transfer features of one language to another with ease as they all speak the languages in question natively or nearly so. The acceptance and durability of features transferred between languages depends on many factors, not just the kind of linguistic feature in question but also others such as the proportions of multilinguals and the distribution of languages among them, factors pertaining to generational differences, social status and social power, domains of language use, and more. These scenarios can, however, have the effect of adding some kinds of complexity to a language, but such an outcome is not necessary.[32] The expected effect of very long-term, multigenerational transfer of features between the same languages in an area of bilingualism or multilingualism is not the drastic reduction of grammatical forms but the production of a *linguistic area* or *convergence area*, also referred to in English by the German term *Sprachbund*, in which languages of separate origins converge in the patterns of their grammatical phenomena, so that they bear many similarities to one another that their ancestor languages did not exhibit in common.[33] These similarities are called areal features. Because there are different ways in which features are transferred from one language to another (discussed later in this chapter), the linguistic area is an umbrella term for several different phenomena with similar outcomes of linguistic convergence. The assumption, however, is that the people in such a society speak more than one language adequately to communicate, usually because they learned their languages at a young age.

---

[32] Trudgill 2010b: 309–310; Parkvall, Bakker, and McWhorter 2018: 231.
[33] Hock 1991: 494–515; Winford 2003: 70–74; Hock 2021: 654–724. Ciancaglini (2011: 10) is right that "the term [*Sprachbund*] seems to denote only approximately a whole group of contact phenomena for which a satisfactory historico-linguistic explanation has not been found," but there is reason to be optimistic about the future of areal linguistic studies, as shown by Muysken (2008) and Heine and Kuteva (2005: 172–218). These studies offer useful definitions of linguistic areas and distinctions between different kinds of them. I discuss linguistic areas more in Chapter 4.

By contrast with these much more frequent circumstances of language use in societies, there is a third and less common situation of *mass nonnative acquisition*. This is when many adults adopt a new language at once. Languages learned by large masses of adult nonnative speakers in a short period tend to become grammatically reduced, particularly in their inflectional morphology. This is because, unlike children, who acquire languages with the fluency of their adult models, adult learners acquire new languages imperfectly with respect to what native speakers hitherto have spoken – with a lexicon more limited than that of natives, with nonnative pronunciation, and with limited command of morphological complexity – as compared with the native usage of the language until that time.[34] They have passed the sensitive period of childhood and early adolescence during which new languages can be learned with native proficiency.[35] The characterization of a nonnative variety as "imperfect" is not a moral evaluation.[36] Imperfect language acquisition by adult learners is normal in historical circumstances of fresh contact between populations with different languages, in which adults hitherto not in contact need to interact. In such conditions, most adult language learners in history did not have access to formal training with carefully designed exercises like those offered today in modern university courses on languages. Most people did not learn languages as educated and literate people tend to learn them today. They did not grow up in a society in which the state instituted mandatory mass schooling in multiple literary languages, as is the case in many countries today. Instead, adult learners in premodern times normally had to pick languages up through casual social exposure, informal instruction, and attentive use with trial and error. They learned languages usually only by necessity or through the ambition to gain a specific advantage. In any case, they usually did so by interacting with other speakers of the language. Under these circumstances, the age of acquisition was especially important. Adult nonnative speakers of a language normally omit its complex features in practice, because those features are cognitively burdensome or they simply have not learned to apply them, and they make do without them, aiming at a functional-level communication recognized by native speakers as foreign.

---

[34] I have heard claims about individuals who attain perfect fluency in a new language as an adult, with no discernible accent and indistinguishable from native speakers. These would be rare exceptions. If they were not, then we would not have a category of nonnative speaker.

[35] Trudgill 2010b: 313: "Simplification in language contact does not result from nonnative language learning as such, but from post-critical threshold nonnative language learning."

[36] Van Coetsem 2000: 82: "The product of second language acquisition . . . is a language in its own right."

Native speakers who need to interact with adult learners of their own language must tolerate the omission of such complex features. They may even simplify their own speech, too, as an expedient for communication with others who do not know their language adequately. Simplification of one's own language is a normal strategy employed by native speakers to facilitate effective communication in their own language and on their own terms – literally – with nonnative speakers. Nonnative speakers learn to speak and understand simplified forms of speech more easily. A form of language with reduced features, such as a simplified range of inflected noun or verb forms, can become routine and normal in a multilingual social setting in which functional communication is the immediate necessity. When the abbreviated, new form of language acquired by adult learners is passed on to younger generations, as, for example, when a large proportion of a population consists of nonnative speakers, all of whom do without the native speakers' inflectional complexities, then children in their midst acquire simplified, nonnative speech as normal and native. Extensive and rapid mass adult acquisition is probably the *only* major driving force behind extensive morphological simplification and restructuring of any language.[37]

It is through new population contact that nonnative speakers – people who learn a language as an adult – come into being. Individual cases are normal, but scale is an issue. A few strangers from a foreign land will not change the grammar of the local language as it is generally used. But when adult language acquisition occurs on a very large scale, as with, for example, migration of numerous people into a social group new to them, suddenly many of the speakers of one language will become nonnative learners of another, and they may often communicate with each other in their shared nonnative variety. This is especially so when the newcomers originated in communities that do not have another common language. Their knowledge of their new language will usually be of the simplest kind necessary to facilitate daily life. That large proportion of speakers will use a new version

---

[37] Trudgill 2011, esp. 62–115; McWhorter 2011a: 2–3. Scattered objections to this discovery have not been adequate. For example, Campbell and Poser (2008: 357–362) discount Trudgill's arguments along these lines largely based on a single case study of Hawai'ian phonology. Their argument does not even mention the historical dimension; synchronic description of a language's complexity alone cannot by itself disprove the thesis about past mass nonnative acquisition leading to simplification of grammar. Trudgill himself addresses these criticisms effectively (2011: 55–60). Moreover, the choice of phonology as the criterion was probably fruitless because complexity of phonology does not appear to be a salient issue in cases such as these (Bakker 2009; Bakker and Daval-Markussen 2017: 79–82). It is possible that phonemic inventories are rather correlated with population size (Hay and Bauer 2007).

of the language, created by the imposition of features of their prior language or languages, giving rise to new pronunciations (foreign accents), abbreviated or neatly analogized paradigms, and regularized or streamlined versions of hitherto irregular grammatical rules and forms. They will misapply or omit word inflection and simplify complexities of the language of the earlier native speakers and they may impose features of their own native languages on their use of the new one. These adult learners will often never have intended to learn the new language fluently, as their goal was not to become a full member of the group of native speakers. In many cases they will not expect ever to be regarded as a full member of the group with which they have come into contact.

The crucial step is that children exposed continually to nonnative speakers will learn from them a restructured form of the language as their own native speech and, in the next generation, they will pass that form of the language on to their own children. In the event of further migrations and contact with still more populations using different languages, newcomers to this linguistic arena will find a simpler variety of the common language available to them. They will more easily learn that variety, if they have a choice and they find it adequate for their aims. It is an easier target with a useful communicative outcome. Within three generations, it is possible for the language in such circumstances to have changed drastically in the direction of inflectional simplification by these processes, to the point that it is mutually incomprehensible with the prior, inflectionally more complex variety of the language. That is, from the old language a new language has arisen on the tongues of newcomers. When children take that new language as their own, it is sustained as a native language to be passed on to the next generation. It is no longer just a strong foreign accent. The morphologically reduced form of the language is now a native tongue.

This kind of language change is not hard to grasp conceptually from ordinary experience. If parents move with their young children to a new locale, where native speakers of the same language speak with a different accent, their children will now learn that accent natively to the extent that they are not confined solely to interaction with their parents and other persons of the same origin. They learn the local accent from those around them. The same phenomenon occurs if the "accent" is, rather, the simplified pronunciation and grammar of foreigners who have moved in around that family and learned the local language nonnatively. The basic process is, therefore, not mysterious, but is easily observable in the world today wherever people are mobile.

In summary, different social conditions tend to give rise to different kinds of language change. For the purpose of illustration, I distinguished three common ideal patterns relevant to this study. Population changes, migration, and demographic upheavals easily interrupt the typically widespread pattern of intergenerational transmission of unchanged grammar from parents to children. They can transform a language because their intergenerational relationships to each other and to their languages shift. As a consequence, languages acquire lastingly different grammatical characteristics that are determined by social events. Large-scale new population contact between adults in effect strips inflectional morphology from the intercommunal language, especially contextual inflection. Drastic grammatical changes induced by those events are permanent in a language within that population, although any language so affected will undergo further changes by all kinds of processes of language change thereafter. Populations will remain linguistically conservative when characterized by (1) closely knit, multiplex social relationships, in which most members know every other member, and (2) little contact, due to any factor, with outsiders attempting to learn their language. Their languages are likewise, in the long run, the most inflectionally complex. At least they retain inherited complex features such as ornate inflectional morphology.[38] The close-knit, closed population of its users seems slowly and gradually to develop increasingly elaborate forms of speech, marking membership in the closed community. In the jargon of linguistics this is "complexification."[39] Different, but not entirely so, are the common cases of populations having numerous contacts with other groups who speak different languages natively. When children in such situations learn more than one language from youth, they become multilingual persons capable of native-like use in each of those languages. Multilinguals are responsible for the transfer of features between these languages, which may foster simplification, new complexities, or both, depending on many

---

[38] The pattern of two tendencies was intuited already by Meillet (1912b: 413): "L'extension d'une langue à une grand nombre d'individus nouveaux en banalise les formes; les langues dont l'aspect est le plus singulier sont celles des plus petits groupes sociaux."

[39] McWhorter and Trudgill both suggest that languages used in such social circumstances slowly become more complex over time, free from the social factors that induce reduction. See Trudgill (2010b: 314). A terminological note: the word complexification is ill-formed. It should be complicification, but this neologism is much less likely to be transparent for English-speakers. Labov (2007: 346) calls it "incrementation." Trudgill (2011: 185) claims that, "Linguistic complexity developed in societies of intimates," and that complexification will occur gradually in social groups with "small size, dense social networks, large amounts of shared information, high stability, and low contact" with outsiders.

factors. They may cause their languages to converge, generating areal features. The third and more distinct pattern occurs when a large population of adults must learn a new language in common at once. Such a language will undergo a potentially drastic degree of morphological reduction. As Wray and Grace put it counterintuitively, languages that many nonnative speakers need to use "will come under pressure to become more learnable by the adult mind" through the elimination of complexity for the sake of the new learners who need to communicate.[40] This is an important pattern of language change arising from the combination of specific social and biological factors: scale of contact and age of acquisition.

Now that I have explained steps (2), (3), and (4), I turn to the fifth step of this part of the linguistic-historical model. It is a caveat.

(5) Languages may be morphologically reduced by this process in *varying degrees*. Reduction of a language's morphology and grammatical restructuring by these intergenerational population changes is not binary: either simplified or not-simplified. Rather, the resulting language may exhibit relative degrees of restructuring and grammatical reduction that vary from instance to instance according to specific historical social factors during the time of large-scale nonnative adult acquisition. Linguists have proposed a few taxonomies of degrees of restructuring in language, but this is work in progress, so we have at our disposal only a limited number of minimally analytical and therefore tentative terms to designate the outcomes of such restructuring. This inhibits our ability to be precise about the character of restructuring in each new historical stage of the evolution of Persian, the subject of this book, but it does not stop us from recognizing the character of partial restructuring that indubitably did occur in a language such as ancient Persian.[41]

To understand this crucial, final step in the model, one must understand the thorny problem of contact languages and especially the *creole*.[42] This will enable one to relate the drastic changes occurring in the history of Persian and other languages to clearly established linguistic categories and living examples of these varieties of language, rather than treating the

---

[40] Wray and Grace 2007: 557.
[41] Holm 2000b; Neumann-Holzschuh and Schneider 2000; Winford 2000; Winford 2003: 300–301, 254–256; Holm 2004; McWhorter 2005: 19–34; McWhorter 2007: 17–18, 252–276; Holm 2010: 258–259; McWhorter 2014.
[42] Holm 2000a offers a responsible introduction to creoles.

Persian language as a sui generis phenomenon, unlike any other language, following natural laws peculiar to it alone.

"Contact Languages" as Comparanda

Some of the discoveries outlined so far arose from the study of the most striking recent historical examples of languages restructured in the wake of intensive, colonial, population contact. These are languages called pidgins and creoles, inflectionally simplified varieties of other languages used in early modern colonial circumstances, which have become entirely new languages in themselves. To varying degrees such languages can seem to be hybrids through the transfer of features from other languages (language mixing through the transfer of features from one to the other being an issue discussed later in this chapter). Creoles arise by the same natural, social, intergenerational processes just outlined. Because most of the recognized living pidgins and creoles came into existence during the recent age of European maritime empires and colonial domination, and not in the ancient past, their genesis is in several cases well documented. Innumerable publications present research on these drastically restructured varieties of Dutch, English, French, Portuguese, Arabic, and other languages. The term creole comes from Spanish and Portuguese, where it referred to persons born in American colonies created by speakers of those languages. Meaning "created, made, begotten," at first it referred to persons of mixed ancestry in these colonies. As new varieties of colonial languages came to be used by these people, the languages soon also acquired the designation "creole," already by the end of the seventeenth century.[43] From these specific languages named Creole, linguists have generalized a category of language, "creole," which has been applied to similarly simplified varieties of languages with analogous origins. It is important to distinguish creole cultures – the cultures of people called creole – from creole languages, which result from the specific processes under discussion. The term "creolization" thus refers to two different things; this present concern is purely the linguistic one.

The focus on creoles in the modern study of language restructuring through grammatical reduction has had, however, two unintended deleterious effects on related scholarship, each of which requires discussion. First, by basing much of their work on creoles – which do provide conspicuous examples of the restructuring or recasting of languages in distinctive,

---

[43] Holm 2000a: 16; Winford 2003: 305–306.

morphologically simpler forms, and of interruptions in the typical intergenerational acquisition of language through social contact – specialists in contact linguistics became mired in ideologically charged debates about the historically particular category of creole itself rather than the phenomena of socially induced language change.[44] It is an emotionally charged debate because the best-known creoles today are radically restructured and morphologically simplified versions of the languages used by European colonial powers. These languages arose as byproducts of social contact often characterized by violence, forced migration, slavery, and oppression, from which descendants of the inhabitants of the colonizing countries continue to benefit, but leaving conditions that have disadvantaged the living descendants of the victims for generations even as they effectively gave rise to new ethnic groups. Humanistic scholars, whose work requires the promotion of cultural understanding, are often interested in defending the dignity of colonized and enslaved peoples and their descendants, and in repelling the disdain and racial bigotry applied unfairly to ethnic groups who had their genesis amid generations of exploitation. In so doing, some have regarded the designation of these colonized peoples' languages, creoles, as the simplest of the world's languages, as adding insult to injury: not only are creole-speakers sometimes treated in appalling, racist ways, but now their languages are deemed "simple"! Because of this, some sensitive defenders of colonized and decolonized peoples have refused to acknowledge that creoles are morphologically simpler, and easier for adults to learn, than their source languages. Naïvely adopting the prejudices of colonizers of bygone times, who disdained simple languages as uncouth or intellectually less capable, they allege that to "exclude" creoles from the rest of languages as belonging to a category of exceptional grammatical simplicity would perpetuate an oppressive colonial discourse and taint this branch of linguistics. This criticism addresses the so-called creole exceptionalism. In so arguing, they fall into the fallacy described under step (1), by assuming that there is any insult at all in declaring that one language is inflectionally simpler than another. They could just as well celebrate the adaptive power of humanity in generating expressive, beautiful languages easily acquired for communication in difficult circumstances, but they do not. Some of them even conflate the views of early colonial scholars of centuries past, who explicitly despised their creole-speaking subjects, with the views clearly expressed by linguists today, whose interest in and fascination with creole-speaking peoples and

---

[44] See, for example, the objections of Mufwene (1997), DeGraff (2003), and some of the studies collected in Ansaldo, Matthews, and Lim 2007.

their languages, as human languages, is hard to describe as colonial, and who explicitly state their belief that there are no "primitive" languages.[45] For those interested in radical language restructuring, and in understanding general linguistic phenomena, as these special cases make them especially clear, the debate makes for a messy and deterring obstacle. It distracts from the actual gains of contact linguistics and obscures the arguments in ongoing debates about the specific processes involved in the genesis of creoles.[46] It makes language use a matter of identity for humanistic scholars, who almost universally ignore the critical issue of age of language acquisition, instead regarding a sense of identity as the leading factor in choosing language use.[47]

The second deleterious side-effect of creole studies on this larger problem of linguistics is that the copious attention to creoles created the implicit impression of a binarism separating creoles and noncreoles, "simplified" versus "normal" languages. The languages called creole today are the most outstanding contemporary examples of "contact languages" in that they are inflectionally radically simpler, restructured varieties of languages used by imperial and colonial powers. Meanwhile, their source languages, such as English and French, are still today the primary media used in instruction in European and American universities and indeed by scholars around the world. The distinction between modern creoles and their widely known source languages is therefore especially conspicuous to scholars today, furthering the impression of scholars that a language is

---

[45] These debates leave interested bystanders like Migge (2019: 862, reviewing McWhorter 2018) wondering about the "absence of hospitality" among those most engaged in the debate. DeGraff, for example, blurs the distinction between folk attitudes toward creole languages with current linguists' stated beliefs about how creoles are exceptional when he claims that linguists "reinforce the belief that Creoles are structurally *inadequate*" (2003: 392; emphasis added). I have not seen any serious linguistic literature from recent times making that claim. Of course, any statement about creoles being "structurally inadequate" would require a demonstration rather than a mere assertion and should be regarded with extreme skepticism. Bakker (2017a: 27) states that "all linguists who have studied creoles agree that creoles are natural languages, with the full range of expressability of the other natural languages of the world." Cf. McWhorter 2007: 272–273; 2018. If creoles are exceptional, then it is not as exceptions to the class of human languages, but as instances of language more exceptionally well characterized by nonnative-learner-induced restructuring. They are exceptional in the sense that the Abkhaz language, for example, is exceptional in respect of its extraordinarily large consonant inventory as compared with those of most other languages.

[46] A less ideologically charged objection to the notion that creoles harbor less complexity has come in the form of studies of creole phonologies. These have demonstrated that such languages tend to have phoneme inventories in the average range of the world's languages. (See, for example, the studies comprised in the first half of Faraclas and Klein 2009.) While these findings are important, they do not address the salient issue of inflectional morphology.

[47] Trudgill 2010a: 184–192, esp. 189: "There is a copious literature ... which suggests that linguistic accommodation is not driven by social factors such as identity at all but is an automatic consequence of human interaction."

either creole or not creole, either like or unlike the languages with which they are personally most familiar.⁴⁸ Since the nineteenth century, however, and especially in the last thirty years, research has recognized the existence of languages between the status of "normal" change – which is not named by a technical term – and the "creole."⁴⁹ These are *partially* restructured languages that vary in degree of inflectional simplification. Only recently has this aspect of the problem come to the fore in concerted discussions, and scholars have begun to search for ways to identify, describe, and even measure *degrees* of simplification or reduction in complexity.⁵⁰ Out of necessity, not preference, this book participates in that effort.

Before describing partially restructured and inflectionally reduced languages, in connection with step (5), and explaining what such changes mean or entail, however, it will help to explain more clearly what a creole is supposed to be in the first place. Understanding the linguistic history of ancient Persian requires this orientation, if we are to analyze Achaemenian society correctly in ways that relate the linguistic history of Persian to other documented natural phenomena in language change. This is especially so when recent studies by specialists in Persian have suggested that Persian – particularly New Persian – may have evolved as something like a creole, but they have done so with hardly any investigation into research on creoles.⁵¹ It is necessary to understand the terms one uses.

---

⁴⁸ Humanists, upon learning about creoles, have sometimes become excited to suggest that the language of their academic specialty is a creole, often without understanding the category adequately. These assertions then draw counterarguments easily demonstrating that it is not a creole in the normal sense of the term. These debates would not play out so inconclusively if participants recognized that there are degrees of restructuring. See, for example, the debate on Middle English as a candidate for creole, summarized dismissively by Watts (2011: 83–113). In my view, Middle English is clearly not a creole, but it has also clearly undergone morphological simplification relative to Old English that absolutely necessitates that it be understood through the historical-linguistic model presented here. Scholars of the history of English must explain the history of the demography of English-speakers better to arrive at a convincing solution. Cf. McWhorter 2007: 59–103 for a linguistic analysis of this problem.

⁴⁹ Earlier, I proposed to call such "normal" languages "intergenerationally stable" so that we have a name for this phenomenon rather than regarding it as a default condition.

⁵⁰ Holm (2004) and McWhorter (2007: 252–265) present the most determined efforts in this direction.

⁵¹ Utas (2006: 246) argues that it is "tempting to see [New Persian] as the result of a process resembling what is known as creolization in modern languages"; later, Utas (2013: 258) backs away slightly from this suggestion, emphasizing that a "great part of the simplification of Old Iranian that final led to the formation of New Persian had obviously already taken place in Middle Persian." Rezakhani (2024: 331) acknowledges that "some" have considered New Persian a creole, but he refuses the term for the discussion of the evolution of New Persian not on analytical grounds but because "creole" "can act as a marker of exceptionalism and indicate a misunderstood social construct," citing Ansaldo, Matthews, and Lim 2007. Yet in 2017 and 2020 he considered New Persian "an almost pidgin form of the language," a "pidginized form of Middle Persian" (Rezakhani 2017; 2020: 263).

Varieties of Contact Languages

Readers already familiar with contact linguistics may wish to skip these substantial sections on the categories of pidgin, creole, bilingual mixed language, and semicreole, as they review what is well known in that subfield of linguistics for specialists in history and for other humanists. Others may find the categories and examples in this section useful for understanding the entire argument of the present work concerning the early history of Persian, and as an orientation to some of the most important issues concerning language restructuring through population contact. It is impossible to grapple with the linguistic history of Persian fully, and to discuss the drastic reduction in its inflectional morphology, without confronting these categories – unless we are to treat Persian as a language unlike any other and not susceptible to the factors involved in change in all other languages.

Practically all languages are shaped in little ways, at least, by their speakers' contact with speakers of other languages, and particularly through the agency of bilingual individuals who replicate features of one of their languages in the other one that they use. The adopted word (usually known as a loanword), transferred from one language into another, is the simplest and most obvious type of such contact-induced change. Some new languages, however, stand out as having arisen precisely because of movements of people or population changes involving speakers of different languages. These are the so-called contact languages: languages profoundly shaped by population contact. By the year 2000, linguists readily acknowledged at least three types of them: pidgin, creole, and bilingual mixed language.[52] Each category entails scholarly debates. I will explain each of the three types just mentioned with specific examples because interested readers familiar with other fields of investigation, such as history and historical linguistics, cannot go far into this topic without encountering the debates about them. These types, as separate categories, are misleading in that they refer to various phenomena that are the outcomes of the same bundle of processes: language acquisition at different times of life, bilingualism, and the transfer of features between languages. The types differ for reasons that have long been difficult to discern because of complex historical social factors not easily measured in each instance. Together, these types still form one of the present bases of research in contact linguistics. Anyone interested in the restructuring of ancient

---

[52] Thomason 1997a; Holm 2000a: 4–12; Winford 2003: 18–22.

Persian, the subject of this book, will want to know whether Persian at any stage fits into these categories. Because I accept the existence of degrees of inflectional reduction – step (5) in the previous section – I hasten to add that I do not consider any stage of Persian directly attested in premodern history to be definitely a pidgin or a creole as the terms are conventionally employed, but to repeat the critical point: creole/noncreole is not a binary phenomenon. As pidgins and creoles represent extreme cases of restructuring via inflectional reduction and other normal changes, the kind of change to which all languages are potentially susceptible in certain social circumstances, it will help the reader unfamiliar with this topic to know about some outstanding instances of this phenomenon. It will put the partial restructuring of Persian into perspective, as virtually on a scale. This scale will be imprecise. Readers oriented toward humanistic disciplines will not be troubled about such a lack of precision. Extremely complex historical human phenomena that cannot easily be measured or quantified, and for which there are many variables, are the staple food of humanistic investigation. Generally, it is linguists, not historians, who aspire to make a more exact science of their material in the history of language. Historians, whose goals and methods differ from those of linguists, may be satisfied with what I have to offer about the history of languages: robust explanatory models based on biological and social facts, supported by the amply tested methods of historical linguistics and philology, offering numerous closely matching parallel instances, and contributing to a historical narrative with verisimilitude that is supported by all available primary sources. Linguists, too, may appreciate the case I make about Persian, although McWhorter's concise, more synchronic and comparative linguistic argument about Persian probably accords more with their own goals, which usually address language itself as a phenomenon and deal with particulars and instances only instrumentally.[53]

The premise to be accepted is that languages can be restructured and simplified in the ways already explained. Historians are used to these sorts of nonquantitative scalar concepts. With the warning that these are not absolute categories, I shall give examples to illustrate each of the three kinds of contact languages generally countenanced by language contact specialists. To this I will add a fourth type, the semicreole, established in the literature but not widely employed in analysis. In each case, it is critical to observe the social contexts in which these kinds of languages develop. Importantly, I need also to define the terms for the purposes of my own

---

[53] McWhorter 2007: 138–164.

discussion, because even specialists in this field have not achieved consensus on the definition of their own primary categories of analysis.

Pidgin

A "pidgin" is a simple language spoken by nobody natively, generated collaboratively and learned by adults for communication primarily with other adult speakers of different languages.[54] Otherwise they cannot understand each other effectively, being limited to gesture, repeated words, and ad hoc jargon.[55] When such jargon (in this technical sense) becomes a linguistic system with a regularly observed, simple grammar, a pidgin has emerged.[56] A pidgin exhibits minimal word inflection or no inflectional morphology at all and begins with a small vocabulary drawn mostly, but not exclusively, from one language in a multilingual environment. The term of art for that main source language is the "lexifier," but pidgins are drastically simpler in inflectional morphology than most other languages including their own lexifiers. At the same time, pidgins often exhibit features of phonology, syntax, or other systems of the first languages of their learners, which they impose on the new pidgin. Sometimes linguists call the latter "substrate" influence, although the term is imprecise and misleading.

Pidgins originate through collaboration in communication. Native speakers of the lexifier deliberately simplify their language to help their adult nonnative speaker interlocutors to understand. This is called "foreigner talk," a term coined on the model of "baby talk."[57] Deliberately simplified foreigner talk is a much easier target of learning to attain for nonnative speakers struggling to understand their foreign interlocutors than the complex natively spoken lexifier. At the same time, a grammatically abbreviated version of a language is a normal outcome of informal adult language learning, as many studies prove, so there are cases in which foreigner talk appears to play no significant role.[58] In any case, for nonnative speakers in

---

[54] Thomason and Kaufman 1988: 167–171; Holm 2000a: 4–6; Winford 2003: 268–303; Myers-Scotton 2006: 278–280; Siegel 2008; Matras 2009: 277–278.
[55] Hock 1991: 522–523; Winford 2003: 268–269; Hock 2021: 724–727.
[56] Much research on pidgins concerns theories of the process, including the cognitive component, by which the language emerges as a language, not on the social context of its emergence. Because I accept it as a fact that pidgin languages, as defined here, exist, these theories are not addressed directly here. Readers may consult Siegel (2008) for a lucid analysis of the problem.
[57] Ferguson and DeBose 1977. See also Romaine 1988: 72–84 and Hock 2021: 640–642.
[58] Siegel 2008: 26–30. Foreigner talk in pidgin generation is real, however; see the present-day Arabic pidgin examples collected by Avram (2014: 33–37).

most historical population contact situations, functional efficiency is often, if not usually, a goal preferable to fluency like that of a native. In many cases, native belonging would not be a feasible or even desirable goal for an outsider. Thus, it is reasonable to suppose that one factor in pidgin formation is that its first users had no intention of complete, native-like acquisition of the lexifier.[59] In sum, pidgin formation is a creative, adaptive process for humans in new social environments, developed through the joint agency of adult speakers of different languages.[60] It becomes regular and systematized through mutual use. Because a pidgin is regular, possessing grammatical rules, however simple, it is not possible for a newcomer fluent in the lexifier to speak it through ad hoc simplifications of the lexifier (mere "foreigner talk"). One must learn a pidgin's grammar and conventions. This is not a difficult task, relatively speaking, because it has deliberately been made easy by the necessity of, or interest in, cooperation. Otherwise, it would not work as a reliable system of communication. Pidgins are thus real languages, but they are nobody's first language, and they are not created by a master plan. Along with their creole offspring, they have been proposed to be the inflectionally simplest known languages.[61] That is, indeed, the purpose of their existence.

The linguistic history of a specific pidgin can illustrate this category better than a theoretical sketch. Let us take the example of Police Motu, a pidgin of Papua New Guinea now disappearing. Papua, also known as New Guinea and Irian, is the second-largest island in the world and is also one of the most linguistically diverse countries in the world. An estimated 750 or 860 languages are spoken in Papua New Guinea, the modern country occupying the eastern half of the island, to the point that one can encounter a different language in practically every village and valley.[62] When the British established a regional base for themselves, Port Moresby, on the southeastern coast of Papua in 1873, staking a claim on the large island's territory, population, and resources in competition with the Dutch and the German governments, they inadvertently caused a new pidgin language to develop and propagated it. The people in the immediate area of the settlement of Port Moresby spoke an Austronesian language called Motu. British visitors and other new settlers learned a simplified Motu as

---

[59] Baker 1990.
[60] Churchill (1911: 1), using the term jargon for pidgin, rightly wrote that "jargon is the speech of necessity."
[61] McWhorter 2001.   [62] Lynch 1998: 34, 61–67; Nettle and Romaine 2000: 80–84.

used by locals to facilitate their communication with them.[63] After Port Moresby became the base for the extension of British control over the surrounding regions of the island, numerous individuals from many different countries in the Pacific and distant continents came to Port Moresby to partake of the new opportunities there and to search for work and resources to exploit. Dutton describes the mix of people consisting of "Chinese, 'Malays,' 'South Sea Islanders,' persons of mixed race, Maltese, Ceylonese, Indians, Filipinos, Europeans, Americans, and a large number of British-Australian origin."[64] The newcomers relied on Motu-speaking locals for necessities, so the pidgin form of Motu found increasingly more speakers among the new arrivals, none of them native speakers of the language. The British government of Papua (1883–1906) created a constabulary to enforce its own claims of government over the island, maintained continuously as a police force under the succeeding Australian government (1906–1975).[65] For this, at first, the British recruited Motu-speaking personnel from the area of their base. The language came to be known as Police Motu from its associations with this organization. As increasingly more people on the island were brought, by hook and by crook, under colonial organization, they found the pidgin Police Motu expedient as a means of communication with authorities and of access to jobs and commodities from the world at large. Representatives of other Papuan communities learned it, even those under British authority who were remote from the Motu-speaking area. Already by 1894, one source reports, Motu had "been carried by retired constables to numerous places where it had never before been heard of."[66] Note that the date of this report means that simplified Motu must have developed, and its use become widely adopted, within ten years of the inception of official British government there. The new language found many more speakers in the decades to follow. In 1928, a government anthropologist noted that the "pidgin-Motuan" "has proved vastly useful," and that "in practice we have made the widest use of Motuan in that simplified (or shall we say degraded?) form which may properly be called pidgin-Motuan."[67] In being shared by many different communities, the pidgin variety of Motu changed and developed in its pronunciation, grammar, and lexicon. Early on it became

---

[63] Some have claimed that a jargon or pidgin of Motu existed before the arrival of the British, a kind of regularized "foreigner talk" facilitating their communication with their linguistically different neighbors for purposes of coastal trade and cooperation. See Dutton 1997: 13–18.
[64] Dutton 1997: 18.   [65] Kituai 1988.   [66] Kituai 1998: 107.
[67] Williams 1928: 7–8. The parenthetical remark of moral evaluation is in the original. It illustrates the tendency to stigmatize new, morphologically simplified languages.

mutually unintelligible with its source and lexifier, the local Motu language from the vicinity of Port Moresby. This was due not just to plentiful words adopted from other languages for colonial novelties, but also, and more importantly, by dropping numerous salient features of Motu grammar and making do without them and using a relatively limited vocabulary. At any time, a few dozen British field officers used it in supervising hundreds of such constables from innumerable different linguistic backgrounds. Through them, Police Motu became a major medium for communication throughout British Papua, easily acquired because of its extreme simplicity.[68] To some extent, it even became a part of the British institutions there, which promoted the use of pidgin Motu while the administrators frowned on pidgin English. For example, uncooperative Papuans put in prison (called *dibura*, or "the dark," in Police Motu) by the British in Port Moresby were expected to learn Police Motu to get by.[69] Some of these prisoners, upon release, went on to work for the constabulary that had recently imprisoned them, carrying the language with them across Papua. In this way, time in prison had taught them a linguistic skill useful for effective British government service. Those who had contact with the British and, subsequently, Australian government became distinguished by this shared language, so the use of Police Motu also signified access to new commodities, technologies, and social authority. This only gave further incentive to Papuans for learning it. British and Australian patrol officers, in charge of the constables, needed a pidgin tongue at least as much as their constables to communicate with them. Recruit Jojoga Yegova recalled that in 1943, in training for the Royal Papuan Constabulary, "Many of us initially used sign language to communicate with each other until we could master Police Motu or New Guinea *Tok Pisin*" (the latter discussed here subsequently).[70] Decisively, many Papuans from different communities who fought alongside each other together with the British in World War II used Police Motu among themselves. Through major shared endeavors, the pidgin Motu became a common link between communities collaborating with the British who could not otherwise communicate directly with one another. In 1963, the authors of an introduction to

---

[68] On Police Motu generally, see Dutton 1985 and 1997. See also Winford 2003: 297–298, who would rather call it a "simplified language" than a "prototypical" pidgin.
[69] Dutton 1985: 74–78. It was a deliberate policy, at least in the 1890s, to put prisoners, "both at work and in the cell," with others who used Motu, so that any prisoner who spent a few months in the Port Moresby prison spoke "Motuan more or less" (i.e., pidgin Motu). By 1905, prisoners were still "picking up" Motu first, then learning a little English.
[70] Kituai 1998: 179.

Police Motu dubbed it simply "the lingua franca of Papua."[71] A Bible translation in Police Motu appeared in 1964.

Upon the political union of Papua in the south and New Guinea in the north in 1972, and with the independence of Papua New Guinea in 1975, its adherents insisted that Police Motu should be one of the three official languages of the new state. They redubbed it Hiri Motu, "Trade-Expedition Motu," to remove possible negative connotations in the name Police Motu. At that time, there were an estimated 120,000 users of the pidgin as a second language.[72] To this day, Hiri Motu still has a special official status in Papua New Guinea. In reality, Hiri Motu has apparently lost most of its ground to a pidgin based on English, Tok Pisin (from English "Talk Business"), which had long been in use in the north part of the island, New Guinea, since the days of German rule there (1884–1919) and, in gradually divergent varieties, in other Pacific islands to the north and east. Pidgin Motu was useful for much of the twentieth century, but now, as far as reports indicate, only a shrinking, aging population retains it, alongside their separate village languages (including the original Motu) and pidgin English. If Christian missionaries and zealous Papuan users of Hiri Motu had not advocated for it so strongly in the 1960s and 1970s, this pidgin would probably be little documented, and it may have disappeared more quickly. It is, however, likely to die out soon, because it never obtained a substantial number of native speakers and the utility of Tok Pisin (the pidgin of English used in Papua New Guinea) has become greater for younger generations.[73] Again, besides the social circumstances in which they arise, and their relative simplicity, that is a fundamental characteristic feature of pidgins: they have a negligible number of native speakers.[74] By their definition, pidgins will tend to disappear unless they are sustained by a continuous stream of new nonnative learners.[75]

---

[71] Wurm and Harris 1963: 1.   [72] Reinecke 1975: 752.
[73] Romaine (1992: 330) suggests that Hiri Motu is (was?) too regionally marked to become a successful lingua franca, unlike Tok Pisin, which is a relatively "ethnically neutral lingua franca." She also demonstrates (1992: 93–94) a distinct drop-off in the percentage of Hiri Motu-speakers in seven major towns of Papua New Guinea from 1966 to 1971 alone. Hiri Motu seems never to have become current in the northern, formerly German-controlled part of the island, or in the more densely populated highlands that were brought under colonial control later. It may be that the social bases of diffusion for these two pidgins also predisposed them to different careers: relatively few Papuans served in the constabulary, whereas many Papuans went out of their villages to work on plantations, where Tok Pisin found its first speakers.
[74] There are a few exceptional reports about multilingual native speakers of Police Motu. For example, Jack Hides (1906–1938), an explorer of Papua New Guinea, "grew up speaking Police Motu" (Franklin 1989: 99). His father was then the head of the prison in Port Moresby, where Police Motu was the common language.
[75] Myers-Scotton 2006: 280: "Pidgins fade away."

Creole

The second widely accepted category of contact language, and the one that has received the most attention, is the creole.[76] It is also a category used recently by historians rather freely without precision or grounding in the study of actual creoles. This undermines the historical study of creole languages by diluting the utility of the term further than linguists already have done (addressed later). I urge fellow historians to understand the term thoroughly before entering into conjectures and debates about its application.

As already mentioned, the term arose in the eighteenth century to designate a number of languages arising among populations of mixed origins, mainly enslaved and subjugated peoples of Africa and the Americas; subsequently, the term was generalized widely to refer to all sorts of cultural and linguistic products of the mixture of different populations.[77] I do not use the term in the historical sense of the specific social origins of languages bearing the proper name "creole," but rather as a linguistic category. For the purposes of this discussion, I adopt a widely used conventional definition of creole. The definition is simple and well known and serves the present purpose. It is that *a creole is a nativized pidgin*. When children learn a pidgin natively, they begin to develop the pidgin beyond its prior range of uses because it is one of their chief means of verbal expression, if not their only means, and human social needs demand the development of rich and nuanced means of expression. Out of necessity, and possibly by their nature, children accomplish this enrichment in their language acquisition and use. Probably every creole specialist today will quibble about such a definition left unqualified, but most creole specialists do not offer or apply a strict definition to their subject.[78] In the same way, creole specialists disagree with each other constantly about their

---

[76] The most concise survey of all the issues pertaining to creole studies is provided soberly by Bakker (2017a).

[77] For orientations to the changing significance and contested meaning of the term creole, see Stewart 2007 and McWhorter 2005. Myers-Scotton (2006: 280) explains the sequence clearly: "Before linguists began studying these languages, the term 'creole' was already in use as the term for people who lived in European colonies, especially people of mixed descent. Then, the language varieties that developed in these colonies came to be called creole."

[78] For example, the useful volume *Comparative Creole Syntax* (Holm and Patrick 2007) presents grammatical summaries of eighteen different creole languages without any declared criterion by which they could be so designated. The recognition that these eighteen languages are "creoles" is based on convention and intuition, for each of them is a recently restructured variety of another well-known language retaining a large native speaker population today (Arabic, Assamese, Dutch, English, French, Portuguese, and Spanish). Blasi, Michaelis, and Haspelmath (2017) suggest that not all languages called creole develop from pidgins. Bakker (2004) makes a sound attempt to sort

respective definitions.[79] Part of the dispute about the definition of creole is due to the evident confusion among creole specialists about how to begin analysis. Some begin with the conventional designation and seek common denominators in those languages already so called; others begin with a theoretical definition and search the data for examples to match the definition. These methods are at odds and are bound to lead to disagreement.[80] But to say that a creole is a nativized pidgin is still probably the closest thing to a generally accepted working definition.[81] We could call it here by a name other than creole, to sidestep the debate, but it seems absurd to invent a new term for an object about which a substantial subfield has developed, and it would be disingenuous, less meaningful, and even misleading to pretend that we are not talking about the same kind of phenomenon. Until creole specialists agree upon a more refined

the terminology, along with specific claims about the nature of the differences between jargon, pidgin, pidgincreole, and creole.

[79] Blasi, Michaelis, and Haspelmath (2017: 724b) note that, "while many authors of contrasting theoretical stances agree on the existence of a distinctive creole profile, they base their arguments on non-overlapping sets of linguistic features and languages."

[80] Creole specialists debating the validity of the category of creole language should realize a distinction between ideological and analytical terms (although see the exception of Bakker 2017a: 15). "Creole" (the word) did originate as a conventional appellation in specific colonial historical circumstances. Winford rightly notes (2003: 269) that such labels as pidgin, creole, and lingua franca "were first used by lay people or non-specialists before they were adapted as technical labels by linguists." Linguists have attempted to define what the term ought to mean in linguistic research, to endow the term with analytical force, as a term of art, and to use it henceforth in a destigmatized way extricated from its history. The sciences are replete with such terms of art. In this case, it is expedient because the languages under discussion are already mostly known as "creoles." The alternative – to give the phenomenon an entirely different name – has not been attempted successfully. But those wanting creole to serve as an analytical term are opposed by those who deny "creole exceptionalism," with the claim that creole is merely an ideological term and that languages so called are like every other language. In opposing such attempts to define "creole," they endorse the term as ideological and forego analytical precision, which, one supposes, is the reverse of their intended effect. See the wise remarks of Holm on terms like "creole" (2004: xi–xvi), the palpable frustration of McWhorter (2011a: 19–27, 103–119) over the studies edited by Ansaldo, Matthews, and Lim (2007) – see also McWhorter 2013b and, more decisively, McWhorter 2018 – and the discerning take of Bakker 2017a. The opponents of "creole exceptionalism" must explain why mass nonnative acquisition (different from regular childhood acquisition) should *not* matter in a language's history. Meanwhile, a strong empirical basis for the category of creole language has been offered by Bakker, Daval-Markussen, Parkvall, and Plag (2011), Bakker and Daval-Markussen (2017), and Bakker (2017b).

[81] E.g., Romaine 1988; Mühlhäusler 1997: 8–10; Holm 2000a: 6–9; van Coetsem 2000: 185; Thomason 2001: 159–160 ("some creoles are nativized pidgins"); Matras 2009: 278–79; Holm 2010: 256; Webb 2013: 304; Bakker 2017a: 6. There are variant definitions based on differing theories of creole formation, clearly and impartially summarized by Matras (2009: 283–288) and Bakker (2017a: 18–19). One notable outlier, offered by Mufwene, is that creoles form no special category, and that they are merely languages like any other, not simpler than others, and which represent merely a different selection of features from a pool of language features in a speech community. This "feature pool" hypothesis has been refuted; see McWhorter 2012; 2018: 33–62 for clear expositions and rebuttals.

definition for their subject, this old definition will have to do for noncreolist historians interested in the history of languages in society generally. To define a creole as a nativized pidgin is, however, meaningful beyond that mere statement, because pidgins are morphologically very simple languages, far simpler than their lexifiers, and purposefully so. Therefore, the definition that I use indicates likewise that creoles originate in a similarly morphologically simple state as divergent varieties of an earlier, more complex, language.

Part of the trouble in defining creoles is that they are conspicuous more by the absence of certain characteristics and by difference from their lexifier rather than by common features that arose in them each independently.[82] McWhorter is one of the few creolists to posit an analytical definition for his subject that can be applied as a categorical check. His definition has not been widely accepted, despite its potential utility, and despite the lack of proposed alternatives.[83] He calls his definition the Creole Prototype. By this model one can identify a creole if it has, all at once, three characteristics. His diagnostic characteristics are really the *relative absence* of features typical in languages.

(a) Morphologically: little or no inflectional affixation.
(b) Phonologically: little or no use of tone to distinguish monosyllabic lexical items or morphosyntactic categories.
(c) Semantically: little or no noncompositional combinations of derivational morphemes with roots.[84]

Restated and simplified, the three criteria have to do with word inflection, lexical tone, and opaque word formation. The less a language exhibits these features, the closer it is to McWhorter's diagnostic Creole Prototype. The critical distinction is undefined: how much constitutes "little."[85] Here the Creole Prototype is blurry, but at least we have working criteria for

---

[82] See Kranich and Breban (2021) on the deceptive inconspicuousness of the loss of features in diachronic linguistics. See also Blasi, Michaelis, and Haspelmath (2017), who show that the category of creole is unlikely to represent a universal default grammar, as once proposed, because of the resemblances of creole grammars to that of their lexifiers.

[83] The neglect seems to be partly because the very idea of a definition of creole came under attack, sometimes in a politically charged way, from a few creole specialists. See McWhorter's discussion (2013b and 2018).

[84] Quoted verbatim from McWhorter 2011a: 39; cf. McWhorter 2005: 9–37. McWhorter 2011b: 111 presents a revised and refined version of this list to account for counterarguments. I have not presented it here because it would require a lengthy explanatory digression.

[85] Cf. Kihm 2012: 658; Thomason 2004: 244. Often creolists assert that creole languages have no inflection, but Bakker (2003) and Holm (2008) point out that some languages conventionally called creole do have minimal inflection. Again, this means that creole/noncreole are not binary states.

discussion. Notably, the definition is synchronic – that is, it is posited regardless of historical data – but creoles are understood as due to historical social processes. In effect, McWhorter posits that we can infer past social events, even undocumented or prehistoric events, from the grammatical state of a language with these characteristics, without reference to the prior historical state of a language's grammar. This proposal is quite meaningful for the methods of linguistic history.

Recent efforts to determine characteristics special to creoles have achieved important results that refine this model. Computational cladistic methods applied to the large data set of a survey of the features of the world's languages show that the languages already called creoles form a typologically identifiable cluster regardless of their respective lexifiers. It is not that there is any one positive characteristic that is common to all languages regarded as creoles, but there are clear tendencies, such as the use of compounding for word formation and reduplication for grammatical purposes (such as plurality of nouns or repeated action), although these are not universal to creoles. As Bakker and Daval-Markusson explain, "There are no linguistic properties that are unique to creole languages. Phonologically, creoles avoid extremes and are average languages." But then, critically, they further indicate a decisive negative feature universal to the morphologies of the set of modern creoles: "Creoles never inherit contextual inflection from their lexifiers, but they may inherit or develop inherent inflection." Here again, the one thing that all the creoles share is the *absence* of a feature of morphology common to many of the world's languages.[86] This last observation is especially important for a historian or a historical linguist attempting to diagnose the status of an ancient language as possibly having arisen as a creole. McWhorter defines creoles as having "little or no inflectional affixation." It is Bakker and Daval-Markusson who specify the kind of inflection involved. Contextual inflection refers to morphemes that are determined by syntax, such as "person agreement markers in the verb linking to nominal elements, agreement markers in adjectives linking to nouns or case markers in nouns linking to their function in relation to the verb."[87] Studies of language acquisition

---

[86] Bakker and Daval-Markussen 2017: 83–85. See also Kihm (2003) and Luís (2010), forerunners in this insight. On the distinction between inherent and contextual inflection, see further Marzi, Blevins, Booij, and Pirrelli (2020).

[87] Bakker and Daval-Markussen 2017: 83–85. On this distinction in morphology, see Booij (1993; 1996). Cf. McWhorter 2011b: 96–98. This sort of inflection is very much like if not identical to Myers-Scotton's "outsider system morphemes" in her 4-M model of code-switching (a refinement to her Matrix Language Frame model) (2006: 241–278); cf. Winford (2005: 418–419). Myers-Scotton

suggest that contextual inflection is indeed acquired later in the process of learning languages.[88] No language conventionally regarded as a creole has preserved contextual inflection from its parent language or lexifier. This supports the notion that creole languages are a byproduct of an episode of mass nonnative acquisition. Future studies are likely to refine these analyses further, but for a historical linguist or a historian of languages, this criterion is clear and easy to apply in tracing the history of a language from one known stage to another.

For a real example of a creole and its emergence from a pidgin, we can remain in Papua New Guinea, with its high density of local languages. The name Tok Pisin is from English "Talk Pidgin" meaning "pidgin speech," the term pidgin coming ultimately from the English word "business." Tok Pisin is an example of a pidgin variety of English that has become a creole.[89] That is, tens of thousands of people now use this pidgin as a native language; hence, a creole. It is a species of the Melanesian Pidgin English still used in Papua New Guinea, Vanuatu, the Solomon Islands, and other South Pacific islands. Its earliest roots seem to be in an English-based jargon used by British sailors in the Pacific in the late eighteenth century. This was used in a variety of far-flung locations around the ocean for trade and basic communication. In the mid nineteenth century, it was developed into a pidgin among sailors, whalers, and gatherers of sandalwood and seaslugs for sale in China. Sydney, Australia, a colony founded in 1788, was a major site for the early diffusion of this pidgin English. Its users interacted with locals in many places, from Canton to Samoa, their medium being this simplified English. It was the European plantations of the South Pacific, however, that formed the main sites for the acquisition and subsequent diffusion of pidgin English by Melanesian islanders. Plantation owners in Queensland, Samoa, and elsewhere derived very cheap labor, if

---

(2008: 22) explains her "outsider system morphemes" with an example: "in German, verbs and prepositions can assign case designations in a clause, but the actual case morpheme (the outsider) appears in elements forming a constituent separate from (i.e., outside) the larger constituent containing the verb or preposition that assigns case." Holm's observations about the presence of inflection in creoles do not cause the "paradigm shift" he supposed (2008) if we distinguish such types of inflection that play syntactic roles of different kinds. None of the features of creole inflection that Holm includes represent contextual inflection bearing agreement with other constituents of a sentence outside of its own phrase, such as case marking on nouns or plural agreement on verbs.

[88] Booij 1996: 11–12. See Slabakova 2008: 100–112 on the bottleneck of "functional morphology" in second-language acquisition, although her focus is limited to the mismatch of morphological inflection and semantics between languages as a hurdle, and not variations in inflectional complexity.

[89] On its development, see Mühlhäusler 1983; Holm 1988–1989: 2.526–551; Crowley 1990; Romaine 1992: 31–54; Mühlhäusler 2003: 5–8; Winford 2003: 291–293; Tryon and Charpentier 2004.

not forced labor, by contracting or kidnapping workers from various Melanesian islands for periods of several years at a time. The labor exchange lasted for decades. These workers, taken abroad from their home islands, rarely shared a common language among themselves, by the employers' design, so they learned the pidgin English made available by their employers in the context of their daily work for those years and, eventually, when some of them returned to their homes, they brought it with them. It remained for them a medium for access to goods and opportunities beyond their immediate locale. Samoan plantations were one of the main sites for the development of Melanesian pidgin in the last quarter of the nineteenth century. The Samoan plantations were run by Germans, where speakers of pidgin English had little linguistic contact with native speakers of English. This allowed the pidgin to develop independently of any native variety of English. The pidgin was adopted further in German-controlled New Guinea (1884–1919), the north side of the island in which British Papua was situated, where new plantations received some of the very same laborers, originally from different islands, who had been employed in Samoa, along with still more imported laborers from other islands. After World War I and the end of German government there, Melanesian pidgin English was adopted more and more widely in villages as a means of access to goods and opportunities outside the village. Christian missionaries also used it to reach polyglot locals, contributing to its standardization. Numerous inhabitants of villages in Papua New Guinea, each of whom spoke a home language with a small number of other native speakers, called a Tok Ples, from English "[the] talk [or speech, of one's home] place [or village]," or "local language," moved to bigger towns, many of them colonial foundations, and to plantations, and mingled with inhabitants of other regions with whom they had little or no contact before. Tok Pisin served, and still serves, to create an ever-broadening speech community in such sites. People who move from the linguistically diverse villages of Papua New Guinea to the towns find Tok Pisin expedient as a common language. When members of different language communities in Papua New Guinea form families and procreate, the common language of their home is sometimes Tok Pisin, the one language held in common by both parents. Children then learn it as their first language of home use. Even when no parents use Tok Pisin as a first language, it can displace the local languages because it represents, to its young speakers, a path to meet their aspirations as inhabitants of the independent state of Papua New Guinea. Villages now witness generation gaps in which the youth are deterred from using the language of their elders, preferring the supralocal Tok Pisin instead.[90] In this way Tok Pisin has become a creole, a pidgin acquired as a native language, in these environments, and shows striking innovations in its usage. For many speakers outside of the cities, however, it is still technically a pidgin, a secondary language not spoken natively. Tok Pisin spoken natively does show new features and developments as it is augmented to serve the communicative needs of those who use it as their dominant language and for every basic human need.[91] Moreover, native speakers of Tok Pisin who learn English, perhaps in school, creatively import nonpidgin English words and features into their dominant language. This is one variety of "decreolization" (discussed here later), the term used for the gradual assimilation of a creole to its lexifier. From the conventional definitions of pidgin and creole, it is evident that pidgin and creole stages of development can coexist, and that one language can be both at the same time for different speakers.[92] Tok Pisin is a pidgin that has also become a creole for many thousands of native speakers.[93]

Linguists have documented many creoles in the world, most of which have arisen as an indirect result of European colonization of the last several centuries and are, hence, young languages with specific, identifiable, sometimes documented, relatively short periods of genesis.[94] What is special about creoles is that, because they are nativized pidgins, and pidgins are drastically simpler in contextual inflection than most other languages, the young creole languages are simpler in the same way, too. Note that pidginization is not the root of all morphological simplification in a language. It is rather nonnative acquisition that appears to be the major cause of such change.[95] Pidginization represents only an unusual but natural occurrence giving rise to radically restructured, and hence especially conspicuous, new languages.[96]

---

[90] Kulick 1992 and 2019.   [91] Smith 2002.
[92] Baker (1997: 92) regards this as a problem for the definition of the terms. I see no problem in it, but rather a useful distinction.
[93] Bakker (2002) has proposed the name "pidgincreole" for such pidgins that acquire native speaker populations, with corresponding effects on the pidgin language. Another common term for the same thing is "expanded pidgin" (Siegel 2008: 4).
[94] Holm 1988–1989.
[95] In a study published posthumously (2017: 160–161), Arends (1952–2005) meticulously showed that, in the genesis of Suriname creoles in the period roughly 1650–1750, "for every locally-born child acquiring the creole as a first language there were around ten African-born adults – for whom learning the creole was a matter of second language acquisition." In this case, these local "creoles" were for a long time, for most of their users, what we would call a pidgin. Arends makes it clear that adult learning is what propagated it not all at once in a single episode but over several generations.
[96] McWhorter 2005 and 2007.

Bilingual Mixed Language

Initially dubbed "intertwined language," this has been proposed as a third kind of contact language, acknowledged as relatively rare. It was claimed as distinct only in the 1990s, beginning with the research of Peter Bakker.[97] The characteristic feature of a bilingual mixed language is that it emerges among children of parents who have two different languages; one language, typically the mother's, provides the grammatical matrix, or the verbs and verbal grammar, while the other language, usually the father's, provides much of the lexicon, or the nouns and nominal inflection. Both components retain most of the grammatical complexity of the two intertwined languages proper to their originally separate systems. Bakker attributes the genesis of such languages to the identity formation of teenaged offspring of immigrant men who marry local women.[98] "These multi-ethnolects," or intertwined languages, Bakker argues, "are used by second-generation immigrants and symbolize their distinctness in society but, at the same time, their connections to both the new land and the parents' country of origin." The available evidence suggests that intertwined languages have their genesis with the formation of a separate ethnic group born of this mixture of populations "within a very short time frame of a few decades."[99] Such languages arise when fully bilingual young people deliberately used elements of the language of their mother and of their father together in the same utterances. Specifically, they have used very large quantities of their father's nominal vocabulary in their mother tongue.

An outstanding example of bilingual mixed language is Michif, used in the prairie lands of Canada, spoken today by several hundred people.[100] It is characterized by Cree verbs and syntax while the great majority of the nouns are from French. Fur hunters and traders from Quebec and Acadia from the seventeenth century onward took Cree-speaking brides as they moved westward in North American land. The mixed-offspring people are known as Métis ("Mixed"), and some of their offspring generated Michif. Bakker argues that what began as an "in-group language" or linguistic code used by a young generation of mixed ancestry to define itself and to express their common identity as mixed became, after a generation, nativized when acquired as native by subsequent children. This resembles the process by

---

[97] Bakker 1997; Matras 2009: 288–306; Bakker 2012: 182–183; Meakins 2013; Hock 2021: 749–757.
[98] Cf. Muysken 2013: 202: "The most complex types of code-mixing have been documented with adolescents and young adults. ... Most cases of complex code-mixing have been recorded with second-generation speakers in immigrant communities."
[99] Bakker 2012: 180.   [100] Bakker 1997; Bakker and Papen 1997.

which a pidgin becomes a creole when acquired by children, but it does not entail significant morphological simplification. Both intertwined languages and creoles are native tongues, but the two have different characteristics. Bilingual mixed languages may remain highly complex in their morphology, for they did not originate as pidgins. Bakker argues that bilingual mixed languages "are associated with very specific social events," such as the intermarriage of immigrant men with local women, within the memory of the first speakers of such languages."[101] Many speakers of Michif have known neither French nor Cree, but only the younger, mixed language formerly comprising parts of both.

Although other examples of this sort of mixed language have been proposed,[102] not all linguists accept the bilingual mixed language as a truly separate category. Winford analyzes intertwined languages simply as extreme cases of lexical borrowing by bilinguals whose shared dominant language is the mother's tongue.[103] Versteegh makes similar observations and is ready to reject the category for this reason. As he points out, Michif and other "mixed languages" are a regular possible outcome of relatively extreme but normal code-switching and word-borrowing by bilinguals.[104] Therefore, they are not a separate species of contact language due to a "new mechanism of language change." Michif represents, therefore, lexical borrowing and transfer between languages used by bilinguals that is unusual only in its extent. After a period of such mixing, the new mixture became permanent and normal. When such extensive code-switching (also known as code-mixing) becomes a fixed norm among children, they can grow up speaking a "mixed language." Michif would therefore be a special variety of Cree with a massive importation of adopted French words brought in by children at one formative stage in the history of a bilingual community.[105]

If pidgins are just the genesis-stage of creoles, and mixed languages are the result of the transfer of a copious lexicon from one language into a matrix language by young bilinguals, we are therefore apparently dealing with a single bundle of language phenomena having different names for different stages of development and different outcomes. The main variable between each of these three is the age of the speakers' language acquisition over more than one generation. Creoles are more likely to be documented than pidgins, as they are more likely to survive by the defining fact that they have acquired native

---

[101] Bakker 2012: 182. [102] Bakker and Mous 1994. [103] Winford 2005: 396–402.
[104] Although today the expression "code-switching" is often used simply to mean signaling competence or participation in more than one culture, it technically refers to embedding words or phrases from one language in the matrix of another. See Hock 2021: 637–640.
[105] Versteegh 2017. Cf. Winford 2003: 168–207; Hock 2021: 757.

speakers. Bilingual mixed languages are relatively rare and arise in special bilingual social groups in which mothers and fathers have different languages. In these cases, language acquisition in childhood plays the main role, rather than adult language acquisition, and accordingly morphological complexity can be maintained. But it is the creoles that have attracted the overwhelming attention of linguists specializing in language contact as they are undeniably restructured, independent, young varieties of other, more morphologically complex, older languages, associated with a group that acquired it in childhood. They are therefore exemplary for theories of the outcome of language contact. The great attention paid to pidgins and their creole descendants has led, however, to a predominant, implicit, binary notion of "normal" languages versus contact languages that are primarily creoles. As I have emphasized, this notion of two states of language is mistaken.

Semicreoles: Partially Restructured Languages

As already explained under (5), plenty of research has demonstrated that there are *degrees of restructuring* toward morphological simplification in languages. Between the outcomes of pidgin/creole formation and the far more ordinary and continuous intergenerationally stable situation of large-scale language acquisition of their parents' language by children everywhere, a variety of degrees of restructuring can occur in different demographic conditions of language contact. New languages arise that are distinctly simpler than their lexifiers, retaining, for example, some minimal noun or verb inflection, but do not seem to have emerged from a pidgin. In view of such languages, the notion of a strict binary opposition of normal language and pidgin/creole should disappear. Some languages not typically regarded as creoles seem very much like creoles in their morphological simplicity, without being quite so reduced as, for example, Tok Pisin vis-à-vis English. These are reduced versions of other languages that have distinctly been transformed through a social event: an episode of large-scale nonnative acquisition of the language (steps (2)–(4) in the model introduced earlier in this chapter).

Creole specialists have long accepted that degrees of creolization are possible, although they disagree about the taxonomy or the factors by which those degrees emerge.[106] Once one accepts that degrees of restructuring exist, one

---

[106] Some creolists use terms like basilectal, mesolectal, and acrolectal, or degrees of "indigenization," to describe the qualitative degree of difference or distance of a creole from its lexifier (Winford 2003: 254–256, 313, 355). Others have occasionally referred to the most radically restructured creoles as "deep creoles," as if far advanced into the process of restructuring, again signifying the existence of degrees. The term decreolization designates a creole's gradual assimilation of more features of its

may attempt to define those relative degrees and to explicate the factors giving rise to variation in degrees of restructuring. Here we arrive at a frontier of research in contact linguistics. Specialists in contact linguistics have not yet formed a consensus on the terms to be used to describe different degrees of restructuring. There are several hindrances to such an agreement. A major one is the matter of assessing morphological complexity and simplicity. Because degrees of restructuring are expressed at least partly in terms of complexity and simplicity, the baseline for measuring change depends on the complexity of the prior state of the language now restructured, as compared with the simplicity of the restructured variety. But the "starting point" of complexity before restructuring varies from language to language in ways hard to measure or compare, and it is likewise conditioned by its own special prior population history. A partially grammatically reduced variety of modern Russian, for example, could, in theory, retain more complex morphology than the literary English of the present, while seeming rather simplified from a Russian point of view. The relativity of changes to a prior state that varies from instance to instance inhibits the development of a general scale of restructuring. Discovering methods to measure complexity, determining the kinds of complexity that should be measured, and the relative significance of the different kinds are unresolved issues on this frontier in linguistics. Still further, the demographic scenarios involved in the partial restructuring of languages vary according to many social factors that are often not discernible either to historians or linguists.

Linguists already employ at least five different terms for partially restructured languages:

(1) new contact vernacular
(2) indigenized variety[107]

On the surface, these first two terms cautiously express ambivalence about the problem of relative simplicity, even though their proponents do acknowledge relative simplicity and complexity. They do no more than to designate a new common variety of an old language as the product of language contact or as having been adopted by a new population. As

lexifier, where the creole coexists socially with its lexifier, again indicating degrees of relative outcomes in restructuring.

[107] Siegel 2013: 517–519; earlier Siegel (1997): 119–125) proposed the term "indigenized variety" with three specific features in mind. (1) "The existence of a continuum of socially and situationally marked varieties, similar to a creole continuum, ranging from a basilect (furthest from standard native varieties) to an acrolect (closest to standard native varieties)." (2) "Formal simplicity in comparison to other varieties [of the language] (especially in the basilect), found in the reduction of categories … optional morphological marking of nouns and verbs and the regularization of paradigms." (3) "Substrate influence in lexicon, morphology, and syntax, as well as in pragmatics."

technical expressions, they merely acknowledge the existence of a new variety of an old language. "Indigenized," as a term by itself, indicates only that the new language appeared when adopted by an "indigenous" population.

(3) partially restructured vernacular

This term also reflects some ambivalence about degrees of complexity, but "restructured" implies fundamental differences between the grammars of the older language and the new variety of language.

(4) creoloid[108]
(5) semicreole[109]

These last two terms have the advantage of concision. More importantly, they directly connect the new, restructured variety of language with the phenomenon of linguistic creolization. They both thereby acknowledge a class of languages called creoles (something not every linguist is willing to do, for reasons already explained), and posit a variety of language that is somehow between creoles and noncreoles. The two terms are in effect synonyms. Both refer to a language that was grammatically reduced and simplified through an episode of mass adult acquisition but that did *not* emerge from a much simpler pidgin. In other words, in its complexity, relative to its lexifier, it is somewhere between the highly reduced variety characteristic of a former pidgin and that of a "normal" language that never arose from a pidgin (at least for many prior generations). Normal, here, of course, refers not to a characteristic of the language as a language but to its social environment. It means just that the great majority of the language's learners have been children for many generations, which is a normal situation for most languages. One must choose between synonyms for the sake of consistency. Creoloid simply means "creole-like," suggesting merely that it is similar to creoles without being identical to them.[110] As a term, semicreole makes the stronger commitment to an explanation in the terms described here: it refers to languages that have undergone processes similar to those leading to creoles – specifically the formation of a new, simple variety of a language in an episode

---

[108] Platt 1975 and 1978; Trudgill 2003: 31; Swann, Deumert, Lillis, and Mesthrie 2004: 62.
[109] Holm 2002; Swann, Deumert, Lillis, and Mesthrie 2004: 274–275.
[110] The term was proposed by Platt in 1975 and 1978, who wrote, "It would seem that a new concept needs to be established for certain speech varieties which are, strictly speaking, neither creoles nor part of a post-creole continuum but which share many features with them. Unlike creoles, these varieties did not develop from a pidgin but by some other process." Trudgill (2011: 67–68) appears to be the only active user of this term. By creoloid he means a language that did not emerge from a pidgin but that shows "relatively undramatic" simplification and hybridity ("admixture").

of mass adult acquisition – but have not attained all of the characteristics of creole, because it did not emerge from an entirely nonnative pidgin.[111] *Semicreole* is therefore the term that I will adopt here. It has the advantage of being associated with the two most cogent efforts to describe and explain partially restructured languages.[112] It is not that I insist on this term for the future, but I do not wish for now to invent a sixth term for the phenomenon of a language that has been grammatically reduced through mass nonnative acquisition without ever having been a pidgin. We need terminological consistency and not the ad hoc proliferation of descriptive explanatory terms for the same phenomena. Trudgill's definition of a creoloid stands also for the semicreole:[113] "A language which, as a result of language contact, has experienced simplification and admixture, but has not undergone the reduction associated with full pidginisation (nor, therefore, the expansion associated with creolisation). Such a language will resemble in its linguistic characteristics a creole which has undergone decreolisation, but will be different in its history." Simply put, a semicreole looks like a creole in its morphological and lexical simplification but it is not so severely reduced and it shows no sign of a pidgin past. Holm has analyzed the process of semicreole formation in two ways. The first is to tease apart the layered linguistic changes involved in partial restructuring through a plausible model. This breaks the bundle of features in a semicreole down into distinct formative linguistic processes acknowledged in studies of language contact.[114] For the formation of a semicreole is not a uniform, single linguistic change, but it depends on many component processes each of which is variable in its extent. Holm's second

---

[111] Holm (2004: 6) notes that Schuchardt was the first to use the term ("halbkreolisch") in 1889.
[112] Holm 2000a: 9–12; Holm 2004: xi–xvi; McWhorter 2007: 252–276. Interestingly, Thomason (2001: 195) has come to hold that "the category 'semi-creole' doesn't really exist," referring to an earlier article of hers in which she rather makes the term useful, writing that "A semi-creole is not a class in itself, but is merely a label that recognizes the possibility of degrees of disruption of a continuous transmission process ... It seems to me that placing such borderline cases on a continuum between the clear noncreoles and the clear creoles is preferable to putting them in classes for which precise characterizations and definite classificatory criteria are lacking" (Thomason 1997b: 84). But the notion of "clear creoles" is not so clear-cut, nor is that of noncreoles. The term semicreole is useful for precisely the reason that Thomason indicates. It recognizes the possibility of degrees of restructuring, in episodes of mass nonnative acquisition, and when the term semicreole is used now in contact linguistics, that is generally how it is used. Watts' objection (2011: 112) to the term creoloid – that the term "only shifts the problem away from looking at language contact as a highly complex area of concern in sociolinguistics" – makes little sense. It is rather that terms like creoloid acknowledge a class of languages that demand more explanation.
[113] Trudgill 2003: 31. Trudgill adds that a semicreole should always be mutually comprehensible with its lexifier, but I do not hold this as necessary.
[114] Holm (2001; 2004; 2013: 258–259) proposes fives component steps in semicreole formation: dialect leveling, language drift (simplification), imperfect language shift with transfer of features between languages, borrowing from short-lived pidgin varieties, and reintroduction of features of the lexifier.

analysis of semicreole formation, like that of Parkvall, is demographic.[115] It shows that the *proportion* of native speakers and nonnative speakers in the environment of language contact is critical in the formation of a partially restructured variety of a language. His compilation of population data from Dutch, English, Spanish, and Portuguese colonies of the eighteenth century – with the rapid increase of Western European maritime colony formation – reveals a correlation of the proportion of the population of Europeans among colonized peoples to the degree of restructuring in the subsequent language of the population. Specifically, where European colonists made up only about 6–8 percent of the population of the colonies, and the rest of the population were locals and imports from elsewhere, a radically restructured creole of the European language developed (such as Negerhollands Creole Dutch, Jamaican Creole English, and Papiamentu Creole Spanish). These creoles bear only superficial resemblance to their lexifier, being essentially entirely new languages. They have all been called creoles initially on the basis of the intuition that they represent similar phenomena. But Holm found that where the Europeans made up 32–59 percent of the population of their colonies, *partially* restructured varieties of the language were the outcome, and he found no evidence for a pervasive pidgin stage (Afrikaans, African American Vernacular English, Brazilian Vernacular Portuguese, and Nonstandard Caribbean Spanish).[116] These are Holm's *semicreoles*. Their morphologies are noticeably reduced, although they retain some older inflectional patterns, and they often show some kind of "hybridity" in the sense that features have been imported from other languages used in the environment of their formation that are not found in the lexifier. Table 2.1 reproduces exactly the contents of Holm's chart on this point.[117]

The first three rows show the proportion of "whites" in these colonial settings where creoles developed. The rest are sites of semicreole formation.

Independently, Trudgill estimates that a proportion of 50 percent non-native speakers visiting a site would reach "a threshold level at which some aspects of the nonnative variety" of a language "could transfer to the native."[118] The reason for the difference in outcome is not difficult to understand. The children of speakers of a pidgin who have very little access to native speakers of the language on which the pidgin is based will elaborate that pidgin into a creole with minimal exposure to the unrestructured variety of the language as spoken by a native speaker. They will perpetuate the pidgin speech as a native tongue without importing features

---

[115] Parkvall 2000.   [116] Holm 2004: 70–71; 135–137.   [117] Holm 2004: 71.
[118] Trudgill 2011: 57–58.

Table 2.1 *"Estimated proportion of whites in various societies in the late eighteenth century" (from Holm 2004)*

Colony	Developing language	Percent
Virgin Islands	Negerhollands Creole Dutch	c. 6
Jamaica	Jamaican Creole English	c. 8
(Rural) Curaçao	Papiamentu Creole Spanish/Portuguese	c. 7
Virginia	African American English	c. 59
Brazil	Brazilian Vernacular Portuguese	c. 32
Cape Colony	Afrikaans	c. 47
Cuba		c. 56
Puerto Rico	Nonstandard Caribbean Spanish	c. 45
Santo Domingo		c. 34

from the lexifier, because the lexifier is not regularly available to them and therefore unfamiliar. In situations where proportionately more native speakers of the target language are available, and in which contact with them is to that extent more regular or intimate, they will have more exposure to nonrestructured speech models in direct transmission, and they will be that much more habituated to the grammatical usages and morphology of the older native speakers. This finding is strongly supported by other, independent research by Bentz and Winter, demonstrating a striking inverse correlation between the number of noun cases in languages of the world today and the proportion of nonnative speakers of those languages. That is, the more adult foreigners learn a given language, the fewer noun cases it is likely to have, an extraordinary finding based on a very large sample of the world's languages.[119] In short, the proportion of native speakers to nonnative speakers seems to be a decisive factor in the degree of restructuring of a language. This happens to cohere with the long-standing theoretical model of pidgin and creole formation, which posits access to native speakers, or the lack thereof, as critical.

The clearest, and perhaps paradigmatic, example of a language regarded as a semicreole is Afrikaans, the divergent form of Dutch that emerged in the polyethnic setting of colonial South Africa.[120] The genesis of Afrikaans offers many close parallels with that of Middle Persian, as I will show. Dutch colonists in Capetown, which they founded in 1652, created an environment in which Dutch was the main medium of communication

---

[119] Bentz and Winter 2013.
[120] Holm 1988: 2.338–352; Thomason and Kaufman 1988: 254–256; de Kleine 1997; Holm 2000b: 27–29; Trudgill 2011: 68 ("creoloid").

but in which a large proportion – as many as two-thirds – of the population spoke other languages natively. As Trudgill explains,[121]

> Dutch was acquired by very large numbers of nonnative speakers, initially speakers of the indigenous Khoi and San languages, and then by speakers of Bantu languages, and immigrant speakers of German, French, the Scandinavian languages, Portuguese, Malagasy, Malay, Indonesian languages, and others. There was much racial mixing and intermarriage, as the current "Coloured" population of South Africa shows. Wives in particular were quite likely to be native speakers of some language other than Dutch. This led to a situation where the nature of transmission became crucial. So many people initially acquired and used Dutch as an L2 [nonnative second language] that, in later generations, children were born who became, as it were, native speakers of nonnative Dutch. A nonnative variety became nativized and in time the dominant, and subsequently only, variety.

The result was a new, divergent species of Dutch with reduced grammatical paradigms, no grammatical gender except in pronouns, and plenty of words adopted from Malay, Khoi, French, German, and other sources.[122] Languages partially restructured in a local setting may eventually spread far and wide. Afrikaans began as a rapidly restructured variety of Dutch in a setting with only hundreds of speakers in southern Africa in the late seventeenth century. From that beginning in 1652, there was a labor shortage relative to the needs and aspirations of the colony. Workers were imported continuously from Europe, Africa, and Southeast Asia. Adult locals began to learn the Dutch of the founders who ran the colony, but they learned it as adults with limited exposure to the language. One generation later, in 1685, "a colonial official reported that the settlers' children were picking up the broken Dutch of the non-whites."[123] The children of Dutch-speaking immigrants were thus learning a different, restructured form of Dutch within a single generation. This was the beginning of the formation of Afrikaans. The "non-whites" just mentioned included slaves, servants, and the nurses of the "white" children, who were of different origins (local and imported) and who learned Dutch partly from other nonnative adult learners. At this point the settlement population still amounted to no more than several hundred, including large

---

[121] Trudgill 2011: 58–60.
[122] As Raidt (1995: 133) describes it, "The main changes that led to the genesis of Afrikaans occurred in the noun and verb systems as a result of morphological reduction, simplification, and regularisation."
[123] Holm 2004: 42, citing Valkhoff.

proportions of both Africans and non-Dutch Europeans, especially French Huguenots, who also had to learn Dutch as adults. The Dutch settlers were mostly men, so they often took mates who did not know Dutch from childhood. The non-Dutch mothers of their children passed on a nonnative adult learner's Dutch language to their children. Archival research by Edith Raidt has demonstrated that women played a pivotal role in the formation of Afrikaans.[124] By 1700, in just two generations, many of the features that distinguish Afrikaans from Dutch language were already established, such as the elimination of case from the pronominal system and the collapse of the present and perfect tenses.[125] By 1800, the grammar of Afrikaans was essentially what it is today and its use had spread hundreds of kilometers beyond the Capetown colony.[126] More than two centuries later still, in the wake of a long-lived political regime in which "white" speakers of Afrikaans enjoyed a disproportionate share of power and wealth in South Africa, there are more than 6 million native speakers of Afrikaans, in a form of Dutch exhibiting many of the changes already present by 1700, during the lifetime of the founders of Capetown. Centuries later, the language still bears the characteristics it acquired during the demographic upheaval of colony formation long before.

Afrikaans is not a creole, because it did not originate directly from a pidgin, as far as the evidence shows, although speakers of a pidgin variety of Dutch probably played a role in its formation. It is also more complex in its morphology than many creole languages, although languages already classed as creoles do exhibit varying degrees of morphological complexity.[127] Afrikaans does, however, resemble creoles in its simplification relative to its lexifier and the social circumstances in which it diverged from Dutch. It represents a class of languages that have become distinctly simpler through mass adult acquisition but not through the extreme reformulation and novelty of a pidgin. It is, in short, a semicreole, bearing this useful name for a type of "contact language."

Semicreole is not the prettiest term in the scholarly lexicon. It does require some explanation. I have found that newcomers to the topic understand the phenomenon of simplification of contextual inflectional morphology most quickly, however, if they learn about creole languages first. This is one reason that I have retained the term semicreole for the

---

[124] Raidt 1993 and 1995.   [125] Holm 2004: 42–43.
[126] Ponelis (1993: 1–67) provides detailed information on demography and language in the development of Afrikaans. See also Combrink 1978: 71, 88n14.
[127] Holm and Patrick (2007) present a volume of summaries of creole syntax, which illustrates variation in complexity.

present analysis. It would be strange to ignore the phenomenon of the creole in explaining what happens to languages that are radically shorn of inflection. The study of creole languages led the way to this kind of analysis, and this term follows from that.

State and Process in Contact Linguistics and Linguistic History

Calling a language creole or semicreole refers to its present state as an outcome of a prior social process.[128] We can call the corresponding historically prior processes *creolization* and *semicreolization*, respectively. Linguists usually address creolization through analytical and descriptive linguistic approaches rather than through social history because their general goal is understanding language as such, not specific events. For linguistic history, by contrast, the process, as an event or series of events, matters more than the resulting state, for history narrates events. To say that history entails diachronic analysis is practically tautological, but the ramifications of this distinction are easy to overlook when we apply the model. The different goals of these research enterprises – the nature of language, on the one hand, for linguists, and the determination and understanding of events of the past on the other, for historians – generate a methodological discrepancy between the two when it comes to studying so-called contact languages as historical subjects. The terms we use matter here. Those concerned with modern languages of recent origin may be satisfied with nearly synchronic categories describing states such as creole and semicreole. Linguistic historians, however, particularly when concerned with premodern languages, will typically be concerned with languages over longer durations. In these cases, the names designating different kinds of contact languages as belonging to a state become much less useful. Designations like "semicreole" imply that specific processes of striking socially induced change had already occurred in a language prior to the time addressed in a language, but the conditions for such processes do not persist forever, and rarely – one would expect – for more than several generations. It is probably adequate to say that a creole five or six generations old is still a creole, especially relative to its extant lexifier, but for how long is it meaningful for an ancient language that has undergone creolization to be known as a creole? I do not imagine that five hundred years from

---

[128] Cf. van Coetsem 2000: 185: "Indeed, the specificity of the creole resides primarily not in its nature, but in its genesis." This is unlike a pidgin, which lasts only as long as it mostly has nonnative speakers.

now it will be useful to describe any future language descendant of Tok Pisin as a creole language, although the creolization in its past will have been one of the most extraordinary determinant events in the history of that language. A language can undergo semicreolization once, itself a process requiring more than one generation of language acquisition, leaving the symptoms of inflectional reduction for all subsequent generations of that language's speakers, long after the social factors of population contact and nonnative language acquisition that made it a semicreole have ceased. But for how many centuries thereafter is such a language to retain the designation "semicreole" after undergoing semicreolization? There is no clear answer to this question because the terms describe outcome states rather than events.

In short, the linguistic historian must beware of using basically synchronic categories for diachronic narrative purposes because the languages will often outlive the meaning of the states designated by those terms. Pidgin, creole, semicreole: these are all terms descriptive of a state of a language consequent to demographic upheavals in a relatively recent past that initiated grammatical reduction. That is, they all refer implicitly to prior intergenerational processes of language change connected with large-scale nonnative language acquisition. Synchronic terms such as these are not useful to describe outcomes the effects of which persist for ten or twenty or forty generations, when a language's later speakers are mostly very remote from the demographic upheavals that shaped their language, despite the clear permanent effects of those past events on their language. The linguistic historian cannot insist, therefore, on these terms as permanent designations of a language that has undergone such contact-induced transformations in the distant past. It is not meaningful to say that a creole remains a creole for a thousand years, even if it remains relatively unadorned with inflectional morphology for that entire time. It is therefore better for the linguistic historian to speak of languages *undergoing the process* of creolization or semicreolization – or other such processes that may be identified – rather than *being* creoles or semicreoles. Afrikaans can now be said just to be a language very closely related to Dutch, or a variety of Dutch, rather than a semicreole of Dutch. Although it was formed through semicreolization, that formative process was long ago.

There is another discrepancy between the methods of contact linguistics and historical approaches to language. Specialists in contact languages have largely ignored the traditional methods of comparative historical linguistics. This seems to be in part because historical linguistics assumes a genealogical framework that creole specialists have struggled to accept, given their different theories about creole-formation. When creolists have emphasized that creoles are "hybrid languages" with grammatical, and not just lexical, genealogies in more than one language, this would appear to pose a challenge to the established methods of historical linguistics, which assume that each language has one ancestor.[129] A related problem is that language genealogies discovered by the methods of historical linguistics depend on shared innovations rather than losses of features, but pidgins, creoles, and semicreoles are most conspicuous in the loss of features – more precisely, by the nonreplication of the contextual inflection – of their lexifiers. For these reasons, historical linguistics does not and perhaps cannot account well for those languages that are mostly the vehicles of nonnative speakers,[130] although the attempt should be made. This helps to explain the reason for the gap between historical linguistics and creole studies. The gap may, however, be filled partly by linguistic history, paying special attention to population history.

Reduction and the Transfer of Features as Concomitant Factors

Now it is necessary to introduce the second part of the linguistic-historical model, which is not a matter of intergenerational patterns of language acquisition, but rather of multilingual usage. Other kinds of changes appear when more than one language is used in the same circumstances by the same people. Understanding the processes by which features are transferred from one language to another requires attention both to the multilingual agent, who enacts this transfer, and to the larger social context of such multilinguals. Linguistic transfer, often construed as language mixture, is another undeniably real kind of socially conditioned language change beyond the sorts of change addressed descriptively by the traditional comparative method of historical linguistics, strictly speaking. Historical linguists have used these obvious kinds of features in their diagnoses of language history since the nineteenth century, but they have not incorporated more recent research findings on the transfer of features between languages.

As explained, Holm employed the category of semicreole to account for languages that have been restructured to some degree in ways resembling

---

[129] Already by 1921 the historical linguist Meillet responded to the early creolist Schuchard over this question. See Meillet (1921: 76–109) in his essays "La problème de la parenté des langues" and "Les parentés de langues." Still recently, Blasi, Michaelis, and Haspelmath (2017: 723), for example, hold that "creoles have more than one language in their ancestry."

[130] Cf. Kranich and Breban 2021.

Table 2.2 *McWhorter's grid of nine types, with some of his examples*[131]

	Mixture: lexicon only	Mixture: lexicon and syntax	Mixture: lexicon, syntax, phonology, morphology
No simplification	Loanwords in any language	Romanian in Balkan linguistic area	Media Lengua
Moderate simplification	NCSL: English, Persian	Semicreole: Afrikaans	Shaba Swahili
Extreme simplification: creoles	Hawai'ian Creole English	Most creoles	"Deep creoles": Tok Pisin

creolization but without qualifying as a creole. This posits a taxonomy of distinctions in three relative degrees: *unrestructured*: *semicreole*: *creole*. McWhorter's treatment of the semicreole goes further than Holm's in giving close attention to this dimension of mixture, the degree to which a language incorporates features from other languages. To achieve a finer typology, he crosses these three qualitative degrees of grammatical reduction, or simplification – none, some, much – with three degrees of mixture of features from other languages – lexicon only, lexicon and syntax, or all subsystems including phonology and morphology – to create a grid of nine types.[132] He then populates these nine proposed types with representative examples of languages familiar to researchers in language contact. A bilingual mixed language might show no simplification but a maximum of "hybridity," whereas a "creole" like Hawai'ian Creole English is extensively simplified but minimally mixed. Other creole specialists appear not to have taken up the challenge of testing it or even addressing this typology. In what follows I discuss it and, ultimately, reject it as it is, while agreeing with the importance of the issues it exemplifies.

Among these nine, reproduced in Table 2.2, McWhorter proposes a new category he calls NCSL, or "Nonhybrid Conventionalized Second Language." For him, this is a close cousin of the semicreole, and the NCSL is especially relevant to the present investigation of Persian because New Persian is one of McWhorter's five main examples of his NCSL. Although his study of Persian takes into consideration changes in prior stages of Persian (Old and Middle) somewhat, the data he uses are

---

[131] McWhorter 2007: 254. [132] McWhorter 2007: 254.

mostly synchronic and modern, comparing the grammar of modern New Persian with that of its closest living modern Iranic relatives to further the case that NCSLs exist.[133] (The NCSLs include some of the world's most-used languages, such as modern English and Malay.) In this taxonomy, what distinguishes an NCSL from a semicreole like Afrikaans is its "Nonhybrid" characteristic. That is, the NCSL was a language acquired nonnatively (as a second language) by many people at once and became a conventional language, and so it is equivalent to a semicreole in its extensive, but not extreme, grammatical reduction, but it is also different in that it exhibits hybridity of lexicon only, not hybridity of phonology, morphology, or syntax. By contrast, McWhorter's semicreole category exhibits hybridity in its syntax as well as lexicon. (By hybrid, the sense here is just that features are transferred from one language to another, not something more essential or profound.)

It is already a challenge to use a tripartite division of languages into creole, semicreole, and unrestructured or "normal." Three degrees of simplification call for a qualitative assessment relative to a prior state differing in each case, making the model fundamentally scalar but its application comparative and therefore slippery and less analytical.[134] To use the ninefold typology is more difficult still, because one must assign a language to one of the categories based on rough comparison with other languages while taking the transfer of features from one or more languages into the new language into account. "Hybridity" or mixture is also hard to measure, but for different reasons. Identifying genuine instances of the transfer of features between languages in context, as opposed to "internal" grammatical change, is not a trivial matter, though methods for doing so have been suggested.[135] Another potential problem here is that the greater the degree of simplification from the lexifier, the more difficult it may be to determine mixture, because greater reduction implies fewer distinct features, which are one basis for identifying mixture. Moreover, degrees of reduction are relative, as already emphasized. Languages that were already simple in morphology before restructuring are not likely to show striking degrees of morphological simplification when they are restructured: there is not as much to lose. The contribution of McWhorter's taxonomy of "contact languages" is that it acknowledges and insists on the existence of degrees of restructuring, formalizes them

---

[133] McWhorter 2007: 266: "the placement of languages in the chart is based on their synchronic character."
[134] Kihm 2012: 658. [135] Heine and Kuteva 2005: 21–34; Bowern 2013: 424–426.

for discussion and analysis, and separates the issue of mixture from reduction of grammatical features while requiring that it enter the discussion

Human Agency in the Transfer of Features and Grammatical Reduction: Three Syndromes

Positing degrees of mixture crossed with degrees of morphological reduction demands that the linguistic model I am using here incorporate findings from other research avenues in contact linguistics and the related field of research on bilingualism. Other researchers have demonstrated languages are not mixed just at random when they "come into contact," but that the transfer of features from one language is specifically conditioned, just as morphological reduction in a language depends on specific variables in the circumstances of social contact and age of language acquisition. The analysis of mixture – more precisely the transfer of features from one language to another – is more complex and entails factors that undermine the utility of the optimistic nine-part grid just examined.

Bilingual or multilingual individuals are the agents of transfer of features from one language to another,[136] but multilingualism is of different varieties in different individuals and operates differently in different settings. One decisive factor is variation in the individual's proficiency in different languages, in turn connected with many other factors such as the individual's age of acquisition, frequency of use, and social domains of use of different languages. A second factor is variation in distribution of the languages spoken by different members of a society. A third is variation in the relative extent and intensity of use of different languages in a society at large. The kinds of crosslinguistic transfer that occur depend on variation in these factors and probably others too. Paying close attention to these complex distinctions can, however, help historians to diagnose aspects of the social history of a language's speakers. As I will explain, the agency of speakers of different languages can sometimes be discerned through the directions of transfer of features from language to language. This tells historians more about the history of the speakers than the mere observation that features were transferred from one language to another as a consequence of population contact. It can also diagnose different kinds of

---

[136] Ringe and Eska (2013: 60–63) consider the limited agency of monolinguals in the transfer of features from another language into their own.

social contact and relationships between speakers of different languages. The transfer of features from one language to another can thus tell us much about the social circumstances of language change. In what follows here, I employ Frans Van Coetsem's (1919–2002) insights into the transfer of features between languages, which focus on the agency of individual speakers. These are supported generally by the research of others, and I build on them further.[137]

One of the critical factors here is called "linguistic dominance."[138] This refers not to social dominance of a language or of its speakers over others but to the language that is the psycholinguistic default for a user, usually the one in which the user is most proficient in a domain of language use. This is the speaker's "dominant language."[139] Although there are apparently exceptions for those who grow up from early childhood with regular exposure to more than one language and become equally fluent in two or even more languages from childhood, most multilingual people have one dominant language, usually the common language of the home early in life, with variable degrees of proficiency in one or more other languages.[140] They may have varying proficiency in different languages according to different, specific domains or contexts of use, such as when one language is used with family and another at work outside of the home.

---

[137] Van Coetsem 1988; 1995; 2000. Van Coetsem created an idiosyncratic terminology and adopted an opaque style of presentation to explain his insights. I have avoided using some of his terms like "SL agentivity" to reduce obfuscation especially for the sake of nonspecialists. Many scholars in contact linguistics have ignored or overlooked his work; his obscure style of presentation may have contributed to that. Van Coetsem's presentation has, however, been clarified by Winford (2005; 2013: 170–172) and Butts (2016: 13–20, also discussing important antecedents of Van Coetsem's model). The latter applies it with important results to the relationship between Syriac and Greek. Henkelman (2011: 588–595) and van Bladel (2021, addressing Henkelman's application) use Van Coetsem's model to consider the history of contact between Elamite and Persian.

[138] Van Coetsem 1995: 70: "A bilingual speaker ... is linguistically dominant in the language in which he is most proficient and most fluent (which is not necessarily his first or native language)." Cf. Winford 2005: 376–377.

[139] Cf. Myers-Scotton (2006: 295–296), who emphasizes that "bilinguals rarely have equal facility with both languages."

[140] Petersen 1988; Van Coetsem 1995: 70–71 and 2000: 32, 52; Winford 2005: 376–377; Myers-Scotton 2006: 3, 295. Van Coetsem (1995: 72; 2000: 93–94) allows the possibility of "neutralization" of linguistic dominance, in which the speaker appears to be dominant in more than one language, or at least dominance cannot be discerned because of near-equivalent proficiency in more than one language. Van Coetsem does not discuss differences between early and late bilingualism (acquiring both languages before the age of seven or afterwards), or, differently, between simultaneous bilingualism, when a child learns more than one language from infancy, and successive or sequential bilingualism, when a child is exposed to a second language from a young age, but after already gaining proficiency in a prior, first language; such differences may matter (Myers-Scotton 2006: 291, 328–329).

The way in which a bilingual person transfers features from one language to another correlates to the speaker's linguistic dominance in the sense just described. Van Coetsem identified different syndromes (as I shall call them) of transfer rooted in the agency of the multilingual individuals who are the living media of such transfer. The two to which he gives the most attention are *adoption* and *imposition*. Speakers of more than one language freely *adopt* (or borrow) so-called loanwords into their dominant language from other languages they speak, which they incorporate into the grammatical matrix of their dominant language, but they can seldom impose and propagate words from their dominant language into another language used by a community that does not need or accept those foreign words.[141] They likewise seldom transfer grammatical features such as word inflection into their dominant language from another language, because they are completely fluent in their dominant language, and so are not motivated, by themselves, to borrow foreign inflectional patterns (though this can happen in some specific social situations, to be discussed). By contrast, speakers of more than one language are prone to *impose* features of the pronunciation (phonology) and usage (such as syntax) of their dominant language onto another language with which they are less proficient, or which they are just learning. They may even reduce unfamiliar grammatical features, especially in inflectional morphology, of their nondominant language(s), in which, by definition, they are less proficient. Their lower proficiency, be it great or slight, is the obvious reason behind imposition; they make up for their lack of proficiency in the one language with patterns imposed from their default, dominant language.[142] In summary, if we pay close attention to the agency of the multilingual individual, we see that features from different modules of a language are transferred differently according to the speaker's language dominance. The typical pattern of transfer is that bilinguals *adopt* "loanwords" from their second language into their dominant language (L2→L1 lexical transfer) and they tend to *impose* features of phonology and syntax from their dominant language onto their nondominant language (L1→L2 phonological and syntactic transfer), which appears as imperfect usage from the point of view of its highly fluent speakers.[143]

---

[141] For this reason, the expression adopted word or borrowed word is preferable to the common term loanword.
[142] Winford 2003: 217–218.
[143] I do not discuss here the concept of the "scale of adoptability" (Haugen 1950) or "stability gradient" (Van Coetsem 1988: 25–45; Van Coetsem 2000: 58–62; Winford 2005: 337; Butts 2016: 18–19), with its antecedents in Whitney 1881, as the matter is explicable without this concept.

Given these two syndromes, the motive for simplification or reduction of the morphology of a language by adult learners, discussed earlier in this chapter, becomes clearer, and a third syndrome emerges. A nonnative speaker who does not know inflectional forms of the target language cannot use them effectively; one has no motive to impose morphology from one's dominant language (L1) onto the target language (L2) because it would hinder communication to use inflectional forms unknown to the L2-speaking audience. Foreign morphology will not be understood by native speakers of the L2.[144] For example, a Russian speaking German to German-speakers would only cause confusion by adding Russian noun case endings to German nouns. Nonnative speakers cannot avoid phonology or syntax – speaking words requires phonology, and using more than one word entails word order and hence syntax – but they can try to communicate without the appropriate inflections of words, *omitting* inflectional morphology when it is not familiar. This can be regarded as a species of imposition not because it must occur in the company of imposition, but because its agent is the speaker whose dominant language is a different one – typically, the nonnative speaker. Nevertheless, this pattern is distinct from other kinds of imposition, because it entails the omission of features in L2 rather than the exportation of features from L1.[145] It often does not involve the transfer of clearly identifiable features from their dominant language.[146] In short, not two but three different kinds of linguistic change result from the agency of the bilingual speaker for whom, in most cases, one language is the dominant language. Put in less precise terms for the sake of concision, hybridity of lexicon occurs largely through *adoption*: taking features, usually words, from a second language into one's dominant language. That is, adoption is enacted by native speakers of the borrowing language (L1). Typically, words adopted from another language will be

---

[144] Muysken (2013: 207) summarizes earlier research: "In L2 learning, there is no transfer of L1 morphology. L1 affixes never appear on L2 lexical items in interlanguage, and a rare L1 lexical item may carry L1 affixes, but then they tend to form part of an unanalyzed whole." That said, Muysken (2013: 200) also notes that in morphological imposition ("insertion" in his usage) in code-mixing, "the most common case involves nominal plural elements." Not surprisingly, this example is a matter of inherent not contextual inflection.

[145] Foreigner talk is an exception to this pattern, whereby the L1-speaker omits features to be accessible to someone who does not know those features.

[146] Van Coetsem (1995: 76): "reduction is a clear sign of SL agentivity [i.e., imposition]." See Van Coetsem 1988; 1995; 2000; Johanson 2000: 165–166; Winford 2005. This model, based on considerations of the transfer of linguistic features from the point of view of contact linguistics, is supported by research on code-switching among bilinguals, specifically the Dominant Language Hypothesis and the Matrix Language Frame theories. See Petersen 1988 and Myers-Scotton 2006: 242–278.

inflected according to the morphological rules of the new recipient language. Hybridity in phonology and syntax tend to occur by *imposition* of features from the speaker's dominant language (L1) onto the speaker's nondominant language (L2). Reduction of inflection, or *omission*, as I dub the third syndrome here, tends likewise to be due to the agency of nonnative speakers.[147] It is therefore not a matter of degree of mixture or hybridity along an axis involving lexicon > then lexicon and syntax > then lexicon, syntax, and phonology, as discussed just now when reflecting on McWhorter's grid of types. This conception of degrees of mixture does not work. Rather, varieties of transfer of features in language change differ due to a combination of the individual speakers' variable proficiency in languages, their agency in language use, and the subsystem of a language affected. Typically, it is simply omission that leads to the reduction of a language's morphology. Where the omission becomes conventional and pervasive, there appear the striking effects seen in the recognized pidgins, creoles, and semicreoles, with their reduced inflectional morphologies relative to their lexifiers.

There is yet another critical variable factor that goes beyond the individual bilingual person's agency. That is the distribution of bilingualism in the individual's society at large, which acts as a condition for the individual speaker's communicative needs. Where people communicating together are multilingual in the same languages at once, they can meaningfully transfer features between the shared languages as a tool of their communication. When they use features from two or more languages at once, this is known as code-switching or code-mixing.[148] Bilinguals who share the same languages have these expanded means of convenient intercommunication at their disposal. Another phenomenon that depends on the distribution of bilingualism in the society at large has been discussed: when a large group of speakers of various languages acquires a new common language as adults, they will show poor proficiency from the point of view of native speakers, and they may even generate a pidgin or semicreole, which may in turn include features imposed and propagated from one of the participants' languages.

Then there are common cases in which speakers dominant in one language all know a second language well, whereas speakers whose dominant language is the second language do not know the other one. These are

---

[147] Van Coetsem (2000: 181–182) calls this "reduction," but that strictly refers the outcome. I prefer to call the act itself "omission."

[148] Myers-Scotton 2006: 239–241; Gardner-Chloros 2010; Muysken 2013.

known as situations of unilateral bilingualism (or "nonreciprocal bilingualism," "unidirectional bilingualism").[149] In this scenario, the monolinguals typically are or are felt to be socially superior in some way, or they speak a language so widely known that they have little need of another language. That is, native speakers of a high-status or high-utility language can expect others to learn their language, not the other way around – so the native speakers of the high-status language do not learn the other language. By contrast, the bilinguals in this scenario sometimes are or feel themselves to be socially inferior or marginal, or they belong to a distinct "minority" community with a language not known by outsiders. In such cases of unilateral bilingualism, borrowing may go far beyond the normal adoption of words from other languages but may involve the transfer of any grammatical feature of a language, even basic patterns of syntax and morphology, into their dominant language. For an example of this more extensive kind of borrowing (L2→L1 transfer), most speakers of Basque in Spain also speak Spanish, whereas those in Spain for whom Spanish is the dominant language seldom speak Basque at all. Basque-speakers may, and do, freely adopt all kinds of Spanish features into their Basque speech – not just adopted words but adapted grammatical constructions and whole phrases – and they can expect fellow Basque-speakers to understand patterns imported from Spanish, because they speak Spanish, too. But Spanish-speakers will not import Basque materials in the same way because generally they do not know the Basque language.

These tendencies in the transfer of features from one language to another, which are rooted in the individual's language dominance and personal agency but are conditioned by the same factors operating on a larger, social scale, turn linguistic mixture and the transfer of features into an important diagnostic tool for linguistic history. The kind of mixture – the result of linguistic transfer – may help to identify the primary agents in the formation of a new contact language. The three positions on McWhorter's hybridity spectrum are "lexicon only," "lexicon and syntax," and "lexicon, syntax, morphology, (and) phonology." Van Coetsem's model calls into question the distinction of the last two types on this spectrum by showing that there is more than one process giving rise to hybridity and these processes affect different modules of a language. For example, imposition of one's dominant-language phonology will often not be accompanied by hybridity of syntax and morphology; it is just a foreign

---

[149] Hock 1991: 492; Winford 2003: 64, "one-way bilingualism"; Myers-Scotton 2006: 48–49; Matras 2009: 57–60. Cf. Heine and Kuteva 2005: 237–238; van Bladel 2021: 458.

accent. Studies of the transfer of features between languages show that the language dominance of participating speakers plays a decisive role in deciding which kind of transfer of features will arise in each language. Reduction in inflectional morphology arises with omission in nonnative use, and this will become conventional in episodes of large-scale adult acquisition of a language. The proportion of nonnative speakers in that episode matters, with the outcomes of pidgin/creole, semicreole, or less pronounced changes. Different kinds of mixture still offer a useful index for explicating a language's social history because it sheds light on human agency. In the next chapter of this book, I will apply both criteria – reduction of inflectional morphology and outcomes of transfer of features between languages – to the analysis of the history of ancient Persian and its speakers. Nevertheless, I will use Holm's concept of semicreole, which does not link that term to hybridity of lexicon and syntax alone, rather than that of McWhorter's, which does. For my analysis, semicreoles constitute a class of languages that have become distinctly simpler in inflectional morphology through mass adult acquisition but not solely from a pidgin origin, regardless of degrees or types of mixture. As emphasized, I think it is more appropriate to discuss language changes as processes, and not to insist on modern terms describing resultant states. Therefore, it is more important for linguistic history to identify episodes of semicreolization than to label a language synchronically as a semicreole, even if the process and the concept are almost identical.

Decreolization

Creole specialists have long recognized linguistic effects due to the ongoing contact of speakers of creoles with speakers of their language's lexifier. Sometimes native speakers of a creole also learn their language's lexifier with high or partial fluency. For example, colonial governments sometimes have instituted language policies to replace creole varieties of the colonial government's language by formal education in the lexifier. The goal is to give access to opportunities through the prestigious and internationally used high-status languages of literary use; the consequence is demoting and reducing the use of the creole and, typically, stigmatizing it. Such efforts have had mixed results due to many factors. The important point here is that bilingual speakers of a creole and its lexifier can and do transfer features between the lexifier and the creole that diverged from it previously, fostering a new mixture of lexifier and already constituted creole. The creole acquires some of the lexifier's characteristics and converges more with it, adding, for example, some of the contextual inflection shorn during pidginization. Creole specialists call this process "decreolization." In the jargon of creole studies, the product of decreolization is called an "acrolect" of the "basilect" creole.[150] As is evident, this phenomenon makes the analysis of the history of creolization muddier. The process seems to reverse itself, but it is due to specific circumstances.

Terms like acrolect and basilect are descriptive and do not account for the agency of the bilingual speaker. That agency is not fixed or implied by these names. Linguistic decreolization can be due to the agency of a speaker whose dominant language is the lexifier, in which case the speaker imposes features of the unrestructured lexifier on the creole. Decreolization can also be due to the agency of a speaker whose dominant language is the creole, who turns to the lexifier to import words for novel goods or technical terminology that did not exist in the prior pidgin, or who adopts features of the lexifier to attract the social status that goes with it. In either of these ways, the morphology of the lexifier can be adopted or imposed in the creole. Because the absence of inherited contextual inflection is a criterion for identifying creoles, restoration of such inflection by contact with the lexifier would tend to obscure the pidgin or creole origin of a language.

The theory of decreolization should apply to semicreoles as well as creoles. These possibilities must be considered in the application of this model to historical instances.

The Pace of Language Change and "Modern" Ancient Languages: A Note for Historical Linguistics

One of the ramifications of the entire foregoing discussion is counterintuitive. When drastic demographic changes occur, languages may change rapidly, too, with the attrition, loss, or new emergence of grammatical structures, phonology, vocabulary, and other features evident within just a few generations, as few as two or three.[151] A new variety of the language, as acquired imperfectly by adults and then natively from them by the children among them, can become notably reduced or changed as compared with that of those children's grandparents and great-grandparents. What is counterintuitive is the speed of the change. Historical linguists have typically fabricated their own rough, ad hoc estimates for the time between

---

[150] Romaine 1988: 158–161; Winford 2003: 314, 354; Hock 2021: 744–745.
[151] Holm (2000a: 3) cites the early creole researcher Reinecke (1937: 6), who stated that "Languages can be observed taking form within a man's lifetime." See Baker 1995 for examples of this chronology, and Daval-Markussen and Bakker 2017: 133–136 for a summary discussion of this issue.

poorly documented or prehistoric stages of a language, but without any evidence.[152] They often guess at periods of several centuries to account for changes in grammatical structure on the assumption that language change is a matter of a very gradual trickle of cumulative effects, like the slow accretion of stalactites in a cave in which water seeps through limestone. When literary standard languages, acquired through schooling, predominate in the record for centuries, the normal assumption is that the vernacular, spoken varieties change gradually in the undocumented background. Rather, it is now clear that abrupt population contact and the ensuing social relations are the primary determinant of language change toward morphological simplicity. The term "abrupt" matters because it refers to the sudden need of adults to learn the language, not necessarily to long-term change over many generations. Language learning by children, in a second generation of population contact, does not lead to extreme morphological simplification. The ongoing entry of foreigners into a society, over more than one generation, however, should entrench the effects of morphological simplification, through a condition of continuously renewed abrupt contact by people who need to learn the new language as adults. While all languages do change slowly and gradually, languages can also change drastically and rapidly in the midst of rapid and drastic population change.[153] Upheavals in populations can act on the elaborate inflections of a language as a hatchet may carve down or truncate an ornate stalactite that has grown slowly by dribbles over centuries or millennia. The signs of those upheavals are permanent, although the reduced stalactite may grow new structures over subsequent centuries and millennia. Instances of languages being restructured radically within three generations of colonial contact are well documented, the most typical being the languages dubbed pidgin and creole that have arisen in recent centuries, for which documentation is sometimes sufficiently ample to illustrate their geneseis. This fact challenges the estimates of some traditional historical linguists that have posited stages of language development over long prehistoric centuries. We should expect that centuries in social

---

[152] This resembles the neglect of population histories by specialists in creoles and contact linguistics. Cf. the critical remark by Yakubovich (2008: 205) about Indo-Europeanists who "use . . . intuitions or makeshift theories as their main guides for drawing sociolinguistic implications from the available data" when many studies of language contact are available to provide a framework for understanding.

[153] Trudgill 2011: 2–13. Already Van Name (1869–1870: 123) remarked that in the case of creole languages, "two or three generations have sufficed for a complete transformation" from their lexifier, due to the "greater violence of the forces at work," as distinct from the slow gradual change found in more familiar cases.

isolation will contribute to the intergenerational replication of a language's archaic features, but that reduction takes place in abrupt episodes.

It is worth remarking, by way of an example not irrelevant to the ancient history of Persian, that this applies to the current estimates for the date of the ancient, orally transmitted Zoroastrian scriptures known as the Avesta, composed in the ancient Iranic language called Avestan, a close relative of Old Persian. Specialists have regularly posited very ancient dates for the composition of the Avestan corpus, in its two linguistic strata called Young and Old, pushing it back even as far as the early or middle second millennium BCE, a thousand years before the Bisitun inscription or more.[154] The argument is nowhere explicit, but the idea seems to be that such an "archaic" kind of Indo-European language must be very ancient on the assumption that significant language change requires long periods. The research on language change in population contact presented here suggests rather that the complexities of Avestan grammatical inflection merely reflect the speech of a community joined by very few outsiders since time of their ancestors' separation from the speakers of Old Indic, whenever that separation occurred. The complexity of Avestan morphology and its similarity to that of the reconstructed Indo-European ancestor *by itself* tells us nothing about its age. Perhaps the Old Avestan Gathas were composed as long ago as 1500 BCE, as some specialists have conjectured; perhaps they were even composed as late as the time of the conqueror Cyrus II of Anshan, as others have supposed. If our only evidence is the language of the Avestan texts themselves, we are simply in the dark about their age without a theory about the history of the speakers of the Avestan language as a population. Other historical evidence, beyond the grammar of the language, is required to make such an estimate. In the case of Avestan, the quotation of Old Avestan texts within Young Avestan texts provides a clinching argument for chronological order that happens to match our expectations in the language's grammatical development. But seemingly archaic, grammatically complex languages can persist for centuries without reductions in complexity if foreigners never learn that language. Indeed, as already said, such languages may become gradually more complex, with innovations, while spoken in relative social isolation. In short, philologists are mostly guessing, almost at random, when they estimate the age of ancient texts solely on the basis of relative states of grammatical change and development, unless they know something about the prehistory of the population of a language's speakers or unless

---

[154] E.g., Boyce 1992: 45; Skjærvø 1994: 201–202; 1999b: 6–7; and 2009a: 46.

something stated in the texts provides a chronological anchor.¹⁵⁵ We cannot be certain of such things without a population history, which is usually not possible for prehistoric societies. That said, the grammatical characteristics of a language may tell us about the prior population history of its speakers.

The foregoing synthesis dispels a second misconception sometimes appearing in the study of the ancient Iranic languages: that simpler languages belong to a "modern" type. In Chapter 4, we will encounter scholars (such as Meillet, Reichelt, and Paul) who have casually regarded simplified ancient Iranic languages like Middle Persian as appearing "modern." As Trudgill has indicated, however, scholars familiar with European languages that have been affected by simplification due to long-term high rates of adult second-language learning "have been tempted to regard" simplification in language over time "as a diachronic universal."¹⁵⁶ This gives the impression that "modern" languages – languages of societies participating vigorously in various kinds of modernity – are generally simpler. Simplification would seem thus to be a universal process into which every language would eventually slide among peoples who adopt "modernity." As is evident by now, this assumption entails numerous problems. Not least among them is the multivalence of the word "modern," which connotes different things in different areas of research. Strictly speaking, the combination of the principles just discovered means that the relative simplicity or complexity of a language cannot tell us how old a language is or how "modern," but rather what kind of social changes its speaker population has undergone.¹⁵⁷ That is, nevertheless, an extraordinary breakthrough for linguistic history.

Exoterogeny and Esoterogeny

In this chapter I have tried to define terms of analysis for future efforts in linguistic history. Most of these terms have been adopted from specialized niches of inquiry in linguistics for the use of historians. I have avoided

---

¹⁵⁵ Kellens (2000: 2) argues that "dating [the Avesta's] constituent parts can be attempted only by approximation, on the basis of linguistic arguments alone." We can be more specific, by saying that this means only the relative dating of the Avesta's constituent parts with respect to each other, not dating according to an established era.
¹⁵⁶ Trudgill 2010b: 313; see also 2012.
¹⁵⁷ It must be acknowledged, however, with Trudgill (2011: 185–189), that the conditions of mass migration with which we associate modernity, eroding the insularity of dense social networks, do correlate with the loss of linguistic complexity. Only in this restricted sense could the term "modern" be applied to this phenomenon; even then it is potentially misleading.

proposing new jargon when so many terms are in use. There are two other terms for which I foresee some utility that I will introduce now, both coined by William G. Thurston in 1987 and used occasionally by other linguists since then.[158] Thurston dubbed languages without an appreciable number of nonnative learners *esoteric* languages, and those with many extracommunal users or nonnative learners *exoteric*. From these uses of those words, he created two neologisms: *esoterogeny* and *exoterogeny*. That is, changes in a language induced by native speakers who live in a relatively closed social network can be described as esoterogenic, in that they are enacted by the linguistic community's insiders, all of whom learned the language from childhood. Thurston's concern in creating these terms was with the deliberate efforts of speakers of a language in a closed community to differentiate their language from that of their neighbors.[159] By contrast, changes induced by those coming from outside of a linguistic community are "exoterogenic." These terms may help linguistic historians within certain limits that I will now discuss.

Earlier, I indicated that we lack a common term for languages that are transmitted "normally" between generations without the interruptions in perfect acquisition by nonnative-speaker outsiders. I proposed calling that process *intergenerationally stable transmission*. Esoterogeny, as coined by Thurston, unfortunately does not adequately describe such transmission; it describes rather the coming into being of new features induced by socially closed communities for their linguistic self-differentiation. Furthermore, in the humanities, to call such languages "esoteric" may give the odd impression that they are used for secret rituals or occult phenomena, because the word esoteric already carries such connotations. Nevertheless, I think the term exoterogeny may have some utility for linguistic history. I acknowledged that it is practically impossible to evaluate the degree of a language's restructuring toward morphological simplicity apart from the useful degrees of *creole*: *semicreole*: *unrestructured*. It may be difficult for linguistic historians to decide whether a language attested in history fits one of these categories because its genesis may be unattested. As Watts rightly warns, "the term 'creole' should not be bent to such an extent that it can be pressed into service to define all the results of all language contact situations."[160] We can use the term exoterogeny as an umbrella term to describe the process by which creoles, semicreoles, and

---

[158] Thurston 1987; McWhorter 2007: 11; Good 2023.
[159] Good (2023: 391–394) claims that this was deliberate in the case of the Cameroonian language Fang.
[160] Watts 2011: 95. Watts summarizes an argument by Görlach (1986) to argue that Middle English could not be a creole, yet the latter concludes by comparing Middle English with Afrikaans, the paradigmatic example of a semicreole.

similar languages come into existence without having to specify whether the language underwent a pidgin stage or not. If a language has undergone a phase of exoterogeny, it means that it became distinct from its ancestor through nonnative use. Thurston defined the term thus: "Exoterogeny is the process of simplifying an esoteric language to create a register that is more easily acquired by outsiders."[161] This definition does not specify speakers' deliberate intention. We are dealing here with the same kind of process that gives rise to pidgins, creoles, and semicreoles, as Thurston indicated when he defined the term. Yet exoterogeny becomes imprecise when we consider that areal features (discussed later) may all be regarded as exoterogenic. Nevertheless, exoterogeny is a term that may bear some utility. For those squeamish about terms like semicreole – despite its clear meaning – "exoterogeny" may provide a refuge.

Ramifications

The synthesis of linguistic research presented here demonstrates strikingly that the linguistic description of a language at a single historical stage permits some inferences about the prior history of the population that spoke it. This is not entirely news for historical linguists, who have long mined ancient languages for linguistic borrowings such as "loanwords" signifying social contact of different kinds. The lexicon of adopted words alone, for example, can signify domains of social contact, as, for example, when terms used for trade, or government, or religion are the ones that are adopted. But the model synthesized here shows that still more can be discerned than mere contact. Even lexical borrowing can indicate more than just the domains of contact. Such phenomena may illustrate the social relationships of those in contact due to the role of different kinds of speaker-agency in the transfer of features. Moreover, when the inflectional morphology of a language appears to have been noticeably reduced in a short period, we should assume that some demographic upheaval has occurred among speakers of the language at some time in the past, and that contact-induced restructuring through mass adult acquisition is behind that. Even when a language is documented at one time only, with no record of its prior history, if its grammar is highly simple relative to its cognates, or even relative to most languages, we may suppose that some such event took place in its undocumented past.[162]

---

[161] Thurston 1987: 150.

[162] This is the main thesis of McWhorter in his work of 2007. McWhorter further suggests (2011a: 17–18), optimistically, that "Grammatical analyticity can be of use in reconstructing population movements for which there is otherwise only fragmentary evidence, or even in directing researchers as to where to look for signs of population movements as yet uninvestigated," and that conspicuous

Fundamentally, it is necessary for linguistic historians to pay close attention to the age of acquisition of a language by historical subjects. This is a diachronic factor that varies according to specific social settings. It is the historian, not the linguist per se, that can perform this analysis best.

Language change due to historical social and demographic factors has fallen between several areas of scholarly investigation. The sound and highly effective methods of traditional historical linguistics do not take social factors much into account. Those methods, which are based on description, are not designed to account for such factors. Contact linguistics and creole studies have, by contrast, with several notable exceptions, lacked historians able to elucidate population histories convincingly in support of their hypotheses, leading to inconclusive debates. When combined, historical research and linguistic models will lead to new results useful to historians, as I will show in the next chapter.

simplicity in a language "is even a scientifically appropriate cause for supposing such rupture [in language transmission] even if other evidence proves unrecoverable."

CHAPTER 3

Middle Persian as a Byproduct of the Social Conditions of the Achaemenian Empire

Now we return to Old Persian and its evolution into Middle Persian. As shown in the first chapter, between about 500 BCE and 350 BCE the grammar of Old Persian changed radically. The frequent irregularities and omissions in the written inflections of the late Achaemenian Persian inscriptions show that its complex inflectional endings had mostly been lost by the end of that period in the living language. The scribes responsible for these inscriptions succeeded in obscuring the extent of this loss from our view when they copied older inscriptional formulae or spelling exactly. They increasingly often failed in this, however, for they also wrote inflectional endings that were not etymological, misapplied inflectional endings by misconstrued analogy, made mistakes by hypercorrection, and, most tellingly, omitted inflectional endings reflecting their living language. As discussed in Chapter 1, there are also signs of general phonological changes affecting Persian words regularly that show through the inscriptions. Mancini has even suggested that the late Achaemenian Persian writing comprised a somewhat regular system of conventional spellings indirectly representing a phonological state of the language much changed from that of the earliest inscriptions.[1] These sorts of changes in morphology and phonology are represented directly in the next attested stage of the language, Middle Persian, apparent fully only in texts surviving from centuries later, written in a different script. The late Achaemenian Persian inscriptions reveal, however, that those changes were well underway, if not substantially complete, by the time of the disastrous invasion of Alexander III of Macedon. The change itself is widely acknowledged among specialists in ancient Iranic languages. In short, we may regard the language of the late Achaemenian Persian inscriptions as Proto-Middle

---

[1] Mancini 2019.

Persian or by a similar term.² That is, this form of Persian expresses the earliest specific characteristics of the language we conventionally call Middle Persian.³

As seen in Chapter 1, the conspicuous omission in Middle Persian of the complex inflections of Old Persian has drawn many remarks and observations but few explanations. Middle Persian appears to have the simplest inflectional morphology of any known ancient Indo-European language (except for the two most closely related known ancient relatives, Parthian and Bactrian, to be discussed in the next chapter). As I remarked, and as specialists in Iranic languages have observed many times, its inflectional morphology is simpler even than that of the great majority of modern Indo-European languages. How did this happen? This chapter answers that question using the explanatory model set out in Chapter 2.

A Nation Morally Corrupted?

There are wrong answers to the question. Let us deal with an old one now. Different strains of modern nationalism have construed a connection between concepts of linguistic vitality and national strength. Often, this is rooted in the implicit notion that conservatism, or resistance to change, signifies the vitality of a people (whatever that would mean), and that real social or cultural power ought to include the ability to keep culture stable and unchanging. From this point of view, if a language changed, or was simplified, it was losing its strength and becoming corrupt. This was a sign of social decay and perhaps even the gradual weakening of a nation. This way of thinking was common in nineteenth-century linguistics, but it is false. These values are not inherent to language of any kind but arise rather from the individual's aversion to social change or from romantic dreams of a history of continuity of a nation's imagined essence as represented by its language. These are the same kinds of attitudes that have made the study of creoles, discussed in the last chapter, a politically charged arena. In an early stage of the study of creole languages, it was normal to dismiss radically restructured languages as uncouth bastard tongues. This judgment was reinforced at times by racist disdain for the populations that lived in colonial sites, whether colonized peoples or imported slave labor

---

² Skjærvø 1999a: 159; Mancini 2019 (who argues against the term "pre-Middle Persian" on the grounds that it is directly attested in the late Achaemenian inscriptions).
³ Korn's descriptive study (2020) of the historical phonology in Persian is complementary with the account here. Korn focuses on carefully ordered accounts of phonological change, not restructuring of morphology.

118   3 Middle Persian a Byproduct of the Persian Empire

populations or mixtures of hitherto unmixed peoples. This old attitude about language change was not peculiar to the study of creoles. Early pioneers in modern linguistics often regarded change from a pristine, ideally unmixed and grammatically complex state as "corruption."[4] Such terms, blending moral judgment with linguistic description, have long intruded into the study of the late Achaemenian Persian inscriptions. In 1852, Oppert regarded later Achaemenian inscriptions as representing a language in decline ("décadence") practically as soon as they were deciphered.[5] Meillet regarded the early inscriptions of Darius I and Xerxes as written in a language "coherent and manifestly correct," whereas the later ones were "very incorrect" and finally "simply barbarous."[6] For Kent, the late Achaemenian inscriptions represented a "corrupted form of the language."[7] Olmstead, even less cogently, held that the late Achaemenian inscriptions "betray a degeneration in literary style."[8] Even for Schmitt, one of the most insightful interpreters of Old Persian, when writing only a few decades ago, late Old Persian had "degenerated" and was "barbaric."[9] These modern philologists were writing descriptively about language forms and not necessarily about moral change, but the two are easily connected by the use of such descriptions. This was typical of nineteenth-century and even twentieth-century linguistics.

This is a sensitive issue for a few different reasons that are mutually entangled. One pertains to the history of the study of the Achaemenian Empire. Some ancient Greek authors – a few of whom appear later in this chapter – created a narrative of moral decay for their contemporary Persian kings and their subjects that European historians, dependent on Greek sources, have echoed until the most recent generation.[10] Ancient Greek authors imagined the Persians, who were an abiding political and military threat to them, as a nation increasingly spoiled by their power and wealth and corrupted thereby in their morals and conduct. These Greeks defended their stubborn independence as the alternative to what they regarded as slavery under eastern despots. While Greek thinkers argued, disagreed, and warred among themselves about the best government for their small-scale states and cities, they used the vastly more powerful

---

[4] Hock 2021: 907–908.   [5] Oppert 1852: 205.   [6] Meillet 1915: 19 §45.
[7] Kent 1950: 6. Mancini (2019: 527) says, "this approach seems unacceptable," and I agree.
[8] Olmstead 1948: 422.
[9] Skjærvø (1999a: 159), echoed by Mancini (2019), criticizes Schmitt's use of terms such as "barbaric," "degeneration (of the language)," etc., to describe the language of the late Achaemenian inscriptions. Schmitt defends this usage (1999: 104) on the theory that foreigners, or "barbarians" to Old Persian-speakers, wrote them, following Meillet's view.
[10] Samieie (2014: 179–234) surveys this kind of historiography.

Achaemenid Persian dynasty as an example in their own arguments about what worked and what did not, and they defined their people and culture by contrast with those who resided in the immense Persian domain. Modern historians of antiquity have struggled to shake off ancient Greek characterizations of the ancient Persians, which they imbibed from their Greek sources. It was all too easy to connect these old attitudes about the gradual moral corruption of the ancient Persians, which is entrenched in modern and ancient literature, with the "corruption" of their language, as if moral corruption and the reduction of grammar were two aspects of the same phenomenon.[11]

Meanwhile, two more modern tendencies have allied in defending the reputation of the Achaemenian Persians against these attitudes, endowing recent historiography on ancient Persia with different, reactive, recent political values. The last generation of specialists in Achaemenian history made great gains in historical interpretation, largely by using a much wider variety of non-Greek sources and perspectives. In doing so, they thoroughly defeated the Hellenocentric and implicitly anti-Persian historical perspective that prevailed earlier. On occasion, this has been carried out to the point of overkill, leading to caricatures of some earlier scholarship on the ancient Persians and even, occasionally, to their own neglect of relevant Greek sources.[12] The aspiration to write Persian history from the tacitly essentialized "Persian point of view," rather than a more obviously essentialized "Western" one, seems to assume that sources such as royal inscriptions really represent a true, general, national, "Persian point of view" or even "Iranian" point of view rather than a specific Achaemenian royal point of view.[13] Alongside this development, Iranian studies today are thoroughly imbued with strains of Iranian nationalistic sentiment that no participant can overlook. The Pahlavi shahs (1925–1979) and their supporters, the leaders of the present Islamic Republic of Iran, and many individual Iranians today in Iran and abroad have fostered their own selective narratives of "ancient Iran," in which "ancient Iran" is

---

[11] On such errors, see Hock 2021: 907–908.
[12] See Harrison's (2011) and Lenfant's (2012) remarks of caution. One of Harrison's most important points is that recent historians of the Achaemenians have, in their treatment of Greek sources, renewed a narrative of East–West (Persian–Greek) division different from that of the classical scholars but no less misleading.
[13] For a recent example, Llewellyn-Jones' lively account of the Achaemenian Empire for a nonspecialist audience claims to offer "the story told by the Persians themselves" rather than being "moulded around ancient Greek accounts" (2022: 5). This laudable goal cannot be accomplished; we have exceedingly few Persian sources, and the book uses ancient Greek and other non-Persian sources throughout.

a glorious property revealing something wonderful about modern Iranian identity, facilitated by silently passing over historical episodes inconvenient to the master narrative of national continuity.[14] In rejecting the point of view of Greek sources, historians of the Achaemenian Persian Empire are able not only to appear as opponents of Western bigotry but also to play the part of cultural champions for modern Iranians by defending their claimed ancient heritage from the Eurocentric bias of classical scholars and the judgmental specter of colonial-period Orientalists.

This present study eschews these nonanalytical tendencies in linguistic history. Whatever the causes of the changes that turned Old Persian into Middle Persian, they did not "corrupt" the language, for no language is corrupt or degenerate. Reduction of Old Persian morphology neither simplified the minds of Persian-speakers nor exalted them. It does, however, reveal something important that will affect our understanding of the Achaemenian Persian Empire. Moreover, the antipathy of ancient Greek sources toward the Persians will not obscure the problem but shed light on it.

What Happened to Old Persian? The Linguistic-Historical Model Alone

If we had no other information about the Persians in the period of the Achaemenian Empire apart from the inscriptions, then the linguistic-historical model presented in the previous chapter should, by itself, lead us to conclude confidently that there had been an extended episode of mass adult acquisition of Old Persian. The inflectional morphology of the language was profoundly simplified within five generations, and the only known, amply documented cause of such a change is mass adult acquisition. Under no other known historical circumstances has this taken place. The speed of the change itself is characteristic specifically of mass adult acquisition, rather than merely a situation of prolonged societal bilingualism or multilingualism, in which the drastic reduction of grammatical features is not expected, but rather two-way borrowings would proliferate leading to grammatical convergence. Grammatically reduced, nonnative speaker varieties of languages are ubiquitous in human societies among adults, but what is also quite remarkable here is that a grammatically simplified, nonnative variety of Persian became the common one for subsequent native speakers of Persian, just as Afrikaans became the normal

---

[14] Marashi 2008; Zia-Ebrahimi 2016. On the creation of "Ancient Iran" as a field, see briefly van Bladel 2024: 3–6.

variety of speech for the descendants of the Dutch colonists in South Africa. Middle Persian, however, is much more reduced from its Old Persian source than Afrikaans is from Dutch. That is partly because Old Persian was much more complex in its inflections than Dutch at the outset of contact. Old Persian had more inflectional complexity to lose, making the transformation much more dramatic. The degree of change is nevertheless remarkable.

Middle Persian, as we know it, does not seem to have evolved from a stabilized pidgin variety. Unlike all modern creoles, it retained a little bit of the contextual inflection from the immediately ancestral form of the language, however minimal. Middle Persian verbs have two stems each that are, synchronically, not transparently derived from the other. Three persons and two numbers are distinguished in the present stem of the verb. The preterit is entirely uninflected by itself but requires an inflected copula to correlate a patient outside of the third-person singular. A simple set of subjunctive verb endings, slightly different from the indicative, is used to indicate the expectation of occurrence (futurity or eventuality) or undefined occurrence (as in indefinite relative clauses). Simple optative forms occur in verbs in the third century CE. An oblique case existed alongside the direct case (former nominative). However minimal this inflection was, based on the linguistic-historical model alone we would assume that Middle Persian, as compared with Old Persian, underwent semicreolization, a term that refers not to its status over the centuries of its existence, but to the social process that shaped it. Middle Persian was drastically reduced to the point that it looks close to a creole but without clear evidence of having emerged from a pidgin. We can say with complete confidence that exoterogeny played a decisive role in the formation of Middle Persian.

The case is not so neatly closed, however. The existence of decreolized "acrolects" of creoles, discussed in the previous chapter, which have emerged through the transfer of grammatical features of the lexifier into the creole derived from it, does prompt the question of whether Middle Persian could have undergone a similar history. For example, the singular and plural of the direct (nominative) case are identical in most, but not all, nouns, as illustrated in Table 1.2. Only plural verb inflection or semantic context marks the plurality of a Middle Persian grammatical subject. In these instances, the noun lacks contextual inflection that cross-references the plurality of the noun phrase with that of the verb. Creole languages do not inherit contextual inflection from their lexifiers. In this specific respect, Middle Persian resembles a true creole. Yet a small number of nouns, like the word for "father," do exhibit a distinct singular nominative (direct case): nom. sing. *pid*, nom. pl. *pidar*. Inherited contextual noun inflection therefore does exist in Middle Persian, at least marginally. For another example, of the two verb stems of Middle Persian, only the present stem takes personal endings, as just mentioned. These present-stem endings are strange, from the point of view of early Old Persian, in deriving from the endings of one verb class of several (the one with the formant -*áya*-), even on the most frequently used verbs (like "to be"), creating an entirely regular, agglutinatively inflected verbal system. Purely hypothetically, this could represent the *re*application of endings generalized from one class of verbs, in a process of decreolization of verbs that had become entirely uninflected in a pidgin form of Old Persian. Only if this sort of speculation were to be verified, then Middle Persian would cross the line from a semicreole into the territory of a true creole in acrolect or decreolized form. It seems impossible to verify or refute this hypothesis, however, so it is not worth pursuing here further. Although it is practically certain that a Persian pidgin of some kind existed at least at royal sites (to be discussed), any popular pidgin based on an Old Persian lexifier is inherently very unlikely ever to have been recorded. With the limited sources of information at our disposal, the more analytically secure solution is to understand Middle Persian as a semicreole, being drastically reduced in its inflectional morphology without having emerged from a prior widespread pidgin, because it does retain some contextual inflection (inflection governed by syntax). If we consider Holm's demographic data on semicreole formation charted in the last chapter, this may give us a vague sense of the proportion of native and nonnative speakers of Persian in Persian households and settlements in the fifth century BCE: something like half and half. This chapter will show that that estimate is quite plausible.

While Middle Persian exhibits extraordinary grammatical simplification in inflectional morphology, its lexicon offers hardly any words at all borrowed from the languages of the subject nations of the Achaemenids.[15] Critically, the near-absence of words adopted from other languages in Old as well as Middle Persian reminds us of the second part of the linguistic model, concerning the agency of speakers in the transfer of features such as words from one language to another. It indicates that few ancient Persians (native speakers of Persian) were highly proficient in foreign languages during the Achaemenian period or perhaps in any ancient period. Like nonimmigrant inhabitants of the USA today who know only English and lack a motive and a social opportunity to learn any other language at a young age, and have little incentive to do so because of the global status

---

[15] Cf. Hübschmann 1895: 118.

of English as a lingua franca, the ancient Persians enjoyed the restricting, dubious benefits of unilateral multilingualism: many others had need of their language, but they had little need of others' languages, and so they spoke just Persian, expecting to be understood sufficiently when they spoke. There is, however, one clear exception to the pattern. The presence of some not strictly Persian Iranic words attested as adopted in Old Persian and Middle Persian demonstrates that some ancient Persian-speakers knew at least one closely related Iranic language. Philologists call such words Median when discovered in Old Persian[16] and Parthian when discovered in Middle Persian.[17] What such words really have in common is that they are Iranic but not Perside. "Perside" is a term of art used to refer to the languages bearing features (usually phonological) reflecting innovations found in Persian and related dialects but not in other Iranic languages. One example is the outcome of Proto-Iranic *ź /dz/ in Persian. In most Iranic languages, this evolved into /z/, but the regular Persian outcome was /d/. As illustrated with a few examples in Table 3.1, however, some Persian words exhibit /z/ where a /d/ is expected by the regular development. Such words in Old Persian have been assumed to be adopted from "Median" because the Achaemenian Persians were political successors of the Arya Medes, making Median (a language scarcely attested directly) the only Iranic language of political significance before Persian. Naming words of this kind adopted in Persian as either Median or Parthian is a convenience, because we do not really know in all cases that they were specifically from one of those two languages, but just that they come from another Iranic language besides Persian.[18]

In this chart one can see that the Old Persian words in three rows exhibit the so-called Median or simply non-Perside /z/ instead of the expected /d/. We see also that in the Middle Persian, other "Median" or "Parthian" forms with /z/ rather than the inscriptional Old Persian reflex /d/ occur. One could multiply this with more examples in which other unexpected phonemes exhibit traces of non-Persian Iranic borrowings. We need not dwell on this longer here, however, as these phenomena have been discussed adequately in reference works just mentioned in note 18. The main point for now is that they demonstrate that some Persians spoke

---

[16] Already Meillet (1915: 9 §16) tentatively suggested calling such words Median: "cette langue n'était pas le perse; tout au plus pourrait-on, sans raison précise, songer au mède." See further Kent 1950: 8–9 §6–11; Brandenstein and Mayrhofer 1964; 12–14; Schmitt 1989c: 87–90. Korn (2019: 254) rightly points out that the distinguishing features of these words show only that they were not Persian, not that they were specifically Median.

[17] Durkin-Meisterernst 2014: 147 §277.

[18] Hübschmann 1895: 220–223 §§110–111; Kent 1950: 33 §88; Brandenstein and Mayrhofer 1964: 53.

Table 3.1 *Reflexes of Proto-Iranic *ź in ancient Iranic languages*

Proto-Iranic *ź	Old Persian	Middle Persian	Avestan	Parthian
*źān- "to know"	dān-	dān-	zān-	zān-
*źrayah- "sea"	drayah-	drayā(b) and zrēh ("Parthian")	zraiiah-	zrēh
*waźr̥ka- "great"	wazarka- ("Median")	wazurg	cf. wazra- "club"	wazurg
*źana- "kind (of person)"	-zana- ("Median")	zanag "kind, sort"	zana-	zanag "kind, sort"
*źūrah "wrongdoing"	zūrah ("Median")	zūr	zūrō	zūr
*źaranya- "golden"	daraniya-	zarrēn ("Parthian")	zaranya-	cf. zarn "gold"
*yaźatai "he worships, sacrifices"	yadatai	yazēd ("Parthian")	yazaite	yazēd

other Iranic languages; if they were not familiar with other Iranic languages, they would not have adopted words or pronunciations from them. The near total absence of words in Old and Middle Persian adopted from other languages, including the languages of their non-Persian subjects, is therefore even more striking.[19] Few Persians knew the languages of most of their subjects; otherwise, they would likely have adopted at least some of their words, beyond proper names. Yet some Persians did know other Iranic languages closely related to Persian.

The combination of the linguistic-historical model of Chapter 2 with the linguistic facts about Achaemenian Persian reviewed in Chapter 1 diagnoses a situation in which many speakers of other languages all at once had to cope with people who spoke Persian, and to learn some of their language immediately as adults, and that the Persians did not have any need of learning the languages of their subjects: a situation of unilateral bilingualism. Nevertheless, some Persians spoke other contemporary Iranic languages, accounting for the "Medianisms." This is what we should assume about the early history of Persian from the linguistic model alone. As it happens, many historical testimonies support this interpretation. The remainder of this chapter will survey those testimonies and discuss their ramifications. The subsequent chapter will discuss the relationship of the socially induced restructuring of Old Persian to other, closely related Iranic

---

[19] De Blois (1994) and van Bladel (2021) analyze the absence of Elamite words in Persian.

languages that show similar characteristics. Before that, however, it is necessary to address a major problem of method and perspective.

Purely Structural Linguistic Alternatives?

Historical linguistics provides descriptions of language change over time without taking social factors much into account. Whether that is enough of an explanation of language change or not depends on the kind of history one wants. I posited in the Introduction that linguistic history should be distinguished from solely structural analysis by its primary and complementary attention to the history of a language's speakers. Taking social factors into account requires the use of contextual primary sources as well as linguistic data. It is possible, however, to construe language change as motivated entirely from within the structure of a language itself. That is what historical linguists normally do. From a strictly descriptive point of view, this is valid. Although many words and word-forms extant in Old Persian are still debated by specialists, the tested methods of historical linguistic analysis of Old Persian work most of the time and have elucidated Old Persian remarkably well. These methods, unfortunately, offer historians almost nothing. The gap between philology and history is not only institutional but a matter of method, too. Before going on, then, let us consider some ways in which this stage in the evolution of Persian has been explained before as the outcome of purely linguistic phenomena, meaning that no social factors play a role in these explanations.

Gernot Windfuhr, a leading specialist in the typology of Iranic languages, has posited a regular pattern of increasing and decreasing morphological differentiation as "typical" of the history of languages. Over centuries, noun case systems would bloom, collapse, and bloom again in a cycle, apparently by the nature of language itself.[20] At first glance, an example of this would be Balochi, an Iranic language spoken today mostly in southeastern Iran and southwestern Pakistan. Balochi, which bears a very close family resemblance to ancient Parthian, exhibits the same direct and oblique noun cases found in most of the other Iranic languages to the west, but has developed new noun cases along with other inflectional novelties.[21] As mentioned, however, research has shown that the number of noun cases in a language tends to hold an inverse correlation with the proportion of nonnative speakers, so it is clear that this is not merely

---

[20] Windfuhr 1990. On this sort of "morphological cycle," see Trudgill 2011: 186 and Hock 2021: 358–361.
[21] Korn 2005b.

a cyclical phenomenon.²² It is rather a matter of population movement and patterns of language acquisition over the long term. Balochi represents an instance in which an ancient episode of grammatical reduction brought on by population mixture, like the kind under discussion here for Persian, was followed by a subsequent period in which speakers of the language migrated to the south and east and pursued a pastoralist economy in relative social isolation.²³ During a long subsequent period of relative social insularity for speakers of Balochi, the inflections of their language became more complex in ways unrelated to the common features of Iranic languages. The inflectional patterns of Balochi reflect not naturally determined cyclical developments but changes in the history of the society of its speakers. I will take up other examples like this in the following chapter.

Geoffrey Haig suggests that the Iranic languages were each somehow preconfigured or programmed to undergo the same sorts of changes because, deriving from a common ancestor language, they reach "remarkably similar" syntactic structures, "although over the course of time the speakers became separated by thousands of miles, and came to speak mutually unintelligible languages."²⁴ The idea that the Iranic languages, or any group of related languages, are genetically predisposed to undergo certain kinds of change by virtue of their cognate relationship is controversial and unproved.²⁵ Of course, the common ancestor of the Iranic languages had specific characteristics, and changes affecting daughter branches of Common Iranic were all changes relative to that shared prior state. A language's grammatical history is, in effect, the descriptive register of the retention, transformation, and omission of the characteristics of the language at an earlier time, as each new

---

[22] Bentz and Winter 2013. It seems, however, that Windfuhr may have intuited the unidirectionality of grammaticalization involved in the evolution of affixes to inflection, which can give grammaticalization the appearance of cyclicality (Hopper and Traugott 2003: 94–129).
[23] Spooner 1988; Jahani and Korn 2009: 634. I discuss other Iranic languages affected by changes like those evident in Persian in the next chapter.
[24] Haig 2008: 325. McWhorter (2007: 138–164) demonstrates that "drift" is not enough to explain the peculiar development of Persian as having a strikingly simplified grammar as compared with the other Iranic languages.
[25] Joseph (2013) proposes to account for the parallel grammatical developments in languages sharing a common ancestor, when the developments appear to take place long after contact between the speakers of the divergent languages has ceased, as the result of undocumented sociolinguistic variation in actual usage of the ancestor language. That is, variation in the ancestor language not attested in the record includes patterns eventually selected for regular use in a later stage of the language. But this is merely to say that the shared developments are not really developments but a shared inheritance from an unrecorded or scarcely recorded register or variety of the common ancestor. See the similar model employed by Jamison (2009), who explains exactly parallel developments in Indic and Iranic languages long after their separation by positing an earlier common vernacular that began to appear in compositions only in a later period.

generation acquired it, replicated it, or employed it differently. Although grammaticalization does appear to be mostly unidirectional in all languages,[26] there is no reason to think that the Iranic languages were all bound to experience the same outcome by inherent tendencies, and, in fact, they did not.[27] Thomas Jügel provides a relevant example in charting the different development of the verbal systems of New Persian and Yaghnobi, and the comparison he illustrates between them is revealing, contradicting the notion of inherent grammatical destiny. Yaghnobi is a modern descendant of an ancient Iranic language closely similar to the Iranic language Sogdian (discussed in the next chapter) that survived in a remote mountain valley of Tajikistan. While its nominal inflection is quite reduced, its speakers retain the ancient Common Iranic imperfect verb, even with the late Proto-Indo-European temporal augment prefix *a-*, used now in Yaghnobi for the simple past (aorist) function and, with new suffix, for continuous past time, in addition to the forms of the verb retained in Middle Persian: the present verb stem and a preterit formed from the ancient perfective verbal adjective in *-ta-*. Persian, by contrast, like most other modern Iranic languages, lost the ancient imperfect verb already in antiquity, leaving New Persian to develop new past-time uses of the verbal stem based on the ancient verbal adjective in *-ta-*.[28] See Table 3.2.

Table 3.2 *Imperfect and perfective forms in Persian and Yaghnobi, greatly simplified from Jügel (2015: 163)*

	Inherited imperfect verb form: "I did" (transitive)	Agent clitics + perfect participle in *-t-*: "It was done by me"
Old Persian	*a-kunaw-am*	*-mai kr̥-ta-*
Yaghnobi	*a-kun-im*	*-m īk-ta-x*
Middle Persian	(lost)[29]	*-m kerd*
New Persian	(lost)	*kard-am* "I did"[30]

---

[26] Haspelmath 1999; Hopper and Traugott 2003: 99–139.
[27] See Korn 2020 for many examples of different outcomes.
[28] Jügel 2015: 163–164. Only two Middle Persian inscriptional texts from the third century exhibit examples of an imperfect verb (Skjærvø 1997b), and the imperfect verbs proposed in one of the two have not been accepted as such by all specialists. Nevertheless, it is clear that the imperfect verb retained marginal existence at least in an insular Middle Persian dialect. The rest of the Middle Persian corpus exhibits no sign of the imperfect.
[29] See the previous note about a few early exceptions.
[30] The New Persian verbal suffix *-am* is not descended from the clitic pronoun *-mai* appearing in the same column; it derives from the copular verb to be in the form *ham*, "I am."

The different social histories of the speakers of Yaghnobi and those of New Persian correspond loosely with the kinds of verbal systems they have inherited. New Persian has been a lingua franca, and it is derived from an ancient language that had undergone semicreolization, Middle Persian. Its verbal system is built on the basis of a drastically simplified ancestor. Yaghnobi's ancestor was spoken in inaccessible mountain valleys of the Zarafshan range, where relatively few visitors ever came, over many centuries as the sole surviving descendant of a once substantially widespread Iranic language.[31] Its verbal system, structurally, resembles that of Old Persian more closely than that of Middle Persian. The language of the isolated population preserved and developed the ancient verbal tense called the imperfect, whereas the common, formerly cosmopolitan dialects had lost that verbal tense already in ancient times. It is therefore not genetic predispositions in the structure of a language but social relationships with newcomers, or lack thereof, that condition this kind of linguistic change. A pattern of preprogrammed attrition and growth may seem to be typical, as Windfuhr supposed, because the Middle Persian verbal system represents the basic type from which most modern Iranic languages have developed their respective verbal systems, characterized by a great reduction of forms long ago followed by subsequent development in varying conditions. An exception like the verbal system of Yaghnobi suggests, however, that something else is at work: social changes conditioned by demography affecting the evolution of languages. We do not have an exact science to say why Yaghnobi's nominal system is greatly reduced whereas its verbal system conserves archaic features preserved nowhere else today – just as we do not have an explanation for why its phonology turned out just as it did – but the point is that the idea of a preprogrammed grammatical fate for the Iranic languages, just because they are Iranic languages, cannot be maintained.[32]

Philologists focus on the purely structural features of language as they change over time to the point that they tend to treat languages as living entities separable from their speakers. When linguists discuss "languages in contact," rather than the use of multiple languages by one person or in one social setting, they too tend to treat languages as separable from users. This

---

[31] From mitochondrial DNA analysis Cilli, De Fanti, Delaini, Panaino, and Gruppioni (2013: 145) conclude that the Yaghnobis "apparently maintain a peculiar biological identity, distinct from other populations" in neighboring regions, so that they genetically "represent an outlier in respect to the other populations examined." If correct, this would corroborate the hypothesis that the Yaghnobis are a population whose ancestors received few outsiders, which is precisely a circumstance that could inhibit the restructuring of their verbal system toward inflectional simplicity.

[32] For sketches of Yaghnobi grammar with bibliographies, see Geiger 1895–1905 and Bielmeier 1989.

is the very gap that necessitates linguistic history. Languages have no agency and are not entities that can come into contact independent of speakers. Languages do not have "self-preserving power" that can become "diluted and weakened" resulting "in their accelerated development or rather decay," as Szemerényi put it in his discussion of the origins of Middle Persian.[33] It is speakers who reproduce languages through learning and who bring their languages into contact, particularly when the brains of individual speakers harbor more than one of them at once. The method of the historical linguist has been to explain changes in a language by terms descriptive of processes that operate on patterns, such as analogy, without regard for the agency of speakers who make choices and errors for mental and social reasons. This has often been necessary, because human choices and agency, normal considerations for historians, are beyond the reach of most of the established methods of comparative historical linguistics. Nevertheless, while languages' inflectional systems may change by analogy (for example), it is the speaker that enacts grammatical analogy in a language, consciously or not. If others repeat an individual's linguistic novelty, an idiosyncrasy may be propagated and adopted by other speakers to become a general feature of the language. It is typically only then that the features appear in written texts available to us, and by the time those texts were written, the inception of the changes was in the unrecorded past.

As pharmacists offer drugs to solve medical problems and surgeons offer the scalpel, historical linguists are predisposed to find phonological solutions to linguistic problems, because the phonological isogloss is rightly their fundamental criterion. The discovery of the regularity of sound change was the foundation of diachronic linguistic research, one of the most important modern insights into the nature of language itself. For all their importance, however, sound laws, being descriptive, do not tell us why a language has changed, but only how the forms and structures differed regularly from period to period.[34] Along these lines, the standard explanation for the loss of inflectional endings in Iranic languages like Persian is that it was simply a matter of the position of a strong stress accent.[35] Iranic language-speakers are thought to have stressed certain

---

[33] Szemerényi 1980: 207.
[34] Similarly, Beekes (1995: 71) writes that "it should be admitted that comparative linguistics is not able to tell us why the changes that do occur, occur at this particular place at this particular point in time, and not somewhere else or some time later."
[35] Müller 1877: 224; Salemann 1895–1904: 1.1.275; Meillet 1900. Back (1978: 30–61) is explicit about this, crediting the transformation of the entirety of Persian morphology and syntax to side-effects of the stress accent. See also Windfuhr 1989: 251 and Mancini 2019: 531. Already von Spiegel (1882: 88),

syllables so heavily that vowels in specific post-tonic phonological conditions were syncopated and the final syllables were dropped. Note that the position of the stress accent is inferred by the loss of syllables, not the other way around. In practice, the argument has been to explain the evolution of Persian by drawing parallels with the evolution of Latin and its Romance descendants.[36] These parallels are real, but pointing to parallel phenomena is explanation by comparison, not by positing a cause. The loss of final syllables in Persian eradicated much of the inflectional morphology, blurring or eliminating distinctions between noun classes and grammatical gender, the distinction between the present and imperfect verbs, built on the same stem but with different verb endings, and in all the other ways discussed in Chapter 1. Understood as a natural and practically inevitable phonological change, the loss of final syllables can even be construed as triggering the rise of the "split-ergative" verbal system common to Middle Iranic languages by leaving only one distinct medio-passive past-time construction standing along with two noun cases, direct and oblique. In short, this purely descriptive explanation based on phonological factors alone indicates that the inflection of Iranic languages came to be extremely pared down, and the verbal system reorganized, just because of a consistently emphatic manner of intonation. One regular sound change would eventually transform the entire grammar.[37]

Such an explanation looks clean and effective, with a single phonological solution to a very complex problem. It is also descriptively correct, as far as it goes, and I endorse it as such. That said, it is insufficient to the point of being misleading. It is not that the stress accent *caused* the loss of subsequent syllables. It was, however, a major *condition* of their loss that followed a regular pattern.[38] Not all languages drop or syncopate post-tonic syllables. Some do so, but only after hundreds of years of intergenerational replication and apparent stability. Why do some speakers of languages

---

at an earlier stage of historical linguistic investigation, drew a connection between phonological change and grammatical change when he wrote that "The later Old Persian inscriptions indicate to us that the decline of the pronunciation went hand in hand with the decline of the language too" ("Die späteren altpersischen Inschriften zeigen uns... dass mit dem Verfall der Aussprache auch der Verfall der Sprache selbst Hand in Hand ging").

[36] Gauthiot (1916–1918: 61) briefly compares the Persian case with that of French. Huyse (2003: 54–60) provides a more detailed comparison of this kind.

[37] As Hock (2021: 99) remarks about general and typical sound changes, "Word-final position is as vulnerable an environment for vowels as it is for consonants and consonant clusters."

[38] Cf. Jespersen 1922: 269: "a 'phonetic law' is not an explanation, but something to be explained; it is nothing else but a mere statement of facts, a formula of correspondence, which says nothing about the cause of change, and we are therefore justified if we try to dig deeper and penetrate to the real psychology of speech."

reduce post-tonic syllables while others do not? Why did they lose those syllables at the specific time in which they did, and not sooner, and not later? The actuation of language change has been extensively discussed for decades; it was one of the main questions that motivated the genesis of sociolinguistics.[39] As Rudi Keller remarked in his treatise on explanations for language change, "Historians of language change have traditionally focused on the aspect of change, perhaps tacitly assuming that 'Where nothing changes, there is nothing to be explained.'"[40] That is a limit of the structural argument about language change. Stasis remains unexplained without taking social factors like those I discussed in Chapter 2 into account. The apparent arbitrariness of the actual occurrence of a generally common tendency to drop post-tonic syllables and its timing must be understood not just as a matter of accentuation but also as the product of speakers' choices and habits and their accommodation to circumstances, including differences in language acquisition. For all we know, the assignment of the stress accent to the received position was simultaneous with the loss of final syllables, not its cause. Ancient records do not otherwise indicate the position of the stress on Old Persian words, but we know that the accentual outcome was not inherited from Proto-Indo-Iranic. The two changes – reassignment of stress and loss of syllables – could have been concomitant, enacted by the very people who dropped final syllables. Researchers like William Labov, who has painstakingly scrutinized phonological change in living progress, have demonstrated that social factors play a primary role in sound changes that originate on idiosyncratic, personal scales before adoption by larger groups, even as the sound changes that are successfully propagated ultimately do follow regular patterns on a large scale that can be described as rules.[41] The social subtleties arising in the communication of individuals with different social roles are usually inaccessible to us who study ancient languages, but, as shown in Chapter 2, large-scale social factors can and should be part of our large-scale analysis. Mass adult acquisition of a language has predictable effects on that language, indeed more predictable than the consequences of a stress accent on its phonological environment. Social factors allow reliable

---

[39] Weinreich, Labov, and Herzog (1968) offer a classic discussion of the problem, calling it "the actuation riddle." Croft (2000: 4) adds that "a theory of language change must explain why languages *do not* change in many ways, sometimes over many generations of speakers" (emphasis added). Accordingly, the observation that post-tonic final syllables in Old Persian were lost does not rest on a complete theory of language change. McWhorter (2007: 139) offers counterexamples of Indo-European languages with strong, regular stress patterns that retain complex inflectional endings.
[40] Keller 1994: 141.
[41] Labov 1994–2010. See also Hock 2021: 925–927 and Ringe and Eska 2013: 45–58.

inferences pinned to knowable historical events. Mass nonnative acquisition is the only known condition under which contextual inflection is drastically reduced in a language. The correlation is so strong that the reverse is true, too: those predictable effects on language allow reliable inferences about the history of a language's acquisition. In other words, social and phonological explanations for language change need not be mutually exclusive. They cannot be mutually exclusive. Both rely on the application of expected tendencies to explain empirical phenomena that are attested on a scale that represents a society. A more comprehensive explanation of systemic language change will consider both our reasonable expectations about what commonly happens to the sounds of languages over time (such as palatalization of consonants before front vowels, or the lenition of postvocalic occlusives)[42] and the social circumstances in which language change of different kinds is facilitated by living speakers responding to their personal circumstances. One may easily regard the omission of all final syllables in Old Persian, most of which were markers of inflection, as a necessary ad hoc choice to simplify a language made by ordinary speakers, people who had no concept of linguistics. Separating the fixation of the stress accent and the utterance of words without final syllables may be impossible, because, as just suggested, they may have occurred simultaneously, the stress shift being enacted when the syllables were dropped, perhaps as its audible cue.[43]

It is clear, however, from the detailed research of scholars such as Sims-Williams and Korn that the loss of final syllables in Old Persian did not occur overnight. This is to be expected when many native speakers of Old Persian were still around. Rather, some ancient Persian final syllables underwent stages of phonological reduction prior to complete omission. This is discernible through later traces. Sims-Williams demonstrated that holdovers of Old Persian final vowels were sometimes preserved in Middle Persian words before bound enclitics (words that are attached to preceding words in a single accentual unit).[44] In a few instances, the combination of inflected form and enclitic may have been in effect lexicalized. For example, the attested Middle Persian form *gawā-m* <gw'm> "tell me," evolved from Old Persian *gawbā-mai. The vowel -ā- here, originally an inflectional ending for the imperative singular, was not lost, despite being the final syllable of a word. It was

---

[42] Hock 2021: 82–87, 91–96.
[43] These general considerations about causation in language change have been basic in historical linguistics for decades. See Hock 1991: 627–661 and Ringe and Eska 2013: 28–44.
[44] Sims-Williams 1981a: 171–176.

preserved at least occasionally in this expression dating back to Achaemenian times – whereas the final diphthong of the enclitic *-mai* was lost, as usual, as a word ending. This is not surprising, as the command "give me!" must have been frequent enough to be treated as a unit. Compare the frequent English vernacular "gimme!" with the English enclitic pronoun "-me" (where the outcome is not the preservation an archaic vowel, but elision of the /v/). Other examples, likewise preserved in Middle Persian before enclitics, show a different phenomenon of change before loss: the endings *-im* and *-am* changed to *-u* before the vowel disappeared entirely.[45] The Middle Persian enclitics thereafter sometimes could occur in a form including the preceding vowel *-u*, now a linking vowel, etymologically derived from the inflectional ending of the preceding word, but later treated as a vowel accompanying the enclitic. Thus Manichaean Middle Persian <qyrdwš> *kerd-u-š*, "he made, it was made by him," would have evolved from Old Persian **kərtam-šai*, where Sims-Williams regards the *-u-* linking vowel as a trace of the ancient neuter singular nominative ending *-am*. Although these vowels survive only because they are preserved at the ends of words before enclitics – to my knowledge, never in Persian without enclitics – it is not unreasonable to assume that the change was taking place even in the absence of an enclitic, before or during the loss of all final syllables. That is, *kərtam* was becoming **kərtu* before the final syllable was lost. These are examples of what Sims-Williams dubbed "isolated archaism" in Middle Persian, and they are valuable for demonstrating that final syllable loss was not a uniform and instantaneous phenomenon simultaneous for all users – as variationist linguistic studies of sound change in living progress also have led us to expect.[46]

A remarkable challenge to the present argument emerges from the fact that final syllables were omitted from all words, even uninflected words such as conjunctions and discourse markers. If the issue was that mass acquisition by nonnative speakers will generalize the omission of inflectional morphology, why should *uninflected* words lose final syllables? This is provisionally best understood as a process of analogy, one of the mainstays of explanation in historical linguistics.[47] When a process of change should affect one instance or several instances but speakers extended it

---

[45] This change, labial assimilation of a final vowel followed by *-m*, occurred word-internally by the time of Middle Persian (Meillet 1900: 268–269) and has exact parallels in other Middle Iranic languages. See Sims-Williams 1981a: 174–176; Huyse 2003: 54; Korn 2021: 12–13.
[46] Labov 1994–2010; Hock 2021: 925–927.
[47] Hock 1991: 45–47; Lehmann 1992: 219–234; Ringe and Eska 2013: 152–153.

to all other parallel instances, that is dubbed analogy. If, according to the descriptive phonological approach, a strong stress on penultimate or antepenultimate syllables rendered final syllables omissible – at a time that could not be predicted by phonology alone, prompted by unspecified factors other than "it just happened"[48] – then for which speakers were they most omissible? There is no motive for native speakers to have enacted this sweeping omission. We know that native speaker children among native speaker adults generally learn the inflections used by adults quite well, because languages with highly complex morphology continue to exist. Bentz and Winter also verified an inverse correlation between the number of nominal cases in a language and the proportion of L2-users.[49] In light of this and everything discussed in Chapter 2, by far the most likely culprits for omission of final syllables are nonnative learners of the language, who benefited pragmatically from such omission, or for those attempting to communicate with them in foreigner talk. If speakers were already propagating a pattern of pronunciation whereby the final syllables on most words – nouns, pronouns, and verbs, including some adverbial inflections – were reduced and then omitted, it is reasonable to suppose that speakers carried out this pattern of clipped pronunciation indiscriminately by analogy on small classes of uninflected words regardless of their grammatical categories, being unconscious of such grammatical categories. It is already by analogy that specialists explain the generalization of the plural oblique noun ending -ān (from genitive plural -ānām after it lost its final syllable) to nouns that belonged historically to noun classes where that ending is not etymological.[50] I must admit, however, that we are reaching an epistemological limit of diachronic linguistics here.[51] While variationist sociolinguistics has shown how speaker choice and conformity in relationships drive the widespread acceptance of a phonological change, the interaction of speaker agency and the *omission* of a language's features is an overlooked topic.[52]

---

[48] Cf. McWhorter 2011a: 225: "To most analysts this would appear not to qualify as a question at all. A common assumption is apparently that these languages simply 'lost their morphology' at some point, in an unremarkable fashion."

[49] Bentz and Winter 2013. They also rule out the counterargument that people choose to learn languages with fewer cases.

[50] Durkin-Meisterernst (2014: 199–201 §422) notes the infrequent exceptions to the analogy (which he describes as "die reguläre Endung des Plurals") where -ûn and -īn correspond to etymological genitive plural forms -ûnām and -īnām.

[51] Newmeyer (2003) outlines the duel between formal and functional explanations, undermining the status of both as explanations, but see Haspelmath 2024 on their reconciliation.

[52] Cf. Ringe and Eska 2013: 209: "As in every area of morphological change, more work needs to be done on the loss of morphosyntactic categories."

It is not new to propose that multiple explanations coexist validly for one phenomenon. During the reign of Artaxerxes III, the philosopher Aristotle distinguished different kinds of causes, or reasons for things becoming as they are. Two of his four causes are known as "formal" and "efficient." A stool at a bar requires at least three legs and a stable, flat surface for sitting. That shape, which is one inevitable reason that it is a stool, is its formal cause. In this sense, its form is the cause of its being a stool. But there was also a carpenter who fashioned it, who caused it to be in another sense. The carpenter is the "efficient cause" of the stool. In the evolution of Middle Persian, the position of the strong stress accent is a part of the formal cause of the reduced inflectional system. The strong stress accent can be linked, by regular rules that describe the pattern of sound change as it occurred, with the loss of subsequent syllables. There is a formal correspondence expressing a determined condition. But there were living speakers who reassigned accents in Iranic languages, giving simple uniformity to a complicated, arbitrary, and various inherited accentual and inflectional system, as they reduced the syllables following those accents. They did so in an effort to communicate. These people were something like an efficient cause of the reduction of Persian inflection. In this way, descriptive (formal) and social (efficient) causal explanations for language change – even if they are not exactly as Aristotle proposed in his theory of causation – must coexist. Both are valid and entail different kinds of causation. Understanding both simultaneously bestows greater comprehension of the problem of language change in history.

Historians do not hesitate to accept that major events, such as wars or famines, do not have just one cause. Philosophers have debated the nature of scientific explanations and how they interact. It is reasonable to conclude, with philosopher of science Chrysostomos Mantzavinos, that explanatory pluralism is not only possible but should be embraced, for different explanatory games each have their own rules without contradicting each other.[53] In linguistics, Haspelmath has argued convincingly against partisanship between different linguistic methods that "different explanations in grammar are mutually compatible." Structural explanations are not necessarily contradicted by functional explanations or biocognitive explanations.[54] In this study of the evolution of ancient Persian, we have all three of these kinds of explanations operating at once.

- Structural explanation: the placement of a heavy stress accent correlated with the reduction and eventual omission of the final syllable of every

---

[53] Mantavinos 2016. [54] Haspelmath 2024.

word. This change follows a regular pattern and has parallels in the evolution of Latin and its descendants. This is the explanation usually offered, partly because it has been the easiest to apply, requiring only intuition and a minimum of linguistic comparison.

- Functional explanation: nonnative speakers and their Persian interlocutors omitted most inflectional syllables because it helped them to communicate more easily by drastically reducing the number of forms needed. The reduction of inflectional morphology induced by mass nonnative acquisition is amply demonstrated in languages around the world.
- Biocognitive explanation: adult humans generally do not learn contextual inflectional morphology as well as children. This is attested universally.

None of these explanations need stand alone.[55] The linguistic history of Persian is more robustly supported by all three at once and is insufficiently explained by just one. The functional and biocognitive explanations are, moreover, necessary for linguistic history, which follows the history of languages as used by speakers.

Already in 1906, Antoine Meillet foresaw that this multiplex kind of explanation would be necessary as linguistics developed into a fully fledged field of inquiry. He anticipated the need for social and biocognitive explanations together with structural linguistic ones.

> Language is an institution with its own autonomy, so it is necessary to determine the general conditions of its development with a purely linguistic point of view, which is the object of general linguistics; it has its anatomical, physiological, and psychic conditions, and it is subject to anatomy, physiology and psychology, which clarify it greatly in many respects, and the consideration of which is necessary to establish the laws of general linguistics. But from the fact that language is also a social institution, it follows that the only variable element to which one can have recourse to account for linguistic change is social change, of which the variations of language are merely the consequences, sometimes immediate and direct, more often mediated and indirect.[56]

---

[55] Burke (2004: 13), discussing the cultural history of languages of Europe, addresses the same problem: "In short, neither structural explanations nor explanations in terms of action seem sufficient by themselves."

[56] Meillet, reprinted 1921: 17. Cf. the partial translation of the same passage by Weinreich, Labov, and Herzog (1968: 176). "Le langage est une institution ayant son autonomie; il faut donc en déterminer les conditions générales de developpement à un point de vue purement linguistique, et c'est l'objet de la linguistique générale; il a ses conditions anatomiques, physiologiques et psychique, et il relève

Imperial Persian, Heterogeneous Persians

The rapid transformation of Old Persian into a radically simpler form of speech was due to the very success of Persian-speaking rulers in dominating so much of the world. Meillet, author of the passage just cited – the same scholar who excluded the late Achaemenian Persian inscriptions from his grammar because they were "incorrect," who deemed the latest inscriptions "simply barbarous," and who insisted that the only possible explanation for the conspicuous palatial inscription of Artaxerxes III (A^3Pa) was that a foreigner had written it – was also the first scholar who understood and expressed the cause and the social context of the changes in ancient Persian correctly. In an essay of 1912, published in a semipopular French scientific and literary journal, Meillet reflected on the recent discovery of Middle Iranic and Tocharian texts in Central Asia, which was shedding new light of the history of the Iranic languages and Indo-European generally. About the ancient Iranic languages, he pointed out that, "In no part of the area of Indo-European was the evolution [of the daughter languages] so rapid as in the Iranic.... The speech of the Sasanian period is of an entirely modern type."[57] His explanation was a surmise:[58]

> The explanation of the fact is found, without doubt, in that the Iranic was the first Indo-European language that had served a great empire, the Achaemenid Empire, and in that successive conquests and above all the foundation of the Achaemenid Empire carried Iranic over an immense domain. For a language, to become imperial is the gravest of crises.... Imposed on diverse populations and serving as a means of communication over vast territories, the Iranic languages tended to become radically transformed.

He added that whatever forces had preserved linguistic standards were soon destroyed with the advent of Alexander. This last point is somewhat

---

de l'anatomie, de la physiologie et de la psychologie qui l'éclairent à beaucoup d'égards et dont la consideration est nécessaire pour établir les lois de la linguistique générale; mais du fait que le langage est une institution sociale, et le seul élément variable auquel on puisse recourir pour rendre compte du changement linguistique est le changement social dont les variations du langage ne sont que les consequences parfois immédiates et directes, et le plus souvent mediates et indirectes."

[57] Meillet 1912: 150–151. "Nulle part sur le domaine indo-européen l'évolution n'a été aussi rapide que dans l'iranien.... le parler de l'époque sassanide est une langue de type tout modern."

[58] Meillet 1912: 151. "L'explication du fait se trouve sans doute en ceci que l'iranien a été la première langue indo-européenne qui ait servi à un grand empire, l'empire achéménide, et à ce que des conquêtes successives et surtout la fondation de l'empire achéménide ont porté l'iranien sur un domaine immense. Devenir impériale est pour une langue la plus grave des crises.... Imposés à des populations diverses et servant de moyen de communication à vastes territoires, les parlers iraniens tendaient à se transformer vivement."

unclear, but it seems that he is referring to the orthography of Old Persian inscriptions. The veneer of the formulaic inscriptions was lost and the real, transformed character of Persian would be henceforth evident, whenever it would be written thereafter.

This brilliant intuition of Meillet was rooted in his comprehensive familiarity with the linguistics of his time, the engine of which was *la grammaire comparée*. Despite his correct hunch, however, Meillet was not able to explain the processes by which language "imposed" as a common tongue might lead to its very rapid evolution into a "modern" type of language.[59] That is because several of the subfields of linguistics, findings of which were synthesized in the preceding chapter, had not even come into existence in Meillet's time.[60] The industry of research devoted in the last several decades to second-language acquisition, bilingualism, language contact, grammatical transfer, creoles, and related problems had not yet been conceived when he wrote this. Nevertheless, Meillet's solution, almost forgotten today and only once partially endorsed,[61] was basically correct: Old Persian – and much of Old Iranic, a point to which I will turn in the next chapter – was transformed when it became a necessary medium of communication for many nonnative speakers gathered at Persian-dominated sites from across the vast territories ruled by the Achaemenid Persians. It metamorphosed abruptly in the direction of inflectional simplicity through mass adult acquisition over a few generations. Perhaps this is something close to what Meillet had in mind when he said that the latest inscriptions were barbarous: they reflected nonnative, foreign acquisition. Whatever he really had in mind, Meillet seems to have abandoned or omitted the idea when he published his grammar of Old Persian a few years later. In any case, now, with the benefit of great advances in the understanding of the interaction of society and language, we can be much more

---

[59] Meillet used the word "imposed" here as if it were imposed forcefully by an empire, not in the sense of "imposition" used in Chapter 2, in the sense employed by Van Coetsem.

[60] That said, Meillet (1921: 76–101) did argue with the early creolist Schuchard about the nature of linguistic "parentage," and was quite aware of creole phenomena. I suspect he considered Middle Persian and creoles of French to be parallels, as languages imposed ("imposés") on subject populations.

[61] Szemerényi (1980) revived Meillet's argument explicitly and discussed the problem of the variation in degrees of simplification of the Iranic languages ("decay" in Szemerényi's terms). He recognized from Meillet's observations that "the linguistic development within the Iranian Empire held an important *general lesson for the theory of evolutionary linguistics*" (emphasis in original). Promisingly, he deemed "imperial aggrandizement" to be the stimulus for the "rapid evolution" of the western Iranic languages, but he concluded, implausibly, merely that contact with Aramaic was the cause behind it and that Western Iranic represented areal features due to that contact. This is an example of the ways in which areal features are invoked without regard for the social circumstances that create areal features. I will discuss the supposed role of Aramaic in the next chapter.

precise about the motivating social context for the phenomenon that Meillet intuitively understood.

Meillet's intuitive solution was mistaken in one subtle but important way. Old Persian was not *imposed* on the subjects of the Achaemenids as a policy decision. As has been well noted, the local languages of the subjects of the Achaemenids continued in use and in writing.[62] The Achaemenids did, however, create a need for many others to learn to speak the Persian language with them. When the Persians and their close Arya allies ruled many other nations, they integrated them, over seven generations of kings, in a vast, durable, ideally unitary network of dominion and interregional contact and exchange, presided over by "one king of many, one commander of many," as Old Persian inscriptions of Darius, Xerxes, and Artaxerxes III declare.[63] We call this an empire. At least two subject regions, Egypt and the Ionian coast, were perpetually restive and prone to rebel, but most of the remainder, from Anatolia and Judaea to Afghanistan, stayed within the realm of the Persian Achaemenid monarchs, even regions that were sometimes almost independent in practice. One result of the unprecedented power of the Persians was a degree of Persification, meaning acculturation to the Persians, and Persianization, meaning the acquisition of some manner of Persian speech. These two allied processes, which should be distinguished from each other, did not much affect the vast majority of the estimated 17 to 35 million regional subjects of the Achaemenids, but rather it mattered most to the elite ruling-class culture of the Achaemenids' delegates, friends, and family that the subjects supported and toward which many of them gradually assimilated.[64] Speaking Persian mattered near the top of the social pyramid. Fostering an interregional ruling-class culture with common values and expectations is itself a source of social power besides typical imperial strategies such as military conquest, direct rule, and rule through clients.[65]

---

[62] Briant 2002: 507–509.
[63] DEa 8–11, DNa 6–8, DSf 4–5, XEa11, XPa 4–6, XPb 8–11, XPc 4–5, XPd 11, XPf 6–8, XPh 5– 6, XVa 7–9, A³Pa 10: *aiwam parūnām xšāyaθiyam, aiwam parūnām framātāram*. The same expression occurs in D²Ha 8 and A²Hc 5–7, but Fattori (2022a) argues convincingly that these are twentieth-century forgeries.
[64] See Wiesehöfer 2009: 77 for the estimated population figures. Tavernier (2017: 341n22) cites other estimates ranging from 10 million to 75 million. In the article just cited, Wiesehöfer (2009: 87) states that there was no Persianization parallel to Romanization, then qualifies it, saying that there was indeed an interregional ruling-class culture fostered by Persian rule. I put emphasis on the latter part of this view.
[65] Mann 2012: 143, 158–161.

Some subjects found opportunities to strive upward socially toward the status of the Persians. Being Persian meant being identified with the ruling regime, but for this reason the ruling regime was not unchanging. It was gradually transformed as subjects actively assimilated themselves to Persian ways. There are always those who aspire to reach new levels of prestige, wealth, and power, and pursue them wherever they are located, opportunity allowing. Many people imitated the manners of the Persian elite – ways which thereafter became synonymous with the behavior of rich rulers, for whom the Persians became the generic model in every country they ruled. Likewise, the bureaucrats and servants of the Persians had to understand their commands. Quite a few of the same Old Persian expressions are found calqued in writing in Aramaic, Elamite, and Babylonian in the Achaemenian period, reflecting the common reception of Persian statements by literate members of these different language communities.[66] This unidirectional borrowing diagnoses a situation of unilateral bilingualism: Persians did not need the languages of others, but others needed to understand the Persians.

What did it mean in practice to be Persian or to do things as the Persians did? From the early fourth century BCE we have the explicit testimony of Xenophon, who briefly served a Persian satrap, closely observed Persian aristocrats, and traveled as a mercenary fighter within the Persian Empire. He describes the imitation of Persian rulers as a custom he believed to have been ordained by Cyrus, the renowned founder of the imperial dynasty.

> He (Cyrus) decreed to all the satraps sent forth (to the provinces) that they should imitate everything they saw him doing. First, they should establish horsemen and charioteers from among the Persians who accompanied them (to the provinces) and the (non-Persian) allies. Everybody who has received land and palaces must go to the court of his satrap, using discretion, and make themselves available for his employment if anything is required. Also, any boys they have should be educated at the court (of the satrap), just as at his (royal) court. Satraps should take those at their courts out hunting, to exercise themselves and those with them in martial pursuits.[67]

---

[66] On this phenomenon, see Tavernier 2017: 344–347, who rightly assumes that the Persian masters were largely monolingual.

[67] Xenophon, *Cyropaideia* 8.6.10. προεῖπε δὲ πᾶσι τοῖς ἐκπεμπομένοις σατράπαις, ὅσα αὐτὸν ἑώρων ποιοῦντα, πάντα μιμεῖσθαι· πρῶτον μὲν ἱππέας καθιστάναι ἐκ τῶν συνεπιστομένων Περσῶν καὶ συμμάχων καὶ ἁρματηλάτας· ὁπόσοι δ' ἂν γῆν καὶ ἀρχεῖα λάβωσιν, ἀναγκάζειν τούτους ἐπὶ θύρας ἰέναι καὶ σωφροσύνης ἐπιμελουμένους παρέχειν ἑαυτοὺς τῷ σατράπῃ χρῆσθαι, ἤν τι δέηται· παιδεύειν δὲ καὶ τοὺς γιγνομένους παῖδας ἐπὶ θύραις, ὥσπερ παρ' αὐτῷ· ἐξάγειν δ' ἐπὶ τὴν θήραν τὸν σατράπην τοὺς ἀπὸ θυρῶν καὶ ἀσκεῖν αὐτόν τε καὶ τοὺς σὺν αὐτῷ τὰ πολεμικά.

Whether his account of the origin of this custom with an edict of Cyrus is correct or not, it describes what was believed, and the practice Xenophon directly observed, in his own day. Each man who was participating in Persian rule seemed to be expected to *imitate* (μιμεῖσθαι) the Persian he served.[68] The locus of imitation was at courts, arranged in a hierarchy of power. Each satrap's court was to mirror the great king's court, and young men of landholding families were expected to be socialized in that environment of shared elite pursuits. Of course, speaking Persian was a basic criterion and requirement for participation. Without a common language, social interaction in any court setting would be extremely restricted. It is difficult to maintain a meaningful relationship solely through a translator. The emphasis on raising boys in this environment suggests that language learning was an implicit part of the education entailed; adults do not learn to speak languages as well as youngsters do. Xenophon did not need to state explicitly that imitating Persian satraps meant at least attempting to speak Persian. There are, nevertheless, clear testimonies in Greek and other sources to bilingualism with Persian and the learning of Persian by adult individuals, most famously by Themistocles of Athens (*circa* 529–455 BCE) in political exile. When he sought refuge with King Artaxerxes I, he asked for a year to learn "whatever he could" of the Persian language and was then admitted to the court. Of what use could he be if he could not communicate with those around him in the Persian setting? He lived out the rest of his life under Persian rule.[69] We can only imagine how many other individuals like Themistocles there were from lands ruled by the Persians or from their frontiers, who came to the court of the king of kings to continue a life in association with power. Assimilating to life among Persian masters must also have meant adopting Persian attire and traditions and participating in the customs that arose in the new political reality of Persian mastery. What such participation required, beyond imitation, learning to speak at least some Persian, ostentatious and obsequious service to Persian kings and lords, and receiving magnificent rewards in return, is not clear, because sources scarcely inform us about Persian culture before the Achaemenids. Certainly, as Xenophon wrote, for the men who wanted

---

[68] Not fortuitously, imitation and mimicry are key terms in postcolonial theory, too: e.g., Bhabha 1994: 85–92.
[69] Kuhrt (2007: 847–848) usefully collects many of these testimonies. The report about Themistocles is from Thucydides 1.138. "In the time that he had [the year of preparation], he apprehended whatever he could both of the Persian language and of the practices of the land" (ὁ δ' ἐν τῷ χρόνῳ ὃν ἐπέσχε τῆς τε Περσίδος γλώσσης ὅσα ἐδύνατο κατενόησε καὶ τῶν ἐπιτηδευμάτων τῆς χώρας). The words ὅσα ἐδύνατο indicate that he was not imagined to have become fluent as an adult learner.

to socialize with Persian elites, it entailed avid horsemanship and interest in the gear necessary for it[70] and martial prowess with spear and bow – skills practiced in frequent hunting. It also probably meant the conspicuous profession of certain moral ideals such as honesty and self-restraint,[71] although these were also values held in common with other ancient peoples. At least from the time of Darius I and Xerxes, it could perhaps entail support for the cult of Ahuramazdā and patronage of the magi, the priests presiding over that god's cult, something held in common with some other Arya peoples,[72] but it is also clear that the early Persian kings and their immediate followers supported the cults of other gods.[73]

More particularly, whatever the Persian rulers and elites adopted from their subjects became Persian in effect because it now belonged to them. It is not that there was ever a Persian essence, before or after the Achaemenids. New peoples and nations are always taking shape; old ones are always evolving. This applies to the Persians at the rise of the Achaemenids, too. Some historians of this period hold that the Persian people from whom Darius I emerged were themselves the product of a hybrid that took shape in the immediately preceding centuries of Arya settlement among Elamite-speakers. The degree and manner of their intermixture and cohabitation before Cyrus and afterwards is a subject of debate.[74] "Persian" came to be, in effect, the term that designated this specific "hybrid" as it developed. Recent scholarship strongly emphasizes the preexistence of Elamite language and culture in pre-Achaemenian Persis. Elamite was the first language of the Bisitun inscription of Darius I and a major language of the administration of Persepolis during his and his successor Xerxes' reign. The name Cyrus was an Elamite name, *Kuraš*,[75] and Cyrus was designated as king of Anshan, an Elamite highland region, in documents contemporary with him, an office he inherited.[76] The earliest Achaemenids are supposed to have worn Elamite formal attire, with a fringe of tassels, but the royal fashion changed to Median robes "after 538, but before work started on the Persepolis reliefs."[77] While some scholars, such as Henkelman, have envisioned a fairly seamless blend of Elamophones and Iranophones giving birth to a vigorous new ethnic group that created an empire, those who regard the Elamite and Persian cultures as distinct components in close contact have given reason to identify

---

[70] Moorey 1985: 22.   [71] Lincoln 2012: 335–353.
[72] Briant 2002: 245–254; Skjærvø 2013; de Jong 2015: 89–93.   [73] Henkelman 2008.
[74] De Miroschedji 1985; Rollinger 1999; Henkelman 2011; Tavernier 2017: 340, van Bladel 2021.
[75] *Pace* Schmitt 2014: 205. See Tavernier 2011: 211–212; also Waters 2011: 289–290 for further references.
[76] Kuhrt 2007: 50, 56, 71, 75.   [77] Sekunda 2010.

Darius I as a transition-figure from predominantly Elamophone rule to Arya Persian rule, a transition obscured by later history as the Elamite background was forgotten and Persian identity was projected back to prehistory. Cyrus, then, would not be a Persian in the sense connoted at a later time, but rather he would come from an Elamite-speaking background, rising to power in service of the Medes.[78]

Less controversially, several textual signs point toward linguistic effects when Elamite-speakers started to learn Old Persian even before the time of Cyrus. Tavernier's detailed study of Iranic names in pre-Achaemenian Elamite administrative texts dating *circa* 590–555 BCE shows that some of the phonological changes later characteristic of Middle Iranic were taking place, at least in one subregion, already a few decades before the Bisitun inscription.[79] These include monophthongization of diphthongs (e.g., *ai* > *ē*),[80] contraction of vowels separated by evanescent consonants (e.g., *iya* > *ī*, *ahya* > *ē*), and loss of final vowels or short unstressed vowels between two syllables. This may be due to "more developed" "Elamite-Iranian acculturation" in the locale from which many of these texts come.[81] The omission of final vowels on a small number of Persian proper names in Elamite texts from the decades before Cyrus suggests that this phenomenon is due to nonnative use. We should expect to see more changes in Old Persian where more individuals learned it as adults as a second language.[82]

The goal here, however, is not to resolve a debate about the ethnic makeup of the Persians at the beginning of the Achaemenid dynasty. The main point is that this was always changing and that there is no such thing as a pure and unchanging ethnicity. Whatever the reality, and however Elamites and Persians had intermixed, in the time of Darius I the outcome was still local and regional. Pārsa was a specific region. The drastic change came with the conquests of Cyrus and Cambyses and the consolidation of

---

[78] Potts 2005; Waters 2004 and 2011.   [79] Tavernier 2011: 239–240.
[80] The cuneiform script may, however, have used the sign transcribed as *i* to indicate *ē* < **ai* already in the earliest Old Persian texts. Strictly speaking, the script is ambiguous. Philologists have assumed the presence of a diphthong merely on etymological grounds.
[81] Tavernier 2011: 243. It may also be that modern philologists have always interpreted the system of the Old Persian cuneiform from the start in a way too archaizing or etymological. There is little to prevent us from interpreting many of the etymological diphthongs in the Bisitun inscription as actual monophthongs. The same process took place in its cousin Sanskrit at some time.
[82] Henkelman has argued for the reverse scenario for Achaemenian Elamite, which exhibits many words adopted from Old Persian and transfers of Persian grammatical features. He regards the changes in Achaemenian Elamite as the result of its acquisition by Iranophones (Henkelman 2011, taking up an argument in the terms articulated briefly by Yakubovich 2008), whereas van Bladel (2021) has made a contrary interpretation, arguing that Elamite speakers adopted Old Persian words and syntagms in a social setting of unilateral bilingualism, in which Persian-speakers seldom learned Elamite but Elamite-speakers needed to learn Persian.

Darius and Xerxes. Then Persian people mastered millions of other people. They became a ruling minority. As his tomb inscription shows, Darius I proudly wanted those after him to know that, although the Persian man was formerly a merely local figure, now he ruled every other nation. Darius declares that when you look at the rock relief of his tomb, where one figure for each of his many distant subject nations is depicted physically supporting his lone royal figure, "then you will recognize, then it will be known to you: the spear of a Persian man went forth far; it will be known to you: a Persian man fought the foe far from Pārsa," *adā xšnāsāhi ada-tai azdā bawāti Pārsahyā martiyahyā dūrai ərštiš parāgmatā ada-tai azdā bawāti Pārsa martiya dūrai hacā Pārsā parataram patiyajatā*.[83] This seems to indicate how hitherto unexpected it was for a Persian, as somebody from a formerly minor nation, to have achieved such extraordinary power. (It also makes Darius appear to be the first truly Persian king.)[84] Representative figures of every other nation are depicted in relief on the rock face of his tomb, elevating the Persian king and contributing to a new royal foundation. But as representatives of the people of one region had become practically universal rulers, they were exposed now to innumerable close contacts with people of other cultures. This had great consequences for the evolution of the Persian language far more than for the languages of the subject peoples.

Several kinds of testimonies indicate the subsequent mixture of the Persians with their subjects, creating circumstances in which many adults had to learn to speak Persian. I turn now to review them. They provide strong primary-source contextual support, beyond the preceding section, for the case that Old Persian became a target of mass acquisition by adult learners, and that the Achaemenian period witnessed the most sweeping changes in the language, giving rise to Middle Persian.

Fighters and Laborers for the Persians

The inscriptions of Darius I and Xerxes I attest to their rule over lands "of people of many kinds," *paruzana-*, or "of all kinds," *wispazana-*.[85] The Akkadian equivalent of this expression, where Akkadian versions survive, says lands "of people of all tongues."[86] At the palatial complex of

---

[83] DNa43–47 (Schmitt 2009: 103).
[84] Cf. Brosius 2021: 63: "Darius I was also the first king to identify himself by his ethnicity as Persian."
[85] These terms, both "Medisms," appear in many inscriptions of Darius I and Xerxes (s.v. in Schmitt 2014: 105 and 116).
[86] *šar ša mātāti naphar lišān(āt)i gabbi* (Weissbach 1911: 87 § 2; 103 §2; 119 § 2). Cf. Panaino 2015: 91.

Persepolis, Xerxes ordered the construction of a portal named in the accompanying trilingual inscription as "the Gate of All Lands," Old Persian *duwarθi- wisadahyu-*. In the early fourth century BCE, Xenophon wrote that Cyrus had "made so many peoples dependent on himself that it was quite a task to traverse them."[87] For the first time, all of these different peoples with different languages now served a common master in circumstances of compulsory cooperation.[88] Members of all these peoples now found themselves face to face at royal sites in large labor crews and marshalled together in massive polyethnic fighting forces.

It is almost needless to say that the military adventures, army camps and marches, and pageants of the Achaemenids and their Persian delegates must have created circumstances in which many individuals from different countries, who spoke different languages, had to learn some Persian as adults. Even if this involved merely individual officers representing the military contingent from one subject country each, the mustering of forces on behalf of the Persian king must have entailed language learning by scores of individuals, if not many more, from different speech communities who now had one thing in common above all: their shared service to the Persians. Such individuals would usually not have been native speakers of Persian, as they came from different countries, and they would themselves then have been a major conduit for information about Persian speech to their followers and companions. Herodotus' famous description goes to great lengths to convey the dazzlingly polyethnic character alleged of the army of Xerxes.[89] Though the numerical scale is not to be believed, the heterogeneous character of the Persian kings' forces cannot be doubted. The contingents of Ethiopians, Thracians, Libyans, Phrygians, Egyptians, Caspians, Indians, Assyrians, Bactrians, Greeks, Arabs, Lydians, and many other groups would each have required at least one interpreter capable of comprehending enough Persian speech to cooperate with the rest. It would have been pointless, let alone impossible, for any of them to learn all the languages of the others. The Persian rulers did need translators, as Cyrus the Younger needed one to communicate with his Greek mercenaries, whereas a Greek officer in his employ, the commander Clearchus,

---

[87] Xenophon, *Cyropaedeia* 1.1.5: ἀνηρτήσατο δὲ τοσαῦτα φῦλα ὅσα καὶ διελθεῖν ἔργον ἐστίν, ὅποι ἂν ἄρξηταί τις πορεύεσθαι ἀπὸ τῶν βασιλείων, ἤν τε πρὸς ἕω ἤν τε πρὸς ἑσπέραν ἤν τε πρὸς ἄρκτον ἤν τε πρὸς μεσημβρίαν.

[88] I borrow the expression "compulsory cooperation" from Michael Mann (2012: 56 and 130–178), who borrowed it in turn from Herbert Spencer.

[89] See Kuhrt 2007: 519–529.

appears to have understood Persian.⁹⁰ For anybody who wanted access to the aristocratic and higher military domains of power, the target of acquisition must have been the Persian language – or rather, an adequate, functional, basic, minimally ornate form of Persian that an adult might learn without modern textbooks and teachers trained in today's communicative methods.

Military organization and the congregation of elite boys at Persian courts thus probably provided one conduit for Persianization, but craftsmen, traders, and many lowly laborers surely participated in their own way, too.⁹¹ The clearest direct Old Persian testimony about the sudden intermixture of people of different tongues occurs in one of the major inscriptions of Darius I at Susa.⁹² This inscription has long served modern historians as an illustration of the cultural workings of early Persian imperialism. It was issued in Babylonian, Elamite, and Old Persian, and survives in different copies at the site of Darius' palace at Susa, city of Elam, the region known in the first millennium CE as Khuzistan. Designated DSf today, the inscription commemorates the construction of the palace there, which must have been gorgeous but is now a bare ruin. One portion describes the ethnic varieties of personnel involved in this undertaking:⁹³

> §8 That the earth was dug downwards and the rubble was poured in and the bricks were molded – the Babylonian people did it.
>
> §9 The cedarwood was brought from a mountain called Lebanon; the Assyrian people brought it as far as Babylon; from Babylon, the Carians and Ionians brought it as far as Susa; the *yaka*-wood was brought from Gandara and Carmania.
>
> §10 The gold which was worked here was brought from Lydia and Bactria; the lapis lazuli and the carnelian which was worked here was brought from Sogdiana; the turquoise which was worked here was brought from Chorasmia.
>
> §11 The silver and the ebony were brought from Egypt; the adornment, with which the walls were ornamented, was brought from Ionia; the ivory which was worked here was brought from Nubia, India and Arachosia.

---

[90] Even the classical scholar E. S. Gehman, who was cautious about Greek–Persian bilingualism, concedes that "we seem obliged to assume that the Greek general Clearchus knew some Persian, at least the Persian of the army" (1914: 10).

[91] See King 2025: 161–169 on the widespread movement of laborers in the Achaemenian Empire. He goes so far as to argue (161) that "The infrastructure of the Achaemenid Empire was, to a large extent, designed to transport groups of dependent laborers to wherever they might be needed."

[92] Inscription DSf; see Schmitt 2009: 127–134. English translation in Kuhrt 2007: 492–495. Cf. also the Elamite and Akkadian texts from Susa, DSz and DSaa (translated by Kuhrt 2007: 495–497).

[93] Translation adapted from that of Kuhrt (2007: 492). Cf. the discussion by King (2025: 167–168).

§12 The stone columns which were worked here were brought from a village called Abiradu in Elam; the masons who crafted the stone were Ionians and Sardians.

§13 The goldsmiths who worked the gold were Medes and Egyptians; the men who worked the wood were Sardians and Egyptians; the men who crafted the bricks were Babylonians; the men who decorated the wall were Medes and Egyptians.

§14 King Darius proclaims: At Susa much that was excellent was commanded, much that was excellent was done. May Ahuramazdā protect me, my father Hystaspes, and my country.

Darius boasts about his palace that it was constructed using rare and costly commodities derived from all parts of his domain: cedar from Lebanon, timber from Gandara (eastern Afghanistan), gold from Lydia (western Turkey) and Bactria (northern Afghanistan), silver and ebony from Egypt, ivory from Kush (northeastern Africa) and India, stone from local quarries, and more.[94] More important for the present argument are Darius' specific statements about the labor force employed in the construction. Assyrians, Babylonians, Carians, Greeks, Medes, Egyptians, Lydians, Hūžes (known today as Elamites) – representatives from many of the nations ruled by Darius – participated in the building project and its adornment. Most of the workers drafted for this purpose will not have used the languages of the others in their collaboration. The one language that would provide the most advantages to all these workers from abroad, who resided together at least for a time at Susa, was Persian, the language of their masters and employers.

The same goes for construction and work at Persepolis. The thousands of Elamite administrative tablets discovered at Persepolis, surviving portions of archives with dates ranging from 509 to 457 BCE, have provided material for a large batch of scholarly articles and books specifically on non-Persians at Persepolis. Judging by their names, at Persepolis there were Babylonians, Cappadocians, Carians, Carmanians, Gandharans, Indians, Lydians, and others.[95] Besides texts in Elamite, the site has provided plentiful short examples of Aramaic writing and individual examples of Greek and Phrygian texts. Other royal bases of operation must have been like Susa and Persepolis, sites of highly heterogeneous populations of immigrant workers serving Persian overlords, generating a new mixed culture. We should expect that the diverse assortment of laborers from different far-off countries would produce an intercommunal language modeled on that of the masters, just as a common Melanesian Pidgin

---

[94] Cf. Esther 1:6. [95] Azzoni, Dusinberre, Garrison, Henkelman, Jones, and Stolper 2017.

English, discussed in the previous chapter, was created by laborers from distant islands and villages in the South Pacific, from New Guinea to Samoa, and just as South and Southeast Asian laborers, of various origins, working today in countries of the Arabian Peninsula have created a new pidgin, called Gulf Pidgin Arabic, based on the Arabic of their employers, a pidgin in formation even now.[96]

Darius' inscription about his palatial construction at Susa is intended to convey the vast extent of Darius' power, but it also indirectly documents an important event in the history of the Persian language.[97] Under the circumstances described, many non-Persian adults will have learned the Old Persian language with limited morphology and native speakers of Persian will have needed to simplify their speech to communicate with many nonnative speakers. At Persepolis, moreover, newly arrived laborers from abroad will have depended on Persian-speakers in their immediate environment for their immediate needs, for they were in Persia proper and so surrounded by local Persian native speakers, but they will not have mastered Persian as native speakers do. Some of them must have stayed in Persia proper and exposed young people with whom they interacted to a nonnative variety of Persian. Perhaps some of them returned to their home countries, where they would be able to serve as representatives of their locality to Persian authorities, because of their experience with Persians. Nonnative learners of Persian who returned home from Persia proper would bring with them their adult-learner, morphologically reduced variety of the language, likely a somewhat restructured nonnative variety acquired during a finite period among the Persians of Pārsa. In this they would resemble the local constables of British Papua who brought Pidgin Motu with them on their return to their villages upon their retirement from government service, where they shared it with young people to groom and prepare them for interaction with the new interregional power and for access to goods and opportunities available outside their own locale.

Alternatives to the hypothesis that the newcomers to Persian royal sites would have learned Persian badly, or even a pidgin variety of Persian, are unlikely. It is not as if the laborers imported to Persepolis and Susa from many different countries were given formal night-classes in Old Persian with instructors trained in modern methods. It is not as if they could all resort to pantomime and would not bother to attempt basic verbal communication, either. It must have been vital for many of the workers to make themselves understood to their Persian-speaking masters. The facts

---

[96] Avram 2014 and 2016; Bizri 2018.   [97] Cf. McWhorter 2007: 156–157.

of human language acquisition, seldom considered by ancient historians, practically require the view proposed here. The inscription of Darius at Susa and the Persepolis administrative archives testify to only two major examples of situations in which non-Persians would have needed to acquire a working, basic ability with Old Persian. There must have been innumerable other such sites like this that have remained undocumented by written sources.[98] Everywhere that Persian rulers and their immediate followers dealt with subjects of different nations, some of those subjects would have required Persian language as the medium of intercommunication. Most of them in the first generation or two will have done so as adults. Thereafter they will often have learned it from fellow countrymen who themselves had learned it as adults.

The large-scale migration of soldiers and workers in imperial labor markets has been a major factor in the genesis of pidgins, creoles, and semicreoles of modern languages. The Persian Empire, a state formed by conquest on a scale unmatched at that time, could not have been an exception to these ordinary and regular social processes. On the contrary, the Persian Empire seems exemplary of this process in ancient history, as illustrated by the evolution of Persian in the inscriptions of the Achaemenids. Achaemenian Persian inscriptions may provide the earliest clear example of morphological reduction through mass nonnative acquisition. The imperial context makes sense of this.

Domestic Personnel of the Persians

Important testimonies to the population mixture of Persians with others survive in the writings of their neighbors on their western frontier, the ancient Greeks. Not all Greek authors were overtly hostile in their accounts of the Persians. Many collaborated with them even in times of war, inspiring Greek accusations of "Medism" against collaborators. Yet even the hostility expressed by well-known ancient Greek authors shed light on what was special about Persian society as compared with that of Greek observers, as I will show.

Around 425 BCE, Herodotus wrote explicitly about the cultural mixture fostered by the Persian rulers.[99]

---

[98] Polybius' description of the royal residence at Hamadān (Ecbatana) provides an example of another such site (Kuhrt 2007: 501).

[99] Herodotus 1.135. ξεινικὰ δὲ νόμαια Πέρσαι προσίενται ἀνδρῶν μάλιστα. καὶ γὰρ δὴ τὴν Μηδικὴν ἐσθῆτα νομίσαντες τῆς ἑωυτῶν εἶναι καλλίω φορέουσι, καὶ ἐς τοὺς πολέμους τοὺς Αἰγυπτίους θώρηκας: καὶ εὐπαθείας τε παντοδαπὰς πυνθανόμενοι ἐπιτηδεύουσι, καὶ δὴ καὶ ἀπ' Ἑλλήνων

> The Persians, of all men, accept foreign customs the most. For they wear Median clothing, thinking it nicer than their own, and they wear Egyptian breastplates into battle. They pursue all kinds of comforts when they find out about them, and they even have sex with boys after they learned it from the Greeks. Each one of them marries many wedded wives, but they acquire still by far more concubines.

This is to say that the Persians selected what they regarded as best from every subject population, including many non-Persian women and boys. They adopted what was best in their view as their own and they made it Persian. Racial purity was evidently not an ancient Persian concept, although legitimacy of patrilineage and family affinity were all-important. Every male Persian aristocrat is evidently supposed to have begotten many children of mixed ancestry raised, often, by non-Persian mothers. Many female mates were brought to them from different home countries where different languages were spoken. Herodotus adds an observation critical for considerations of language acquisition: a Persian child "does not come into his father's sight before he turns five years old but lives with the women. They do this in order not to strike the father with grief if it should die young."[100] Strabo, centuries later, reports the same details, apparently on the basis of an earlier source of the Achaemenian period shared with Herodotus, and adds that Persian men were rewarded for having many babies.[101] "They marry many women, and they keep more concubines at the same time, in order to have many children. The kings set annual prizes for those who beget many, but the children are not brought into their parents' sight until they are four years old."[102] Other ancient Greek authors on the Persians, such as Dinon[103] and Heracleides[104] (both mid fourth century BCE), remark on the hundreds of concubines of the Persian kings. Herodotus elsewhere adds the detail that "the women sleep with the Persian men in rotation."[105]

μαθόντες παισὶ μίσγονται. γαμέουσι δὲ ἕκαστος αὐτῶν πολλὰς μὲν κουριδίας γυναῖκας, πολλῷ δ᾽ ἔτι πλεῦνας παλλακὰς κτῶνται.

[100] Herodotus 1.136.1. πρὶν δὲ ἢ πενταέτης γένηται, οὐκ ἀπικνέεται ἐς ὄψιν τῷ πατρί, ἀλλὰ παρὰ τῆσι γυναιξὶ δίαιταν ἔχει. τοῦδε δὲ εἵνεκα τοῦτο οὕτω ποιέεται, ἵνα ἢν ἀποθάνῃ τρεφόμενος, μηδεμίαν ἄσην τῷ πατρὶ προσβάλῃ.

[101] On Strabo's sources on the Persians (but not concerning this specific statement), see de Jong (1997: 127).

[102] Strabo 15.3.17. γαμοῦσι δὲ πολλὰς καὶ ἅμα παλλακὰς τρέφουσι πλείους πολυτεκνίας χάριν. τιθέασι δὲ καὶ οἱ βασιλεῖς ἆθλα πολυτεκνίας κατ᾽ ἔτος. τὰ δὲ τρεφόμενα μέχρι ἐτῶν τεττάρων οὐκ ἄγεται τοῖς γονεῦσιν εἰς ὄψιν. Cf. the verbal parallels with Herodotus 1.135: γαμέουσι δὲ ἕκαστος αὐτῶν πολλὰς μὲν κουριδίας γυναῖκας, πολλῷ δ᾽ ἔτι πλεῦνας παλλακὰς κτῶνται.

[103] Almagor 2018a (F 27 = Athenaeus).   [104] Almagor 2018b (F 1 = Athenaeus, 12.8 p. 514 BC).

[105] Herodotus 3.69.6. ἐν περιτροπῇ γὰρ δὴ αἱ γυναῖκες φοιτέουσι τοῖσι Πέρσῃσι.

Many, perhaps most, of these numerous concubines – women enslaved for sexual companionship, a practice that was normal in many societies including the one under discussion – were imported from non-Persian-speaking societies into wealthy Persian households as young women who had entered sexual maturity and likewise had passed the early age of sensitivity to fluent language acquisition, as adolescents or adults. The wives, who may have been mostly Persian by birth, were outnumbered,[106] and like the European wives of Dutch colonists at Capetown in the seventeenth and eighteenth centuries discussed in the previous chapter, Persian women would have been at the center of domestic language contact, surrounded by speakers of other languages, adult learners of Persian, and widespread linguistic variation.[107] One thinks also of the portrayal of concubines in the fictional Hebrew Book of Esther, set in the empire of the Achaemenids, in which numerous selected good-looking girls from various countries, like the book's Judaean heroine Esther, were carefully prepared at the city of Susa for their roles as royal mates. M. Brosius, the author of the only monograph on women in the Achaemenian Empire, concludes on this matter, "To have concubines

---

[106] Lenfant (2020: 23) writes about the Greek perspective of the Achaemenian period that it was not concubinage itself that awed the Greeks but rather the sheer numbers of concubines held by Persian royals. Elsewhere Lenfant (2019) expresses skepticism about the extent of Persian royal polygamy (as opposed to concubinage). Of the Persian kings themselves, she writes, "All in all, the Persians who are pictured by Greeks as having several wives at the same time are five – which is not very many." But out of the twelve kings she counts, we can exclude very short reigns as unlikely to provide evidence of royal polygamy. Cambyses' short-lived disputed successor, the "false Smerdis," and the brief reign of Arses (338–336) are unlikely to have provided data. Put differently, then, Greek sources attest positively to polygamy (and not just concubinage) for half of the remaining ten Persian kings. The reigns of kings for whom polygamy is positively attested amount to 131 years of the 220 Achaemenian years from 550 BCE to the death of Darius III in 330. That is, Achaemenian Persian kings were reportedly polygamists just as often as not. If we assume that our sources, being far from comprehensive, sometimes do not provide attestations to multiple wives when they were there, then probably the majority of the kings were polygamous. In short, the polygamy of the Persians is not an ancient Greek exaggeration. This is especially so when sources from the same region in subsequent periods specifically remark on Parthian and Persian polygamy as a well-known custom. In the second-century-CE epitome of the first-century-BCE history of Pompeius Trogus, we are told that the Parthians "individually have many wives to enjoy a changeable desire, and they punish no offense more seriously than adultery. For this reason, they forbid the women not only to socialize with men, but also their even looking at them," *uxores dulcedine variae libidinis singuli plures habent, nec ulla delicta adulterio gravius vindicant, quamobrem feminis non convivia tantum virorum, verum etiam conspectum interdicunt*. In the fourth century CE, Ammianus remarks that the men of the Persian Kingdom may take multiple wives, according to their means (23.76): *pro opibus quisque adsciscens matrimonia plura vel pauca*. The seventh-century Armenian history attributed to Sebēos states of Xusrō II (regn. 590–628) that "he had many wives in accordance with the tradition of their magism, but he had Christian wives, too," *ēin sora kanaykʿ bazowm ǝst awrini mogowtʿean iwreancʿ baycʿ aṙ sa ew kanays kʿristoneays* (Sebēos 1979: 85, trans. Thomson 1999: 29).

[107] Raidt 1993.

was not the privilege of the king alone. By all accounts they were to be found in the palaces of the satraps and Persian nobles. The presence of concubines therefore must be seen as a characteristic of Persian society."[108] Foreign concubines and maidservants necessarily came late to the acquisition of Persian speech, as nonnative speakers. If the reports of Greek authors are correct, some Persian kings were routinely accompanied by dozens of pretty foreign girls of this kind. These attractive young women not only contributed to the ostentatious display of social power by a small number of men who increasingly owed their high rank to mere patrilineage rather than to force of arms, but they also bore the babies of the Persian men who acquired them. The children of Persian men will therefore have had many nonnative speakers as their first models for Persian language acquisition. If the report shared by Herodotus and Strabo is true, then concubines, wet-nurses, nannies, and eunuchs, all of various origins and language backgrounds, were caring for the children of the Persian men in women's quarters along with what was probably a minority of Persians who spoke Persian natively.[109] Nonnative speakers of Persian must have predominated numerically in many Persian homes, and they were also more responsible for early childcare.[110]

As mentioned, eunuchs must have played a role in this, too.[111] They were gatekeepers and attendants of night quarters[112] and companions and

---

[108] Brosius 1996: 191.
[109] Some years after writing this sentence, I read Beeta Baghoolizadeh's similar description of more recent use of enslaved people in Iran (2024: 2): "During the nineteenth century, elite and wealthy Iranians enslaved people in their domestic spaces as nannies, wet nurses, eunuchs, cooks, and other jobs critical to the maintenance of a healthy household that are often socially undervalued.... these individuals were seen as critical for the preservation of the family and the royal court. They were generally symbols of power and status, not economic slaves, despite some examples of chattel slavery." Suffice it to say that nineteenth-century practices like these have a millennia-long history in the region of Iran, older even than the Achaemenian Empire. That history easily eludes discussion by those concerned with modernity. The "erasure of enslavement," to use Baghoolizadeh's expression, works differently in discussions of ancient empires.
[110] Versteegh 2013: 70: "In patrilocal communities, the wife coming from outside affects her children's speech to a much larger degree than the incoming husband in a matrilocal system, because in most societies, whether matrilocal or patrilocal, the mother is the one responsible for the primary socialisation of the children."
[111] See the fresh discussion of Lenfant (2021), based on a review of primary sources, who shows that eunuchs were not solely guardians of women's quarters, as has commonly been assumed.
[112] Llewellyn-Jones' plea (2013: 97–102) to continue using the word "harem" for the quarters of the aristocratic women of the Persians should be declined, not because of the "Orientalist clichés" that he hopes to sidestep, but because it is misleading in blurring distinctions between the historical ḥarīm or dār al-ḥuram (not "the Arabic ha'ram," a word seemingly invented here) and the much less well-known ancient Persian private quarters of women. There surely were similarities between the harems of Muslim caliphs and the quarters of the women of Persian king, but to speak of an enduring Near Eastern "ideology of the harem" is a misapplication of terms and wipes away relevant

servitors of kings and lords.¹¹³ Enslaved eunuchs were given as the payment of tribute to the Persian kings. Herodotus mentions an annual tribute of five hundred boys from Babylon as well as boys from Ethiopia and Colchis; he also mentions the punishment of Ionian rebels through the castration and enslavement of the best-looking boys (τοὺς εὐειδεστάτους).¹¹⁴ If the Babylonian tribute just mentioned had lasted just as described even for twenty years, that would populate Persian sites with 10,000 castrated young speakers of Aramaic, possibly as well as Akkadian, who had to learn some Persian speech to adapt. The Platonic *First Alcibiades* informs us that expensive eunuchs of good character, and not female "nurses of little value," raised the king's own eldest heir and groomed him, but eunuchs, too, were probably mostly non-Persian by origin, and often must have been nonnative speakers of Persian.¹¹⁵ One expects that more ordinary Persian household lords would have had female nurses and the mothers of the babies themselves to care for their children. In any case, Persian boys from powerful families reportedly would not have had much interaction with their Persian-speaking fathers during the initial period of language acquisition, their first four or five years according to the Greek sources just mentioned. We must not believe that this alleged five-year rule was strictly observed at all times just as described. Rather it was a noticeable

differences and innovations, such as the role of Islamic law in the Islamic context. As El Cheikh remarks (2010: 87), "The harem cannot be understood apart from its historical specificity." See also El Cheikh 2018 and the convincing arguments of Lenfant 2020. Llewellyn-Jones is right, strictly speaking, that the Old Persian name for ancient Persian women's private quarters does not survive directly, but the Old Iranic word has long been known to have been *xšapastāna-, "night quarters" (Henning 1958: 45n3; it is not "hard to substantiate," as Llewellyn-Jones [2013: 98] holds), on the basis of later Middle Persian <špstn>, <špst'n'>, and New Persian *šabestān*. The term for the eunuchs working in these quarters was derived from *xšapastān* by the ancient Indo-Iranic adjective formation with *vṛddhi*-grade vowel applied to the first syllable (Kent 1950: 44–45 §126; Maricq 1958: 330n5 on this very word), evident in Middle Persian <š'pstn>, *šābistān*. Henning (1964: 95–96n1) claims that *vṛddhi*-adjectives of this kind were productive in Middle Iranic, but there is no evidence for this in Middle Persian. Compare also the later borrowings from Middle Persian: Bactrian þαβαστανο, þαβιστανο (Sims-Williams 2007: 283a), earlier Armenian *šapstan takaṙapet*, "eunuch cup-bearer" (in *P'awstos*; see Garsoïan 1989: 556). As this method of noun derivation did not exist in Middle Persian, we can be confident that the early Old Persian term for the eunuchs of the private quarters was *xšāpastāna-, and that this was derived from *xšapastāna-, an ancient Iranic term for such quarters. For some real Sasanian instances of the eunuch called *šābistān*, see Shaked 1975: 223–225, Huyse 1999: 2.176, and Gyselen 2001: 27–28; see also Harmatta-Pékáry 1971: 471 for an early attestation of the word in Middle Persian.

¹¹³ Lenfant 2012; Waters 2017: 20–44; de Araujo 2024.
¹¹⁴ Herodotus 3.92, 3.97, 6.9, 6.32. See also Dandamaev 1998, Kuhrt 2007: 588–592, and Llewellyn-Jones 2013: 38–40.
¹¹⁵ *First Alcibiades* 121d: "Then the child [*scil.* the royal heir, ὁ παῖς ὁ πρεσβύτατος οὕπερ ἡ ἀρχή] is raised not by a nurse of little value, but by the eunuchs around the king who appear to be the most excellent"; μετὰ τοῦτο τρέφεται ὁ παῖς, οὐχ ὑπὸ γυναικὸς τροφοῦ ὀλίγου ἀξίας, ἀλλ' ὑπ' εὐνούχων οἳ ἂν δοκῶσιν τῶν περὶ βασιλέα ἄριστοι εἶναι.

cultural difference from the Greek point of view, remarked upon because Persian fathers tended to have so many children that they could not know them all well. The point is again that nonnative speakers played an outsized role in providing linguistic models of a variety of Persian that the children of Persian fathers would learn.[116] The large place of non-Persian domestics in the household inevitably must have had major effects on the language of each new generation of Persian elite youth. Such Persian boys would be fluent from childhood in nonnative varieties of Persian, with reduced morphology, learned from the women and eunuchs who nurtured them, from servants who supplied their needs and cleaned up after them, and from laborers who built and repaired their domiciles.

Plato clarifies these matters. Hardly any more explicit testimony could be wanted for the mixture of population and culture taking place in the homes of Persian lords, and the role of foreign women and eunuchs in that mixture, than that provided by Plato in the third scroll of his dialogic treatise *Laws*. He wrote it *circa* 357–347,[117] during the reign of Artaxerxes III. This is the very Persian king for whom the latest extant Old Persian inscription was carved, exhibiting Old Persian grammar at its most divergent from that of Darius I and at the attested point of greatest development toward Middle Persian. At just that time, Plato characterizes the nations (γένη) ruled by the Persians, which "are settled, now spread around and jumbled together," as ethnically mixed (μεμειγμένα) and thus "ill-begotten" (κακῶς ἐσπαρμένα).[118] The crass expression "ill-begotten" here is literally "ill-seeded," referring to the father's seed in the combination of parents of different ethnic origins. Plato is proud that Athenian

---

[116] It is reasonable to suppose that such children could easily make up for the lack of native-speaker input after the age of five through interaction with older Persian males (Ringe and Eska 2013: 39). Why should a delay in early childhood have posed a problem? Myers-Scotton (2006: 323–339) summarizes research showing that the decline of ability to learn a second language can set on as early as seven to nine years of age. Ringe and Eska (2013: 34) write that "Children invariably acquire the inflectional system(s) of their native language(s) by about the age of 5." Any widespread yearslong delay in the acquisition of complex Persian morphology by Persian children would predictably have some general linguistic effect over a few generations. This must have been reinforced when Persians who grew up in such early childhood conditions were subsequently surrounded by nonnative speakers of Persian from adolescence to the end of life, not to mention peers also constantly exposed to simplified Persian usage.

[117] It is generally agreed that the *Laws* was one of Plato's latest works, if not the latest (Kahn 2002: 95). Plato died in 348/347 BCE. Aristotle calls it a work written by Plato "later" (ὕστερον) (*Politics*).

[118] Plato, *Laws* 3, 692e–693a. ἀλλ' εἰ μὴ τό τε Ἀθηναίων καὶ τὸ Λακεδαιμονίων κοινῇ διανόημα ἤμυνεν τὴν ἐπιοῦσαν δουλείαν, σχεδὸν ἂν ἤδη πάντ' ἦν μεμειγμένα τὰ τῶν Ἑλλήνων γένη ἐν ἀλλήλοις, καὶ βάρβαρα ἐν Ἕλλησι καὶ Ἑλληνικὰ ἐν βαρβάροις, καθάπερ ὧν Πέρσαι τυραννοῦσί τε νῦν διαπεφορημένα καὶ συμπεφορημένα κακῶς ἐσπαρμένα κατοικεῖται. Tuplin (2018: 594–595), who made a thorough study of all of Plato's references to the Persians, regards this remark as unusual and atypical. It therefore deserves this close attention.

and Spartan defenses against the Persians had kept the Greeks pure of such mixing in previous generations, so that the Greeks remained a distinct people. This, at any rate, is Plato's ideal, also expressed in the Platonic speech called *Menexenus*.[119] In his view, the Persians in his day presided over a people now blended into something new, indicating that their former national distinctions were to an extent lost. For Plato, the blending of peoples had consequences for the Persian rulers themselves: it corresponded with a dilution of Persian manliness. The Persian kings lost their original Persian virtue, he went on to say, when they were raised in comfort by women and eunuchs. Plato's main purpose in this passage was not to discuss the Persians, but to discuss the proper education of the young. He condemned royal luxury as a source of corruption in the Persian princes' upbringing. This is an example of the ancient Greek antipathy toward the Persians that influenced modern historiography, a tendency that predominated as long as classically trained historians relied almost entirely on Greek perspectives. But Plato's words, suited for modern nationalism, too, were not merely expressing anti-Persian sentiment without an argument. Plato could have chosen traits to criticize besides their jumbled ethnic mixture. For example, he could have followed the diatribe at the end of his acquaintance Xenophon's *Cyropaedeia*, a work he knew,[120] against the latter-day Persians, and found fault with them for such unmanly luxuries as wearing gloves in winter, using carpets on the floor, or sitting too long at meals, or for their perceived cowardice in combat or the mismanagement of charioteers, or some other particular.[121] Plato rather deemed virtue to have been lost by the Persian dynasty through the effect of women and eunuchs who raised the royal boys in childhood. As this passage follows immediately his observation that the Persian subjects are an ethnically mixed nation, it is evident that here, too, Plato was thinking of mixing. For he must have known the obvious fact that Persian concubines, nurses, and slaves were drawn from different subject nations. Plato judged the outcome to be degeneration and corruption of character, whereas the Greeks, he held, avoided such corruption by holding off foreign rule and consequent intermixture of Greek with foreigner. We will dismiss the negativity of

---

[119] *Menexenus* 245d: "But we reside as real Greeks who have not been mixed with foreigners," ἀλλ' αὐτοὶ Ἕλληνες οὐ μειξοβάρβαροι οἰκοῦμεν.
[120] Hirsch 1985: 97–100.
[121] Xenophon, *Cyropaedeia* 8.8. Some classical scholars have doubted authenticity of this passage, which is the conclusion of Xenophon's work. Others accept it, as I do, too, as an integral part of this treatise on strategy and leadership. See Due 1989: 16–25; Gera 1993: 299–300; Sancisi-Weerdenburg 1993.

Plato's evaluation as merely a matter of his personal judgment, but we should not regard his observation about the mixture of the subject nations of the Persians as creative invention, especially as he presented it in the manner of a fact that his contemporary reader is expected to know already. For Plato's critical evaluation to be meaningful, it had to be founded on a generally accepted observation about Persian society. It is this mixing that necessitated large-scale adult acquisition of the Persian language. More than army camps and teams of ethnically mixed laborers, foreign women and eunuchs in Persian homes must have played a large role in generating a drastically reduced form of the language, ultimately the beginnings of Middle Persian. If an adult learners' form of Persian had remained restricted to the barracks of warriors and builders, Persian boys would not likely have acquired it as their own, except when involved in war. It is the domestics who must have played the biggest role.

Historians Amélie Kuhrt and Josef Wiesehöfer, knowing sources like these, both emphasize that local elites intermarried with Persian royals and that Persian royals took many provincial concubines.[122] Herodotus records a case in which a Greek man married a Persian woman, and their children were regarded as Persian.[123] Modern historians wonder about the "identity" of such people, but events like these necessarily have more salient linguistic effects. The Persian kingdom promoted the integration of local elites in a common ruling-class culture. Being allowed to join the Persians and to sit with them was regarded as an honor. Although in the time of Darius I being Persian seems to have become a special and exclusive privilege, it was possible to join the ranks of the Persians, and especially to have one's sons raised as Persian, through imitation of and socializing with Persian aristocrats. That was one function of the "king's gate," a term usually rendered as "the court" today.[124] The most promising young men from local elites, many of whom

---

[122] Kuhrt 1995: 2.696–697; Wiesehöfer 2009: 89.
[123] Herodotus 6.41. Briant (2002: 350) has to regard this as "extremely rare" to maintain his concept of the dominant ethno-class of Persians, discussed later in this chapter.
[124] Xenophon (*Cyropaedia* 8.5–6) credits this custom to the dynasty's founder, Cyrus. "'Therefore, let us remain by these headquarters here, as Cyrus bids, and let us train ourselves through those things which we will most be able to hold fast as we should, and let us offer ourselves for Cyrus to use however he should require.' ... It seemed best that those of high rank should always remain at the gates and make themselves available to be employed for whatever is wanted until Cyrus should send them away. As they agreed then, so also those throughout Asia who are under the king still do now. They attend to the gates of the rulers." παρῶμέν τε οὖν, ὥσπερ Κῦρος κελεύει, ἐπὶ τόδε τὸ ἀρχεῖον, ἀσκῶμέν τε δι' ὧν μάλιστα δυνησόμεθα κατέχειν ἃ δεῖ, παρέχωμέν τε ἡμᾶς αὐτοὺς χρῆσθαι Κύρῳ ὅ τι ἂν δέῃ. ... καὶ ἔδοξε τοὺς ἐντίμους ἀεὶ παρεῖναι ἐπὶ θύραις καὶ παρέχειν αὑτοὺς χρῆσθαι ὅ τι ἂν βούληται, ἕως ἀφείη Κῦρος. ὡς δὲ τότε ἔδοξεν, οὕτω καὶ νῦν ἔτι ποιοῦσιν οἱ κατὰ τὴν Ἀσίαν ὑπὸ βασιλεῖ ὄντες, θεραπεύουσι τὰς τῶν ἀρχόντων θύρας.

will not have spoken Persian at home, were sent to attend at the "king's gate," where they vied for royal favor through assiduous service to the king. Here, too, was another site in which a common variety of Persian speech would have been shared by men of different origin interacting with servile non-Persians. The royal family and its privileged Persian and Iranic-language speaking counterparts such as Medes, in and around their own homes, must have been outnumbered, perhaps drastically, by servants, workers, concubines, and others who came from other language communities. Persians purchased, imported, attracted, and accommodated outsiders and the result was a hybrid that soon became the elite standard.

The rapid grammatical transformation of the Old Persian language indicates that the successful practice of populating elite Persian households with foreign domestics and sexual mates who raised Persian children contributed to a transformation of the Persians themselves. Persians actively drew into their midst visitors, followers, and household members from every land, many of whom became permanent attendants, courtiers, and even close relatives. It was simply expected that Persian leaders would promiscuously enjoy the company of the most pleasing of the conquered peoples. They chose slaves, brides, and concubines for themselves (not to mention boys) in numbers quite surprising by today's most widespread standards, and they had very large numbers of children by them.[125] A special title applied to the male and female scions of so many royal children: "son/daughter of the (royal) house," a term widely used and subsequently retained in local languages from Armenian to Sogdian and Bactrian.[126] But Persian elite men were not changing diapers or chasing

---

[125] These things should not surprise us. The Qajar king Fatḥ-ʿAlī (regn. 1779–1834) had many hundreds of concubines, in addition to four lawful wives, and fathered, according to Amanat (1999), "at least 260 children of whom sixty sons and fifty-five daughters survived their father." This led to "a huge royal family, which by the time of shah's death reached one thousand in number and by the middle of the 19th century exceeded ten thousand." Examples from beyond Iran are not hard to find, either. At the time of this writing, King Mswati III (regn. 1986–) of Eswatini reportedly has fifteen wives and forty-five children. I suppose he will have more by the time of publication. Abdulaziz Ibn Saud (regn. 1932–1953) had many wives and concubines and about ninety children. Jacob Zuma, former president of South Africa, from 2009 to 2018, currently has four wives remaining of six women he married and, reportedly, about twenty children. When the Indian polygamist Ziona Chana died in 2021, he had accumulated thirty-eight wives, eighty-nine children, and thirty-six grandchildren. In 2021, Canadian polygamist Latter-Day Saint leader Winston Blackmore reportedly had one hundred and fifty children from twenty-seven wives. These sorts of figures must not have been rare among rich Persians of antiquity. See also Llewellyn-Jones 2022: 177–178 for more ancient examples of kings with extremely large numbers of female sexual partners and offspring.

[126] Henning 1964; Benveniste 1966: 22–26 and 34–50; Huyse 1999: 2.119–120; Colditz 2000: 328–356; Sims-Williams and Grenet 2022–2023: 136. The Middle Persian *wispuhr*, for the male, and *duxš* and *wisduxt* for the female, are commonly translated as "prince" and "princess" but evidently developed

defiant toddlers. They brought non-Persian-speakers into their palaces, audience halls, and homes, as companions, flunkies, and mates, so their own children were frequently raised, at least in their early years, by women and eunuchs who were foreigners, who therefore must have learned Persian mostly only as adults, and who thus certainly spoke a nonnative sort of Persian. As discussed in Chapter 2, it is nonnative learners, not native speakers, who reduce and even drop contextual inflection in a language, the very effect observed in Middle Persian.

Modern scholars have sometimes seemed embarrassed about the hundreds of beautiful women and castrated males reported to abide in the fancy halls of Persian lords.[127] Either they have been interpreted as a source of corruption, as Plato saw it, or they need to be explained away or minimized, as a misunderstanding, a distasteful exaggeration, or a mirage arising from bigoted perceptions and orientalist bias. But all the sources together have not lied. Such human beings have existed in many societies, for many different reasons. Close to the epicenter of Persian power, concubines and eunuchs, who evidently greatly outnumbered their masters in their private quarters, surely played a large role, not only as foils for lordly Persian manhood, but also in the nurture of Persian boys, the creation of elite Persian culture, and the evolution of the Persian language. Plato did not like it, but that does not mean that we should dislike it – or deny the sources that testify to it.

The Testimony of Material Culture

Besides the ample testimonies from sources pertaining to the world of men employed at war and in construction work, on the one hand, and the domestically employed women and eunuchs, on the other, a third testimony to the cultural mixture of rulers and ruled comes from the material remains of durable precious objects and architecture from the Achaemenian Empire. These pertain less to language, so I will linger here more briefly, but they buttress the case that the Persians were not just willing but interested in fostering a new cultural blend of the things that

in the Achaemenian period as something more like "royals," applied, it seems, to relatives by patrilineal descent from the Persian monarchical line.

[127] On vindicating the existence of the special quarters for numerous concubines from the skepticism of recent scholars, which has been motivated by misleading good intentions, see Llewellyn-Jones 2013: 99–102 (although he insists on using the term "harem," which should rather be dropped for this context). Lenfant (2012; 2013; 2014) writes persuasively of the reality of the eunuchs. For a survey of eunuchs in history and the biology of eunuchs, see Tougher 2008: 7–35.

pleased them. Material remains have testified to art historians and archaeologists that the Achaemenids produced a mixture of hitherto regional cultural forms. Mixture has long been a keyword in the history of Achaemenid royal material culture. Formerly this mixing ran against the tastes of art historians seeking neat, distinct national types of art. Herzfeld, the pioneering archaeologist of Iran, wrote that Persian art was "a hybrid art, if art it can be called, worthy to be studied only out of scientific and historical, not of aesthetic, interest."[128] Roes complained that "if Achaemenid art was not regarded [by modern scholars] as the work of foreigners, it has generally been called a hodgepodge of foreign elements that hardly deserves the name of art and seems to have been regarded by many scholars as an affront to their artistic sensibilities."[129] Ghirshman admitted but defended the apparently "dependent" character of Persian art, which relied on "borrowing from other peoples": "There is a tendency to criticize Achaemenian civilization for depending too much on the achievements of others, particularly in the sphere of art. But even if a study of the surviving monuments lends support to this view, it only illustrates the old truth that peoples living in close relationship inevitably exert a reciprocal influence."[130] A half century later, Boardman showed that art historians finally had to acknowledge that "Persian" meant "mixture," when it came to material culture. He wrote, "It must soon have become a matter of indifference whether any given Mesopotamian, Egyptian or Anatolian was carving a figure composed of elements of Anatolian, Egyptian or Mesopotamian style. It was by then all Persian."[131] For Henkelman, "Persepolitan art is willfully synthetic," and art at Pasargadae synthesizes a "coherent vision" appropriated from elements of "eclectic origins."[132] From points of view beyond imperial centers, Khatchadourian, using sophisticated language, emphasizes the agency of local elites in adopting forms of material goods in architecture and ornament that emphasize their participation in a larger imperial culture,[133] and Colburn probes the possibilities of describing such Achaemenian material production with the term globalization.[134] We see in such statements from over decades an evolution from distaste for the mixture of regional forms into understanding based on appreciation, but the basic idea of synthesis remains.

In my view, some historians of art go too far in supposing that every aspect of Persian art and architecture was part of a master plan of "imperial

---

[128] Herzfeld 1935: 52.   [129] Roes 1952: 17.   [130] Ghirshman 1954: 181, 351.
[131] Boardman 2000: 219.   [132] Henkelman 2012: 947.   [133] Khatchadourian 2013.
[134] Colburn 2016.

ideology," as if the kings and their ministers were informed architects and decorators who carefully planned the "ideological" import of every statue's minute characteristics. Instead, the mixture of forms evident to art historians were more probably the result of a collaboration of intelligent artisans of different regional origins who developed something new and distinctive to please their kings, deliberately suited to the purpose of their employment. Ultimately, for the present argument, one should note that although art historians have disagreed over the decades in their personal evaluation of artistic quality in the mixture of regional styles and forms in objects from imperial Persian sites, they agree in the fact of that mixture.[135] Considering these consistent observations by archaeologists and historians of art, the material environment of royal Persian sites likewise shows that Persian soon meant hybrid. This was not regarded as something bad, but as prestigious. It was a demonstration of the universality of Persian power, but it was human individuals who had to bring the regional expertise required to fashion such objects synthesizing previously separate forms. Population contact of this kind also naturally and necessarily had striking linguistic effects.

The Testimony of the Language of the Late Achaemenian Inscriptions

To summarize the foregoing, three sorts of testimonies to the mixture of peoples brought about by Persian rule have long been available. First, the early Achaemenian royal inscriptions and Elamite administrative texts tell how the people of one region became rulers of many far-flung peoples who spoke different languages. Persian kings commanded workers and craftsmen from distant countries and united them all in sites of royal display as ostentatious demonstrations that they had indeed taken the best of all and used them together in an awe-inspiring mixture. Elamite administrative texts on clay tablets likewise reveal how workers from many different subject populations, who did not originally share a common language, collaborated in managing the Persian state and found employment in labor forces at sites ruled by Persians. We can add to this the obvious role that shared military pursuits must have played in fostering a common speech among martial servants of the kings. Fighting men from different countries

---

[135] Khatchadourian (2016: 86–87) acknowledges these customary terms in art historical discussions of Achaemenian architecture and visual culture but avoids them, holding that "Achaemenid cultural production was not unimaginatively derivative, nor is it best understood as the impressive result of creative borrowings."

serving Persian masters would need to learn just enough Persian to do their jobs, and more if they wanted to communicate directly with their masters. Second, with regard to the Persian domestic domain, Greek authors comment explicitly on the willingness of the Persians to accept the customs of others and to mix socially with them, especially their taking numerous foreign females and eunuchs into their homes. Herodotus states it as an obvious fact. Plato and other Greek authors disdained such mixing as impure, fearful of the mixing that was the outcome of the worldly success and power that inspired their jealousy and especially their feelings of political insecurity. But it was obvious to them that the mixture was real. Third, modern art historians and archaeologists testify to a blend of regional cultural forms into something new and synthetic as the outcome of the material production that they fostered, as far as durable material media preserve them for us to see today. These varieties of available evidence support the argument that by the fourth century BCE, the Persians, as people with imperial privilege, had willfully taken the best of everything they ruled and incorporated choice objects and people into their own. Thus, they had evolved and changed over several generations.

The ruling elite called Persian in the fourth century BCE, whose domain stretched from the Mediterranean to Afghanistan, were different from the Persians local to Pārsa of the early sixth century BCE. Their empire had promoted and homogenized local elites into a new synthesis with less conspicuous regional variation among themselves and, as argued here, a new form of Persian language. One might say, speaking loosely, that they fostered a hybridized pan-Near Eastern elite culture, while retaining the name and meaning of "Persian," and they bequeathed its amalgamated forms to later elites as cultural norms for the rulers of successor states. We can call this tendency *Persism*,[136] a term on the model of "Hellenism," to focus the investigation of the impact, influence, and reception of ancient Persian people and their culture in the world around them. As a descriptive

---

[136] "Persianism," a term promoted by a recent volume (Strootman and Versluys 2017; also Strootman 2020), is not as apt as Persism. The English neologism "Persism" makes a better parallel with Hellenism, based on the name Persia, as well as the ancient Greek word περσίζειν, "to imitate the Persians, speak Persian." Compare this with the English word adopted from ancient Greek: Medism (rather than Medianism, a term not used in this sense). Moreover, Talattof (2000: 4, 19–65) already used the term Persianism/*Pārsīgīrā'ī* extensively to refer to an early twentieth-century literary movement aiming to purify, modernize, and secularize Persian literature through the purgation of Arabic words and writing in a more vernacular Persian style, among other means. The term Persism will be more precise also because it will be more clearly distinguished from Persianization, which should refer to the adoption of the Persian language in a population, just as Arabicization, in English, refers to the adoption of Arabic, as opposed to Arabization, the assimilation to Arab ethnicity and culture (van Bladel 2022: 92n13).

neologism serving as an umbrella for several different phenomena, Persism can be used to characterize the elite cultural blend that arose as an effect of Persian power and practices of rule during the period of the Achaemenids and lingering long after them. The phenomenon of population change here should not come as a surprise. No nation today is the same as it was one hundred and fifty years ago. Immigration and population movements have created great demographic changes, even when the names and sometimes even governments of these nations remain apparently consistent and stable. The Achaemenian Persians clearly experienced such changes on a scale never seen before them in history but seen many times since then. Those changes did not affect all their provincial subjects nearly so much as it affected their own Persian people.

The clinching testimony comes from the Persian language itself. This is the focus of this study, and it also offers the decisive argument that shows that the other testimonies just reviewed reflect not just the perspectives of onlookers but substantial social changes evident to contemporaries. Corresponding to the changes in population, Old Persian grammar exhibits drastic changes in the direction of inflectional simplicity within a few generations. By the late fourth century BCE, the old inflectional system of the Persian language had been reduced to a minimal state (Chapter 1). Middle Persian had emerged in some sense. Knowing now what we know about the social factors in language change (Chapter 2), we should already expect this to be due to the sudden mixture of populations and the concomitant acquisition of Old Persian by large numbers of adult learners. The combination of clear linguistic effects and explicit ancient sources is conclusive. The changes in the Persian language become, in effect, yet another witness to the changing constitution of Persianness in the Achaemenian period, from numerous regional sources. The testimony of the changes to the grammar of Old Persian is even more important than the contemporary witnesses, in that it is based not on third-party description but on modern grammatical analysis combined with a robust theory of language change based on facts about human language acquisition.

Dominant Ethno-Class or Domestic Melting Pot?

Pierre Briant, a leading historian of the Achaemenian Persians, posed a model to understand the culture of Achaemenian Persian rule in which the Persians constituted a "dominant ethno-class" that insisted on Persian superiority to and difference with those ruled. Being ethnically Persian would be a prerequisite to true participation in the ruling elite.¹³⁷ In this view, Persian ethnicity was an essential attribute for members of the elite ruling class. It is hard to argue against this. Briant goes further, however, in holding that Persianness was exclusive to Persians and the Persians remained quite distinct. He holds that the Persians did not preside over "an imperial melting pot" (his expression).¹³⁸ Even the Persian language is supposed to have been exclusive to this dominant ethno-class. "With only a few exceptions, only the Persians spoke Persian," Briant writes.¹³⁹ Perhaps on the basis of a similar estimation, Mancini recently interpreted the history of Old Persian with the idea that the Persian language persisted in "a rigidly close-knit network" of speakers.¹⁴⁰ Part of Briant's argument is based on the analysis of the names of the satraps, generals, and high officials from the reigns of Darius I and Xerxes; these names are overwhelmingly Old Iranic names (Persian or Median). This is indeed striking.¹⁴¹ The present discussion, however, shows that there is a limit to which we should accept this analysis.¹⁴² Although "the Persians" were always identified as the rulers of the Achaemenian Empire, the six royal generations comprising the kings from Darius I to Artaxerxes III entailed great demographic changes that transformed what it meant to be Persian. That is because the Achaemenian state, as the kings' inscriptions explicitly state, was not only a state of Persians or Aryas (*Ariyā*), but it included many peoples of different kinds (*paruzana-*). The early testimonies from the times of Darius I and his son Xerxes do clearly express Persian difference and dominance. They did so in the decades immediately after the formation of the empire by conquest and by crushing subsequent resistance raised by local rulers, when differences between rulers and ruled were at their most conspicuous. Their inscriptions and rock reliefs, especially those of Darius I, depict

---

[137] Briant 1988, 2002: 82, 334, 350–352; Lavan, Payne, and Weisweiler 2016: 17–19.
[138] Briant 1988: 137.
[139] Briant 2002: 77. Briant describes some of these exceptions in which non-Persians learned Persian. For his theory of the dominant ethno-class to endure, he must regard the testimonies that contradict it as "anecdotal and isolated" (2002: 508–509). Given the general paucity of the sources for the period in general, reports like this should not be disregarded as few.
[140] Mancini 2019: 226n4. Such a social network would indeed tend to conserve a language and inhibit the transfer of features and morphological reduction (Milroy and Llamas 2013). But the record of grammatical change in Old Persian by itself makes the idea of such a close-knit social network impossible.
[141] Tavernier (2017) also shows that administrative commands came mostly from persons bearing Iranic names.
[142] Already Sancisi-Weerdenburg (1990: 268) pointed out that "a growth of the 'ethno-classe dominante' applies mostly to the first phase of the conquests. There are indications, in later stages, that the 'ethno-classe' was not an impenetrable entity ... and that at least some elements from the indigenous population made their way into this select group."

subject ethnic groups in carved relief in stereotyped appearances and attire. This striking overt display of ethnic domination supports the idea that this "ethno-class" was a political regime characteristic of Persian rule for its duration. Others have adopted Briant's idea. It is now a standard view about the history of the Persians of the Achaemenian period. Just before Briant began to publish his views on the dominant ethno-class, however, an earlier view was that Achaemenid rule "induced racial and cultural fusion,"[143] and that "the Achaemenid period is characterized by intensive processes of ethnic mixing and syncretism of the cultures and religious concepts of various peoples,"[144] just as Plato said that the Persians ruled people who had been "spread around and brought together," διαπεφορημένα καὶ συμπεφορημένα. This chapter reminds us that the rock relief images of Darius' tomb, clearly depicting Persian dominance over other many distinct ethnic groups, were established near the beginning of Achaemenid rule, and cannot be used to explain the meaning of Persian ethnicity for its entire duration. After one hundred years, and still more after two hundred years, members of Persian aristocratic families and households surely included many men and women of mixed descent and heterogeneous family origins. If, in a later period, a Greek name used by a follower of the Seleucids does not necessarily convince us that its bearer was a native speaker of Greek – or even Greek in ancestry at all – or an Arabic name borne by a servant of the caliphs that he was of pure Arabian ancestry, why should the Persian name of an Achaemenian satrap necessitate that its bearer belonged to an ancestral exclusive Persian ethnic class that always excluded non-Persians? What made someone Persian was success in assimilation to the ruling class, which itself changed over time. As Xenophon said, those who served the satraps were supposed to imitate their Persian rulers. Persian nomenclature from the Achaemenian period therefore reveals little about the family background of individuals. It tells us only that people adopted Persian names or gave such names to their children in hope of their future social success.

Of course, this is not to say that the Persians shared their supreme power with non-Persians. In a sense, it was lastingly true that there was a dominant class of Persians, for the rulers were always known as Persian.[145] That was their identity. Briant and others are surely right that they had no specific, deliberate imperial policy of programmatic Persism or

---

[143] Cook 1985: 290.
[144] Dandamaev and Lukonin 1988: 292–293, translated from the original Russian of 1980.
[145] In fact, they were often known as Medes, as was normal in Egypt, for example (Graf 1984).

Persianization, nor any intention of making the generality of their subjects Persian. Nevertheless, they created the circumstances through which Persian demography and culture were bound to change drastically. The melting pot happened more covertly, from the point of view of the sources surviving today: in the night quarters and the halls of Persian manors and palaces, in the army camps between ethnically different units, and in the work yards where men from different nations collaborated in creating monuments to the Persian kings and the royal family. The preceding discussion demonstrates that what it meant really to be Persian was not static. By the time of Artaxerxes III, Persian men were probably mostly of an ancestry that would be considered mixed by comparison with their forebears of the time of Darius I, just as Plato described them with his contemporary negative evaluation. This is not a matter of biological race, a false concept.[146] The point is that the Persians readily accepted cultural goods and customs from other peoples. They took on new customs and acquired new luxuries, just as happily as we today adopt new technologies that transform our lives with hitherto unimagined comforts and conveniences, without our considering much how our culture is thereby transformed. Most importantly for the history of the Persian language, Persians accepted thousands of non-Persians into their households and made thousands of children with them, and these numerous children, raised in large part by non-Persian servants, were often accepted as Persian. The Persians were thus, in fact, assimilated to those they ruled, in their own palaces, just as local elites gradually Persified themselves to maintain and promote their status. It could hardly be otherwise in the multilingual, polyethnic social conditions of the Achaemenian centers of power. The transformation of the Old Persian language into Middle Persian is a clearer testimony to this internal metamorphosis than even the direct statement of contemporary observers. The concept of a Persian "ethno-class," if one wishes to retain it, cannot refer to something static, and so becomes much less useful for historians today. Individuals could join the Persians, intermarry with them, and their progeny could be raised as Persian, speaking a new, current, simpler kind of vernacular Persian language. There was indeed a melting-pot of heterogeneous ingredients right in the homes of Persian kings and lords. While most local peoples under Persian rule retained their own languages and regional identities, what being Persian looked like and sounded like in 350 BCE must have been quite different from what it was in 500 BCE. This is inherently plausible or even obvious when we consider the

---

[146] Yudell 2011; Tattersall and DeSalle 2011.

rearrangement of ethnicities in the one hundred and fifty years of imperial processes and population mixtures preceding our own time. It seems, then, that historians should allow for more social and cultural change among the Persians of the Achaemenid period. Historians have followed the two largest textual corpora from royal centers within the Persian Empire – the royal inscriptions and the Elamite administrative tablets from Persepolis – but these have skewed our attention toward the earliest decades of the empire and away from the ensuing changes that imperial organization brought with it. One cannot expect the snapshot of a few major early inscriptional sources, despite their inestimable importance, to account for change across two centuries of Persian rule.

In the end, what makes the hypothesis of population mixing accompanied by unilateral nonnative bilingualism not just plausible, but certain, is the combination of the evidence of the history of the grammar of the Achaemenian Persian inscriptions with a host of testimonies about the social facts of the Achaemenian period.

Modern Terms for Imperial Population Mixture

Recent historians of ancient empires have adopted comparative approaches to discover common patterns and special characteristics in empires. This has required a definition of empire to establish a set of comparable cases. They have usually defined empire as a state formed by one people or ethnic group through conquest of others, typically on a large scale. Empires, understood in this way, are distinguished by conspicuous ethnic difference between the rulers and the ruled. One weakness of this definition is that these differences erode over time as the populations remain in contact, cooperate, and share goods and practices, so that by this defining feature, the older the empire, the less "imperial" it will be.[147] Accordingly, the idea that difference between ruler and ruled is the core feature of empire has turned the attention of these historians toward the terms in which that difference is characterized and how imperial states maintained their integrity along with the ethnic differences. If empire is defined by ethnic differences along a scale of power, then should it not be that a long-lived empire maintained ethnic difference? That would be a false assumption arising from this concept of empire created for comparative purposes.

---

[147] Barfield (2001: 29) regards the changeability of the ruling elite, without causing the collapse of the imperial state, as a characteristic of empire, saying that "empires are organized both to administer and exploit diversity."

One attempt to solve this problem of historians' own making, by insisting on this definition of empire, relies on a concept of "cosmopolitanism." A group of ancient historians have recently taken "cosmopolitan" to designate "persons and polities that freely cross cultural boundaries." They posit an imperial cosmopolitanism that works in two ways: by *assimilation*, whereby the differences between local elites and universal rulers are blurred, and by *subordination*, whereby the preeminence of the culture of the rulers over others is continually reasserted.[148] Either way, cosmopolitanism entails the creation of a new, common ruling-class culture with elements that pass over and erode former boundaries. Ancient empires fostered cosmopolitan ruling classes by necessity because their control of many ethnically different populations required individuals who could mediate between the rulers and the subjects. Rulers rely on such people. In this sense, the regime of the Achaemenids clearly produced a cosmopolitan culture – one that created a model for ruling elites that lasted for centuries after them – and they belong in this comparative discussion.[149] But because of the widespread acceptance of Briant's idea of an ancient Persian dominant ethno-class, Achaemenian Persian cosmopolitanism is deemed to have been strictly one of subordination, wherein the Persians always remained sharply distinct masters of the rest, not an empire of cosmopolitan assimilation.[150] The preceding discussion of Persism and Persianization undermines the meaning of this by showing that the lines between subject populations and masters were blurrier than has been assumed. The conduits for assimilation were personal and often intergenerational, formed by marriages and concubinage and the birth of children into a Persian identity assigned mostly by patrilineage, carried out by foreign-born eunuchs and servants who surrounded Persian masters, not merely through the occasional promotion of non-Persian individuals through the favor of the king. Without understanding the very large scale

---

[148] Lavan, Payne, and Weisweiler 2016. The cosmopolitanism discussed in their edited volume has little to do with other recent discussions about "cosmopolitanism" and ethics, such as those stimulated by Martha Nussbaum and Kwame Anthony Appiah. They owe more rather to the historical sociology of Michael Mann. The word cosmopolitanism is serving different purposes in different fields.

[149] See also Colburn 2016, which proposes globalization as a parallel way to consider the contrast between the abiding ethnic diversity of the Persians' subjects and the growing homogeneity of "visual vocabulary" in their increasingly shared material culture. The issues are the same as those under discussion here.

[150] Briant's idea that the Achaemenian Persians constituted a lastingly distinct "dominant ethno-class" has even been used as a model for the role of Greek Macedonian ethnicity in the cosmopolitanism of the successor states to the Achaemenids (e.g., Richter 2011: 15–16). Classical scholars must investigate more thoroughly the ways in which Greek elites and subject populations were, and were not, integrated in the period after Alexander. See Fischer-Bovet 2014 for an exemplary study of this kind, focused on Ptolemaic Egypt.

of servitude and of sexual and reproductive access to women enjoyed by privileged Persian masters, we cannot understand the scale of the corresponding Persianization.

Linguists, by contrast, do not normally discuss "cosmopolitan" languages. Their category is "contact languages," with the creole as a distinct phenomenon among them. Creolization is a specific linguistic process, as discussed in the previous chapter, and not a moral evaluation. Along with linguistic creolization, however, scholars specializing in the cultures of speakers of modern creoles sometimes discuss "creolization of culture." The use of the term as applied to language and culture differs very distinctly, though, because the discussions of creolization of culture do not usually refer to reduction of inflected forms through nonnative acquisition, as discussions of creolization of language do. "Creolization of culture" usually refers to mixing and hybridization, not to simplification or reduction of a culture's complexity (whatever that might be) on the model of grammatical, morphological reduction.[151] This makes discussion of linguistic creolization and cultural creolization fundamentally incompatible at an analytical level, even though they can be said to happen simultaneously in one population. One could, however, very nearly equate the concept of cultural creolization in some form with cosmopolitanism. Both are terms of description referring to different kinds of hybridization of cultures; both lack analytical precision.[152] At the same time, the two terms carry distinct values. Cosmopolitanism refers to the creation of an elite ruling-class culture bridging formerly separate groups, whereas creolization is typically conceived as a phenomenon among subordinate, conquered groups who have been forcibly mixed. These connotations are due to the modern histories of the two words. Creole-speakers were colonial subjects of European empires; European imperialists generated a cosmopolitan, colonial culture for themselves.[153] Despite the difference in valuation, the names nevertheless refer to similar processes. Both arose through mixing and homogenization of various components: practices, habits, products, words, relationships. Hybridity is one outcome of both. It

---

[151] Thus, e.g., Chaudensen 2001. A sounder approach is to apply anthropological methods to the social circumstances of pidgin and creole formation. We can see how the term creolization signifying "simplification" of culture would be objectionable, whereas the simplification or reduction of morphological inflection is a matter of description and quantification. It is critical to distinguish these two different phenomena. See Jourdan 2004.

[152] The goal of Lavan, Payne, and Weisweiler (2016: 9–10) to give "cosmopolitanism" new analytical utility in the study of ancient empires has been met only minimally. As for creole, the fraught debate about its definition in creole studies, discussed in the previous chapter, speaks for itself.

[153] Thomas 1994.

is arresting to think that by this similarity we might invert the values of these terms and designate the later Achaemenid Persian rulers "creole kings," thinking of the imperial mixture of cultures that they propagated for their own glorification and private enjoyment. One specific example jumps out of the pages of history. Darius II (regn. 423–405) had a Babylonian mother; with this in mind, his contemporary Greeks entitled him *Nóthos*, νόθος, "bastard," "born of a foreign concubine." Would his royal great-grandfather, Darius I, have thought, if he could have met him, that this descendant of his spoke a "bastard tongue" as well?[154] Through this bastard king every subsequent Achaemenid king shared Babylonian ancestry. Of course, mixed ancestry alone does not make a subject "creole" in any of the senses current today. The royal environment of the Persians was, nevertheless, supported by non-Persian subjects who, coming from other backgrounds, brought new cultural goods to enhance the majesty of Persian rulers. Thereby we simultaneously force ourselves yet again to think of ancient Persian culture not as pure but as a hybrid[155] – like nearly all cultures and peoples, but in relatively sudden and high degree – in which the relationship of Persian cultural contributions to the cosmopolitan culture fostered by the Achaemenian regime is analogous to the relationship of the "lexifier" to its pidgin and creole offspring. It must be emphasized that this is merely an analogy. One must not speak of a corresponding "simplification" of a "cultural grammar." Thinking about imperial hybrids is not new, but few such ruminations are genuinely useful here for my purposes.[156] For historians, designating the culture of the Achaemenids as hybrid, or perhaps better, suddenly heterogeneous, or even exoterogenic (to use Thurston's neologism discussed briefly at the end of Chapter 2), facilitates two elements in our account of the Achaemenids. For us, it acknowledges the blending of local elite cultures

---

[154] The term "bastard tongue" figures in the title of two popularizing works by creole specialists: Bickerton 2008 and McWhorter 2008.

[155] My view of cultural hybridity is in line with Renato Rosaldo's characterization in his foreword to García Canclini's *Hybrid Cultures* in English (1995: xv): "hybridity can be understood as the ongoing condition of all human cultures, which contain no zones of purity because they undergo continuous processes of transculturation (two-way borrowing and lending between cultures). Instead of hybridity versus purity, this view suggests that it is hybridity all the way down." Taking a further tip from Rosaldo (2005: xvi), we should ask who determined what counted as Persian in the Achaemenian Empire. We should ask who today determines what counted as Persian then. Asking the questions is probably more important than any answer.

[156] Bhabha (1994) wrote the seminal work on the ambiguities of cultural hybridity in imperial contexts. It would be unproductive to indulge in a tone of dissatisfaction or outrage about the use of terms like "hybridity" here on the grounds that it may obscure the inequalities and injustices inherent in the Achaemenian Persian Empire. In any case, nobody will doubt that the Achaemenids and their servitors presided over a violent regime built on slavery and oppression.

that resulted in what was effectively an evolving new elite superculture with an old name – Persian – and that this blending occurred within the period of a few generations, even while Persian people were regarded as distinct and retained privileges under the Achaemenid kings. The Persian language itself testifies to this. In the end, this experimental line of thought is not especially productive, because it is based on terms that lack analytical power. As with many arresting ideas, that of the Achaemenids as living in a creole culture offers a perspective that does not bear satisfying fruit. It does not change the facts of history but only the terms of our description. The linguist S. Mufwene, active in the analysis of creolization, rightly warns against the overgeneralization of a historically specific term for basically unrelated phenomena.[157] Yet, as history creates a narrative, the terms of our narration do matter, and sometimes new perspectives are illuminating. I leave it to the readers to contemplate what "Persian" may have meant by the time of Artaxerxes III, and how that meaning has changed, and continues to change, over time.

---

[157] Mufwene 2009: 105. His insistence that we use the term "hybridize" rather than "creolize" is not, however, without undisputed theoretical baggage. See McWhorter's argument (2012; 2018: 33–62) against Mufwene's "feature pool" hypothesis, in which the formation of a creole language is nothing other than an *unreduced* hybrid. In most specialists' views, the formation of a creole is not just splicing features from different sources, but at least also simplification of inflectional morphology.

CHAPTER 4

Common and Remote Varieties of Iranic-Language Speech

Readers already familiar with ancient Iranic languages and Iranic linguistics are likely to have become frustrated by now that I have not yet addressed a glaring fact: Middle Persian is not the only Iranic language that was shaped by drastic reduction of grammatical inflection. Two other known but less well-attested ancient Middle Iranic languages – Parthian and Bactrian – clearly have much in common with Middle Persian in their grammatical structures.[1] This chapter addresses this phenomenon. I claim that both Parthian and Bactrian were shaped by a similar process – grammatical reduction through mass adult acquisition – as well as by convergence due to individuals who spoke more than one of these languages at once. I also posit that the Achaemenian period is the time when these regional varieties of Old Iranic were grammatically reduced along the same lines, or at least the period in which this process was well underway. In other words, Parthian and Bactrian took on most of their characteristic grammatical shapes in tandem with the transformation of Old Persian to Middle Persian, and they continued to be used in contact with each other thereafter. I argue that the clear discrepancy in morphological complexity between these three ancient attested Iranic languages, on the one hand, and other ancient and modern Iranic languages used outside of or on the periphery

---

[1] Parthian and Middle Persian are so similar that they are often treated side-by-side in the same reference works and dictionaries (Boyce 1977; Brunner 1977; Sundermann 1989; Durkin-Meisterernst 2004; 2014; Skjærvø 2009b). Sundermann (1989: 108) explicitly stated that Parthian and Persian "went in the same direction" in their morphology. The analysis of Bactrian has only recently been made possible through the discovery and decipherment of a substantial corpus of texts. Cf. Skjærvø 2009b: 196: "The two languages [Middle Persian and Parthian] are closely similar in structure, though Parthian shares some features with its eastern neighbors, notably with Bactrian, rather than with Middle Persian." Ideally, however, each of these languages should be treated separately, so that their distinctive features are clearly comprehended.

of the Achaemenian Empire, on the other, is due to this social aspect of the ancient history of their speakers.[2]

It was necessary to base the study so far on Persian alone because there are no contemporary Old Parthian or Old Bactrian texts illustrating the regional varieties of Old Iranic from which they descended or a securely dated set of changes in their inflectional systems. It may be that such regional varieties in the Achaemenian period, including Old Persian, were mutually comprehensible dialects of Old Iranic. This study had to begin, rather, with the observation of attested, chronologically anchored changes to the Persian language and the puzzle posed by the rapidity and severity of those changes evident within the Achaemenian Persian inscriptions over a century and a half. Combined with the synthesis of various findings of recent research in linguistics (Chapter 2) and a new look at long-known sources of Achaemenian history (Chapter 3), the Achaemenian Persian inscriptions and their variation over time are what has made it possible, and indeed necessary, to argue that mass adult acquisition of Old Persian did occur and that the result was a semicreolized version of Persian, the directly attested descendent of which we call Middle Persian. Integrating Parthian and Bactrian into this analysis is more difficult, because the oldest extant texts in these two Iranic languages are later by centuries than the latest Old Persian inscriptions and they are both more scantily attested than Middle Persian. When they do appear in the record, however, they stand out as conspicuously simplified in their inflections as compared with all other attested ancient Iranic languages except Middle Persian. The linguistic model presented in Chapter 2, by itself, could support the hypothesis that mass adult learning led to the grammatical reduction of Parthian and Bactrian, but with small, later corpora of texts and few relevant historical sources, it would remain merely a highly likely hypothesis. As it is, this chapter will necessarily conclude with somewhat less certainty than there is for the case of Persian, but it does support the argument of the previous chapter that the social circumstances of population mixture that characterized the lives of the Achaemenian elite was the factor that induced drastic morphological reduction in Persian.

---

[2] Earlier, Szemerényi (1980: 210) supposed that the "decay" of forms was general to Western Iranic languages (Persian and Parthian), and that this was due to contact with Aramaic, but Bactrian was not then well known. The alleged role of Aramaic in these processes is discussed later in this chapter.

Parthian and Bactrian

Parthian was a distinct Iranic language attested in scattered texts discovered across much of what is today Iran. When it first appears in our extant records, it is written in a regional variety of the Achaemenian Aramaic script distinct from the one used for Middle Persian. The two are different enough that they can be distinguished on sight. Parthian is assumed to have been adopted and used by the administration of the Arsacid kings, a dynasty that first emerged on the Central Asian steppes in the third century BCE and that lasted until the Persian Sasanids usurped their role as overlords in the early third century CE. The Arsacids gradually dominated the lands of modern Iran and Iraq by conquest from the Greek-speaking Seleucids, the dynasty of kings founded by Seleucus (d. 281 BCE), one of Alexander's prominent generals. Eventually, the Arsacids ruled the territory of Iran, Iraq, and adjacent regions, particularly from the time of Mithridates I (regn. 171–132 BCE). The oldest evidence of the Parthian language is in scattered texts from the late second century BCE onward. These early Parthian texts include a small number of very short inscriptions, coin legends, a single document on parchment from the northern Zagros Mountains, and a few thousand inscribed ostraca. The last of these, tersely recording transactions such as the transfer of food commodities and wine, were found at Nisa, the site of an ancient city in present-day Turkmenistan near the border of Iran. The oldest substantial surviving Parthian texts were written much later. Several of the Middle Persian inscriptions of early Sasanid kings, in the third century CE, are accompanied by Parthian versions.[3] The bulk of the extant Parthian corpus, however, consists of many hundreds of fragmentary Manichaean manuscripts discovered in Central Asia. Parthian had been used for the Manichaean mission from the late third century CE onward.[4] Mani, the founder of the religion Manichaeism, is supposed to have dispatched Ammo, his evangelist to northeastern Iran and Central Asia from Ḥulwān (today's Sarpul-i Ḏahāb), at the western edge of modern Iran. Some extant Parthian compositions are attributed to Ammo.[5] The apparent presence of Parthian-speakers from Ḥulwān to Nisa suggests that Parthian was used very widely from east to west in the course of its history. A language with such extensive geography should have exhibited dialectal variation, but the limited texts available do not give us an adequate basis for discerning that.

---

[3] Huyse 2009: 86–90.   [4] Sundermann 2009.   [5] Sundermann 1981: 27.

Bactrian was an Iranic language widespread in what is today northern Afghanistan, a populous and prosperous region in antiquity. The corpus of Bactrian texts now known has mostly become available and comprehensible only in the last thirty years, the texts having emerged during the relentless wars in Afghanistan.[6] Bactrian was written in the Greek script, in handwriting a distinct semi-cursive variety that had evolved locally from a ligatured Seleucid Greek hand.[7] This writing system had been brought there originally by large numbers of Greek-speaking colonists in the wake of Alexander's conquests.[8] The Greek language did not persist there, but the script remained to be used for the Iranic language of regional currency. Bactrian is attested in a small number of inscriptions, graffiti, and words on coin legends and seals from the second century CE to the ninth.[9] More substantial are more than 150 handwritten instrumental and communicative texts (contracts, correspondence, and the like) mostly on leather, from the fourth to the eighth century CE, in a tradition of literacy that continued through many different local dynasties of different origins: Kushans, Persians, Huns, Hephthalites, Turks, and Arabs. A new batch of Bactrian texts on birch bark, from southern Afghanistan, has now come to light.[10] There is also one small fragment of a Bactrian text in the Manichaean script found in Central Asia with more extensive Manichaean texts in other languages, such as Middle Persian and Parthian. All these texts, which were recently deciphered, edited, and translated largely through the philology and erudition of Nicholas Sims-Williams, not to mention others, have resulted in the exposition of this hitherto almost unknown Middle Iranic language, its grammar and lexicon, and have triggered recent efforts to build a new, revised family tree of the Iranic languages (discussed further in this chapter under the heading "The Hypothesis of Central Iranic and Areal Features").

A very recent development must be mentioned here. Scholars have made a breakthrough in the decipherment of hitherto unreadable ancient inscriptions in the region of Bactria, evidently older than the Bactrian texts in Greek letters, written in an abugida script derived from the Aramaic, for now known as the "(Issyk-)Kushan script." The language

---

[6] Sims-Williams 1997.
[7] Examples of this "missing link" semicursive Seleucid hand were found in the two Greek documents from Avroman, dated to the first century BCE, and reproduced by Minns (1915).
[8] Lurje and Yakubovich (2017: 327–333) hypothesize that Bactrian was written earlier in a variety of the Aramaic script.
[9] Sims-Williams and de Blois (2018) establish the chronology of most of the texts.
[10] Sims-Williams and Grenet 2022–2023.

has now been determined to be an old form of Bactrian, although the decipherment is ongoing.[11] We can now anticipate that it will be possible to augment our understanding of the earlier history of Bactrian grammar in the future. For now, however, and until the inflectional morphology of this older Iranic language of the region becomes clear, we must base our analysis on what is clearly known and understood.

Bactrian, Parthian, and Middle Persian are three different languages, not dialects of one language.[12] Although they share innumerable cognate words, they became strongly differentiated and were surely mutually incomprehensible before the second and third centuries CE, a period from which enough known texts survive to compare them meaningfully. Corresponding perhaps with their geographic distribution, they exhibit a continuum of features, with Bactrian and Middle Persian as the most mutually dissimilar of the three and Parthian sharing features with the other two but tending more toward Bactrian in resemblance, at least superficially. A major characteristic of all three together, though, is the striking reduction of their grammatical inflection. Not only is it extensive, but the grammatical reduction they share is of the same kind in each, as compared with the features we know for certain to have characterized three other sets of Iranic languages: (1) their reconstructed shared ancestor, late Common Iranic, the grammar of which is best represented in its oldest attested offshoots, Old Persian and Avestan; (2) Middle Iranic languages contemporary with them used in Central Asia: Sogdian, Chorasmian, Khotanese, and Tumshuqese; and (3) most other modern languages of the Iranic family, from Turkey and Iraq to Pakistan. Although the ancestors of most of the modern Iranic languages shared in the loss of much of the same inflectional complexity – so that, for example, they have just two inherited noun cases and two verb stems of the same ancient derivation like Middle Persian – they also frequently preserve grammatical features lost in Middle Persian, Parthian, and Bactrian, like distinct masculine and feminine grammatical genders. This demonstrates that most modern Iranic languages besides New Persian must have descended from extensively reduced varieties of Old

---

[11] Bonman, Halfmann, Korobzow, and Bobomulloev 2023; Sims-Williams 2025.
[12] Henning (1958: 102–104) showed that a Parthian translation of a Manichaean Middle Persian hymn relied on its own vocabulary rather than exact cognates with Persian, even when those cognates were available. This indicates that the highly similar cognate words that they shared bore different senses or were words differing in the appropriateness of their contextual use in their respective languages.

Iranic, but not from varieties that had been reduced to the extent that Parthian or Bactrian were.[13]

One of Paul's studies of the taxonomy of Western Iranic languages remarked on this discrepancy between modern Iranic languages of western Iran and the relative simplicity of Parthian morphology, saying "a still unanswered question of West Iranian dialectology" is "why Parthian, spoken nearly 2000 years ago, should be in its noun morphology more modern than any of the closely related N(orth)W(estern) dialects spoken today."[14] Paul's question, expressed casually, was not new. Otto Jespersen (1860–1943) wrote in 1894 on the distinction between "modern" and "ancient" languages, the difference being that the latter had many more numerous forms of a single word.[15] We saw that Meillet, in 1912, considered the Middle Iranic languages to seem "modern." In 1927, Hans Reichelt (1877–1939) also wrote that "decay" caused the ancient Middle Iranic languages – especially the western ones, Middle Persian and Parthian – to enter "the state of almost modern languages" already before the Christian era.[16] Likening these languages to modern languages implies that modern languages constitute a morphologically analytical and inflectionally bare type. The concept of a distinct modern type of language is ill-founded, however. It is not modernity per se but widespread adult acquisition that induces language change in the direction of inflectional simplicity. This is surely the reason for the character of Parthian grammar, just as it was for Middle Persian. If we restate Paul's unanswered question, though, it is effectively the same one that I am attempting to answer here: why was ancient Parthian more morphologically simplified and less characterized by contextual inflection than its closest living cousins more than a thousand years later? Now that its ancient neighbor and sibling, Bactrian, is much better known, we can pose the same question of Bactrian, too.

---

[13] On the typology of the modern Western Iranic languages, see Windfuhr 1989. Cf. Korn 2016: 408–409.
[14] Paul 1998: 172.
[15] Jespersen 1894: 345–346. "Ancient languages have several forms where modern languages content themselves with fewer; ... Where the modern language has one or two cases, in an earlier stage it had three or four, and still earlier even seven or eight." Jespersen (1894: 337) explicitly compares Modern Persian with Zend (Avestan) in discussing this point. On this, see also Trudgill 2011: 185–186.
[16] Reichelt 1927: 4. "Denn der Verfall, dessen Merkmale schon die höfische Sprache der Achämeniden an sich trägt, ist zum mindesten im Westen sehr früh eingetreten, da feststeht, daß sich die Dialekte der Persis und Parthiens schon vor dem Beginn der christlichen Ära im Zustande fast moderner Sprachen befunden haben."

Systemic Similarities between Middle Persian, Parthian, and Bactrian

Middle Persian, Parthian, and Bactrian appear, superficially, to be cut from the same material. Of course, most of their similarities are due to their derivation from a Common Iranic ancestor, but that is not what I mean. It is not just a matter of lexical and formal cognates of the sort found in all Iranic languages. It is morphological reduction on a similar pattern. The noun systems of all three were reduced to one declension of two numbers and two cases with the same functions and the same case-marking suffixes (further eroded in Middle Persian and Parthian; Bactrian noun inflectional endings became as simple as those of the other two in the third century CE).[17] Members of the same small class of nouns for family relations (father, mother, sister, etc.) constitute a special type in each, as expected from the regular patterns of syllable loss. Grammatical gender disappeared from Middle Persian and Parthian; it appears evanescent in a few second-century Bactrian inscriptions, absent thereafter. The verbal systems of all three languages lost the ancient perfect and aorist verb stems (like all Iranic languages classified as Middle and New Iranic) and then lost the imperfect verb (the normal one used for past narration in the Old Persian corpus), with the exception of imperfect forms of "to be" and trace examples of imperfect verbs in two specific Middle Persian texts of the third century CE.[18] This left only a completely uninflected perfective participle

---

[17] Kreidl (2024), following Sims-Williams (2015: 258), shows that five third-century Bactrian texts of the Kushan period show some irregularly occurring traces of the old instrumental-ablative nominal and pronominal case in the singular (not plural), in an agent function in a preterit ergative construction and somewhat more often with locational prepositions. This calls to mind the parallel restricted use of the Old Persian instrumental-ablative only with prepositions from Artaxerxes I onward (Cantera 2009: 26–28). Noun phrases in Kushan-period Bactrian with these instrumental-ablative cases do not show clear concord of case from word to word within the same noun phrase. Kreidl (2024: 217) considers as one possibility "attributing this bewildering variety to the increasing uncertainty regarding case usage in the grammatical system" on the part of Bactrian-speakers. These Kushan Bactrian texts may thus reflect something like the state of Persian in the early fourth century BCE.

[18] The handful of examples of the surviving Middle Persian imperfect verb, if Skjærvø (1997b) has identified them correctly (see earlier Henning 1958: 101–102), occur only in the late-third-century inscriptions of the priest Kirdēr and on an inscribed fire altar from Pārs at the very onset of Sasanian rule. Imperfect verbs other than a few forms of "was" otherwise occur neither in the third-century Sasanian Middle Persian royal inscriptions nor in the Manichaean Middle Persian texts, both being much more extensive sets of texts. This suggests that the imperfect was harbored only in a less cosmopolitan dialect of Middle Persian and had become defunct elsewhere. See Durkin-Meisterernst's caution (2014: 244–245 §491), as well as MacKenzie's skepticism (1993: 105, 107) and Skjærvø's response (1997b: 183–184), about the reading of some of these inscriptional forms as imperfect verbs. Weber ignores the issue in her interpretation of the Barm-i Dilak inscription (2016).

combined with present-stem copulas as the basis for past-time reference.[19] In Middle Persian and Parthian, the plural forms of the clitic pronouns are formed agglutinatively with the addition of the same suffix, *-ān*, which was imported to the pronouns from the nouns; Bactrian shows a closely parallel development.[20] The present-stem verbs of all three were conjugated with the same generalized suffix, *-áya-*, a single common morphological reduction out of several possibilities from the inherited verbal inflection classes.[21] Examples of verbs conjugated in the third-person singular present without this generalized suffix do appear in Bactrian and possibly in Middle Persian (as well as other Iranic languages).[22] All three retained a subjunctive mood, exhibit an uncommonly used optative (more productive in Bactrian) restructured along mutually parallel lines,[23] and imperative verbs, all used and formed nearly the same way, based on an unchanging present verb stem, with a few exceptions.

These languages each reflect sweeping changes leading to an outcome of extraordinary mutual similarity in type, in each case apparently formally correlating with the position of the stress accent. (I discussed the relative value of structural explanations of this kind in Chapter 3.) Sims-Williams refers to the "severe simplification of the inflectional system" in Bactrian,[24] the least reduced of the three, and we have already seen similar assessments for the other two languages. The features mentioned in the preceding paragraph, moreover, concern inflectional morphology alone. More changes common to the three could be listed, as well as many features in which they diverge significantly from one another, differentiating the three as distinct languages.

While the imperfect verb did exist in a dialect of early third-century Middle Persian, this may have been marginal (Durkin-Meisterernst 2014: 246 §493, "sehr eingeschränkt").

[19] The sole surviving past-time construction, based on the perfective participle, was normal in Old Persian. The "rise of the ergative" is best understood as the outcome of the attrition of all other distinct past-time forms.

[20] A few traces of plural endings *-ūn* and *-īn* are attested in Middle Persian, vestiges of different ancient noun declensions (Durkin-Meisterernst 2014: 199–201 §422).

[21] Tedesco 1923: 302; Sims-Williams 1989: 235; Durkin-Meisterernst 2014: 243 §489. Gholami (2014: 107), implicitly contra Sims-Williams, interprets the Bactrian verb endings rather as copulas derived from demonstrative pronouns, but this seems unlikely.

[22] Sims-Williams (2007: 41–42) dubbed these "Class B" verbs. See Gershevitch 1970; for Middle Persian examples, see Skjærvø 2009b: 217 §3.2.4.1. Durkin-Meisterernst (2014: 240 §485) suggests that the shorter third-person singular endings in Middle Persian represent interference from New Persian as used by later Zoroastrian copyists of Middle Persian books, not a direct ancient inheritance.

[23] Korn (2019: 267) rightly interprets the pattern of the development of the Middle Persian, Parthian, and Bactrian optative verb morphology as an areal feature. I discuss this later in this chapter.

[24] Sims-Williams 1989: 234.

It is unlikely, however, that all three languages, spoken in adjacent regions, evolved just so independently of each other and happened to end up so very alike fortuitously, while other Iranic languages did not. There are only two plausible explanations to account for their uncannily common developmental outcomes. Either they took their shape in the same period under the same or closely similar circumstances to those described in the last chapter, as contemporary shared phenomena due to common causes in their historical social context, or they are the result of linguistic convergence over time due to extensive social contact between their speakers. Each of these two explanations requires that real, specific social phenomena occurred: mass adult acquisition in the one case and large-scale intergenerational bilingualism in the other. Either explanation has a strong bearing on ancient social history. Importantly, they are not mutually exclusive explanations. Both may be true, but they should be considered separately for the sake of clarity of analysis.

Common Achaemenian Social Conditions

In this scenario, Arya peoples (Iranic language-speakers) like the Medes, Bactrians, and others shared in the benefits of empire along with the Persians, including the importation and employment of foreign slaves, laborers, household servants, and sexual mates, and they collaborated in military endeavors with many others who did not speak their language at first. Mass nonnative acquisition ensued, as deduced in Chapter 3, but, on this explanation, it was not only adult learning of Persian but also of other regional Old Iranic dialects. This entailed "severe simplification" (as Sims-Williams put it) of the immediate ancestors of the attested Parthian and Bactrian texts, just as it did for Persian. This explanation is supported generally by the geography of the Iranic languages over time. Most known Iranic languages from former Achaemenian territory retained only two nominal cases from Old Iranic, the direct (from the nominative) and oblique (from different cases, especially the genitive).[25] Some of these languages, later, generated new cases as they evolved, as the speech of eventually more socially remote communities, but those two noun cases were the only inherited ones. Most known Iranic languages in former Achaemenian territory have built their past-time verbs from the perfective patient participle in *-t- together with copulas, although they have later evolved into more complex systems from that foundation, with innovated prefixes, periphrastic constructions, and other new features. At the same

---

[25] Klingenschmitt 2000; Cantera 2009.

time, while all these languages shared in the loss of many grammatical features, the reduction of inflectional systems was not all equally far-reaching. Many modern Iranic languages have retained some major Old Iranic features, like grammatical gender distinctions with corresponding inflections, which were lost by Middle Persian, Parthian, and, by the third century CE, Bactrian. The linguistic principles (Chapter 2) suggest that the less-reduced varieties, whose descendants survive to this day, derive from dialects learned by fewer new contacts. These were Iranic dialects spoken in less socially accessible places in mountains and deserts or in villages away from major routes of transit. The effects of mass adult acquisition on ancient varieties of Iranic were therefore not uniform. The languages were affected according to specific population movements and social contacts about which we know few specific facts. This is one hypothesis.

Long-Term (Intergenerational) Bilingualism

Convergence probably also contributed somewhat to the shared, common reduction of Middle Persian, Parthian, and Bactrian, as well as of the generality of modern Iranic languages used in contact with the rest. The main indication of convergence is the phenomenon called areal features: an areal feature means a linguistic feature held in common by languages with a geographical area of use in common without necessarily having common ancestry for that feature. For historical linguists, invoking areal features is a last resort, sometimes when the comparative method does not seem to produce neatly distinct developments for related languages. Dubbing a shared feature areal, however, postulates a lived social history that is rarely discussed explicitly. Areal features always implicitly propose a hypothesis of widespread bilingualism over generations fostered by meaningful social ties between groups using different languages in their most local environments.[26] It is such conditions in which bilingual individuals can enact the slow convergence of languages. That said, convergence is often a misleading term, because it is typically not a reciprocal process, but is based on unilateral copying of features from the language of a socially powerful group and their replication in the home language of a bilingual.[27] All-pervasive bilingualism need not be

---

[26] Muysken 2008. Heine and Kuteva's (2005: 175–177) pessimism about the value of a linguistic area for shedding light on the history of the speakers of languages involved in it is not warranted, because the kinds of features that are transferred between languages can tell us about the social relations between their users; see Chapter 2.

[27] Ross 2007: 133.

a characteristic of either group, but lasting and widespread areal features, representing the convergence of two or more languages, probably do not come about through the speech of a very small number of individuals, either. Many should be bilingual with the other language. It is the bilinguals who replicate features of their second language in their own dominant language. Widespread bilingualism is a realistic historical social model for the geographically contiguous pairs of Middle Persian-Parthian and Parthian-Bactrian. As the Achaemenian state and subsequent imperial dynasties facilitated conduits of communication and exchange, masses of people fluent in more than one species of Iranic language will likely have transferred features from one similar language to another, generating areal features. One might assume this to have been more easily accomplished with languages that are as closely cognate as the Iranic ones, but social proximity, not common ancestry, has priority as the fundamental requirement for the replication of features from one language in another.[28] Areal features do not inherently entail grammatical simplification, however. They may represent reduction of grammatical complexity or, by contrast, proliferation of grammatical complexity, or both.[29] In this case, areal features may nevertheless be behind some of the grammatical reduction in Iranic languages. We can imagine how this might work. If, for example, the much-reduced late Achaemenian Persian, an incipient Middle Persian, was a prestigious language, as speaking it signified belonging to the dominant class of Persian rulers, then speakers of other Iranic dialects may well have replicated simplified paradigms analogically from it in their own regional language.[30] They may have simply omitted features of their own language to match the pattern of late Achaemenian Persian. This would also facilitate their efforts to make themselves understood in speech with Persians and non-Persians, along the lines of foreigner talk. Persian-speakers, native or nonnative, on the other hand, also must have spoken reduced varieties of other Iranic dialects, when they felt motivated to attempt their use, imposing inflectional reduction or simplification as already found in Persian onto other Iranic languages. Convergence by itself does not explain sweeping grammatical reduction, but it may have been a way in which the reduced inflectional patterns of one language, presumably

---

[28] Bowern (2013) gives reasons to doubt that relatedness of languages is the chief factor in the transfer of features, emphasizing rather proximity.
[29] Van Coetsem 2000: 181; Trudgill 2011: 42.
[30] On L2→L1-replication, see Heine and Kuteva 2005: 237–239. See also Matras 2009: 235–266 and Butts 2016: 139–152.

Persian, were transferred to another.³¹ In short, bilingualism among these languages could account for the evolution of some of the systemic similarity between Middle Persian, Parthian, and Bactrian. It is difficult to decide between the two. The problem deserves more analysis.

Both Mass Adult Acquisition and Convergence

Without further discoveries – such as earlier texts in Parthian or Bactrian – it is likely to be difficult for researchers to distinguish which of these two possible social factors in grammatical reduction is more responsible for the closely parallel losses of features in two languages when one of them is not attested until centuries after that loss. Part of the problem is that the common loss of complex features – just the kind of change fostered by adult acquisition – does not guarantee common ancestry, whereas shared morphological innovations usually do. A further difficulty is the possibility that both social patterns leading to the reduction of grammar, just described, were sometimes combined. What would happen if a new speaker of the reduced Proto-Middle Persian – say, a Babylonian or Greek maid taken captive by Persians – were suddenly to find herself in the service of a Bactrian lady through sale, gift, inheritance, or change of employer?³² Her efforts to learn the local Iranic language, Bactrian, are likely to rely on some of the same linguistic strategies she used in speaking incipient Middle Persian: grammatical imposition and omission. If adult learners of Old Iranic dialects were especially common in the Achaemenian period, as the late Old Persian inscriptions and the sources reviewed in the last chapter require us to accept, and some of them had to use more than one dialect, as must have happened sometimes, then the same specific linguistic strategies, in the vein of foreigner talk and pidginization, may well have been widely employed in the context of different Iranic languages in neighboring regions at the same time. It depends partly on how much migration of workers and other non-Arya subjects we imagine having occurred. In any case, the kinds of grammatical simplification that

---

[31] Ross' (2007: 124) concise term *metatypy* may prove useful here, which he defines as "a diachronic process whereby the morphosyntactic constructions of one of the languages of a bilingual speech community are restructured on the model of the constructions of the speakers' other language, such that the constructions of the replica language come to more closely match those of the model language in both meaning and morphosyntax." Ross' example concerns metatypy between unrelated languages. The case is blurrier for these three very closely related languages.

[32] This kind of thing evidently happened. I think of Herodotus' characterization of a threat posed to Greek rebels of Ionia that their boys would be turned into eunuchs and their unwed daughters "hauled off inland to Bactra (Balkh)" (τὰς δὲ παρθένους ἀναστπάστους ἐς Βάκτρα, Herodotus 6.9.4).

adult learners imposed on the one dialect out of convenience and necessity could be transferred by adult learners from one to the other. This would make adult learners the source of convergence as well as morphological simplification, combining both social causes in the same individuals' agency.

It is conceivable, along the same lines, that the similar outcomes in these three languages were due not to their convergence with each other, but rather to their convergence with an otherwise unattested reduced vehicular variety of Iranic, such as a pidgin that may have been used as a medium of communication primarily by servile peoples who did not speak an Iranic language natively. Then features of this purely hypothetical variety could have become entrenched permanently in the speech of the most cosmopolitan Iranic language-speakers. Here, it is worthwhile to note that one of Holm's components in the generation of a semicreole is "incorporating structural features from fully pidginized or creolized varieties of the target language spoken by newcomers or found locally but confined to contiguous areas where sociolinguistic conditions were favorable to full restructuring."[33] That is, if certain classes of people were speaking fully fledged pidgin varieties of Old Persian, this may well have contributed to the reduction of the variety spoken natively by those raised as Persian as well as that of speakers of Old Parthian and Old Bactrian.

There is a consideration that seems to give more weight to a common social cause as the explanation rather than convergence over time. It seems unlikely that the noun and verb systems of both Parthian and Bactrian would have converged with Middle Persian due to bilingualism as areal features so extensively without other glaring signs of features transferred between them. There are some Parthian (non-Perside) words adopted in Persian and there are Persian words adopted in Bactrian (from the Sasanian period, much later than the Achaemenids), for example, but lexical transfer between these languages is not nearly so conspicuous as their similar patterns of grammatical reduction. This suggests that imposition of adult learners was the chief force behind this, rather than long-term bilingualism. As Thomason surmises about language contact generally, "if we can establish significant structural interference, but there are few or no loanwords, then interference must have come about via imperfect learning of a target language during shift [of a population to the target language from one or more other languages], not through borrowing."[34] That is, the linguistic phenomena signal not adoption of linguistic features but imposition and omission.

[33] Holm 2000b: 32. [34] Thomason 2001: 80.

Comparisons with Languages from the Outer Achaemenian Domain and Beyond

Comparison of the inflectional morphology of Middle Persian, Parthian, and Bactrian with their other known contemporary Middle Iranic languages to the east offers a strong indication that it was social mixture and consequent mass nonnative acquisition fostered by Achaemenian society that generated grammatically reduced regional Iranic languages.[35] We see, roughly, that the farther they lay from the centers of Achaemenian power, the more inherited inflectional complexity they retained. Such observations do not provide for an exact science, but they nevertheless show a striking correspondence between the grammars of the specific languages and the social-linguistic principles introduced in Chapter 2.

Sogdian was an Iranic language spoken to the north of Bactria in what is today eastern Uzbekistan, in a prosperous country of developed towns along the Zerafshan and Kashka rivers. The region of Sogdia was thus on the northeastern outskirts of the Achaemenian domain. Sogdian came to be written in a derivation of the Aramaic script, like Middle Persian and Parthian. There are a few short Sogdian inscriptions surviving from as early as the second century CE,[36] but the oldest extant substantial texts are remarkably well-preserved letters from the early fourth century CE, found in the ruin of a Chinese frontier fortification. Still in the time of these letters, contemporary with Middle Persian, Parthian, and Bactrian texts and their reduced grammar, Sogdian retained two to six of the Common Iranic noun cases, depending on the noun, as well as the three common Indo-European grammatical genders (masculine, feminine, and neuter), and a specialized function of the dual inflection for counted nouns.[37] Like Old Persian and Avestan, Sogdian retained the imperfect verb and elaborate distinctions of verbal mood. Sogdian also underwent various other modifications conditioned by the position of the ancient lexical stress accent: when it fell on inflectional endings, those endings tended to be preserved, but when it was on noun or verb stems, the endings were reduced or lost, as in Middle Persian. This meant the development of two separate inflectional classes of verbs and nouns depending on the position of the accent, one more like that of Middle Persian and the

---

[35] These kinds of comparisons are not new. See, e.g., Henning 1958: 89–92, "Ganz anders das Ostiranische, dessen Sprachtyp dem des Mittelwestiranischen in manchen Punkten diametral entgegengesetzt ist." See also Szemerényi 1980; Sims-Williams 1981a: 165.
[36] Grenet, Sims-Williams, and Podushkin 2007; Sims-Williams 2022.
[37] On this function of the ancient dual form and its presence in different Iranic languages, see Sims-Williams 2019.

other more conservative. Along with this, Sogdian exhibits further modest reduction as well as distinct innovation.[38] The conservative features of early Sogdian as well as its complexifying innovations imply that it was a language learned by relatively few outsiders before the fourth century CE. When Alexander's armies arrived in Sogdia, they reportedly required a special interpreter for the speech of the people of Samarkand, suggesting that the Iranic speech of this outlying country remained distinct at the end of the Achaemenian period.[39]

Chorasmian, a close cousin of Sogdian, was spoken in the towns and farms along the river delta that formerly existed to the south of the Aral Sea, in northwestern Uzbekistan. This was the northernmost province of the Achaemenids, virtually an oasis of settlements surrounded by desert and seashore, connected to the rest of the empire by the Amu Darya river flowing from Bactria to its south, north of the oasis of Marw. The extant ancient Chorasmian texts are very few and limited, telling us little about the grammar of the language in antiquity. Whatever Chorasmian texts were written are now mostly lost. Much later, a few thirteenth- and fourteenth-century Chorasmian texts preserved in the Arabic script are the most extensive and latest known texts in language. These attest to the state of Chorasmian after centuries of Arab, Turk, and Mongol invasions and many changes of government. Even in this much later period, Chorasmian still retained two genders, five noun cases (though with only two or three inflectional endings between them for any declension), the imperfect verb along with the present stem as well as the expected preterit stem, and numerous innovations.[40]

Because extensive, sudden grammatical reduction is induced by mass adult acquisition, any hypothesis about the nonreduction of Sogdian and Chorasmian should be contextualized with evidence that these two languages were more isolated from numerous outsiders than Persian, Parthian, and Bactrian. In these cases, it is obvious: Sogdia and Chorasmia

---

[38] Yoshida 2009. The large Sogdian noun-class bearing just two cases, called heavy stems, is formed quite differently from that of the two-case system of Bactrian, Parthian, and Middle Persian nouns, all of which use the inherited genitive for the oblique case.

[39] For some reason, a Lycian bearing an Iranic name spoke that language. Perhaps his mother was Sogdian. Arrian 4.3.7: ἐπιτάσσει δὲ αὐτοῖς Φαρνούχην τὸν ἑρμηνέα, τὸ μὲν γένος Λύκιον τὸν Φαρνούχην, ἐμπείρως δὲ τῆς τε φωνῆς τῶν ταύτῃ βαρβάρων ἔχοντα. This does suggest a distinct Sogdian speech already in the fourth century BCE. Briant (2002: 509) mentions this testimony to the existence of a form of Sogdian speech unintelligible to outsiders in his argument that "there is nothing to indicate widespread use of the Persian language among the Iranian peoples." This claim must now be diminished, if not abandoned, considering the preceding discussion.

[40] Durkin-Meisterernst 2009.

were remote northeastern regions of the Achaemenian Empire and were probably not places receiving frequent visitors from the main part of it. La Vaissière characterizes Achaemenian Sogdia as "a distant frontier province" governed from Bactria "in constant contact with the nomads of the steppe."[41] Its provincial isolation would limit the causes of linguistic reduction that prevailed in imperial centers to the west and south. Chorasmia may even have been more in the nature of a client country peripheral to the Achaemenian domain rather than a tightly integrated province.[42] A few scholars have supposed that it became independent sometime during or after the reign of Artaxerxes II, which would naturally cut it off from some of the causes of grammatical reduction proposed here.[43] In the end, we know very little about the social history of the speakers of Sogdian and Chorasmian, apart from what the conservatism of their inflectional morphology shows us. Here, it is the linguistic theory applied to these two languages that offers insight into the history of the populations of their speakers. Yet there are many possibilities. Perhaps the movement of nomadic speakers of relatively unreduced Iranic languages into these regions could have displaced older, more reduced varieties of regional Iranic speech that are not otherwise attested. Such speculation aside, what the extant data do show is a couple of languages infrequently learned by adults from other countries.

Two other Middle Iranic languages are attested from a region never controlled by the Achaemenids. Khotanese and Tumshuqese were Iranic languages used outside of the Achaemenian domain, spoken by ancient immigrants who founded settlements at the desert oases in what are today the western edges of the Xinjiang Uygur Autonomous Region of the People's Republic of China. These languages remained in use there for centuries. Tumshuqese is too poorly known to form a useful comparand here, but Khotanese illustrates the present point clearly. The Iranic language of Khotan was used by a local monarchy and for an extensive Buddhist literature in the first millennium of the common era, contemporary with texts extant in Middle Persian, Parthian, Bactrian, and Sogdian. Substantial Khotanese texts survive. Early Khotanese texts distinguish two grammatical genders, masculine and feminine, with traces of the old neuter gender, and at least six different ancient noun declensions (*a*-, *ā*-, *i*-, *nd*-, *n*-, and *r*-stems) as well as innovated new declensions. Nouns differ by as many as six inherited cases. Although the ancient imperfect verb has been lost,

---

[41] De La Vaissière 2011. [42] Minardi 2015: 84.
[43] Frye 1984: 112; Rapoport 1991; Wiesehöfer 1996: 108.

verbs generally are inflected for all the moods attested in Avestan, with separate active and middle endings for several conjugations. The level of inflectional complexity is very high compared with Bactrian, Parthian, and Middle Persian.[44]

Modern Iranic languages that evolved in places remote from the centers of ancient Achaemenian power show similar distinctions in inflectional complexity. Yaghnobi has already been mentioned, but we can add the testimony of Pashto, the Iranic language of a numerous population who had been, until the eighteenth and nineteenth centuries, "people at the margins" of empires, as Thomas Barfield put it, living in tribes based on egalitarian lineages.[45] D. N. MacKenzie sketched the "remarkably complex nominal and verbal morphology" of Pashto, spoken today by millions in southern and eastern Afghanistan and western Pakistan.[46] Pashto retains the ancient Iranic masculine and feminine genders, the ancient class of $\bar{a}$-stem nouns as a separate declension, and, remarkably, traces of the ancient pattern of accentuation on some words. Georg Morgenstierne wrote, "Nowhere in Iran, and hardly in any modern I(ndo-)E(uropean) language, do we find such a bewildering variety of nominal plural endings" as in Pashto.[47] Much of this variety is innovation, not due to inheritance from Common Iranic, but MacKenzie remarked casually that "If we compare the archaic structure of Pashto with the much simplified morphology of Persian, the leading modern Iranian language, we see that it stands to its 'second cousin' and neighbour in something like the same relationship as Icelandic does to English."[48] Such remarks by specialists in Iranic languages reveal unstated suspicions about the social factors that play a role in conditioning the morphology. MacKenzie's remark is cited by McWhorter in his study of the contrast between Pashto and New Persian, which singles New Persian out as having been reduced by nonnative acquisition (see Chapter 2).[49] Pashto looks like a language removed from the morphology-reducing effects of the sudden arrival of populations of foreigners at Iranophone sites, induced by the reign of the Achaemenids.

The Hypothesis of Central Iranic and Areal Features

Alternatively, one could imagine that both Parthian and Bactrian became grammatically reduced only after the downfall of the Achaemenian Empire

---

[44] Emmerick 2009. [45] Barfield 2010: 78–80, 90. [46] MacKenzie 1987.
[47] Morgenstierne 1942: 90.
[48] MacKenzie 1987: 554 and 565; Morgenstierne 1973 and Cheung 2009–2010 (on accent).
[49] McWhorter 2007: 140.

and before both languages are attested. For this to work in the case of Parthian, we would have to posit that it shed its complex inflections between Alexander and the earliest attested Parthian texts from the first century BCE, under Seleucid rule. This seems much less plausible, unless we assume that few foreigners learned the ancestor of Parthian during Achaemenian times, and the reduction occurred only when many Greek-speaking newcomers in the wake of Alexander learned Parthian at once. In that case, we should expect to find features from Greek transferred into Parthian, and Parthian words adopted in Greek. But we do not find them. The unattested Old Parthian is therefore likely to have been restructured into the Parthian we know in tandem with Old Persian's transformation into Middle Persian, in the Achaemenian period. The morphology of Bactrian may have diminished from its prior Common Iranic state during the comings and goings of invading peoples and new dynasties from Alexander to the Kushans. The linguistic model suggests that people at social crossroads should be expected to speak languages with reduced inflection, regardless of other factors. But it is less plausible that Middle Persian, Parthian, and Bactrian lost the same features in the same way, and generalized the same features in morphological reduction, for entirely separate reasons that left no trace in each instance. This suggests common circumstances in the formation of each of these languages.

All offshoots of a prior single language initially share in its earlier innovations. What they retain of these innovations is a sign for historical linguists of the former unity of their speech community. That is, shared morphological innovations in two related languages strongly indicate common ancestry in a society of people who could speak to each other and understand each other because they spoke more or less the same language, a language that changed eventually for all its speakers systematically, as languages do. Therefore, shared morphological innovations serve as a strong criterion for determining the affiliation and the order of separation of the descendant languages from their common stock. When shared innovations cannot be accounted for by the comparative method, however, because they seem to have crossed language boundaries or to have arisen separately in two related but adjacent languages, historical linguists invoke areal features as described. Areal feature is a term describing an outcome, not the process by which they originated. As already discussed, to call on areal features as an explanation is to assert a specific social scenario of multigenerational bilingualism, because only bilinguals can transfer features like morphological innovations from one language into another. It is now generally agreed that even fundamental features of morphology are susceptible to transfer,⁵⁰ but one expects this only when bilingualism with the two languages involved is widespread in a society.

In 1976, Robert Hetzron rightly insisted that shared morphological innovation is an especially strong criterion for determining the affiliation of the Semitic languages.⁵¹ His article expressing this had the effect of rewriting the family tree of the Semitic languages, relocating Arabic away from the branch of the family called South Semitic, where it had been regarded as closely connected with the Ethiopic languages, into a new Central Semitic group, together with Hebrew and Aramaic. In the decades since then, his revised model has become the consensus on the reconstructed Semitic family tree and Central Semitic is a generally acknowledged subgrouping of Semitic. Not dissimilarly, in an article of 2016, Agnes Korn used the new data from Bactrian and the principle of shared morphological innovations to propose a Central branch of the Iranic languages.⁵² Her partially revised family tree, which focuses on the Middle Iranic languages, is based on phonological and morphological innovations shared between Parthian, Bactrian, and Sogdian. These three appear to share not just grammatical reduction but also certain common innovatory features. Applying the principle that affinity is demonstrated by shared innovations, she shows that Sogdian probably diverged earlier from Bactrian and Parthian. (Previously, Bactrian had been assumed to belong to an Eastern Iranic branch of languages, a subgrouping that no longer has any sure empirical basis.)⁵³ Korn's proposal of a Central Iranic subgroup is promising, and it appears that more insights are yet to come from this direction.

One noteworthy aspect of her proposed configuration of the branching trees leading to Middle Iranic is, however, the inference of areal features. In Korn's analysis, Middle Persian clearly belongs to a separate branch of Middle Iranic. This coheres with the long-standing recognition of decisive phonological isoglosses that mark Persian (and its phonologically closest cousins, called Perside languages) apart from its neighbors to the north, discussed in Chapter 3. For example, Middle Persian has *dil* for "heart" whereas Parthian has *zird*, both from an earlier **źṛd* (cf. Avestan *zərəd-*, Balochi *zird*,⁵⁴ Pashto *zṛə*).⁵⁵, ⁵⁶ The initial consonant of the Persian word

---

⁵⁰ Heine and Kuteva 2005. ⁵¹ Hetzron 1976; see also Hetzron 1974.
⁵² Korn 2016, followed by Korn 2019 on the same problem.
⁵³ Sims-Williams 1996: "However, it does not seem possible to regard the Eastern Iranian group as a whole ... as a genetic grouping." See also Wendtland 2009, Novák 2014, and Korn 2019: 248–250.
⁵⁴ Korn 2005a: 295. ⁵⁵ Morgenstierne 2003: 103.
⁵⁶ Hübschmann 1895: 220–221 §110, 263 §160; Sadovsky 2017: 582.

sets the history of other Iranic languages that systematically share this feature into a group apart from their relatives but together with Persian. At the same time, however, Korn recognizes affinity between Persian and Parthian, and to a lesser extent Bactrian, crossing between the separate branches and making the lines of descent unclear. Without many specifics, she turns to areal features in her explanation for these phenomena: "there is sufficient motivation at hand to justify the attempt of a different family tree, and of an approach that combines it with areal features."[57] Not only does she hypothesize areal features shared between the three languages under discussion here – Middle Persian, Parthian, and Bactrian – but also another set of areal features shared separately among Bactrian and "some Pamir languages" of the Iranic family. In her second contribution directed at this problem, Korn proposes that a wave model, based on the geographical distribution of isoglosses among the Iranic languages, may describe their interrelationships better than the traditional branching tree model. She suggests that apparent waves of features that spread from Persian are "possibly attributable to the periods of Persian as official language in Achaemenid and Sasanian times."[58] Although in neither time was Persian the "official" language, strictly speaking, of the domain ruled by the Persians – there was no constitution or decree stipulating an official language – the basic idea has been corroborated by my findings in the present study. All one needs to do is change the word from "official" language to "ruling-elite" language.

Korn has opened a new and exciting phase in the study of Iranic historical linguistics that will require more research for its ramifications to be traced. It is likely to change our comprehension of many specific and general features in the historical relationships of the Iranic languages. Readers can join me in holding high hopes for more results along these lines. The present concern, however, is with reconciling social history and linguistic history. Again, areal features automatically imply long-term bilingualism or multilingualism in some past period. Korn's hypothesis of widespread areal features shared in the formation of Middle Persian, Parthian, and Bactrian, which she arrives at by the methods of comparative historical linguistics, matches the present thesis based on correlation between the linguistic models and the history of the inflection of these languages. Areal features point to social factors and language contact,

---

[57] Korn 2016: 418. Extensive and lasting ancient contact among Western Iranic languages is also posited by Jügel 2014. Bowern (2013: 426–428) discusses other cases in which the transfer of features between related language due to population contact impedes genealogical subgrouping.
[58] Korn 2019.

The Hypothesis of Central Iranic and Areal Features 191

specifically bilingualism, and the restructuring and diminishment of inflectional morphology in these Iranic languages was due to social factors. The period in which these factors played a role must have been one in which the populations that spoke the immediate ancestors of Middle Persian, Parthian, and Bactrian were united in one political domain, before they came to be attested directly. That can be only the Achaemenian period.

Like the concept of "Central Iranic," or indeed that of any proposed linguistic group, the argument I have advanced here is ultimately inferential,[59] but it does find support from these distinct lines of inquiry. It helps us to reconcile known ancient history with specific characteristics of the languages involved. In the comparative method of historical linguistics, shared innovations typically indicate a common social historical stage. The common loss of final syllables after or in tandem with the common repositioning of the accent in Persian, Parthian, and Bactrian therefore suggests a common social history. A major theoretical question requiring further research is whether co-occurring reductions or losses of the same sets of features in different systems can be diagnostic in the strong way that shared phonological and morphological innovations are.

As discussed here previously, languages do not inherently and automatically undergo a cycle of decay and regeneration of inflectional morphology. These variations over time correspond only with the social history of the speakers of the languages. This may make sense of the evolution of the generality of the Iranic languages. For a time, many Iranic language-speakers, with the Persians leading them, presided over and participated in the most extensive empire in the history of the world until that time. An age of population movement and mixing set in, not among all the subject peoples but among the beneficiaries of the empire and their polyethnic servitors, leading to grammatical reduction and widespread areal features among the Iranic languages of the masters. In subsequent ages, speakers of these languages were only rarely united in one political domain. Meanwhile, the Iranic languages spoken in places remote from population movement remained more morphologically conservative. Some, like (Proto-)Balochi, took on a much-reduced form – in this case extremely close to ancient Parthian – but subsequently evolved into new levels of inflectional complexity, "mutating normally," in McWhorter's catchy phrase,[60] among relatively insular pastoralists during and after their

---

[59] Ringe and Eska (2013: 32) note that in all historical linguistics "we are constrained to *infer* the origins not only of all linguistic changes of the past, but also of all or most of the changes in progress that we can still observe" (emphasis in original).
[60] McWhorter 2007: 151.

migration to the region now called Balochistan. On the hypothesis that the Achaemenian Empire created the circumstances for the reduction of the Iranic languages, as postulated first by Meillet, these modern Iranic languages should serve as important examples in future studies of the gradual growth of inflectional complexity from reduced states.

An Achaemenian Common Tongue?

The ancient Greek scholar Eratosthenes (*circa* 275–*circa* 195 BCE), in a report preserved by Strabo, stated that the geographical name Ariana (ἡ Ἀριανή), which referred to a region of what is today western Afghanistan, could be extended to include the Medes, Persians, Bactrians, and Sogdians, "for they speak just about the same language, with small differences."[61] The remark is clearly based on an awareness that the term Arya referred also to a larger group of people, whom we designate as ancient Iranic language-speakers. Eratosthenes surely derived this report from an earlier source, so it probably reflects the linguistic situation around the end of the Achaemenids' dynasty. As Panaino rightly recognizes, this ambiguous statement may be interpreted variously.[62] The possibility that jumps to mind first is that the four peoples named here, for each of whom a distinct Iranic language is attested in later centuries, were indeed recognized as speaking closely cognate languages with a common name, Arya. Inscriptions in two of these languages, Old Persian (Bisitun, 521 BCE) and Bactrian (Rabatak, second century CE), both refer to their own language as "Arya,"[63] suggesting that this was indeed the name of the common ancestor of the Iranic languages (spoken by the people known in Avestan as *airiia-*), and that at least two of these languages retained that common name as they diverged into separate species over time. Eratosthenes says that this name may apply to all of them. Panaino doubts this interpretation because he holds that Sogdian, Bactrian, Median, and Persian could not have been mutually comprehensible at the end of the Achaemenian period. Amid other speculation, Panaino offers a second plausible hypothesis to explain the statement of Eratosthenes, and this is

---

[61] Strabo 15.2.9: ἐπεκτείνεται δὲ τοὔνομα τῆς Ἀριανῆς μέχρι μέρους τινὸς καὶ Περσῶν καὶ Μήδων καὶ ἔτι τῶν πρὸς ἄρκτον Βακτρίων καὶ Σογδιανῶν· εἰσὶ γάρ πως καὶ ὁμόγλωττοι παρὰ μικρόν. It seems that the source is conflating the region of Haraiwa, the valley of modern Herāt, with the Arya. The lack of an /h/ in eastern dialects of Greek may have contributed to this conflation as the two words are more alike without that /h/.

[62] Panaino 2015.

[63] Schmitt 2009: 87 (DNb §70); Sims-Williams and Cribb 1996: 83; Sims-Williams 2004: 56.

the interpretation that he prefers. If the Iranic languages of the four peoples named must have been mutually incomprehensible, as he supposes, then the claim that they all shared more or less the same language would imply the existence of a "prestigious *passpartout*" variety of the Persian language, a common Iranic tongue.

Both hypotheses have explanatory merits, despite Panaino's doubts about the former. It is entirely possible that the observer originally behind this report reached the conclusion that four ancient regional Iranic languages, despite their evident differences, were basically similar enough to consider them a unit, approximately, and that would help to explain why these four were all known as Arya. The Greek expression "with small differences," παρὰ μικρόν, may simply have been an exaggeration by somebody who noticed shared vocabulary and cognates either without any profound knowledge of any of these languages or, just as plausibly, with knowledge of all of them. In my life, I have heard scholars claim casually that the Romance languages are "basically all the same," even though we observe their mutual incomprehensibility, or quite limited mutual comprehensibility. Such remarks were also possible for polyglots in distant antiquity. But it is also possible that Panaino is right, and that a common lingua franca variety of Persian was employed across all these domains. A further complication is that, although Eratosthenes or his informant must have intended only one of these possibilities, both interpretations still may have been true.

Underlying Panaino's judgment against the first possibility is the widespread but unsupported assumption that language changes are uniformly gradual over time. This is a problem discussed already in Chapter 2. It is impossible to be certain about the pace of change in languages from an unattested, prehistoric state (although sweeping simplification implies rapid change in one episode). The social-linguistic considerations suggest that all these languages may have been mutually comprehensible at an early time in the Achaemenian period, and they may have become quite different by the end of the fourth century BCE. Yet it is precisely the role of Old Persian as a common medium between communities that must account for the degree and rapidity of its restructuring during the same time. Pavel Lurje and Ilya Yakubovich refer to a "Late Old Persian *koine*," apparently positing a similar concept,[64] and recently Yakubovich more explicitly suggests the existence of a "lingua franca" of "the Achaemenid provincial elites, which can be called for

---

[64] Lurje and Yakubovich 2017: 331.

convenience Peripheral Old Persian, and which anticipated the evolution of Late Old Persian," without elaborating its character.[65] This is almost exactly the hypothesis I have been discussing at length. If Old Persian had not been widely adopted by many adult non-Persian-speakers, then there would not be such an enormous discrepancy between the Old Persian of the time of Darius I and that of Artaxerxes III, and we would be at a loss to explain the widely noted early simplification of the inflections of ancient Iranic languages among all the other Indo-European languages. Panaino supposes further, as most plausible among the possibilities, that a form of Old Persian was known widely wherever Persians ruled, and that "necessarily, [this widely used form of Old Persian] should have been known for practical reasons throughout the whole empire, in particular in the higher strata of the Irano-Aryan ethne and in the local administrations of the different satrapies."[66]

This is supported by anecdotes like one in Xenophon's *Anabasis*, in which Xenophon reports that he relied on a Persian-speaking interpreter to communicate with an Armenian village leader and a group of Armenian women at a well in 400 BCE.[67] Here, a form of Persian was the linking language between a Greek mercenary leader and Armenian locals. Neither of the two parties included native speakers of Persian, but Persian was their common medium. Circumstances like these must have been quite common across the Achaemenian Empire. Indeed, native speakers must have been a diminishing proportion of the total number of Persian-speakers for as long as the importation of fighters, workers, slaves, eunuchs, and concubines by the hundreds and thousands was ongoing. Such persons as Xenophon's interpreter and his Armenian interlocutors would not require the highly inflected noun and verb endings natural to the language of Darius I. They simply needed to communicate, and to communicate simply. In conclusion, I do not know exactly what Eratosthenes' remark means, when he says that these peoples could all be called "Arya" because they speak the same language, with small differences, but either of the two most likely interpretations supports the arguments I have been making.

---

[65] Yakubovich 2020: 109.   [66] Panaino 2015: 96.
[67] Xenophon, *Anabasis* 4.5.34. ἐπεὶ δ' ἀλλήλους ἐφιλοφρονήσαντο Χειρίσοφος καὶ Ξενοφῶν, κοινῇ δὴ ἀνηρώτων τὸν κώμαρχον διὰ τοῦ περσίζοντος ἑρμηνέως τίς εἴη ἡ χώρα. ὁ δ' ἔλεγεν ὅτι Ἀρμενία. 4.5.10. αὗται ἠρώτων αὐτοὺς τίνες εἶεν. ὁ δ' ἑρμηνεὺς εἶπε περσιστὶ ὅτι παρὰ βασιλέως πορεύονται πρὸς τὸν σατράπην.

The Putative Role of Aramaic as an Achaemenian Lingua Franca

Meanwhile, some historians of the Achaemenids have held that the language of written communication among the Persian rulers and their agents was not Persian but Aramaic, even claiming that Aramaic was the lingua franca of the Achaemenian Empire. The latter cannot be true in the conventional sense of the term lingua franca.[68] It applies only with respect to writing for bureaucratic purposes, and, even then, certainly not in every domain. The languages of the provinces continued to be written, as extant texts and subsequent linguistic history show. There was no Achaemenian constitution declaring Aramaic to be the "official language," though many scholars have stated that it was the official language of the empire (thus ignoring the languages of the royal inscriptions and many texts in different languages used for government purposes under Achaemenian rule).[69] One should specify, rather, that it was a "highly standardized supra-regional chancellery language," as Holger Gzella puts it.[70] Jan Tavernier meticulously shows that Aramaic seems to have been used particularly for writing at the satrapal level of administration, meaning that of provincial governors. Documents serving lower levels of administration were written in regional languages.[71] Aramaic letters and documents reflecting the Achaemenian government and its activities have been discovered at opposite ends of the empire, in southern Egypt and in Bactria, where accidents of climate preserved them. These exhibit a remarkably uniform language of business and correspondence. All the Iranic languages that came to be written in antiquity, except perhaps for Bactrian,[72] were rendered in regional varieties of the Aramaic secretarial script of Achaemenian times, which evolved into distinct letter-shapes in the post-Achaemenian age of regional powers. This indicates the widespread use of Aramaic for the ends of the government scribes at a certain high administrative level, but that is all. One might guess that the large-scale importation of eunuchs from Aramaean Assyria and Babylonia may have provided personnel for this kind of standardized Aramaic chancellery with uniform writing, orthography, and style, for some time, but we are not well informed about the subsequent history of this kind of literacy.

---

[68] Hock 1991: 522–523; Winford 2003: 268–269.
[69] Reichelt 1927: 3. Some call Persian "the official language" instead, which is also untrue.
[70] Gzella 2015: 165.   [71] Tavernier 2017.
[72] When the decipherment of the Kushan inscriptions, written in a derivative of the Aramaic script, is complete, this exception may be removed. See Bonman, Halfmann, Korobzow, and Bobomulloev 2023.

In any case, it is quite clear from several facts that Aramaic was never a general vernacular lingua franca across the domains of the Achaemenids.[73] First, Aramaic did not become a common language of any non-Aramaean population, Iranic-speaking or otherwise, under the Achaemenids, except the Judaeans and Babylonians, peoples who already had intensive contacts with Aramaic-speakers under the Assyrian and Babylonian Empires.[74] As just mentioned, Xenophon used a Persian-speaking interpreter to communicate with an Armenian village leader, not a Syrian-speaking (Aramaic-speaking) interpreter. No language of the populations ruled by the Persians, such as Armenian, or indeed any Iranic language, is full of words adopted from Aramaic from this period, as we should expect to find if Aramaic was the common spoken tongue.[75] Instead, Armenian is full of words adopted from Persian and Parthian – a sign of widespread unilateral bilingualism, wherein Armenians knew Western Iranic languages but not vice versa.[76] Old Iranic words were adopted and naturalized in Aramaic already in Achaemenian times.[77] By contrast, Middle Persian exhibits practically no Aramaic adopted words except specifically in Manichaean texts, many of which are found in translations from Aramaic and so probably do not represent ordinary Middle Persian usage; rather it is the transfer of Aramaic terms for

---

[73] Some scholars who have argued that the use of Aramaic was restricted to a specific, high-level part of the administration nevertheless call it a lingua franca. The term lingua franca, however, usually refers to a simplified common vernacular of communication between groups, not to an administrative link language used in writing by a specific stratum of administrators (Thomason 2001: 269; Matras 2009: 275).

[74] On the chronology of the shift to Aramaic from Akkadian, see Brown 2008.

[75] See Chapter 2 on the conditions in which words are adopted. Shaked's short list of Aramaic words adopted in Persian (2009) reveals only a few in Middle Persian and more in New Persian, most of which refer to cultural and material aspects of Judaism and Christianity, and thus is not indicative of interaction in general domains. See also Nöldeke 1892.

[76] Scholars have long noted that the Armenian noun-stem classes assigned to words borrowed from Iranic languages exhibit a degree of formal correspondence with their original Iranic noun-stem classes at a rate too high to be random. This has been taken to suggest that Armenians adopted Iranic words when they were still more fully inflected. (Examples of such arguments can be found with Olsen 1999: 859; 2005 and Korn 2013.) If this were true, it should indicate that many of the adopted words were taken by Armenian-speakers while the Old Iranic nominal declensional types were still alive. Given the reduction of Old Persian in the Achaemenian period, we would have to assume therefore that they are words adopted in the early part of the Achaemenian period, unless they are construed as borrowings from outlying, conservative dialects. Fattori (2023b), however, has shown convincingly that the noun-stem classes could easily be inferred from the Middle Iranic oblique plural case. Early Achaemenian-period adoptions of Iranic words are therefore not ruled out, but they are not required, either.

[77] Ciancaglini (2008: 27) counts thirty-nine Old Iranic words that survive adopted in Syriac (Syrian Aramaic). That is, she deems them, by virtue of their phonology, as clearly having been adopted earlier than Middle Persian and Parthian (from which a great many more words were adopted in Syriac).

specifically Manichaean phenomena, including technical terms of the religion, into Manichaean Middle Persian.[78] It seems likely, therefore, that outside of Syria and Iraq, where it was becoming the common vernacular already before Cyrus, Aramaic was, as far as the government was concerned, no more than a language of professional scribes and secretaries. At most, it was a language used to link levels of administration under the Achaemenids, but even this is not certain.[79] The reports that are available about the use of language in the Persian Empire do not characterize Persian elites as using Aramaic as their primary language. Nevertheless, there is no doubt that Aramaic was used for correspondence, record-keeping, and formal documents. Such texts do survive in sufficient numbers to be sure of this.

Szemerényi proposed that the "decay" and "disintegration" of inflections in western Iranic languages was due to the role of Aramaic, which, he supposed, formed the influential member of a *Sprachbund* (linguistic area) with Middle Persian and Parthian.[80] Although we can assume that Babylonians and other Aramaic-speakers played a role, among many others, in the formation of Middle Persian, as adult learners of Persian, the case is not so decisively clear as Szemerényi held. More recent research has amply demonstrated that Aramaic was affected by the transfer of features from western Iranic languages into Aramaic, but it is not apparent that the reverse was true.[81] We can abandon the hypothesis that Old Iranic languages were restructured due specifically to bilingualism with an "official" Aramaic. Mass nonnative acquisition reduced the Old Persian morphology, not areal phenomena due to bilingualism with Aramaic.

Socially Remote and Socially Common Iranic Languages

Viacheslav Chirikba remarks about the languages of the Caucasus that "It has been noted that multilingualism in the Caucasus has a certain vertical dependency: the population of the mountains knew the language(s) of their heterolingual neighbours in the foothills and lowlands, but not vice versa."[82] This condition of unilateral bilingualism is likely also to have been

---

[78] Shaked 2009. More remarkable is how frequently Manichaean Middle Persian texts deploy venerable Persian words to translate technical concepts coined in Aramaic.
[79] Tavernier 2017: 342–343.
[80] Szemerényi 1980. This view was hinted at already by Müller (1877: 224).
[81] This does not strictly hold for much later historical periods of Persian history. Ciancaglini 2008: 28–37; 2011; Coghill 2016: 162–249; Khan 2017. See also Geller 2005, though he may place too much weight on the theory that Semitic verb stems were exclusively aspectual.
[82] Chirikba 2008: 31.

common throughout the domain of the Iranic languages in antiquity as it is today, for the signs of this occur in their relative grammatical complexity and simplicity and the direction of the movement of word-adoption ("loanwords"). Most, if not all, of even the most socially remote modern Iranic languages – remote by geography or by community boundaries, such as endogamous religious or tribal boundaries – have received vocabulary from New Persian (in its different regional varieties, including the ones called Tajik and Dari today), because speakers whose dominant language was not New Persian have been likely to learn New Persian as a vehicle for socially transcending their locale and gaining access to a wider range of goods and opportunities. New Persian-speakers, by contrast, generally have not needed those parochial languages used only in a remote place or in a cluster of villages. In a way supportive of the present argument, New Persian inflectional grammar is famously simple, while the Iranic languages not learned by outsiders often retain older grammatical inheritances, such as distinct grammatical genders, lost in Persian and Parthian already two thousand years ago. This is due to the distribution of multilingualism in Iran. Learners of Persian as a second language have steadily maintained its inflectional simplicity, while the relative lack of learners of the socially remote modern Iranic "dialects" and non-Iranic languages of the region have not subjected them to imposition by outsiders to such an extent.[83] This is a description of universal tendencies, which will certainly vary in each case, according to their respective social histories. It is possible, nevertheless, to see a correspondence between the social connectedness and remoteness of the speakers of Iranic languages today and their grammatical complexity.

This chapter has shown that Iranic languages other than Persian were affected by changes very close to those that befell Persian in the Achaemenian period. The causes of the morphological reduction in these cases were the same: mass nonnative acquisition triggered by the demographic upheaval induced by empire. Areal features are clearly a factor, too, but differently. The strongest argument for the role of the Achaemenian Empire in the common linguistic effects is that the Iranic languages spoken on the Achaemenian periphery or beyond its domain were not affected in the same way, retaining a relatively high degree of morphological complexity instead. These observations firmly support the thesis of Chapter 3.

[83] Perry (2003) explains the "homoglossia" (as opposed to diglossia) of New Persian as a result of its complementary relationship with Arabic and Turkic. I add that the other Iranic languages of Iran, with which many speakers of New Persian are bilingual, should also be considered in this model.

Conclusion

For centuries, language experts and casual learners alike have recognized Persian as a "simple" language, referring to the morphology that must be learned to speak or read it. As specialists in ancient Persian have known for some time, the Persian language took on most of this inflectional simplicity more than two thousand years ago. I have argued here that the transformation of Persian from a typically highly inflected ancient Indo-European language into one of the inflectionally simplest known ancient languages – the change from Old Persian to Middle Persian – was a side-effect of the Persian imperial society created by the Achaemenids. Their empire created conditions in which many adults who spoke many different languages needed to learn to speak at least some Persian with their new masters and even with each other in specific imperial sites. The unprecedented reach of the Persian Empire created conditions for intensive and extensive contact between native speakers of Persian and diverse foreigners who had to learn Persian language to participate in the new society either as elites or as their servants. The latter probably outnumbered the former in many places where Persian was current. Some of the most important sites of this intergenerational change in Persian inflectional morphology were the palaces and mansions of the Persians themselves. Persians populated their own homes, even their most private residences, with many foreign servants, slaves, eunuchs, and concubines taken from distant lands. The armed men who served the Persians likewise came from many different linguistic backgrounds and some of them needed to learn Persian to cooperate in that service. Persians probably simplified their own speech as foreigner talk, while a large wave of nonnative learners of Persian transformed the language by reducing its morphology to make it easier to speak as adults who did not grow up speaking Persian. This is the well-documented normal effect of such an event. It is likely that the influx into these sites of adults who needed to learn Persian never ceased for the duration of Achaemenian power. All later forms of Persian exhibit the same simplified morphology, demonstrating that the grammatical changes were not just the nonnative usages of foreigners, but that they were learned as native speech by later generations of Persians generally. Within decades, Persian children were learning Persian from nonnative speakers as much as from native speakers. In about five generations, the native varieties of Persian had lost most of the inflectional morphology that Persian had exhibited about the year 500 BCE. By the time of Alexander's invasion, it had become an early form of Middle Persian, or something close to the Middle Persian attested in later centuries.

The conclusion just stated is based on the application of a complex model of social factors in language change to a complex set of data. About the data there has been widespread agreement since the nineteenth century. It has long been noted that something unusual happened to some of the ancient Iranic languages, and particularly to Persian for which Achaemenian written records are available, as compared with other ancient Indo-European languages. The inscriptions of the Achaemenids provide the clearest testimony to this. Scholars have concurred that most of the Old Persian grammatical inflection had disappeared by the end of the Achaemenids' dynasty, and that this indicated the genesis of Middle Persian. Although they have sometimes described this variously with evaluative terms current in the nineteenth and early twentieth centuries, such as "decay," they were nevertheless correct that the change had substantially occurred already in the Achaemenian period and that it was therefore a rapid transformation. They also have sometimes agreed that Iranic languages other than Persian have been affected by a similar process before the times of their earliest attestation in writing, making some ancient Iranic languages seem to resemble "modern languages," meaning, implicitly, those of contemporary Western Europe.

What has been missing is an explanation for the apparent grammatical aberrancy of Persian. Historical comparative linguistics, the main tool used in deciphering the ancient Iranic languages with remarkable success, has lacked models adequate to explain this event in the history of Persian and other Iranic languages. Instead, there have been only moral evaluations or tentative guesses, as well as a few intuitive hypotheses that language contact was somehow responsible. It was necessary here, therefore, to use complementary material synthesized from several sub-branches of linguistics to assemble a cogent model that could account for the rapid transformation of Old Persian into Middle Persian. These derived principles are much newer than the decipherment of Old Persian and are related to debates about general issues in linguistics. They have not been digested hitherto by most scholars of ancient languages, be they Iranic languages or others. Nevertheless, the principles are sound, and they are corroborated as complementary findings from related areas of linguistic research. The combination of the long-established inscriptional data and the labors of generations of philologists with the new linguistic-historical model synthesized here has created a historical account that is furthermore supported by what has long been known from familiar primary sources. The Achaemenian royal inscriptions in Persian represent perhaps the earliest clearly documented instance of semicreolization, a social process tied to patterns of abrupt population contact and large-scale adult language acquisition. In this case the process was induced by the use of imperial power to gather linguistically diverse subject peoples at sites presided over by Persian speakers, rapidly and naturally triggering a transformation of the language of the imperial masters through the nonnative varieties of Persian by the newcomers. It is often remarked that the Achaemenian Persian Empire was imperial on a scale far greater than that of any prior empire. "World empire," a nonanalytical category, has often been invoked to convey the idea that the Persian dominion was unprecedented in scale. The coincidence between this common observation and the restructuring of the Persian language of the rulers is telling. It supports Meillet's intuition, when discussing the Iranic languages, that "To become imperial is, for a language, the most serious of crises."[1] More precisely, "the most serious of crises" for the *inflectional morphology* of a language is a demographic upheaval in which mass adult acquisition of a language is necessary, although Meillet's formulation sounds better.

Generations of historians of this Persian Empire have already intensively analyzed numerous sources about social arrangements in Achaemenian Persian society, so that the Achaemenian Empire is better known than many much later empires in human history. Here, the interpretation of some of these sources has been improved through the combined application of the specific linguistic data and the linguistic principles. Together they illustrate change in the constitution of the Persian ruling class, and they happen to shed some light on members of Achaemenian society that normally stand in the shadow of the kings who predominate in our narratives, almost completely ignored in the sources. This tells us something genuinely new. The assumption that only Persians spoke Persian and that there was no imperial melting-pot must be strongly qualified if not discarded. It is true that most of the subjects of the Persians had little close

[1] Meillet 1912: 151.

contact with the ethnic elite of the empire, as has been the case in most empires. Such people continued to work in their fields, tend their flocks, or do whatever it was that provided them with a living, and they also continued to speak the languages of their parents. But the view is mistaken if we look at the sites in which Persians themselves lived. We can infer confidently that workers, concubines, and eunuchs – newcomers, foreigners, people enslaved after being taken as tribute and as captive – played a large part in the reshaping of the language at the center of the elite Persian culture that they nurtured and the elite culture of this mighty empire. This research thus gives voice, albeit very indirectly, to those forced into servitude. The grammar of the language itself testifies to their presence in Persian mansions and palaces. It was the imperial power of the Persian kings, and the patriarchy and slavery that has prevailed in most complex societies, that subjugated these people and united them in royal sites. The Persians' free enjoyment of that power over others inadvertently led their own language to evolve into a form that would be easier for adults to learn as they entered their service. The ensuing unilateral bilingualism – others had to learn Persian, but Persians seldom had to learn other languages – meant that speakers of other languages would adopt Persian vocabulary, but by contrast the Persian language would be grammatically reduced. Exposed to exoterogenic forces, Old Persian underwent semicreolization; it emerged as Middle Persian, an ancient Indo-European language with drastically reduced inflectional morphology. To say that Middle Persian is a semicreole of Old Persian is, however, only to classify it with respect to its origins. By the Sasanian period in the third century CE, after hundreds of years of use, Middle Persian's origin in semicreolization was already ancient history. That is the character of languages transformed through episodes of morphological reduction induced by mass nonnative acquisition. They retain creole-like characteristics long after the formative population event has ceased. To use the term semicreolization here is to accept that creolization is a predictable phenomenon in language change consequent to uncommon but normal social changes, and moreover that languages do not belong to two sets, creole or noncreole, but that degrees of restructuring are possible. As explained in Chapter 2, to invent another term for this phenomenon would obfuscate the relationship between the effects of a demographic upheaval in the history of Persian and the effects of similar events on other languages. Persian is a language like any other, susceptible to the same processes as other languages in specified conditions.

In his book *The Growth and Maintenance of Linguistic Complexity*, Östen Dahl posited that linguistic complexity, such as ornate inflectional morphology, "may even be negatively correlated with the rise of large-scale societies with highly mobile populations."[2] This book supports that informed hypothesis with a major case study from ancient history. When the ancient Persians created an empire necessitating long-distance mobility and sudden population mixing on a scale unprecedented in human history, they triggered drastic effects in their own language. Persian became, in a word, imperial. This event also explains why some specialists in Iranic languages – as discussed in Chapters 2 and 4 – have been inclined to see Middle Persian as virtually a "modern" language. Their intuition correlates with Dahl's hypothesis in that the "modern" languages that one has in mind for such comparisons exist in the wake of more recent extensive empires that have facilitated mobility on a truly global scale, involving a larger population of humans than has ever been sustained on earth before. This suggests that one may speak loosely of "imperial languages" under certain circumstances. Such a term is not an analytical category. It is descriptive of a tendency at best, because not all languages of imperial elites will undergo the same effects. In the case of the ancient Persian language, nevertheless, it seems quite appropriate.

Trudgill reflects that "in the future, we are increasingly unlikely ever again to see the development of highly inflectional, fusional language varieties" with very complex morphology – at least in the foreseeable future.[3] That is because we live in a period of increasingly global communication. We benefit and suffer from networks of exchange that extensively surpass any sort of imperial pattern hitherto known. We are witnesses to mass migration and population contact in many directions on a scale never seen before. Beyond the large-scale relocations of people themselves, electronically mediated nonlocal or long-distance relationships are replacing many of the face-to-face interactions hitherto normal for all people of history. The intimate societies of isolated groups and thick, dense social networks based on physical propinquity, which ensured constant small-scale conflict between little self-supporting communities, are eroding in different places at different rates. They are being exchanged for what seem like surrogates for the relationships in which humans have evolved, along with inequalities vaster than any known before and conflicts now on global scales. Following the lines of linguistic history, we could point at the empire of the Achaemenians as one of the earliest monumental

---

[2] Dahl 2004: 296. Dahl calls grammatical complexity of this kind "mature phenomena" in language, in the sense that the transmission of the language was not interrupted by demographic upheavals triggering "young" phenomena.
[3] Trudgill 2011: 188. See also Ostler 2010.

landmarks on this path toward mass migration, population scrambling, and pervasive open social networks, with their expected linguistic effects. The case of the Old Persian language shows us that the first so-called world empire of the Persians was a harbinger of these social changes that predictably leave a language with reduced morphology in its wake, shaped by the forces of functionality to satisfy the urgent need of adults to learn it. It is with the Achaemenian Persian Empire that the correlation of patterns of grammatical reduction with a demographic upheaval first comes into clear historical view. It will be interesting if older examples of this syndrome can be detected by those studying still earlier language records, but it is fair to say that it is the mighty Persian Empire that marks for us the beginning of a new age of imperial demographics tumultuous enough to leave traces even in the grammar of its rulers' language.[4]

More precisely, I have made the case that ancient Persian exhibits the oldest clearly documented instance of the semicreolization of a language, the drastic but incomplete reduction of its inflectional morphology, due particularly to the imperial status of its users and the demographic mixture induced by extensive and intensive coercion – with all the caveats and pointers supplied about the term semicreole provided in Chapter 2. The evolution of Persian from the fourth century BCE until today has retained the clear signs of that event ever after in the relative learnability of its morphology, a vestige of ancient Persian imperial culture still reaching students in Persian classrooms today.

---

[4] Aramaic is a conspicuous contender for an older example, but through different imperial conditions. The Assyrian or Neo-Assyrian Empire was famous for the mass relocation of populations that refused to submit absolutely. An estimated 1.5 to 4.5 million people, mostly Syrians speaking early varieties of Aramaic and other Northwest Semitic dialects, were forcibly relocated to Iraq between the ninth and the seventh centuries BCE (Oded 1979). Even if this number is an overestimate, as Bedford supposes (2009: 33), the numbers of Syrians and others forcibly relocated to Iraq made up a significant portion of the population of their new destination. See Frahm 2023: 146–151 for a judicious summary of this history. As he rightly notes, in subsequent centuries most of Iraq's population would shift from Akkadian and other languages to Aramaic, the language of people imported on such a massive scale. This matches the linguistic evidence: Aramaic itself was evidently affected by extensive nonnative acquisition, for if we compare the grammar of Aramaic to that of any other ancient Semitic language, we see that it is conspicuously reduced. When comparative Semitist John Huehnergard wrote his essay "What Is Aramaic?" (1995), he found it difficult to identify innovative features constituting specific differences with other Semitic languages. That is, Aramaic became grammatically the least marked of the ancient Semitic languages not only in the paucity of innovative features within ancient Semitic but also by the reduction of ancient inflectional patterns, including noun case. This is a clear sign of dialect leveling and grammatical reduction through forced migration and subsequent mass nonnative acquisition. We have an instance in which a language of conquered people was grammatically reduced as its speakers were imported, and their language eventually became the common language of the region of the conquerors themselves. Others will have to evaluate this hypothesis.

References

Adone, Dany. 2012. *The Acquisition of Creole Languages: How Children Surpass Their Input*, Cambridge: Cambridge University Press.

Aikhenvald, Alexandra. 2013. "Areal Diffusion and Parallelism in Drift: Shared Grammaticalization Patterns," in Martine Robbeets and Hubert Cuyckens (eds.), *Shared Grammaticalization with a Special Focus on Transeurasian Languages*, Amsterdam: John Benjamins, 23–41.

Almagor, Eran. 2018a. "Deinon of Kolophon (690)," in Ian Worthington (ed.), *Brill's New Jacoby*, brill.com, http://dx.doi.org/10.1163/1873-5363_bnj_a690.

Almagor, Eran. 2018b. "Herakleides of Kyme (689)," in Ian Worthington (ed.), *Brill's New Jacoby*, brill.com, http://dx.doi.org/10.1163/1873-5363_bnj_a690.

Amanat, Abbas. 1999. "Fatḥ-ʿAlī Shah Qājār," *Encylopædia Iranica*, Vol. IX, Fasc. 4, Leiden: Brill, 407–421.

Ammianus. 1871. *Ammiani Marcellini Rerum gestarum libri*, ed. Franz Rudolph Eyssenhardt, Berlin: Vahlen.

Anonymous. 1857. "Prof. Mírza Ibrahím," *The Gentleman's Magazine and Historical Review* 203 (July), 679.

Ansaldo, Umberto, Stephen Matthews, and Lisa Lim (eds.). 2007. *Deconstructing Creole*, Amsterdam: John Benjamins.

Arends, Jacques. 2017. *Language and Slavery: A Social and Linguistic History of the Suriname Creoles*, Amsterdam: John Benjamins.

Aristotle. 1957. *Politica*, ed. William David Ross, Oxford: Clarendon Press.

Arrian. 1907. *Anabasis*, ed. Antoon Gerard Roos, Leipzig: Teubner.

Avram, Andrei A. 2014. "Immigrant Workers and Language Formation: Gulf Pidgin Arabic," *Lengua y Migración* 6.2, 7–40.

Avram, Andrei A. 2016. "On the Developmental Stage of Gulf Pidgin Arabic," in George Grigore and Gabriel Biţiună (eds.), *Arabic Varieties Far and Wide: Proceedings of the 11th International Conference of AIDA*, Bucharest: Editura Universităţii din Bucureşti, 87–97.

Azzoni, Annalisa, Elspeth R. M. Dusinberre, Mark B. Garrison, Wouter F. M. Henkelman, Charles E. Jones, and Matthew W. Stolper. 2017. "Persepolis Administrative Archives," *Encylopædia Iranica*, online edition, www.iranicaonline.org/articles/persepolis-admin-archive (accessed June 9, 2017).

Back, Michael. 1978. *Die sassanidischen Staatsinschriften: Studien zur Orthographie und Phonologie des Mitttelpersischen der Inschriften zusammen mit einem etymologischen Index des mittelpersischen Wortgutes und einem Textcorpus der behandelten Inschriften*, Leiden: Brill.

Baerman, Matthew, Dunstan Brown, and Greville G. Corbett (eds.). 2015. *Understanding and Measuring Morphological Complexity*, Oxford: Oxford University Press.

Baghoolizadeh, Beeta. 2024. *The Color Black: Enslavement and Erasure in Iran*, Durham, NC: Duke University Press.

Baker, Philip. 1990. "Off Target?" *Journal of Pidgin and Creole Languages* 5.1, 107–119.

Baker, Philip. 1995. "Some Developmental Inferences from Historical Studies of Pidgins and Creoles," in Jacques Arends (ed.), *The Early Stages of Creolization*, Amsterdam: John Benjamins, 1–24.

Baker, Philip. 1997. "Directionality in Pidginization and Creolization," in Arthur K. Spears and Donald Winford (eds.), *The Structure and Status of Pidgins and Creoles*, Amsterdam: John Benjamins, 91–109.

Bakker, Peter. 1997. *A Language of Our Own: The Genesis of Michif, the Mixed Cree-French Language of the Canadian Métis*, Oxford: Oxford University Press.

Bakker, Peter. 2002. "Some Future Challenges for Pidgin and Creole Studies," in Glenn Gilbert (ed.), *Pidgin and Creole Linguistics in the Twenty-First Century*, New York: Peter Lang, 69–92.

Bakker, Peter. 2003. "Pidgin Inflectional Morphology and Its Implications for Creole Morphology," in Geert Booij and Jaap van Marle (eds.), *Yearbook of Morphology 2002*, Dordrecht: Kluwer Academic Publishers, 3–33.

Bakker, Peter. 2004. "Pidgins versus Creoles and Pidgincreoles," in Silvia Kouwenberg and John Victor Singler (eds.), *The Handbook of Pidgin and Creole Studies*, Oxford: Blackwell, 130–157.

Bakker, Peter. 2009. "Phonological Complexity in Pidgins," in Nicholas Faraclas and Thomas B. Klein (eds.), *Simplicity and Complexity in Creoles and Pidgins*, London: Battlebridge, 7–27.

Bakker, Peter. 2012. "Ethnogenesis, Language, and Identity: The Genesis of Michif and Other Mixed Languages," in Nicole St.-Onge, Carolyn Podruchny, and Brenda Macdougall (eds.), *Contours of a People: Metis Family, Mobility, and History*, Norman: University of Oklahoma Press, 169–193.

Bakker, Peter. 2017a. "Key Concepts in the History of Creole Studies," in Peter Bakker, Finn Borchsenius, Carsten Levisen, and Eeva Sippola (eds.), *Creole Studies: Phylogenetic Approaches*, Amsterdam: John Benjamins, 5–33.

Bakker, Peter. 2017b. "Feature Pools Show that Creoles Are Distinct Languages Due to Their Special Origin," in Peter Bakker, Finn Borchsenius, Carsten Levisen, and Eeva Sippola (eds.), *Creole Studies: Phylogenetic Approaches*, Amsterdam: John Benjamins, 369–373.

Bakker, Peter, and Aymeric Daval-Markussen. 2017. "Creole Typology I: Comparative Overview of Creole Languages," in Peter Bakker, Finn Borchsenius, Carsten Levisen, and Eeva Sippola (eds.), *Creole Studies: Phylogenetic Approaches*, Amsterdam: John Benjamins, 80–101.

Bakker, Peter, Aymeric Daval-Markussen, Mikael Parkvall, and Ingo Plag. 2011. "Creoles Are Typologically Distinct from Non-Creoles," *Journal of Pidgin and Creole Languages* 26, 5–42.
Bakker, Peter, and Marten Mous (eds.). 1994. *Mixed Languages: 15 Case Studies in Language Intertwining*, Amsterdam: IFOTT.
Barfield, Thomas. 2001. "The Shadow Empires: Imperial State Formation along the Chinese-Nomad Frontier," in Susan E. Alcock, Terence N. D'Altroy, Kathleen D. Morrison, and Carla M. Sinopoli (eds.), *Empires: Perspectives from Archaeology and History*, Cambridge: Cambridge University Press, 10–41.
Barfield, Thomas. 2010. *Afghanistan: A Cultural and Political History*, Princeton, NJ: Princeton University Press.
Basello, Gian Pietro. 2021. "Hierarchy and *ethno-classe dominante*," in Bruno Jacobs and Robert Rollinger (eds.), *A Companion to the Achaemenid Persian Empire*, 2 vols., Hoboken, NJ: Wiley Blackwell, Vol. 2, 859–870.
Bedford, Peter R. 2009. "The Neo-Assyrian Empire," in Ian Morris and Walter Scheidel (eds.), *The Dynamics of Ancient Empires*, Oxford: Oxford University Press, 30–65.
Beekes, Robert S. P. 1995. *Comparative Indo-European Linguistics: An Introduction*, Amsterdam: John Benjamins.
Benes, Tuska. 2008. *In Babel's Shadow: Language, Philology, and the Nation in Nineteenth-Century Germany*, Detroit: Wayne State University Press.
Bentz, Christian, and Bodo Winter. 2013. "Languages with More Second Language Learners Tend to Lose Nominal Case," *Language Dynamics and Change* 3, 1–27.
Benveniste, Émile. 1966. *Titres et noms propres en Iranien ancien*, Paris: Librairie C. Klincksieck.
Bertrand-Bocandé, Emmanuel. 1849. "Notes sur la Guinée portugaise ou Sénégambie méridionale," *Bulletin de la Societé de géographie*, ser. 3.12: 57–93.
Bhabha, Homi K. 1994. *The Location of Culture*, London: Routledge.
Bickerton, Derek. 2008. *Bastard Tongues: A Trailblazing Linguist Finds Clues to Our Common Humanity in the World's Lowliest Languages*, New York: Hill and Wang.
Bielmeier, Roland. 1989. "Yaghnōbī," in Rüdiger Schmitt (ed.), *Compendium Linguarum Iranicarum*, Wiesbaden: Dr. Ludwig Reichert, 480–488.
Birdsong, David. 2006. "Age and Second Language Acquisition and Processing: A Selective Overview," *Language Learning* 56.s1, 9–49.
Bizri, Fida. 2018. "Pidgin as Counterlanguage: Asian Labour Migrants and Arab Employers Speaking," *Language Ecology* 2.1/2, 128–146.
Black, Jeremy. 2008. "The Obsolescence and Demise of Cuneiform Writing in Elam," in John Baines, John Bennet, and Stephen Houston (eds.), *The Disappearance of Writing Systems: Perspectives on Literacy and Communication*, London: Equinox, 45–72.
Blasi, Damián E., Susanne Maria Michaelis, and Martin Haspelmath. 2017. "Grammars Are Robustly Transmitted Even during the Emergence of Creole Languages," *Nature Human Behavior* 1, 723–729.

Boardman, John (ed.). 1988. *The Cambridge Ancient History. Volume IV: Persia, Greece and the Western Mediterranean, c. 525 to 479 B.C.*, 2nd edn., Cambridge: Cambridge University Press.

Boardman, John. 2000. *Persia and the West: An Archaeological Investigation of the Genesis of Achaemenid Art*, London: Thames and Hudson.

Bonman, Svenja, Jakob Halfmann, Natalie Korobzow, and Bobomullo Bobomulloev. 2023. "A Partial Decipherment of the Unknown Kushan Script," *Transactions of the Philological Society* 121.2, 293–329.

Booij, Geert. 1993. "Against Split Morphology," in Geert Booij and Jaap van Marle (eds.), *Yearbook of Morphology 1993*, Dordrecht: Kluwer, 27–49.

Booij, Geert. 1996. "Inherent versus Contextual Inflection and the Split Morphology Hypothesis," in Geert Booij and Jaap van Marle (eds.), *Yearbook of Morphology 1995*, Dordrecht: Kluwer, 1–16.

Bowern, Claire. 2013. "Relatedness as a Factor in Language Contact," *Journal of Language Contact* 6, 411–432.

Boyce, Mary. 1977. *A Word-List of Manichaean Middle Persian and Parthian*, Tehran: Bibliothèque Pahlavi.

Boyce, Mary. 1992. *Zoroastrianism: Its Antiquity and Constant Vigour*, Costa Mesa: Mazda.

Brandenstein, Wilhelm, and Manfred Mayrhofer. 1964. *Handbuch des Altpersischen*, Wiesbaden: Otto Harrassowitz.

Briant, Pierre. 1988. "Ethno-classe dominante et populations soumises dans l'empire achéménide: Le cas de l'Égypte," in Amélie Kuhrt and Heleen Sancisi-Weerdenburg, *Method and Theory: Proceedings of the London 1985 Achaemenid History Workshop*, Leiden: Nederlands Instituut voor het Nabije Oosten, 137–173.

Briant, Pierre. 2002. *From Cyrus to Alexander: A History of the Persian Empire*, translated by Peter T. Daniels, Winona Lake, IN: Eisenbrauns.

Briant, Pierre. 2005. "History of the Persian Empire (550–330 BCE)," in John Curtis and Nigel Tallis (eds.), *Forgotten Empire: The World of Ancient Persia*, Berkeley: University of California Press, 12–17.

Brosius, Maria. 1996. *Women in Ancient Persia 559–331 BC*, Oxford: Clarendon.

Brosius, Maria. 2006. *The Persians: An Introduction*, London: Routledge.

Brosius, Maria. 2021. *A History of Ancient Persia: The Achaemenid Empire*, Hoboken, NJ: Wiley-Blackwell.

Brown, David. 2008. "Increasingly Redundant: The Growing Obsolescence of the Cuneiform Script in Babylonia from 539 BC," in John Baines, John Bennet, and Stephen Houston (eds.), *The Disappearance of Writing Systems*, London: Equinox, 73–101.

Brunner, Christopher J. 1977. *A Syntax of Western Middle Iranian*, Delmar, NY: Caravan Books.

Brust, Manfred. 2018. *Historische Laut- und Formenlehre des Altpersischen*, Innsbruck: Institut für Sprachen und Literaturen der Universität Innsbruck.

Burke, Peter. 2004. *Languages and Communities in Early Modern Europe*, Cambridge: Cambridge University Press.

Butts, Aaron Michael. 2016. *Language Change in the Wake of Empire: Syriac in Its Greco-Roman Context*, Winona Lake, IN: Eisenbrauns.

Callieri, Pierfrancesco, and Alireza Askari Chaverdi. 2013. "Media, Khuzestan, and Fars between the Achaemenids and the Rise of the Sasanians," in Daniel T. Potts (ed.), *The Oxford Handbook of Ancient Iran*, Oxford: Oxford University Press, 690–717.

Campbell, Lyle, and William J. Poser. 2008. *Language Classification: History and Method*, Cambridge: Cambridge University Press.

Cantera, Alberto. 2009. "On the History of the Middle Persian Nominal Inflection," in Werner Sundermann, Almut Hintze, and François de Blois (eds.), *Exegisti Monumenta: Festschrift in Honour of Nicholas Sims-Williams*, Wiesbaden: Harrassowitz, 17–30.

Chaudenson, Robert. 2001. *Creolization of Language and Culture*, revised in collaboration with Salikoko S. Mufwene, translated from the French original of 1992 by Salikoko S. Mufwene, Sabrina Billings, and Michelle AuCoin, London: Routledge.

Cheung, Johnny. 2007. *Etymological Dictionary of the Iranian Verb*, Leiden: Brill.

Cheung, Johnny. 2009–2010. "Selected Pashto Problems I: The Accent in Pashto," *Persica* 23, 109–121.

Chirikba, Viacheslav A. 2008. "The Problem of the Caucasian Sprachbund," in Pieter Muysken (ed.), *From Linguistic Areas to Areal Linguistics*, Amsterdam: John Benjamins, 1–23.

Churchill, William. 1911. *Beach-La-Mar: The Jargon or Trade-Speech of the Western Pacific*, Washington, DC: The Carnegie Institution.

Ciancaglini, Claudia. 2008. *Iranian Loanwords in Syriac*, Wiesbaden: Dr. Ludwig Reichert.

Ciancaglini, Claudia. 2011. "The Formation of the Periphrastic Verbs in Persian and Neighbouring Languages," in Mauro Maggi and Paola Orsatti (eds.), *The Persian Language in History*, Wiesbaden: Dr. Ludwig Reichert, 3–21.

Cilli, Elisabetta, Sara De Fanti, Paolo Delaini, Antonio Panaino, and Giorgio Gruppioni. 2013. "A Contribution to the Genetic History of the Yaghnobis of Tajikistan through Mitochondrial DNA Analysis," in Antonio Panaino, Andrea Gariboldi, and Paolo Ognibene (eds.), *Yaghnobi Studies I: Papers from the Italian Mission to Tajikistan*, Milan: Mimesis, 141–150.

Coghill, Eleanor. 2016. *The Rise and Fall of Ergativity in Aramaic: Cycles of Alignment Change*, Oxford: Oxford University Press.

Colburn, Henry. 2016. "Globalization and the Study of the Achaemenid Persian Empire," in Tamar Hodos, Alexander Geurds, Paul Lane, Ian Lilley, Martin Pitts, Gideon Shelach, Miriam Stark, and Miguel John Versluys (eds.), *The Routledge Handbook of Archaeology and Globalization*, Routledge: New York, 871–884.

Colditz, Iris. 2000. *Zur Sozialterminologie der iranischen Manichäer: Eine semantische Analyse im Vergleich zu den nichtmanichäischen iranischen Quellen*, Wiesbaden: Harrassowitz.

Combrink, Johan. 1978. "Afrikaans: Its Origin and Development," in Len W. Lanham and Keith P. Prinsloo (eds.), *Language and Communication Studies in South Africa: Current Issues and Directions in Research and Inquiry*, Cape Town: Oxford University Press, 69–95.

Cook, John M. 1985. "The Rise of the Achaemenids and the Establishment of Their Empire," in Ilya Gershevitch (ed.), *The Cambridge History of Iran, Volume 2: The Median and Achaemenian Periods*, Cambridge: Cambridge University Press, 200–291.

Coupland, Nikolas, and Adam Jaworski. 2009. "Social Worlds through Language," in Nikolas Coupland and Adam Jaworski (eds.), *The New Sociolinguistics Reader*, Houndmills: Palgrave Macmillan, 1–21.

Croft, William. 2000. *Explaining Language Change: An Evolutionary Approach*, Harlow: Longman.

Crowley, Terry. 1990. *Beach-la-Mar to Bislama: The Emergence of a National Language in Vanuatu*, Oxford: Clarendon.

Dahl, Östen. 2004. *The Growth and Maintenance of Linguistic Complexity*. Amsterdam: John Benjamins Publishing Company.

Dandamaev, Muhammad A. 1989. *A Political History of the Achaemenid Empire*, English trans. Willem J. Vogelsang, Leiden: Brill.

Dandamaev, Muhammad A. 1998. "Eunuchs i: The Achaemenid Period," *Encylopædia Iranica*, Vol. IX, Fasc. 1, 64–69.

Dandamaev, Muhammad A., and Vladimir G. Lukonin. 1988. *The Culture and Social Institutions of Ancient Iran*, Cambridge: Cambridge University Press.

Darmesteter, James. 1883. *Études iraniennes*, 2 vols., Paris: F. Vieweg.

Daryaee, Touraj. 2008. *Sasanian Iran (224–651 CE): Portrait of a Late Antique Empire*, Costa Mesa, CA: Mazda.

Daval-Markussen, Aymeric, and Peter Bakker. 2017. "Creole Typology II: Typological Features of Creoles: From Early Proposals to Phylogenetic Approaches and Comparisons with Non-Creoles," in Peter Bakker, Finn Borchsenius, Carsten Levisen, and Eeva Sippola (eds.), *Creole Studies: Phylogenetic Approaches*, Amsterdam: John Benjamins, 103–140.

De Araujo, Metheus Treuk Medeiros. 2024. "Male Homoerotic Practices in Achaemenid Persia: An Overview," *Archai* 34, 1–38.

De Blois, François. 1994. "Elamite Survivals in Western Iranian: A Preliminary Survey," *Studia Iranica, Mesopotamica, et Anatolica* 1, 13–19.

De Jong, Albert. 1997. *Traditions of the Magi: Zoroastrianism in Greek and Latin Literature*, Leiden: Brill.

De Jong, Albert. 2015. "Religion and Politics in Pre-Islamic Iran," in Michael Stausberg and Yuhan Sohrab-Dinshaw Vevaina (eds.), *The Wiley Blackwell Companion to Zoroastrianism*, Chichester: John Wiley & Sons, 85–101.

De Mauro, Tullio. 1970. *Storia linguistica dell'Italia unita*, 2nd edn., Bari: Laterza.

De Miroschedji, P. 1985. "La fin du royaume d'Anšan et de Suse et la naissance de l'empire Perse," *Zeitschrift für Assyriologie* 75, 265–306.

DeKeyser, Robert. 2005. "What Makes Learning Second-Language Grammar Difficult? A Review of the Issues," *Language Learning* 55.S1, 1–25.
DeGraff, Michel. 2003. "Against Creole Exceptionalism," *Language* 79.2, 391–410.
De Vaan, Michiel, and Alexander Lubotsky. 2012. "Old Persian," in Holger Gzella (ed.), *Languages from the World of the Bible*, Berlin: Walter de Gruyter, 194–208.
Dixon, Robert M. W. 2016. *Are Some Languages Better Than Others?*, Oxford: Oxford University Press.
Due, Bodil. 1989. *The Cyropaedia: Xenophon's Aims and Methods*, Esbjerg: Aarhus University Press.
Durkin-Meisterernst, Desmond. 2004. *Dictionary of Manichaean Middle Persian and Parthian*, Dictionary of Manichaean Texts III: Texts from Central Asia and China, Part 1, Turnhout: Brepols.
Durkin-Meisterernst, Desmond. 2009. "Khwarezmian," in Gernot Windfuhr (ed.), *The Iranian Languages*, London: Routledge, 336–376.
Durkin-Meisterernst, Desmond. 2014. *Grammatik des Westmitteliranischen (Parthisch und Mittelpersisch)*, philosophisch-historische Klasse, Sitzungsberichte, 850. Band, Vienna: Verlag der Österreichische Akademie der Wissenschaften.
Dutton, Tom. 1985. *Police Motu: Iena Sivarai (Its Story)*, Port Moresby: University of Papua New Guinea Press.
Dutton, Tom. 1997. "Hiri Motu," in Sarah G. Thomason (ed.), *Contact Languages: A Wider Perspective*, Amsterdam: John Benjamins, 9–41.
El Cheikh, Nadia Maria. 2010. "Caliphal Harems, Household Harems: Baghdad in the Fourth Century of the Islamic Era," in Marilyn Booth (ed.), *Harem Histories: Envisioning Places and Living Spaces*, Durham, NC: Duke University Press, 87–103.
El Cheikh, Nadia Maria. 2018. "Guarding the Harem, Protecting the State: Eunuchs in a Fourth/Tenth-Century Abbasid Court," in Almut Höfert, Matthew M. Mesley, and Serena Tolina (eds.), *Celibate and Childless Men in Power: Ruling Eunuchs and Bishops in the Pre-Modern World*, London: Routledge, 65–98.
Emmerick, Ronald E. 2009. "Khotanese and Tumshuqese," in Gernot Windfuhr (ed.), *The Iranian Languages*, London: Routledge, 377–415.
Faraclas, Nicholas, and Thomas B. Klein. 2009. *Simplicity and Complexity in Creoles and Pidgins*, Plymouth: Latimer Trend and Company.
Fattori, Marco. 2022a. "A Scribal School of Forgers in 'Hamadān,'" *Rivista degli Studi Orientali* 95.3, 27–44.
Fattori, Marco. 2022b. "Persiano antico in lettere aramaiche: pratiche redazionali nell'epigrafia tardoachemenide," *Archivo Glottologico Italiano* 107.1, 3–36.
Fattori, Marco. 2023a. "Some Remarks on the Proto-Middle Persian Inscription Persis 2 and the Oblique Case," *Acta Orientalia Academiae Scientiarum Hungaricae* 76.4, 511–527.
Fattori, Marco. 2023b. "Armenian Stem Classes and the Western-Middle Iranian Oblique Plural Case," *Studi e Saggi Linguistici* 61 1, 107–122.

Fenk-Oczlon, Gertraud, and August Fenk. 2014. "Complexity Trade-Offs Do Not Prove the Equal Complexity Hypothesis," *Poznań Studies in Contemporary Linguistics* 50.2, 145–155.

Ferguson, Charles, and Charles E. DeBose. 1977. "Simplified Registers, Broken Language, and Pidginization," in Albert Valdman (ed.), *Pidgin and Creole Linguistics*, Bloomington: Indiana University Press, 99–125.

Field, Fred. 2004. "Second Language Acquisition in Creole Genesis: The Role of Processability," in Geneviève Escure and Armin Schwegler (eds.), *Creoles, Contact, and Language Change: Linguistic and Social Implications*, Amsterdam: John Benjamins, 127–160.

Finkel, Irving L. 2005. "The Decipherment of Achaemenid Cuneiform," in John E. Curtis and Nigel Tallis (eds.), *Forgotten Empire: The World of Ancient Persia*, Berkeley: University of California Press, 25–29.

Finkel, Rafael, and Gregory Stump. 2009. "Principal Parts and Degrees of Paradigmatic Transparency," in James P. Blevins and Juliette Blevins (eds.), *Analogy in Grammar: Form and Acquisition*, Oxford: Oxford University Press, 14–53.

Fischer-Bovet, Christelle. 2014. *Army and Society in Ptolemaic Egypt*, Cambridge: Cambridge University Press.

Fisher, Michael Herbert. 2001. "Persian Professor in Britain: Mirza Muhammad Ibrahim at the East India Company's College, 1826–44," *Comparative Studies of South Asia, Africa and the Middle East* 21, 24–32.

Foy, Willy. 1898. "Beiträge zur Erklärung der altpersischen Keilinschriften," *Zeitschrift für vergleichende Sprachforschung auf dem Gebiete der indogermanischen Sprachen* 35.1, 1–78.

Frahm, Eckart. 2023. *Assyria: The Rise and Fall of the World's First Empire*, New York: Basic Books.

Franklin, Karl J. 1989. "Jack Hides's Visit to the Kewa Area," *The Journal of Pacific History* 24.1, 99–105.

Frye, Richard. 1984. *The History of Ancient Iran*, Munich: C. H. Beck.

García Canclini, Néstor. 1995. *Hybrid Cultures: Strategies for Entering and Leaving Modernity*, translated by Christopher L. Chiappari and Silvia L. López, Minneapolis: University of Minnesota Press.

Gardner-Chloros, Penelope. 2010. "Contact and Code-Switching," in Raymond Hickey (ed.), *The Handbook of Language Contact*, Chichester: Wiley-Blackwell, 188–207.

Garsoïan, Nina. 1989. *The Epic Histories Attributed to Pʻawstos Buzand (Buzandaran Patmutʻiwnkʻ)*, Cambridge, MA: Harvard University Press.

Gauthiot, Robert. 1916–1918. "De la reduction de la flexion nominale en iranien," *Mémoires de la Société linguistique de Paris* 20, 61–76.

Gehman, Henry S. 1914. "The Use of Interpreters by the Ten Thousand and by Alexander," *The Classical Weekly* 8.2, 9–14.

Geiger, Wilhelm. 1895–1905. "Über das Yaghnōbī," in Wilhelm Geiger and Ernst Kuhn (eds.), *Grundriss der iranischen Philologie*, Strassburg: Karl J. Trübner, 1.334–344.

Geldner, Karl Friedrich. 1885. "Persian: Part III. Language and Literature. Section I. Persian (Iranian) Languages," *Encyclopedia Britannica*, 9th edn., Vol. 18, New York: Scribner's, 653–655.
Geller, Mark J. 2005. "Persian Influence on Aramaic?" *Electrum* 10, 32–39.
Gera, Deborah Levine. 1993. *Xenophon's* Cyropaedia: *Style, Genre, and Literary Technique*, Oxford: Clarendon.
Gerlee, Philip, and Torbjörn Lundh. 2016. *Scientific Models: Red Atoms, White Lies and Black Boxes in a Yellow Book*, Cham: Springer.
Gershevitch, Ilya. 1964. "Zoroaster's Own Contribution," *Journal of Near Eastern Studies* 23.1, 12–38.
Gershevitch, Ilya. 1970. "The Crushing of the Third Singular Present," in Mary Boyce and Ilya Gershevitch (eds.), *W.B. Henning Memorial Volume*, London: Lund Humphries, 61–74.
Ghirshman, Roman. 1954. *Iran from the Earliest Times to the Islamic Conquest*, Baltimore, MD: Penguin.
Gholami, Saloumeh. 2014. *Selected Features of Bactrian Grammar*, Wiesbaden: Harrassowitz.
Glassner, Jean-Jacques. 2021. "The Interplay of Languages and Communication," in Bruno Jacobs and Robert Rollinger (eds.), *A Companion to the Achaemenid Persian Empire*, 2 vols., Hoboken, NJ: Wiley Blackwell, 1.737–747.
Good, Jeff. 2023. "Language Change in Small-Scale Multilingual Societies: Trees, Waves, and Magnets?" in Darya Kavitskaya and Alan C. L. Yu (eds.), *The Life Cycle of Language: Past, Present, and Future*, Oxford: Oxford University Press, 386–398.
Görlach, Manfred. 1986, "Middle English: A Creole?" In Dieter Kastovsky and Aleksander J. Szwedek (eds.), *Linguistics across Historical and Geographical Boundaries: In Honor of Jacek Fisiak on the Occasion of his Fiftieth Birthday*, Berlin: Mouton de Gruyter, 329–344.
Graf, David F. 1984. "Medism: The Origin and Significance of the Term," *Journal of Hellenic Studies* 104, 15–30.
Greenfield, Jonas C., and Bezalel Porten (eds.). 1982. *The Bisitun Inscription of Darius the Great: Aramaic Version*, London: Lund Humphries on behalf of Corpus Inscriptionum Iranicarum.
Greenfield, William. 1830. *A Defence [sic] of the Surinam Negro-English Version of the New Testament*, London: Samuel Bagster.
Grenet, Frantz, Nicholas Sims-Williams, and Aleksandr Podushkin. 2007. "Les plus anciens monuments de la langue sogdienne: les inscriptions de Kultobe au Kazakhstan," *Comptes rendus des séances de l'Académie des Inscriptions et Belles-Lettres* 151–2, 1005–1034.
Guha, Sumit. 2024. "Empires, Languages, and Scripts in the Perso-Indian World," *Comparative Studies in Society and History* 66.2, 443–469.
Gyselen, Rika. 2001. *The Four Generals of the Sasanian Empire: Some Sigillographic Evidence*, Rome: Istituto Italiano per l'Africa e l'Oriente.
Gzella, Holger. 2015. *A Cultural History of Aramaic: From the Beginnings to the Advent of Islam*, Leiden: Brill.

Hahn, E. Adelaide. 1965. "On Alleged Anacoloutha in Old Persian," *Journal of the American Oriental Society* 85, 48–58.
Haig, Geoffrey L. J. 2008. *Alignment Change in Iranian Languages: A Construction Grammar Approach*, Berlin: Mouton de Gruyter.
Harmatta-Pékáry, Margaret. 1971. "The Decipherment of the Pārsīk Ostracon from Dura-Europos and the Problem of the Sāsānian City Organization," in *Atti del Convegno Internazionale sul Tema: La Persia nel Medioevo (Roma, 31 marzo-5 aprile 1970)*, Rome: Accademia Nazionale dei Lincei, 467–475.
Harrison, Thomas. 2011. *Writing Ancient Persia*. London: Bristol Classical Press.
Hartshorne, Joshua K., Joshua B. Tenenbaum, and Steven Pinker. 2018. "A Critical Period for Second Language Acquisition: Evidence from 2/3 Million English Speakers," *Cognition* 177 (August), 263–277.
Haspelmath, Martin. 1999. "Why Is Grammaticalization Irreversible?" *Linguistics* 37.6, 1043–1068.
Haspelmath, Martin. 2019. "Can Cross-Linguistic Regularities Be Explained by Constraints on Change?," in Karsten Schmidtke-Bode, Natalia Levshina, Susanne Maria Michaelis & Ilja A. Seržant (eds.), *Explanation in Typology: Diachronic Sources, Functional Motivations and the Nature of the Evidence*, Berlin: Language Science Press, 1–23.
Haspelmath, Martin. 2021. "General Linguistics Must Be Based on Universals (or Non-Conventional Aspects of Language)," *Theoretical Linguistics* 47.1–2, 1–31.
Haspelmath, Martin. 2024. "Разные объяснения совместимы: структурные, эволюционные и биокогнитивные объяснения в грамматике/Different Explanations in Grammar Are Mutually Compatible: Structural, Evolutionary and Biocognitive," *Типология морфосинтаксических параметров (Typology of Morphosyntactic Parameters)* 7.2, 133–151.
Haugen, Einar. 1950. "The Analysis of Linguistic Borrowing," *Language* 26.2, 210–231.
Hay, Jennifer, and Laurie Bauer. 2007. "Phoneme Inventory Size and Population Size," *Language* 83.2, 388–400.
Heine, Bernd, and Tania Kuteva. 2005. *Language Contact and Grammatical Change*, Cambridge: Cambridge University Press.
Henkelman, Wouter F. M. 2008. *The Other Gods Who Are: Studies in Elamite-Iranian Acculturation Based on the Persepolis Fortification Texts*. Leiden: Nederlands Instituut voor het Nabije Oosten.
Henkelman, Wouter. 2011. "Cyrus the Persian and Darius the Elamite: A Case of Mistaken Identity," in Robert Rollinger, Brigitte Truschnegg, and Reinhold Bichler (eds.), *Herodot und das Persische Weltreich/Herodotus and the Persian Empire*, Wiesbaden: Harrassowitz, 577–634.
Henkelman, Wouter F. M. 2012. "The Achaemenid Heartland: An Archaeological-Historical Perspective," in Daniel T. Potts (ed.), *A Companion to the Archaeology of the Ancient Near East*, Malden, MA: Wiley-Blackwell, 931–962.
Henning, Walter. 1933. "Das Verbum des Mittelpersischen der Turfanfragmente," *Zeitschrift für Indologie und Iranistik* 9, 158–253.

Henning, Walter. 1940. Review of *Archaeologische Mitteilungen aus Iran*, vols. vii–ix, 1934–8, in *Bulletin of the School of Oriental Studies* 10.2, 501–507.
Henning, Walter. 1958. "Mitteliranisch," in Bertold Spuler and Herbert Kees (eds.), *Iranistik 1. Linguistik*, Handbuch der Orientalistik 1.4, Leiden: Brill, 20–130.
Henning, Walter. 1964. "The Survival of an Ancient Term," in *Indo-Iranica: Mélanges présentés à Georg Morgenstierne*, Wiesbaden: O. Harrassowitz, 95–97.
Hernández-Campoy, Juan Manuel, and Juan Camilo Conde-Silvestre. 2012. *The Handbook of Historical Sociolinguistics*, Malden, MA: John Wiley & Sons.
Herodotus. 1871. *Herodoti Historiarum libri IX*, ed. Heinrich Rudolf Dietsch, Leipzig: Teubner.
Herzfeld, Ernst. 1935. *Archaeological History of Iran*, London: British Academy.
Herzfeld, Ernst. 1937. "Die Silberschüsseln Artaxerxes' des I. und die goldene Fundamenturkunde des Ariaramnes," *Archaeologische Mitteilungen aus Iran* 8, pp. 5–51.
Hetzron, Robert. 1974. "La division des langues sémitiques," in André Coquet and David Cohen (eds.), *Actes du premier Congrès International de Linguistique Sémitique et Chamito-Sémitique, Paris, juillet 1969*, The Hague: Mouton, 181–194.
Hetzron, Robert. 1976. "Two Principles of Genetic Reconstruction," *Lingua* 38, 89–108.
Hirsch, Steven. 1985. *The Friendship of the Barbarians: Xenophon and the Persian Empire*, Hanover, NH: University Press of New England.
Hock, Hans Henrich. 1991. *Principles of Historical Linguistics*, 2nd edn., revised and updated, Berlin: Mouton de Gruyter.
Hock, Hans Henrich. 2021. *Principles of Historical Linguistics*, 3rd edn., revised and updated, Berlin: Walter de Gruyter.
Holm, John. 1988–1989. *Pidgins and Creoles*, 2 vols., Cambridge: Cambridge University Press.
Holm, John. 2000a. *An Introduction to Pidgins and Creoles*, Cambridge: Cambridge University Press.
Holm, John. 2000b. "Semi-Creolization: Problems in the Development of Theory," in Ingrid Neumann-Holzschuh and Edgar W. Schneider (eds.), *Degrees of Restructuring in Creole Languages*, Amsterdam: John Benjamins, 19–40.
Holm, John. 2001. "The Semicreole Identity of Afrikaans Lects: Parallel Cases of Partial Restructuring," *Journal of Germanic Linguistics* 13.4, 353–379.
Holm, John. 2002. "The Study of Semi-Creoles in the 21st Century," in Glenn Gilbert (ed.), *Pidgin and Creole Linguistics in the Twenty-First Century*, New York: Peter Lang, 173–197.
Holm, John. 2004. *Languages in Contact: The Partial Restructuring of Vernaculars*, Cambridge: Cambridge University Press.
Holm, John. 2008. "Creolization and the Fate of Inflections," in Thomas Stolz, Dik Bakker, and Rosa Salas Palomo (eds.), *Aspects of Language Contact: New*

Theoretical, Methodological and Empirical Findings with Special Focus on the Romancisation Process, Berlin: Mouton de Gruyter, 299–324.

Holm, John. 2013. "Contact and Change: Pidgins and Creoles," in Raymond Hickey (ed.), *The Handbook of Language Contact*, Malden, MA: Wiley-Blackwell, 252–261.

Holm, John, and Peter L. Patrick. 2007. *Comparative Creole Syntax: Parallel Outlines of 18 Creole Grammars*, London: Battlebridge.

Hopper, Paul L., and Elizabeth Closs Traugott. 2003. *Grammaticalization*, 2nd edn., Cambridge: Cambridge University Press.

Huart, Clément. 1927. *Ancient Persia and Iranian Civilization*, translated from French by Mary R. Dobie, London: Keegan Paul, Trench, Trübner and Company.

Hübschmann, Heinrich. 1875. *Zur Casuslehre*, Munich: Theodor Ackermann.

Hübschmann, Heinrich. 1895. *Persische Studien*, Strasbourg: Karl J. Trübner.

Hübschmann, Heinrich. 1895–1897. *Armenische Grammatik*, 2 vols., Leipzig: Breitkopf & Härtel.

Huehnergard, John. 1995. "What Is Aramaic?" *Aram* 7, 261–282.

Humboldt, Wilhelm von. 1999. *On Language: On the Diversity of Human Language Construction and Its Influence on the Mental Development of the Human Species*, ed. Michael Losonsky, trans. Peter Heath from the German original of 1836, Cambridge: Cambridge University Press.

Huyse, Philip. 1999. *Die dreisprachige Inschrift Šabuhrs I. an der Kaʿba-i Zardušt (ŠKZ)*, 2 vols., London: Corpus Inscriptionum Iranicarum.

Huyse, Philip. 2003. *Le Y Final dans les inscriptions moyen-perses et la 'loi rythmique' proto-moyen-perse*, Paris: Association pour l'Avancement des Études Iraniennes.

Huyse, Philip. 2009. "Inscriptional Literature in Old and Middle Iranian Languages," in Ronald E. Emmerick and Maria Macuch (eds.), *The Literature of Pre-Islamic Iran*, London: I.B. Tauris, 72–115.

Ibraheem, Meerza Mohammad. 1841. *A Grammar of the Persian Language*, London: Wm. H. Allen and Company.

Jahani, Carina, and Agnes Korn. 2009. "Balochi," in Gernot Windfuhr (ed.), *The Iranian Languages*, London: Routledge, 634–692.

Jamison, Stephanie. 2009. "Sociolinguistic Remarks on the Indo-Iranian *-ka-Suffix: A Marker of Colloquial Register," *Indo-Iranian Journal* 52.2/3, 311–329.

Jespersen, Otto. 1894. *Progress in Language*, London: Swan Sonnenschein.

Jespersen, Otto. 1922. *Language: Its Nature, Development, and Origin*, London: George Allen & Unwin Ltd.

Johanson, Lars. 2000. "Linguistic Convergence in the Volga Area," in Dieter G. Gilbers, Jan Nerbonne, and Jan Schaeken (eds.), *Languages in Contact*, Amsterdam: Rodopi, 165–178.

Johnson, Edwin Lee. 1917. *Historical Grammar of the Ancient Persian Language*, New York: American Book Company.

Jones, William. 1809. *A Grammar of the Persian Language*, 7th edn., London: W. Bulmer and Co.

Joseph, Brian. 2013. "Demystifying Drift: A Variationist Account," in Martine Robbeets and Hubert Cuyckens (eds.), *Shared Grammaticalization with a Special Focus on Transeurasian Languages*, Amsterdam: John Benjamins, 43–65.

Josephson, Judith. 2011. "Definiteness and Deixis in Middle Persian," in Mauro Maggi and Paola Orsatti (eds.), *The Persian Language in History*, Wiesbaden: Dr. Ludwig Reichert, 24–39.

Jourdan, Christine. 2004. "The Cultural in Pidgin Genesis," in Silvia Kouwenberg and John Victor Singler (eds.), *The Handbook of Pidgin and Creole Studies*, Oxford: Blackwell, 359–381.

Jügel, Thomas. 2014. "On the Linguistic History of Kurdish," *Kurdish Studies* 2.2, 123–142.

Jügel, Thomas. 2015. *Die Entwicklung der Ergativkonstruktion im Alt- und Mitteliranischen: Eine korpusbasierte Untersuchung zu Kasus, Kongruenz und Satzbau*, Wiesbaden: Harrassowitz.

Justi, Ferdinand. 1879. *Geschichte des alten Persiens*, Berlin: G. Grote.

Kahn, Charles. 2002. "On Platonic Chronology," in Julia Annas and Christopher Rowe (eds.), *New Perspectives on Plato, Modern and Ancient*, Cambridge, MA: Center for Hellenic Studies, Harvard University Press, 93–127.

Kellens, Jean. 2000. *Essays on Zarathustra and Zoroastrianism*, trans. and ed. Prods Oktor Skjærvø, Costa Mesa, CA: Mazda.

Keller, Rudi. 1994. *On Language Change: The Invisible Hand in Language*, London: Routledge.

Kent, Roland G. 1950. *Old Persian: Grammar, Texts, Lexicon*, New Haven, CT: American Oriental Society.

Khan, Geoffrey. 2017. "Ergativity in Neo-Aramaic," in Jessica Coon, Diane Massam, and Lisa Demena Travis (eds.), *The Oxford Handbook of Ergativity*, 873–899.

Khatchadourian, Lori. 2013. "An Archaeology of Hegemony: The Achaemenid Empire and the Remaking of Fortresses in the Armenian highlands," in Gregory E. Areshian (ed.), *Empires and Diversity: On the Crossroads of Archaeology, Anthropology, and History*, Los Angeles, CA: Cotsen Institute of Archaeology Press, University of California, 108–145.

Khatchadourian, Lori. 2016. *Imperial Matter: Ancient Persia and the Archaeology of Empires*, Oakland: University of California Press.

Kihm, Alain. 2003. "Inflectional Categories in Creole Languages," in Ingo Plag (ed.), *Phonology and Morphology of Creole Languages*, Tübingen: Max Niemeyer, 333–363.

Kihm, Alain. 2012. Review of McWhorter 2011, *Language* 88.3, 657–660.

King, Rhyne. 2025. *The House of the Satrap: The Making of the Ancient Persian Empire*, Oakland: University of California Press.

Kituai, August. 1988. "Innovation and Intrusion: Villagers and Policemen in Papua New Guinea," *The Journal of Pacific History* 23.2, 156–166.

Kituai, August Ibrum K. 1998. *My Gun, My Brother: The World of the Papua New Guinea Colonial Police, 1920–1960*, Honolulu: University of Hawai'i Press.

Klein, Wolfgang, and Clive Perdue. 1997. "The Basic Variety (or: Couldn't Natural Languages Be Much Simpler?)," *Second Language Research* 13.4, 301–347.

De Kleine, Christa. 1997. "The Verb Phrase in Afrikaans: Evidence of Creolization?" in Arthur K. Spears and Donald Winford (eds.), *The Structure and Status of Pidgins and Creoles*, Amsterdam: John Benjamins, 289–307.

Klingenschmitt, Gert. 2000. "Mittelpersische," in Berndt Forssman and Rolf Plath (eds.), *Indoarisch, Iranisch und die Indogermanistik: Arbeitstagung der Indogermanischen Gesellschaft vom 2. bis 5. Oktober 1997 in Erlangen.* Wiesbaden: Reichert, 191–229.

Korn, Agnes. 2005a. *Towards a Historical Grammar of Balochi: Studies in Balochi Historical Phonology and Vocabulary*, Wiesbaden: Dr. Ludwig Reichert.

Korn, Agnes. 2005b. "Das Nominalsystem des Balochi, Mitteliranisch betrachtet," in Günter Schweiger (ed.), *Indogermanica: Festschrift Gert Klingenschmitt*, Taimering: Schweiger VWT, 289–302.

Korn, Agnes. 2013. "Final Troubles: Armenian Stem-Classes and the Word-End in Late Old Persian," in Sergei Tokhtas'ev and Pavel Lur'e (eds.), *Commentationes Iranicae, Vladimiro f. Aaron Livschits nonagenario donum natalicium*, St. Petersburg: Nestor-Istorija, 74–91.

Korn, Agnes. 2016. "A Partial Tree of Central Iranian: A New Look at Iranian Subphyla," *Indogermanische Forschungen* 121, 401–434.

Korn, Agnes. 2017. "The Evolution of Iranian," in Jared Klein, Brian Joseph, and Matthias Fritz (eds.), *Handbook of Comparative and Historical Indo-European Linguistics*, Vol. 1, Berlin: De Gruyter Mouton, 608–624.

Korn, Agnes. 2019. "Isoglosses and Subdivisions of Iranian," *Journal of Historical Linguistics* 9.2, 239–281.

Korn, Agnes. 2020. "Grammaticalization and Reanalysis in Iranian," in Walter Bisang and Andrej Malchukov (eds.), *Grammaticalization Scenarios: Cross-Linguistic Variation and Universal Tendencies, Volume 1: Grammaticalization Scenarios from Europe and Asia*, Berlin: De Gruyter, 465–498.

Korn, Agnes. 2021. "Contributions to a Relative Chronology of Persian: The Non-Change of Postconsonantal y and w in Middle Persian in Context," *Indo-European Linguistics* 8, 1–43.

Kranich, Svenja, and Tine Breban. 2021. "Introduction: Lost in Change," in Svenja Kranich and Tine Breban (eds.), *Lost in Change: Causes and Processes in the Loss of Grammatical Elements and Constructions*, Amsterdam: John Benjamins, 1–18.

Kreidl, Julian. 2024. "On the Kushan Bactrian Ablative-Instrumental Case," *Iran and the Caucasus* 28, 206–228.

Kuhrt, Amélie. 1995. *The Ancient Near East c. 3000–330 BC*, 2 vols., London: Routledge.

Kuhrt, Amélie. 2007. *The Persian Empire: A Corpus of Sources from the Achaemenid Period*, Abingdon: Routledge.
Kulick, Don. 1992. *Language Shift and Cultural Reproduction: Socialization, Self, and Syncretism in a Papua New Guinea Village*, Cambridge: Cambridge University Press.
Kulick, Don. 2019. *A Death in the Rainforest*, Chapel Hill, NC: Algonquin.
Kusters, Wouter. 2003. *Linguistic Complexity: The Influence of Social Change on Verbal Inflection*. Utrecht: Landelijk Onderzoekschool Taalwetenschap.
Labov, William. 2007. "Transmission and Diffusion," *Language* 83.2, 344–387.
Labov, William. 1994–2010. *Principles of Linguistic Change*, 3 vols., Chichester: Wiley-Blackwell.
Laplantine, Chloé. 2023. "Émile Benveniste on the Relation between Linguistic and Social Structures," in *The Limits of Structuralism*, ed. James McElvenny, Oxford: Oxford University Press, 267–297.
Lass, Roger. 2000. "Language Periodization and the Concept of 'Middle,'" in Irma Taavitsainen, Terttu Nevalainen, Päivi Pahta, and Matti Rissanen (eds.), *Placing Middle English in Context*, Berlin: Mouton de Gruyter, 7–41.
Lassen, Christian. 1836. *Die Altpersischen Keil-Inschriften von Persepolis. Entzifferung des Alphabets und Erklärung des Inhalts*, Bonn: Eduard Weber.
Lavan, Myles, Richard E. Payne, and John Weisweiler (eds.). 2016. *Cosmopolitanism and Empire: Universal Rulers, Local Elites, and Cultural Integration in the Ancient Near East and Mediterranean*, Oxford: Oxford University Press.
Lazard, Gilbert. 1975. "The Rise of the New Persian Language," in Richard N. Frye (ed.), *The Cambridge History of Iran, Volume 4: The Period from the Arab Invasion to the Saljuqs*, Cambridge: Cambridge University Press, 595–632.
Lazard, Gilbert. 1983. Review of Back 1978, *Indo-Iranian Journal* 25.1, 51–53.
La Vaissière, Étienne de. 2011. "Sogdiana III: History and Archeology," *Encyclopædia Iranica*, online edition, available at www.iranicaonline.org/articles/sogdiana-iii-history-and-archeology (accessed March 4, 2011).
Lehmann, Winfred P. 1992. *Historical Linguistics*, 3rd edn. New York: Routledge.
Lenfant, Dominique. 2012. "Ctesias and His Eunuchs: A Challenge for Modern Historians," *Histos* 6, 257–297.
Lenfant, Dominique. 2013. "Des eunuques dans la tragédie grecque: L'orientalisme antique à l'épreuve des textes," *Erga-Logoi* 2, 2–30.
Lenfant, Dominique. 2014. "La mépris des eunuques dans la Grèce Classique: orientalisme ou anachronisme?" in A. Queyrel Bottineau (ed.), *La representation négative de l'autre dans l'Antiquité: Hostilité, réprobation, dépréciation*, Dijon: Éditions universitaires de Dijon, 423–442.
Lenfant, Dominique. 2019. "Polygamy in Greek Views of the Persians," *Greek, Roman, and Byzantine Studies* 59, 15–37.
Lenfant, Dominique. 2020. "The Notion of the Harem and Its Irrelevance to Women of the Persian Court," *Ancient Society* 50, 13–27.

Lenfant, Dominique. 2021. "Eunuchs as Guardians of Women in Achaemenid Persia: Orientalism and Back Projection in Modern Scholarship," *Greek, Roman, and Byzantine Studies* 61, 456–474.

Lincoln, Bruce. 2012. *"Happiness for Mankind": Achaemenian Religion and the Imperial Project*, Leuven: Peeters.

Llewellyn-Jones, Lloyd. 2013. *King and Court in Ancient Persia 559 to 331 BCE*, Edinburgh: Edinburgh University Press.

Llewellyn-Jones, Lloyd. 2022. *Persians: The Age of the Great Kings*, New York: Basic Books.

Luís, Ana R. 2010. "The Loss and Survival of Inflectional Morphology: Contextual vs. Inherent Inflection in Creoles," in Silvina Colina, Antonio Olarrea, and Ana Carvalho (eds.), *Romance Linguistics 2009*, Current Issues in Linguistic Theory 315, Amsterdam: John Benjamins, 323–336.

Lupyan, Gary, and Rick Dale. 2010. "Language Structure Is Partly Determined by Social Structure," *PLoS One* 5.1, 1–10.

Lurje, Pavel, and Ilya Yakubovich. 2017. "The Myth of Sogdian Lambdacism," in Alberto Cantera and Maria Macuch (eds.), *Zur lichten Heimat: Studien zu Manichäismus, Iranistik und Zentralasienkunde im Gedenken an Werner Sundermann*, Wiesbaden: Harrassowitz, 319–341.

Lynch, John. 1998. *Pacific Languages: An Introduction*. Honolulu: University of Hawai'i Press.

MacKenzie, David N. 1987. "Pashto," in Bernard Comrie (ed.), *The World's Major Languages*, Oxford: Oxford University Press, 547–565.

MacKenzie, David N. 1993. "The Fire Altar of Happy *Frayosh," *Bulletin of the Asia Institute*, New Series 7, 105–109.

Maggi, Mauro, and Paola Orsatti. 2018. "From Old to New Persian," in Anousha Sedighi and Pouneh Shabani-Jadidi (eds.), *The Oxford Handbook of Persian Linguistics*, Oxford: Oxford University Press, 7–51.

Maghbouleh, Neda. 2017. *The Limits of Whiteness: Iranian Americans and the Everyday Politics of Race*, Stanford, CA: Stanford University Press.

Malkiel, Yakov. 1953. "Language History and Historical Linguistics," *Romance Philology* 7.1, 65–76.

Mancini, Marco. 2019. "Middle-Persian Morphology and Old Persian Masks: Some Reflections on 'Proto-Middle Persian,'" in Sabir Badalkhan, Gian Pietro Basello, and Matteo De Chiara (eds.), *Iranian Studies in Honour of Adriano V. Rossi*, Vol. 2, Naples: Unior Press, 523–564.

Mann, Michael. 2012. *The Sources of Social Power, Volume 1: A History of Power from the Beginning to AD 1760*, new edn., Cambridge: Cambridge University Press.

Mantzavinos, Chrystostomos. 2016. *Explanatory Pluralism*, Cambridge: Cambridge University Press.

Marashi, Afshin. 2008. *Nationalizing Iran: Culture, Power, and the State, 1870–1940*, Seattle: University of Washington Press.

Maricq, André. 1958. "Classica et Orientalia 5," *Syria* 35.3, 295–360.

Marx, Karl, and Frederick Engels. 1983. *Marx & Engels Collected Works Vol. 39: Marx and Engels: 1852–1855*, London: Lawrence & Wishart.
Marzi, Claudia, James P. Blevins, Geert Booij, and Vito Pirrelli. 2020. "Inflection at the Morphology-Syntax Interface," in Vito Pirrelli, Ingo Plag, and Wolfgang U. Dressler, *World Knowledge and Word Usage: A Cross-Disciplinary Guide to the Mental Lexicon*, Berlin: Walter de Guyter, 228–294.
Matras, Yaron. 2009. *Language Contact*, Cambridge: Cambridge University Press.
McWhorter, John. 2001. "The World's Simplest Grammars Are Creole Grammars," *Linguistic Typology* 5.2, 125–166.
McWhorter, John. 2005. *Defining Creole*, Oxford: Oxford University Press.
McWhorter, John. 2007. *Language Interrupted: Signs of Non-Native Acquisition in Standard Language Grammars*, Oxford: Oxford University Press.
McWhorter, John. 2008. *Our Magnificent Bastard Tongue: The Untold History of English*, New York: Avery.
McWhorter, John. 2011a. *Linguistic Simplicity and Complexity. Why Do Languages Undress?* Boston, MA: De Gruyter Mouton.
McWhorter, John. 2011b. "Tying Up Loose Ends: The Creole Prototype After All," *Diachronica* 28.1, 82–117.
McWhorter, John. 2012. "Case Closed? Testing the Feature Pool Hypothesis," *Journal of Pidgin and Creole Languages* 27.1, 171–182.
McWhorter, John. 2013a. "Why Noncompositional Derivation Isn't Boring: A Second Try on the 'Other' Part of the Creole Prototype Hypothesis," *Journal of Pidgin and Creole Languages* 28.1, 167–179.
McWhorter, John. 2013b. "It's Not Over: Why It Matters Whether There Is Such Thing as a Creole," *Journal of Pidgin and Creole Linguistics* 28.2, 409–423.
McWhorter, John. 2014. "Mesolect as the Norm: Semi-Creoles Revisited," *PAPIA: Revista Brasileira de Estudos do Contato Linguístico* 24.1, 7–25.
McWhorter, John. 2018. *The Creole Debate*, Cambridge: Cambridge University Press.
Meakins, Felicity. 2013. "Mixed Languages," in Peter Bakker and Yaron Matras (eds.), *Contact Languages: A Comprehensive Guide*, Berlin: De Gruyter, 159–228.
Meillet, Antoine. 1900. "La déclinaison et l'accent d'intensité en Perse," *Journal Asiatique*, 9th series, 15.2, 254–277.
Meillet, Antoine. 1912. "Les nouvelles langues indo-européens trouvées en Asie Centrale," *Revue du Mois* 14, 135–152.
Meillet, Antoine. 1915. *Grammaire du vieux-perse*, Paris: Librarie orientale et américaine.
Meillet, Antoine. 1921. *Linguistique historique et linguistique générale*, Paris: Édouard Champion.
Meillet, Antoine. 1931. *Grammaire du vieux-perse*, 2nd edn., fully corrected and augmented by E. Benveniste, Paris: Champion.
Miestamo, Matti, Kaius Sinnemäki, and Fred Karlsson (eds.). 2008. *Language Complexity: Typology, Contact, Change*, Amsterdam: John Benjamins Publishing Company.

Migge, Bettina. 2019. Review of McWhorter 2018, *Journal of Language Contact* 12, 857–863.
Milroy, James, and Lesley Milroy. 1985. "Linguistic Change, Social Network and Speaker Innovation," *Journal of Linguistics* 21, 339–384.
Milroy, James. 2002. "The Legitimate Language: Giving a History to English," prologue to Richard J. Watts and Peter Trudgill (eds.), *Alternative Histories of English*, London: Routledge, 7–25.
Milroy, Lesley, and Carmen Llamas. 2013. "Social Networks," in Jack K. Chambers and Natalie Schilling (eds.), *The Handbook of Language Variation and Change*, 2nd edn., Chichester: John Wiley & Sons, 409–427.
Minardi, Michele. 2015. *Ancient Chorasmia: A Polity between the Semi-Nomadic and Sedentary Cultural Areas of Central Asia*, Leuven: Peeters.
Minns, Ellis H. 1915. "Parchments of the Parthian Period from Avroman in Kurdistan," *Journal of Hellenic Studies* 35, 22–65.
Misteli, Franz. 1891. "Neupersich und Englisch," *Philologische Abhandlungen Heinrich Schweizer-Sidler zur Feier des fünfzigjährigen Jubiläums seiner Docententhäthigkeit an der Zürcher Hochschule, I*. Zürich: Zürcher und Furrer, 28–35.
Misteli, Franz. 1893. *Charakteristik der hauptsächlichsten Typen des Sprachbaues*, Berlin: F. Dümmlers.
Moorey, Peter Roger Stuart. 1985. "The Iranian Contribution to Achaemenid Material Culture," *Iran* 23, 21–37.
Morgan, Gary. 2014. "Critical Period in Language Development," in Patricia Brooks and Vera Kempe (eds.), *Encyclopedia of Language Development*, Thousand Oaks, CA: SAGE Publications, 115–118.
Morgenstierne, Georg. 1938. *Indo-Iranian Frontier Languages, Vol. II: Iranian Pamir Languages: Yidgha-Munji, Sanglechi-Ishkashmi and Wakhi*, Oslo: Universitetsforlaget.
Morgenstierne, Georg. 1942. "Archaisms and Innovations in Pashto Morphology," *Norsk Tidsskrift for Sprogvidenskap* 12, 88–114.
Morgenstierne, Georg. 1973. "Traces of Indo-European Accentuation in Pashto?," *Norsk Tidsskrift for Sprogvidenskap* 27, 61–65.
Morgenstierne, Georg. 2003. *A New Etymological Vocabulary of Pashto*, ed. John Elfenbein and David N. MacKenzie, and Nicholas Sims-Williams, Wiesbaden: Dr. Ludwig Reichert.
Morpurgo Davies, A. 1998. *History of Linguistics Volume IV: Nineteenth-Century Linguistics*, London: Longman.
Motadel, David. 2013. "Iran and the Aryan Myth," in Ali M. Ansari (ed.), *Perceptions of Iran: History, Myths and Nationalism from Medieval Persia to the Islamic Republic*, London: I.B. Tauris, 119–146.
al-Muḥibbī, Muḥammad Amīn ibn Faḍlallāh. 1966. *Khulāṣat al-aṯar fī aʿyān al-qarn al-ḥādī ʿašar*, 4 vols., Beirut: Maktabat Ḥayyāṭ.
Mufwene, Salikoko. 1997. "Jargons, Pidgins, Creoles, and Koines: What Are They?" in Arthur K. Spears and Donald Winford (eds.), *The Structure and Status of Pidgins and Creoles*, Amsterdam: John Benjamins, 36–70.

Mufwene, Salikoko. 2009. "Review of Charles Stewart, 2007, Creolization: History, Ethnography, Theory, Walnut Creek, CA: Left Coast Press," *Journal of Anthropological Research* 65.1, 105–109.
Mühlhäusler, Peter. 1983. "Samoan Plantation Pidgin English and the Origin of New Guinea Pidgin," in Ellen Woolford and William Washabaugh (eds.), *The Social Context of Creolization*, Ann Arbor, MI: Karoma, 28–76.
Mühlhäusler, Peter. 1997. *Pidgin and Creole Linguistics*, expanded and revised edition, London: University of Westminster Press.
Mühlhäusler, Peter. 2003. "Sociohistorical and Grammatical Aspects of Tok Pisin," in Peter Mühlhäusler, Thomas E. Dutton, and Suzanne Romaine (eds.), *Tok Pisin Texts from the Beginning to the Present*, Amsterdam: John Benjamins, 1–34.
Müller, Friedrich. 1877. "Bemerkungen über den Ursprung des Nominalstammes im Neupersischen," *Sitzungsberichte der Kaiserlichen Akademie der Wissenschaften, Philosophisch-Historische Classe* 88, 223–228.
Muysken, Pieter. 2017. "Using Scenarios in Language Contact Studies," in Eitan Grossman, Peter Dils, Tonio Sebastian Richter, and Wolfgang Schenkel (eds.), *Greek Influence on Egyptian-Coptic: Contact-Induced Change in an Ancient African Language*, Hamburg: Widmaier, 3–16.
Muysken, Pieter. 2008. "Introduction: Conceptual and Methodological Issues in Areal Linguistics," in Pieter Muysken (ed.), *From Linguistic Areas to Areal Linguistics*, Amsterdam: John Benjamins, 1–23.
Muysken, Pieter. 2013. "Two Linguistic Systems in Contact: Grammar, Phonology, and Lexicon," in Tej K. Bahtia and William C. Ritchie (eds.), *The Handbook of Bilingualism and Multilingualism*, 2nd ed., Chichester: Wiley-Blackwell, 193–215.
Myers-Scotton, Carol. 2006. *Multiple Voices: An Introduction to Bilingualism*, Malden, MA: Blackwell.
Myers-Scotton, Carol. 2008. "Language Contact: Why Outsider System Morphemes Resist Transfer," *Journal of Language Contact* 2: 21–41.
Nettle, Daniel, and Suzanne Romaine. 2000. *Vanishing Voices: The Extinction of the World's Languages*, Oxford: Oxford University Press.
Neumann-Holzschuh, Ingrid, and Edgar W. Schneider (eds.). 2000. *Degrees of Restructuring in Creole Languages*, Amsterdam: John Benjamins Publishing Company.
Nevalainen, Terttu, and Helena Raumolin-Brunberg. 2012. "Historical Sociolinguistics: Origins, Motivations, and Paradigms," in Juan Manuel Hernández-Campoy and Juan Camilo Conde-Silvestre (eds.), *The Handbook of Historical Sociolinguistics*, Malden, MA: John Wiley & Sons, 22–40.
Newmeyer, Frederick J. 2003. "Formal and Functional Motivation for Language Change," in Raymond Hickey (ed.), *Motives for Language Change*, Cambridge: Cambridge University Press, 18–36.

Nöldeke, Theodor. 1892. "Persische Studien II," *Sitzungsberichte der kaiserlichen Akademie der Wissenschaften in Wien, philosophisch-historische Classe* 126.12, 1–46.
Novák, Ľubomír. 2014. "Question of (Re)classification of Eastern Iranian Languages," *Linguistica Brunensia* 62.1, 77–87.
Oded, Bustenay. 1979. *Mass Deportations and Deportees in the Neo-Assyrian Empire*, Wiesbaden: Reichert.
Olmstead, Arthur T. 1948. *History of the Persian Empire*, Chicago, IL: University of Chicago Press.
Olsen, Birgin Anette. 1999. *The Noun in Biblical Armenian: Origin and Word-Formation*, Berlin: Mouton de Gruyter.
Olsen, Birgit Anette. 2005. "On Iranian Dialectal Diversity in Armenian," in Gerhard Meiser and Olav Hackstein (eds.), *Sprachkontakt und Sprachwandel. Akten der XI. Fachtagung der Indogermanischen Gesellschaft, 17.–23. September 2000, Halle an der Saale*, Wiesbaden: Dr. Ludwig Reichert, 473–481.
Oppert, Jules. 1852. "Études sur les Inscriptions des Achéménides, conçues dans l'Idiome des anciens Perses," *Journal Asiatique*, fourth series, 19, 140–213.
Ostler, Nicholas. 2010. *The Last Lingua-Franca: English until the Return of Babel*, New York: Walker & Co.
Panaino, Antonio. 2015. "Ὁμόγλωττοι παρὰ μικρόν?" *Electrum* 22, 87–106.
Parkvall, Mikael. 2000. "Reassessing the Role of Demographics in Language Restructuring," in Ingrid Neumann-Holzschuh and Edgar W. Schneider (eds.), *Degrees of Restructuring in Creole Languages*, Amsterdam: John Benjamins, 185–213.
Parkvall, Mikael, Peter Bakker, and John McWhorter. 2018. "Creoles and Sociolinguistic Complexity: Response to Ansaldo," *Language Sciences* 66, 226–233.
Paul, Ludwig. 1998. "The Position of Zazaki among West Iranian Languages," in Charles Melville (ed.), *Proceedings of the Third European Conference of Iranian Studies held in Cambridge, 11th to 15th, 1995*, Wiesbaden: Dr. Ludwig Reichert, 163–177.
Paul, Ludwig. 2019. "Persian," in Geoffrey Haig and Geoffrey Khan (eds.), *The Languages and Linguistics of Western Asia: An Areal Perspective*, Berlin: De Gruyter Mouton, 569–624.
Perry, John. R. 1998. "Languages and Dialects: Islamic Period (A Review of the Encyclopædia Iranica)," *Iranian Studies* 31.3/4, 517–525.
Perry, John R. 2003. "Persian as a Homoglossic Language," in Bernard Hourcade (ed.), *Iran: Questions et connaissances. Actes du IVe congrès européen des études iraniennes, vol. III: Cultures et sociétés contemporaines*, Studia Iranica, Cahier 27, Leuven: Peeters, 11–28.
Petersen, Jennifer. 1988. "Word-Internal Code-Switching Constraints in a Bilingual Child's Grammar," *Language* 26, 479–493.
Pīrniyā, Ḥasan. 1933 (1311). *Īrān-i bāstān yā tārīx-i mufaṣṣal-i Īrān-i qadīm*, 3 vols., Tehran: Majlis. Reprint with introduction and commentary by Bāstānī Pārīzī, 1994 (1373), Tehran: Dunyā-yi Kitāb.

Plato. 1903. *Platonis Opera*, ed. John Burnet, Oxford: Oxford University Press.
Platt, John T. 1975. "The Singapore English Speech Continuum and Its Basilect 'Singlish' as a 'Creoloid,'" *Anthropological Linguistics* 17.7, 363–374.
Platt, John T. 1978. "The Concept of a *Creoloid* – Exemplification: Basilectal Singapore English," *Papers in Pidgin and Creole Linguistics* 1, Canberra: Pacific Linguistics A-54, 53–65.
Ponelis, Fritz. 1993. *The Development of Afrikaans*, Frankfurt am Main: Peter Lang.
Potts, Daniel T. 2005. "Cyrus the Great and the Kingdom of Anshan," in Vesta Sarkhosh Curtis and Sarah Stewart (eds.), *Birth of the Persian Empire*, London: I.B.Tauris, 7–28.
Raidt, Edith H. 1993. "The Role of Women in Linguistic Change," in Henk Aertsen and Robert J. Jeffers (eds.), *Historical linguistics 1989: Papers from the 9th International Conference on Historical Linguistics, Rutgers University, August 14–18, 1989*, Amsterdam: John Benjamins, 371–388.
Raidt, Edith H. 1995. "Women in the History of Afrikaans," in Rajend Mesthrie (ed.), *Language and Social History: Studies in South African Sociolinguistics*, Cape Town: Oxford University Press, 129–139.
Rapoport, Yuri Aleksandrovich. 1991. "Chorasmia i: Archeology and Pre-Islamic History," *Encyclopædia Iranica*, Vol. V, Fasc. 5, 511–516.
Reichelt, Hans. 1927. "Iranisch," in Albert Debrunner and Ferdinand Sommer (eds.), *Geschichte der indogermanischen Sprachwissenschaft* II.4^2, Berlin: De Gruyter, 1–84.
Reinecke, John E. 1937. "Marginal Languages: A Sociological Survey of the Creole Languages and Trade Jargons," PhD Dissertation, Yale University.
Reinecke, John E. 1975. *A Bibliography of Pidgin and Creole Languages*, Oceanic Linguistics Special Publications No. 14, Honolulu: The University Press of Hawai'i.
Rezakhani, Khodadad. 2017. "The Arab Conquests and Sasanian Iran (Part 2): Islam in a Sasanian Context," *History Today* 67.4, www.historytoday.com/archive/arab-conquests-and-sasanian-iran (accessed February 29, 2019).
Rezakhani, Khodadad. 2020. "West Asia," in Eric Hermans (ed.), *A Companion to the Global Early Middle Ages*, Leeds: Arc Humanities Press, 253–276.
Rezakhani, Khodadad. 2024. "Navigating Persian: The Travels and Tribulations of Middle Iranian Languages," in Antoine Borrut, Manuela Ceballos, and Alison M. Vacca (eds.), *Navigating Language in the Early Islamic World: Multilingualism and Language Change in the First Centuries of Islam*, Turnhout: Brepols, 329–363.
Richter, Daniel S. 2011. *Cosmopolis: Imagining Community in Late Classical Athens and the Early Roman Empire*, Oxford: Oxford University Press.
Ringe, Don, and Joseph F. Eska. 2013. *Historical Linguistics: Toward a Twenty-First Century Reintegration*, Cambridge: Cambridge University Press.
Roes, Alfred. 1952, "Achaemenid Influence upon Egyptian and Nomad Art," *Artibus Asiae* 15, 17–30.

Rollinger, Robert. 1999. "Zur Lokalisation von Parsu(m)a(š) in der Fārs und zu einigen Fragen der frühen persischen Geschichte," *Zeitschrift für Assyriologie* 89, 115–139.
Romaine, Suzanne. 1982. *Socio-Historical Linguistics: Its Status and Methodology*, Cambridge: Cambridge University Press.
Romaine, Suzanne. 1988. *Pidgin and Creole Languages*, London: Longman.
Romaine, Suzanne. 1992. *Language, Education, and Development: Urban and Rural Tok Pisin in Papua New Guinea*, Oxford: Clarendon.
Ross, Malcolm. 2007. "Calquing and Metatypy," *Journal of Language Contact* 1.1, 116–143.
Sadovsky, Velizar. 2017. "The Lexicon of Iranian," in Jared Klein, Brian Joseph, Matthias Fritz, and Mark Wenthe (eds.), *Handbook of Comparative and Historical Indo-European Linguistics*, Berlin: De Gruyter Mouton, vol. 1, 566–599.
Salemann, Carl. 1895–1904. "Mittelpersisch," in Wilhelm Geiger and Ernst Kuhn (eds.), *Grundriss der iranischen Philologie*, Strasbourg: Karl J. Trübner, 1.249–331.
Samiei, Sasan. 2014. *Ancient Persia in Western History: Hellenism and the Representation of the Achaemenid Empire*, London: I.B. Tauris.
Sampson, Geoffrey, David Gil, and Peter Trudgill (eds.). 2009. *Language Complexity as an Evolving Variable*, Oxford: Oxford University Press.
Sancisi-Weerdenburg, Heleen. 1990. "The Quest for an Elusive Empire," in Heleen Sancisi-Weerdenburg and Amélie Kuhrt (eds.), *Achaemenid History IV: Centre and Periphery: Proceedings of the Groningen 1986 Achaemenid History Workshop*, Leiden: Nederlands Instituut voor het Nabije Oosten, 263–274.
Sancisi-Weerdenburg, Heleen. 1993. "Cyropaedia," *Encyclopædia Iranica*, Vol. VI, Fasc. 5, 512–514.
Schlegel, Friedrich. 1808. *Über die Sprache und Weisheit der Indier*, Heidelberg: Mohr und Zimmer.
Schmitt, Rüdiger. 1980. "Zu Sprache und Wortschatz der Sāsānideninschriften," *Wiener Zeitschrift für die Kunde des Morgenlandes* 72, 61–82.
Schmitt, Rüdiger. 1983. "Achaemenid Dynasty," *Encyclopædia Iranica*, Vol. I, Fasc. 4, 414–426.
Schmitt, Rüdiger. 1989a. "Altpersisch," in Rüdiger Schmitt (ed.), *Compendium Linguarum Iranicarum*, Wiesbaden: Dr. Ludwig Reichert, 56–85.
Schmitt, Rüdiger. 1989b. "Mitteliranische Sprachen im Überblick," in Rüdiger Schmitt (ed.), *Compendium Linguarum Iranicarum*, Wiesbaden: Dr. Ludwig Reichert, 95–105.
Schmitt, Rüdiger. 1989c. "Andere altiranische Dialekte," in Rüdiger Schmitt (ed.), *Compendium Linguarum Iranicarum*, Wiesbaden: Dr. Ludwig Reichert, 86–94.
Schmitt, Rüdiger. 1999. *Beiträge zu altpersischen Inschriften*, Wiesbaden: Reichert.
Schmitt, Rüdiger. 2000. *The Old Persian Inscriptions of Naqsh-i Rustam and Persepolis*, London: Corpus Inscriptionum Iranicarum and School of Oriental and African Studies.

Schmitt, Rüdiger. 2004. "Old Persian," in Roger Woodard (ed.), *The Cambridge Encyclopedia of the World's Ancient Languages*, Cambridge: Cambridge University Press, 717–741.
Schmitt, Rüdiger. 2009. *Die altpersischen Inschriften der Achaimeniden: Editio minor mit deutscher Übersetzung*, Wiesbaden: Reichert.
Schmitt, Rüdiger. 2011. *Iranische Personennamen in der griechischen Literatur vor Alexander d. Gr.*, Iranisches Personennamenbuch Band V, Faszikel 5A, Vienna: Österreichische Akademie der Wissenschaften.
Schmitt, Rüdiger. 2014. *Wörterbuch der altpersischen Königsinschriften*, Wiesbaden: Reichert.
Schmitt, Rüdiger. 2021. "The Achaemenid Empire and Forgery: Inscriptions," in Bruno Jacobs and Robert Rollinger (eds.), *A Companion to the Achaemenid Persian Empire*, 2 vols., Hoboken, NJ: Wiley Blackwell, 2.1545–1550.
Sebēos. 1979. *Patmowt'iwn Sebēosi*, ed. Grigor V. Abgaryan, Yerevan: Armenian Academy of Sciences.
Sekunda, N. V. 2010. "Changes in Achaemenid Royal Dress," in John Curtis and St John Simpson (eds.), *The World of Achaemenid Persia: History, Art and Society in Iran and the Ancient Near East*, London: I.B.Tauris, 255–272.
Shahbazi, Shapur. 2011. "The Achaemenid Persian Empire (550–330 BCE)," in Touraj Daryaee (ed.), *The Oxford Handbook of Iranian History*, Oxford: Oxford University Press, 120–141.
Shaked, Shaul. 1975. "Some Legal and Administrative Terms of the Sasanian Period," in Jacques Duchesne-Guillemin (ed.), *Monumentum H.S. Nyberg*, 4 vols., Vol. 2, Tehran: Bibliothèque Pahlavi, 213–225
Shaked, Shaul. 2009. "Aramaic Loan-Words in Middle Persian," *Bulletin of the Asia Institute* 19, 159–168.
Shosted, Ryan. 2006. "Correlating Complexity: A Typological Approach," *Linguistic Typology* 10, 1–40.
Siegel, Jeff. 1997. "Mixing, Leveling, and Pidgin/Creole Development," in Arthur K. Spears and Donald Winford (eds.), *The Structure and Status of Pidgins and Creoles*, Amsterdam: John Benjamins, 111–149.
Siegel, Jeff. 2008. *The Emergence of Pidgin and Creole Languages*, Oxford: Oxford University Press.
Siegel, Jeff. 2013. "Multilingualism, Indigenization, and Creolization," in Tej K. Bhatia and William C. Ritchie (eds.), *The Handbook of Bilingualism and Multilingualism*, 2nd edn., Chichester: Blackwell, 517–541.
Sims-Williams, Helen, and Matthew Baerman. 2021. "A Typological Perspective on the Loss of Inflection," in Svenja Kranich and Tine Breban (eds.), *Lost in Change: Causes and Processes in the Loss of Grammatical Elements and Constructions*, Amsterdam: John Benjamins, 22–49.
Sims-Williams, Nicholas. 1981a. "Notes on Manichaean Middle Persian Morphology," *Studia Iranica* 10, 165–176.
Sims-Williams, Nicholas. 1981b. "The Final Paragraph of the Tomb-Inscription of Darius I (Dnb, 50–60): The Old Persian Texts in the Light of the Aramaic Version," *Bulletin of the School of Oriental and African Studies* 44.1, 1–7.

Sims-Williams, Nicholas. 1989. "Bactrian," in Rüdiger Schmitt (ed.), *Compendium Linguarum Iranicarum*, Wiesbaden: Dr. Ludwig Reichert, 230–235.

Sims-Williams, Nicholas. 1996. "Eastern Iranian Languages," *Encyclopædia Iranica*, Vol. 7, Leiden: Brill, 649–652.

Sims-Williams, Nicholas. 1997. *New Light on Ancient Afghanistan: The Decipherment of Bactrian*, London: School of Oriental and African Studies (University of London).

Sims-Williams, Nicholas. 2004. "The Bactrian Inscription of Rabatak: A New Reading," *Bulletin of the Asia Institute* 18, 53–68.

Sims-Williams, Nicholas. 2007. *Bactrian Documents from Northern Afghanistan II*, Studies in the Khalili Collection Volume III, London: Azimuth Editions.

Sims-Williams, Nicholas. 2015. "A New Bactrian Inscription from the Time of Kanishka," in Harry Falk (ed.), *Kushan Histories: Literary Sources and Selected Papers from a Symposium at Berlin, December 5 to 7, 2013*, Bremen: Hempen, 255–264.

Sims-Williams, Nicholas. 2019. "Dual and Numerative in Middle and New Iranian," in Sabir Badalkhan, Gian Pietro Basello, and Matteo De Chiara (eds.), *Iranian Studies in Honour of Adriano V. Rossi*, Vol. 2, Naples: Unior Press, 955–970.

Sims-Williams, Nicholas. 2021. "Another Pre-Sasanian Middle Persian Inscription," *Journal of the Royal Asiatic Society* 3, 1–8.

Sims-Williams, Nicholas. 2022. "The Proto-Sogdian Inscriptions of Kultobe: New Fragments and New Reconstructions," in Deborah G. Tor and Minoru Inaba (eds.), *The History and Culture of Iran and Central Asia from the Pre-Islamic to the Islamic Period*, Notre Dame, IN: University of Notre Dame Press, 41–56.

Sims-Williams, Nicholas. 2025. "Bactrian in Two Scripts," *Indo-Iranian Journal* 68, 185–214.

Sims-Williams, Nicholas, and François de Blois. 2018. *Studies in the Chronology of the Bactrian Documents from Northern Afghanistan*, Vienna: Österreichische Akademie der Wissenschaften.

Sims-Williams, Nicholas, and Joe Cribb. 1996. "A New Bactrian Inscription of Kanishka the Great, Part 1: The Rabatak Inscription, Text and Commentary," *Silk Road Art and Archaeology* 4, 75–96.

Sims-Williams, Nicholas, and Frantz Grenet. 2022–2023. "A New Collection of Bactrian Letters on Birchbark," *Bulletin of the Asia Institute* 31, 135–144.

Skjærvø, P. Oktor. 1989. "Verbal Ideograms and the Imperfect in Middle Persian and Parthian," in Charles-Henri de Fouchécour and Philippe Gignoux (eds.), *Études irano-aryennes offertes à Gilbert Lazard*, Paris: Association pour l'avancement des études iranniennes, 333–354.

Skjærvø, P. Oktor. 1994. "Hymnic Composition in the Avesta," *Die Sprache* 36, 199–243.

Skjærvø, P. Oktor. 1997a. "The Joy of the Cup: A Pre-Sasanian Middle Persian Inscription on a Silver Bowl," *Bulletin of the Asia Institute* 11, 93–104.

Skjærvø, P. Oktor. 1997b. "On the Middle Persian Imperfect," in Éric Pirart (ed.), *Syntaxe des langues indo-iraniennes anciennes*, Barcelona: AUSA, 161–188.
Skjærvø, P. Oktor. 1999a. "Methodological Questions in Old Persian and Parthian Epigraphy," *Bulletin of the Asia Institute* 13, 157–167.
Skjærvø, P. Oktor. 1999b. "Avestan Quotations in Old Persian? Literary Sources of the Old Persian Inscriptions," *Irano-Judaica* 4, 1–64.
Skjærvø, P. Oktor. 2007. "Avestan and Old Persian Morphology," in Alan S. Kaye (ed.), *Morphologies of Asia and Africa*, 2 vols., Vol. 2, Winona Lake, IN: Eisenbrauns, 853–940.
Skjærvø, P. Oktor. 2009a. "Old Iranian," in Gernot Windfuhr (ed.), *The Iranian Languages*, London: Routledge, 43–195.
Skjærvø, P. Oktor. 2009b. "Middle West Iranian," in Gernot Windfuhr (ed.), *The Iranian Languages*, London: Routledge, 196–278.
Skjærvø, P. Oktor. 2013. "Avesta and Zoroastrianism under the Achaemenids," in Daniel T. Potts (ed.), *The Oxford Handbook of Ancient Iran*, Oxford: Oxford University Press, 547–565.
Slabakova, Roumyana. 2008. *Meaning in the Second Language*, Berlin: Mouton de Gruyter.
Slabakova, Roumyana. 2016. *Second Language Acquisition*, Oxford: Oxford University Press.
Smith, Geoff P. 2002. *Growing Up with Tok Pisin: Contact, Creolization, and Change in Papua New Guinea's National Language*, London: Battlebridge.
Spiegel, Friedrich von. 1871–1878. *Erânische Alterthumskunde*, 3 vols., Leipzig: Wilhelm Engelmann.
Spiegel, Friedrich von. 1881. *Die altpersischen Keilinschriften*, 2nd edn, Leipzig: Wilhelm Engelmann.
Spiegel, Friedrich von. 1882. *Vergleichende Grammatik der altérânischen Sprachen*, Leipzig: Wilhelm Engelman.
Spooner, Brian. 1988. "Baluchistan i: Geography, History and Ethnography," *Encyclopædia Iranica*, Vol. III, Fasc. 6, 598–632.
Stewart, Charles. 2007. "Creolization: History, Ethnography, Theory," in Charles Stewart (ed.), *Creolization: History, Ethnography, Theory*, Walnut Creek, CA: Left Coast Press, 1–25.
Strootman, Rolf. 2017. "Imperial Persianism: Seleukids, Arsakids and *Fratarakā*," in Rolf Strootman and Miguel John Versluys (eds.), *Persianism in Antiquity*, Stuttgart: Franz Steiner, 177–200.
Stootman, Rolf. 2020. "Hellenism and Persianism in Iran: Culture and Empire after Alexander the Great," *Dabir* 7, 201–227.
Sturtevant, E. H. 1928. "The Misuse of Case Forms in the Achaemenian Inscriptions," *Journal of the American Oriental Society* 48, 66–73.
Strabo. 1877. *Geographica*, ed. August Meineke. Leipzig: Teubner.
Strootman, Rolf, and Miguel John Versluys (eds.). 2017. "From Culture to Concept: The Reception and Appropriation of Persia in Antiquity," in Rolf Strootman and Miguel John Versluys (eds.), *Persianism in Antiquity*, Stuttgart: Franz Steiner, 9–32.

Strootman, Rolf, and Miguel John Versluys (eds.). 2017. *Persianism in Antiquity*, Stuttgart: Franz Steiner.
Sundermann, Werner. 1981. *Mitteliranische manichäische Texte kirchengeschichtlichen Inhalts*, Berlin: Akademie-Verlag.
Sundermann, Werner. 1989. "Westmitteliranische Sprachen," in Rüdiger Schmitt (ed.), *Compendium Linguarum Iranicarum*, Wiesbaden: Dr. Ludwig Reichert, 106–113.
Sundermann, Werner. 2009. "Manichaean Literature in Iranian Languages," in Ronald E. Emmerick and Maria Macuch (eds.), *The Literature of Pre-Islamic Iran*, London: I.B. Tauris, 197–265.
Swann, Joan, Ana Deumert, Theresa Lillis, and Rajend Mesthrie. 2004. *A Dictionary of Sociolinguistics*, Edinburgh: Edinburgh University Press.
Szemerényi, Oswald. 1980. "Language Decay: The Result of Imperial Aggrandisement?" in Jean Bingen, André Coupez, and Francine Mawet (eds.), *Recherches de linguistique: hommages à Maurice Leroy*, Brussels: Éditions de l'Université de Bruxelles, 206–214.
Szmrecsanyi, Benedikt, and Bernd Kortmann. 2012. "Introduction: Linguistic Complexity: Second Language Acquisition, Indigenization, Contact," in Bernd Kortmann and Benedikt Szmrecsanyi (eds.), *Linguistic Complexity: Second Language Acquisition, Indigenization, Contact*, Berlin: De Gruyter, 6–34.
Talattof, Kamran. 2000. *Politics of Writing in Iran: A History of Modern Persian Literature*, Syracuse, CA: University of Syracuse Press.
al-Ṭāluwī, Darwīš Muḥammad ibn Aḥmad. 1983. *Sāniḥāt dumā l-qaṣr fī muṭāraḥāt banī l-ʿaṣr*, 2 vols., ed. Muḥammad Mursī al Ḫūlī, Beirut: ʿĀlam al-Kutub.
Tattersall, Ian, and Rob DeSalle. 2011. *Race? Debunking a Scientific Myth*, College Station: Texas A&M University Press.
Tavernier, Jan. 2007. *Iranica in the Achaemenid Period (ca. 550–330 B.C.): Lexicon of Old Iranian Proper Names and Loanwords, Attested in Non-Iranian Texts*, Leuven: Peeters.
Tavernier, Jan. 2011. "Iranians in Neo-Elamite Texts," in Javier Álvarez-Mon and Mark B. Garrison (eds.), *Elam and Persia*, Winona Lake, IN: Eisenbrauns, 191–261.
Tavernier, Jan. 2013. "Old Persian," in Daniel T. Potts (ed.), *The Oxford Handbook of Ancient Iran*, Oxford: Oxford University Press, 638–657.
Tavernier, Jan. 2017. "The Use of Languages on the Various Levels of Administration in the Achaemenid Empire," in Bruno Jacobs, Wouter F. M. Henkelman, and Matthew W. Stolper (eds.), *Die Verwaltung im Achämenidenreich: Imperiale Muster und Strukturen/Administration in the Achaemenid Empire: Tracing the Imperial Structure*, Wiesbaden: Harrassowitz, 337–412.
Tavernier, Jan. 2021. "Peoples and Languages," in Bruno Jacobs and Robert Rollinger (eds.), *A Companion to the Achaemenid Persian Empire*, 2 vols., Hoboken, NJ: Wiley Blackwell, 1.39–52.
Tedesco, Paul. 1923. "a-Stämme und aya-Stämme im Iranischen," *Zeitschrift für Indologie und Iranistik* 2, 281–315.

Thomas, Nicholas. 1994. *Colonialism's Culture: Anthropology, Travel, and Government*, Princeton, NJ: Princeton University Press.

Thomason, Sarah G. 1997a. "Introduction," in Sarah G. Thomason (ed.), *Contact Languages: A Wider Perspective*, Amsterdam: John Benjamins, 1–7.

Thomason, Sarah G. 1997b. "A Typology of Contact Languages," in Arthur K. Spears and Donald Winford (eds.), *Pidgins and Creoles: Structure and Status*, Amsterdam: John Benjamins.

Thomason, Sarah G. 2001. *Language Contact*, Washington, DC: Georgetown University Press.

Thomason, Sarah G., and Terrence Kaufman. 1988. *Language Contact, Creolization, and Genetic Linguistics*, Berkeley: University of California Press.

Thomason, Sarah G. 2004. "Pidgins/Creoles and Historical Linguistics," in Silvia Kouwenberg and John Victor Singler (eds.), *The Handbook of Pidgin and Creole Studies*, Oxford: Blackwell, 242–262.

Thomson, Robert W. (trans.). 1999. *The Armenian History Attributed to Sebeos*, 2 vols., translated with notes by Robert W. Thomson, historical commentary by James Howard-Johnston, Liverpool: Liverpool University Press.

Thucydides. 1942. *Historiae*, ed. Harold S. Jones, Oxford: Oxford University Press.

Thurston, William R. 1987. *Processes of Change in the Languages of North-Western New Britain*, Canberra: Australian National University.

Tougher, Shaun. 2008. *The Eunuch in Byzantine History and Society*, London: Routledge.

Trudgill, Peter. 2003. *A Glossary of Sociolinguistics*, Edinburgh: Edinburgh University Press.

Trudgill, Peter. 2009. "Sociolinguistic Typology and Complexification," in Geoffrey Sampson, David Gil, and Peter Trudgill (eds.), *Language Complexity as an Evolving Variable*, Oxford: Oxford University Press, 98–109.

Trudgill, Peter. 2010a. *Investigations in Sociohistorical Linguistics: Stories of Colonisation and Contact*, Cambridge: Cambridge University Press.

Trudgill, Peter. 2010b. "Contact and Sociolinguistic Typology," in Raymond Hickey (ed.), *The Handbook of Language Contact*, Chichester: Wiley-Blackwell, 299–319.

Trudgill, Peter. 2011. *Sociolinguistic Typology: Social Determinants of Linguistic Complexity*, Oxford: Oxford University Press.

Trudgill, Peter. 2012. "On the Sociolinguistic Typology of Linguistic Complexity Loss," in Frank Seifart, Geoffrey Haig, Nikolaus P. Himmelmann, Dagmar Jung, Anna Margetts, and Paul Trilsbeck (eds.), *Potentials of Language Documentation: Methods, Analyses, and Utilization*, Honolulu: University of Hawai'i Press, 90–95.

Tryon, Darrell T., and Jean-Michel Charpentier. 2004. *Pacific Pidgins and Creoles: Origins, Growth and Development*, Berlin: Mouton de Gruyter.

Tuplin, Christopher. 2018. "Plato, Xenophon and Persia," in Gabriel Danzig, David Johnson, and Donald Morrison (eds.), *Plato and Xenophon: Comparative Studies*, Leiden: Brill, 576–611.

Utas, Bo. 2006. "A Multiethnic Origin of New Persian," in Lars Johansen and Cengiz Bulut (eds.), *Turkic-Iranian Contact Areas: Historical and Linguistic Aspects*, Wiesbaden: Harrassowitz, 241–251. Reprinted in Carina Jahani and Mehrdad Fallahzadeh (eds.), *From Old to New Persian: Collected Essays*, Wiesbaden: Ludwig Reichert, 181–191.

Utas, Bo. 2013. "The Grammatical Transition from Middle to New Persian," in Carina Jahani and Mehrdad Fallahzadeh (eds.), *From Old to New Persian: Collected Essays*, Wiesbaden: Ludwig Reichert, 251–259.

Van Bladel, Kevin. 2021. "The Language of the Xūz and the Fate of Elamite," *Journal of the Royal Asiatic Society*, 1–16.

Van Bladel, Kevin. 2022. "Arabicization, Islamization, and the Colonies of the Conquerors," in Josephine van den Bent, Floris van den Eijnde, and Johan Weststeijn (eds.), *Late Antique Responses to the Arab Conquests*, Leiden: Brill, 89–119.

Van Bladel, Kevin. 2024. *Written Middle Persian Literature under the Sasanids*, AOS Essay 16, New Haven, CT: American Oriental Society, https://dx.doi.org/10.5913/aos16.2024036.

Van Coetsem, Frans. 1988. *Loan Phonology and the Two Transfer Types in Language Contact*, Dordrecht: Foris.

Van Coetsem, Frans. 1995. "Outlining a Model of the Transmission Phenomenon in Language Contact," *Leuvense Bijdragen* 84, 63–85.

Van Coetsem, Frans. 2000. *A General and Unified Theory of the Transmission Process in Language Contact*, Heidelberg: Winter.

Van Name, Addison. 1869. "Contributions to Creole Grammar," *Transactions of the American Philological Association* 1, 123–167.

Versteegh, C. H. M. (Kees), 2013. "Your Place or Mine? Kinship, Residence Patterns, and Language Change," in Wim Vandenbussche, Ernst Hakon Jahr, and Peter Trudgill (eds.), *Language Ecology for the 21st Century: Linguistic Conflicts and Social Environments*, Oslo: Novus, 65–93.

Versteegh, Cornelis H. M. (Kees), 2017. "The Myth of the Mixed Language," in Benjamin Saade and Mauro Tosco (eds.), *Advances in Maltese Linguistics*, Berlin: De Gruyter, 217–238.

Waters, Matt. 2004. "Cyrus and the Achaemenids," *Iran* 42.1, 91–102.

Waters, Matt. 2011. "Parsumaš, Anšan, and Cyrus," in Javier Álvarez-Mon and Mark B. Garrison (eds.), *Elam and Persia*, Winona Lake, IN: Eisenbrauns, 285–296.

Waters, Matt. 2014. *Ancient Persia: A Concise History of the Achaemenid Empire, 550–330 BCE*, Cambridge: Cambridge University Press.

Waters, Matt. 2017. *Ctesias'* Persica *and Its Near Eastern Context*, Madison: The University of Wisconsin Press.

Watts, Richard J. 2011. *Language Myths and the History of English*, Oxford: Oxford University Press.

Webb, Eric Russell. 2013. "Pidgins and Creoles," in Robert Bayley, Richard Cameron, and Ceil Lucas (eds.), *The Oxford Handbook of Sociolinguistics*, Oxford: Oxford University Press, 301–320.

Weber, Dieter. 2007. "Pahlavi Morphology," in Alan S. Kaye (ed.), *Morphologies of Asia and Africa*, 2 vols., Winona Lake, IN: Eisenbrauns, 2.941–973.
Weber, Ursula. 2016. "The Inscription of Abnūn and Its Dating to the Early Days of Šābuhr I," in Rika Gyselen (ed.), *Words and Symbols: Sasanian Objects and the Tabarestān Archive*, Bures-sur-Yvette: Group pour l'Étude de la Civilisation du Moyen-Orient, 107–118.
Weinreich, Uriel, William Labov, and Marvin I. Herzog. 1968. "Empirical Foundations for a Theory of Language Change," in Winfrid P. Lehmann and Yakov Malkiel (eds.), *Directions for Historical Linguistics*, Austin: University of Texas Press, 95–195.
Weissbach, Franz Heinrich. 1895–1904. "Die altpersischen Inschriften," in Wilhelm Geiger and Ernst Kuhn (eds.), *Grundriss der iranischen Philologie*, Strasbourg: Karl J. Trübner, 2. 54–74.
Weissbach, Franz Heinrich. 1911. *Die Keilinschriften der Achämeniden*, Leipzig: J. C. Hinrichs.
Wendtland, Antje. 2009. "The Position of the Pamir Languages within East Iranian," *Orientalia Suecana* 58, 172–188.
Whitney, William Dwight. 1881. "On Mixture in Language," *Transactions of the American Philological Association* 12, 5–26.
Wiesehöfer, Josef. 1994. *Die 'dunkeln Jahrhunderte' der Persis*, Zetemata: Monographien zur klassischen Altertumswissenschaft 90, Munich: C.H. Beck.
Wiesehöfer, Josef. 1996. *Ancient Persia*, London: I.B. Tauris.
Wiesehöfer, Josef. 2000. "Frataraka," *Encyclopædia Iranica*, Vol. X, Fasc. 2, Leiden: Brill, 195.
Wiesehöfer, Josef. 2009. "The Achaemenid Empire," in Ian Morris and Walter Scheidel (eds.), *The Dynamics of Ancient Empires: State Power from Assyria to Byzantium*, Oxford: Oxford University Press, 76105.
Wiesehöfer, Josef. 2013. "Frataraka and Seleucids," in Daniel T. Potts (ed.), *The Oxford Handbook of Ancient Iran*, Oxford: Oxford University Press, 718–727.
Wiesehöfer, Josef. 2021. "Demoscopy and Demography," in Bruno Jacobs and Robert Rollinger (eds.), *A Companion to the Achaemenid Persian Empire*, 2 vols., Hoboken, NJ: Wiley Blackwell, 1.27–38.
Williams, Frederick E. 1928. *Native Education: The Language of Instruction and Intellectual Education*, Territory of Papua Anthropology Report No. 9, Port Moresby: Edward George Baker.
Windfuhr, Gernot. 1979. *Persian Grammar: History and State of Its Study*, The Hague: Mouton.
Windfuhr, Gernot. 1989. "New West Iranian," in Rüdiger Schmitt (ed.), *Compendium Linguarum Iranicarum*, Wiesbaden: Ludwig Reichert, 251–262.
Windfuhr, Gernot. 1990. "Cases," *Encyclopædia Iranica*, Vol. V, Fasc. 1, pp. 25–37.
Winford, Donald. 2000. "'Intermediate' Creoles and Degrees of Change in Creole Formation: The Case of Bajan," in Ingrid Neumann-Holzschuh and Edgar W. Schneider (eds.), *Degrees of Restructuring in Creole Languages*, Amsterdam: John Benjamins, 215–246.
Winford, Donald. 2003. *An Introduction to Contact Linguistics*, Oxford: Blackwell.

Winford, Donald. 2005. "Contact-Induced Changes: Classification and Processes," *Diachronica* 22.2, 373–427.

Winford, Donald. 2013. "Contact and Borrowing," in Raymond Hickey (ed.), *The Handbook of Language Contact*, Chichester: Wiley-Blackwell, 170–187.

Wray, Alison, and George W. Grace. 2007. "The Consequences of Talking to Strangers: Evolutionary Corollaries of Socio-Cultural Influences on Linguistic Form," *Lingua* 117, 543–578.

Wurm, Stephen Adolphe, and John B. Harris. 1963. *Police Motu: An Introduction to the Trade Language of Papua (New Guinea) for Anthropologists and Other Field Workers*, Canberra: Linguistic Circle of Canberra.

Xenophon. 1910. *Opera omnia*, Oxford: Clarendon Press.

Yarshater, Ehsan. 1989. "Communication," *Iranian Studies* 22.1, 62–65.

Yakubovich, I. 2008. Review of Seth L. Sanders (ed.), Margins of Writing, Origins of Cultures, Chicago: Oriental Institute 2005, *Journal of Indo-European Studies* 36, 202–211.

Yakubovich, I. 2020. "Persian *Ezāfe* as a Contact-Induced Feature," *Voprosy Jazykoznanija* 5, 91–114.

Yoshida, Yutaka. 2009. "Sogdian," in Gernot Windfuhr (ed.), *The Iranian Languages*, London: Routledge, 279–335.

Yudell, Michael. 2011. "A Short History of the Race Concept," in *Race and the Genetic Revolution: Science, Myth, and Culture*, ed. by Sheldon Krimsky and Kendrick Sloan, New York: Columbia University Press, 13–30.

Zia-Ebrahimi, Reza. 2011. "Self-Orientalization and Dislocation: The Uses and Abuses of the 'Aryan' Discourse in Iran," *Iranian Studies* 44.4, 445–472.

Zia-Ebrahimi, Reza. 2016. *The Emergence of Iranian Nationalism: Race and the Politics of Dislocation*, New York: Columbia University Press.

Zimmermann, Carl. 1842. *Der Kriegs-Schauplatz in Inner-Asien*, Berlin: E.H. Schroeder.

Index

Page numbers with 't' are tables; with 'n' are notes

abrupt population contact, 110, 201
abugida script, 174
Achaemenids, 19, 201
   Achaemenian royal inscriptions, 40–46
   common tongue, 192–194
   and Aramaic, 195–197
   term, 16
   see also linguistic-historical model
acrolects, 109, 121–122
adoption, 104–107, 114
adults, learning new languages, 60, 61–69
Afrikaans, 91–97, 98, 100t
agency, human, 102–108, 109, 129
Ahuramazdā (god), 20, 21–22, 142
Akkadian, 20–21, 144
Alexander of Macedon, 22
Aramaic, 55–56, 195–197, 204n4
areal features, 63, 68, 180–182, 187–192
Arends, Jacques, 86n95
Aristotle, 135
Armenian, 157, 194, 196
Arsacids, 48, 173
Artaxerxes I, 27
Artaxerxes II, 21–22, 27–28, 30
Artaxerxes III, 21–22, 28–32, 33, 137, 154
Arya peoples, 142–143, 179–180, 192–193
Aryan (term), 15–16
assimilation, 164, 167–168
athematic nouns, 24t, 25, 29, 38
athematic verbs, 55
Avesta (Zoroastrian scriptures)/Avestan, 5, 23, 111–112

Babylonian, 20–21
Bactrian, 174–176, 187–188, 189, 190
   compared to Middle Persian and Parthian, 177–183
Baghoolizadeh, Beeta, 152n109
Bakker, Peter, 71n45, 83, 87–88

Balochi, 125–126
Barfield, Thomas, 187
basilects, 109
Beekes, Robert S. P., 129n34
Bentz, Christian, 94, 134
bigotry, 58–59
bilingual mixed language, 73–74, 87–89
bilingualism, 140, 141–142, 166, 202
   and Iranic languages, 179, 180–182, 197–198
   and linguistic history, 10
biocognitive explanations, 135–136
biology, 61
Bisitun (Behistun) monument, 20–22, 23, 31
Boardman, John, 159
borrowing
   and bilinguals, 88, 104–107
   loanwords, 73, 104–105, 114
   unidirectional, 140
bowls, silver, 47–48
Briant, Pierre, 162–165
Brosius, Maria, 151–152

Cantera, Alberto, 27
Central Iranic, 187–192
children, 110
   and bilingual mixed language, 87, 88
   learning new languages, 60, 61–69
   and pidgin, 80
   raising of, 150–154, 157–158, 165
   and simplified forms of languages, 61
Chirikba, Viacheslav, 197
Chorasmian, 185–186
Churchill, Winston, 58
code-switching/mixing, 106
Colburn, Henry, 159
colonization, 58–59, 69–71, 86
   and semicreoles, 93, 94t, 97
Common Iranic, 126–127, 175

comparative linguistics *see* historical linguistics
complexification, 67
complexity
  grammatical, 53–68
    and creoles, 71n46
    and semicreoles, 90–91
concubines, 150–152
contact
  languages in, 128–129
  population, 5, 9, 51, 61, 65, 67, 69, 73, 98, 102, 110–111, 160, 190n57, 201, 203
contact languages, 69–72, 73–75, 128–129
  see also bilingual mixed language; creole; pidgin; semicreoles
contact linguistics, 12–13, 114–115
  state and process, 97–99
contextual inflection, 57, 132, 136
  and creole languages, 83–84, 121–122
convergence, 63, 171, 179–183
corruption
  moral, 117–120
  Old Persian inscriptions, 32
  Plato on Persian, 155–156, 158
cosmopolitanism, 167–170
creole languages, 69–72, 73–74, 80–86
  as corrupt, 117–118
  and decreolization, 108–109
  Middle Persian as, 121–122
Creole Prototype, 82–83
creolization, 97–98, 168–170
creoloid, 91–92
Crowley, Terry, 8
culture
  and creolization, 168–170
  ruling-class, 139–140
cuneiform script, 20–22, 34
Cyrus of Anshan, 19–21

Dahl, Östen, *The Growth and Maintenance of Linguistic Complexity*, 202–203
Darius the Persian (Darius I), 19–22, 142–144, 164
  inscriptions, 20–22, 31
Daval-Markusson, Aymeric, 83
Dāwūd of Antioch, 4
decreolization, 108–109
DeGraff, Michel, 71n45
diversity, of fighters and laborers for the Persians, 144–149
domestic personnel, 149–158, 199
dominance, linguistic, 103–108
Dutton, Tom, 77

Elamite, 20, 142–143, 160

elites
  local, 156–158, 165, 169–170
  see also ruling-class
empire, 166–170, 199
enclitics, 132–133
Engels, Friedrich, 4
English grammar, 4
equal complexity hypothesis, 56–61
Eratosthenes, 192–193, 194
Eska, Joseph F., 59n24
Esther, Book of, 151
ethno-class, 162–166
eunuchs, 152–156
exceptionalism, creole, 70–71
exoterogeny and esoterogeny, 112–114
explanatory pluralism, 13–14, 135–136

Fattori, Marco, 27n14, 44–45n78
fighters, 144–149, 199
First Alcibiades (Ps.-Plato), 153
first-language acquisition, 60n25, 62–63
foreigner talk, 75–77, 105n145, 134, 181, 182, 199
forgeries, of inscriptions, 27, 28–29n21, 30n23, 139n63
Foy, Willie, 45n79
functional explanations, 135–136

Geldner, Karl, 35
Ghirshman, R., 159
global communication, 203–204
Grace, George W., 68
grammatical reduction, 5–6, 35–38
  and contact languages, 69–72, 99–102
  and social factors, 53–69, 99–102
  see also Iranic languages; simplification
Greek
  sources on the Persians, 118–120, 149, 150
  see also Aristotle; Herodotus; Plato; Strabo; Xenophon
  verbs, 54–55
Greenfield, William, 58–59
Guinea-Bissau Creole Portuguese, 58
Gulf Pidgin Arabic, 148
Gzella, Holger, 195

Hahn, E. A., 27
Haig, Geoffrey, 126
Haspelmath, Martin, 135
Henkelman, Wouter, 143–144n83, 159
Henning, Walter, 5
Herodotus
  on concubines, 150
  cultural mixture, 149–150, 156
  diversity of the army of Xerxes, 145
  on eunuchs, 153

Index

Histories, 26
Herzfeld, Ernst, 45n79, 159
Hetzron, Robert, 189
Hiri Motu, 79
historical linguistics, 7–9, 125–136, 127t,
    and linguistic history, 10–11
Holm, John, 83–84n87, 92–93, 99–100, 108, 183
Hübschmann, Heinrich, 45n79
hybridity *see* linguistic transfer
hybridity spectrum (McWhorter), 100t, 102, 107

Ibraheem, Meerza Mohammad, 4
imitation, of Persian rulers, 140–142, 156–157, 164
imperial languages, 203
imperial Persian, 137–144
imposition, 104–106, 139
inflectional reduction, degrees of, 68, 72, 74
inscriptions, 32, 40–46, 160–162, 200–201
    Artaxerxes I, 27
    Artaxerxes II, 21–22, 27–28, 30
    Artaxerxes III, 21–22, 28–32, 33, 137, 154
    Darius I, 20–22, 31, 144, 146–147
    forgeries of, 27, 28–29n21, 30n23, 139n63
    mistakes, 33
    Old Persian, 20–22
    Xerxes I, 21–22, 31, 145
Insler, Stanley, 46–47
intelligence, and language complexity, 58–59
intergenerationally multilingual transmission, 63, 180–182
intergenerationally stable transmission, 62–63
intertwined language *see* bilingual mixed language
Iran, ancient, 119–120
Iranic languages, 16, 123–125, 124t, 126–130, 171–172, 200–201,
    Achaemenian common tongue/lingua franca, 192–194
    and Aramaic, 195–197
    Bactrian, 174–176, 187–188, 189, 190
    compared to Middle Persian and Parthian, 177–183
    Balochi, 125–126
    Central Iranic, 187–192
    Parthian, 123, 124t, 171–176, 187–188, 189–190,
    compared to Middle Persian and Bactrian, 177–183
    remote varieties, 184–187
    socially remote/common, 197–198
    Yaghnobi and New Persian, 127t, 128
Iranic (term), 14–16

Jespersen, Otto, 176

Johnson, Edwin Lee, 4
Jones, William, 3–4
Joseph, Brian, 126–127n26
Josephson, Judith, 35
Jügel, Thomas, 127

Kaufman, Terrence, 8
Keller, Rudi, 131
Kent, Roland G., 118
Khatchadourian, Lori, 159
Khotanese, 186–187
king's gate, 156–157
Korn, Agnes, 189–191
Kreidl, 177–178n18

de La Vaissière, Étienne, 186
laborers, 144–149
Labov, William, 13–14
language acquisition
    and bilingual mixed language, 88–89
    first-, 60n25, 62–63
    intergenerational patterns, 61–69
Lassen, Christian, 15
late Achaemenian Persian, 49–50, 116–117, 118, 160–162
learning new languages, 60, 61–69, 136
Lenfant, Dominique, 151n106
lexifier, 75–76
lingua franca, an Achaemenian, 192–194
linguistic dominance, 103–108
linguistic history
    general discussion, 9–14
    state and process, 97–99
linguistic transfer, 99–102
linguistic-historical model, 51–53
    contact languages, 69–72
        types, 73–75
        bilingual mixed language, 87–89
        creole, 80–86
        pidgin, 75–79
        semicreoles, 89–97, 94t
    and grammatical reduction, 53–69
    and Old Persian, 120–125, 124t
    reduction and transfer of features, 99–102
    state and process, 97–99
loanwords, 73, 104–105, 114

MacKenzie, D. N., 187
McWhorter, John, 59n24, 82–83, 100–102, 107, 187, 191
    Language Interrupted, 6
Mancini, Marco, 35, 41–42, 116, 163
Manichaean script/manuscripts, 43, 133, 173–174, 196–197
Mantzavinos, Chrysostomos, 135

mass adult language acquisition, 60, 65, 131
  and Iranic languages, 171–172, 179, 180, 182–183
  and Old Persian, 120–121
  and semicreoles, 91–92, 96, 108
mass nonnative acquisition, 64–69, 132, 179, 197
material culture, 158–160, 165
Median 160.20nt, 123–125
Meillet, Antoine, 32–33, 118, 136, 137–139, 176, 201
Michif, 87–88
Middle English, 72n48
Middle Iranic, 175, 176, 186–187, 189
Middle Persian, 2–3, 175–176, 189–191
  and Aramaic, 196–197
  compared to Parthian and Bactrian, 177–183
  in late Achaemenian royal inscriptions, 40–46
  transformation from, 34–40
Migge, Bettina, 71n45
migration, 65–67, 126, 191, 204n4, 204
  soldiers and laborers, 149
mistakes, and inscriptions, 33
Misteli, Franz, 4
mixture *see* linguistic transfer; population mixture
"modern" ancient languages, 109–112
Modern Iranic languages, 187
moral corruption, 32, 117–120
Morgenstierne, Georg, 187
Mufwene, Salikoko, 81n81
Müller, Friedrich, 34
multilingualism, 67–68, 197–198
  intergenerational, 63
  linguistic transfer, 99–102
Muysken, Pieter, 105n144
Myers-Scotton, Carol, 57n20, 80n77, 83–84n87

names, 143, 163–164
Nevalainen, Terttu, 11–12n31
New Persian, 2–3, 198
  as Nonhybrid Conventionalized Second Language, 100–101
  and Yaghnobi, 127t, 128
ninefold typology (McWhorter), 100–102, 107
Nonhybrid Conventionalized Second Language (NCSL), 100–101
nonnative acquisition *see* mass nonnative acquisition
nonnative speakers, and raising of Persian children, 153–154
nouns
  Khotanese, 186–187
  Middle Persian, 35–40, 42–43
  and Bactrian and Parthian, 177–178, 183
  Old Persian, 23–25, 24t, 27–30, 36–38, 121–122, 125
  Sogdian, 184–185

Old Iranic, 163, 171–172, 175–176, 179–180, 182, 196, 197
Old Persian, 2–3, 19–22, 163, 193–194
  early explanations of changes, 32–34
  grammar, 23–32, 162
  and the linguistic-historical model, 120–125, 124t
  and Middle Persian in late Achaemenian royal inscriptions, 40–46
  transformation to Middle Persian, 34–40
Oppert, 118

Pahlavi shahs, 15, 119–120
Panaino, Antonio, 192–194
Papua New Guinea, 76–79, 84–86
Parthian, 123, 124t, 171–176, 187–188, 189–190,
  compared to Middle Persian and Bactrian, 177–183
Pashto, 187
Paul, Ludwig, 35, 176
Peripheral Old Persian, 194
Persepolis (Iran)
  inscriptions, 21–22, 28–30, 31, 33, 145
  laborers at, 147–149
Persianism (term), 161–163n137
Persianization, 139, 146, 164–165, 167–168
Perside, 123
Persification, 139
Persism, 161–162, 164–165, 167–168
philology, 13–14
pidgins, 69, 73–74, 75–79
Plato, 154–156, 164
  see also First Alcibiades
Police Motu, 76–79
population mixture, 137–144, 162–166
  domestic personnel, 149–158
  fighters and laborers, 144–149
  and the late Achaemenian inscriptions, 160–162
  and material culture, 158–160
  modern terms, 166–170
Port Moresby *see* Papua New Guinea
preterit, 39t, 40, 121
process, and state, 97–99
pronunciation *see* sound changes
Proto-Middle Persian, 40–42

Raumolin-Brunberg, Helena, 11–12n31
reduction *see* grammatical reduction; inflectional reduction
Reichelt, Hans, 176
restructuring, 65, 68, 69–72
  see also semicreoles
Rezakhani, Khodadad, 72n51
Ringe, Don, 59n24
Roes, A., 159

Romaine, Suzanne, 79n73
Rosaldo, Renato, 169n155
Ross, Malcolm, 182n31
ruling-class, 139–140, 156–157, 163–164, 201–202

Sancisi-Weerdenburg, Heleen, 163–164n143
Sasanids, 16, 48, 49
Schmitt, Rüdiger, 34–35, 49, 118
semicreoles, 74, 89–97, 100t, 102, 108
semicreolization, 97–98, 121, 201, 202, 204
shared morphological innovations, 182, 188–189
Siegel, Jeff, 90n107
simple, creoles as, 70
"simple" grammar hypothesis, 3–6, 35–38, 46–50
simplification, 112, 199–200
  by native speakers, 65–68
  and Iranic languages, 179–180
  and McWhorter, 100t, 102
  and Parthian, 176
  see also complexity; reduction
Sims-Williams, Nicholas, 35, 132–133, 178
Skjærvø, P. Oktor, 49
social factors, 7–8, 52–53, 114–115, 200
  decreolization, 108–109
  exoterogeny and esoterogeny, 112–114
  and grammatical reduction, 53–69
  and Iranic languages, 179–180
  pace of language change, 109–112
  reduction and transfer of features, 99–102
  see also contact languages
social/moral corruption, 32, 117–120
sociohistorical linguistics, 11
sociolinguistics, 11, 13
Sogdian, 184–186, 189
soldiers *see* fighters
sound changes, 7, 129–135
  Middle Persian, 41, 43–44
Spiegel, Friedrich von, 34, 129–130n36
split-ergative verbal system, 130
state, and process, 97–99
Strabo, 150
stress accents, 129–136
structural explanations, 9, 11, 125–136, 178
Sturtevant, E. H., 27
subordination, 167
Susa (Iraq), inscriptions, 21–22, 30, 146–147, 148–149

syllables, final, 130–136, 191
Szemerényi, Oswald, 35, 129, 197

Tavernier, Jan, 143, 195
terminology, 14–16
Themistocles of Athens, 141
Thomason, Sarah G., 8, 92n112, 183
Thurston, William G., 113–114
Tok Pisin, 84–86
transfer, linguistic, 99–108, 100t,
transmission, intergenerationally stable, 62–63
Trudgill, Peter, 59n24, 92, 93, 95, 112, 203
Tumshuqese, 186–187

universal tendencies, 52
Utas, Bo, 72n51

van Coetsem, Frans, 103–104, 107
verbs
  Aramaic, 55–56
  Greek, 54–55
  Iranic, 130
  Middle Persian, 38–40, 39t, 121–122,
    and Bactrian and Parthian, 177–178, 179, 183
  New Persian and Yaghnobi, 127–128
  Old Persian, 23, 27–28, 30
  Sogdian, 184–185
Versteegh, C. H. M., 88, 152n110

Watts, Richard, 92n112, 113
wave model, 190
Western Iranic, 176, 196
Windfuhr, Gernot, 125
Winford, Donald, 81n80
Winter, Bodo, 94, 134
women, 150–152
workers *see* laborers
world empire, 1–2n2, 201, 204
Wray, Alison, 68

Xenophon, 140–142, 145, 164, 196
  Anabasis, 194
  Cyropaedia, 155, 156–157n125
Xerxes I, inscriptions, 21–22, 31, 145

Yaghnobi, and New Persian, 127t, 128
Yakubovich, I., 110n152, 193–194

For EU product safety concerns, contact us at Calle de José Abascal, 56–1°, 28003 Madrid, Spain or eugpsr@cambridge.org.

www.ingramcontent.com/pod-product-compliance
Ingram Content Group UK Ltd.
Pitfield, Milton Keynes, MK11 3LW, UK
UKHW022317240426
470365UK00021B/660